# Nuclear Terror

# Nuclear Terror

## The Bomb and Other Weapons of Mass Destruction in the Wrong Hands

Al J. Venter

Pen & Sword
MILITARY

First published in Great Britain in 2018 by
PEN & SWORD MILITARY
An imprint of Pen & Sword Books Ltd
Yorkshire - Philadelphia

ISBN: 978 1 52672 304 8

A CIP catalogue record for this book is
available from the British Library

Typeset in Ehrhardt MT 11/13.5 by
Aura Technology and Software Services, India

Printed and bound in India by Replika Press Pvt. Ltd.

Pen & Sword Books Ltd incorporates the Imprints of Aviation, Atlas, Family
History, Fiction, Maritime, Military, Discovery, Politics, History, Archaeology,
Select, Wharncliffe Local History, Wharncliffe True Crime, Military Classics,
Wharncliffe Transport, Leo Cooper, The Praetorian Press, Remember When,
Seaforth Publishing and Frontline Publishing. For a complete list of
Pen & Sword titles please contact

PEN & SWORD BOOKS LTD
47 Church Street, Barnsley, South Yorkshire, S70 2AS, England
E-mail: enquiries@pen-and-sword.co.uk
Website: www.pen-and-sword.co.uk <http://www.pen-and-sword.co.uk/>

Or
PEN AND SWORD BOOKS
1950 Lawrence Rd, Havertown, PA 19083, USA
E-mail: Uspen-and-sword@casematepublishers.com
Website: www.penandswordbooks.com

For David Albright, who has led the pack in creating an international awareness of illegal nuclear weapons proliferation

# Also by the Author

# Contents

# Acknowledgements

This book would never have appeared in print without solid help over many years from David Albright, who heads Washington's Institute for Science and International Security (ISIS), though these days David likes to stress 'the *good* ISIS'. So it is too, because the three nuclear-related books I published over the years would never have materialised had it not been for him. A totally committed and focused individual, David has spent much of his professional career highlighting illegal or devious nuclear efforts, not only in the Third World but also in the Former Soviet Union, China and elsewhere. We have seen him interviewed often enough on BBC, CNN, MSNBC, ABC News and the rest and he rarely comes away without having pushed a rather worrying button or two.

I must also acknowledge the role – and this is going back a bit – of a delightful lady who initially assisted in putting my *Iran's Nuclear Option* on the shelves. Corey Hinderstein was long tasked with helping David Albright in administering ISIS efforts at promulgating efforts in many remote parts of the globe. She was, and still is a leading authority on what is going on in North Korea as well as Iran. Corey moved on from ISIS and is now Senior Coordinator for Nuclear Security and Nonproliferation Policy Affairs at DOE/NNSA: Iran Task Force as well as President of Institute of Nuclear Materials Management (INMM), both in Washington DC.

Over many years I received a lot of help from the people at Britain's Jane's Information Group, today IHS/Jane's. I was writing for *Jane's Intelligence Review, Jane's Defence Weekly, Jane's Islamic Affairs Analyst, Jane's Security and Terrorism Monitor* and quite a few others. That was when I was doing the occasional report on some of the more esoteric threats – prior to 9/11 – on subjects like chemical and biological warfare as well as nuclear issues. The truth is, I would never have had the access I did to quite a few sensitive establishments in the United States that today need extremely intrusive security clearances to access and here I must thank another old friend who goes way back, Peter Felstead, editor of IHS *Jane's Defence Weekly*.

When I first put the idea of this book to Chris Cocks, who has moved across to Britain from South Africa, I suggested the title *Nuclear Rogues*. Chris talked to Claire Hopkins, commissioning editor at Pen and Sword Books and they decided that the subject demanded something stronger and came up with *Nuclear Terror*. I expect that was what swung it with the folks at marketing and I am grateful to them for bringing this title to fruition.

On the editorial side, I have Carol Trow  to thank for keeping my sometimes unbridled enthusiasm in check. She is a seasoned wordsmith and while working with her I confess, even in my dotage, to learning a lot. Book production was handled by Janet Brookes and I would like to thank her for the help and support she gave.

Once again Jerry Buirski in Cape Town did a preliminary read – and in the process, a good job of it all.

Finally, with a subject as vast and complex as this, the occasional untoward error is bound to happen, especially since things change or (we hope) improve with time. My footnotes have credited those who have been asked for assistance, or offered advice or information over the years. If I have left somebody out or misconstrued, that fault is entirely mine.

Al J. Venter, Downe, England January 2018

# Author's Note

The Washington-based Institute for Science and International Security (ISIS, or more appropriately, as its website suggests, 'The good ISIS') has disclosed the names of some thirty countries that have nuclear weapons or may seek to acquire them in the future. Some of the more prominent players are from the Middle East and, as a consequence, have been branded 'rogue'. Others have been accused of supporting terrorist organizations by the US State Department.

During a visit to his home in Old Town, Alexandria just outside Washington, David Albright, President of ISIS told me that the actual number of countries in search of nuclear weapons was difficult to determine, adding that 'traditionally much secrecy has surrounded nuclear weapons programmes, particularly in their early stages and this secrecy often continues long after a particular program had ended.' Of the ten that succeeded, only South Africa had voluntarily dismantled its nuclear weapons program, he declared.

Countries with successful on-going nuclear weapons programs, said Albright, were the US, Russia, Britain, France, China, India, Israel and Pakistan. North Korea must now be added to that list, at least being able to build atom bombs similar to those dropped on the Japanese cities of Hiroshima and Nagasaki by the Americans at the end of the Second World War. There had been hope that after its most important nuclear facilities were 'frozen' by the 1994 US/North Korea Agreed Framework, it could be dissuaded from building a nuclear arsenal. Unfortunately, that 'freeze' did not succeed, nor did the later one under the Six Party Talks in the 2000s. Albright warned that some aspects of nuclear developments in North Korea were still subject to confirmation, including its efforts to try to acquire thermonuclear capability – the ability to build crude hydrogen bombs which have anything up to 200 times more destructive power than fissile bombs. That, as we have recently observed, North Korea has achieved.

Currently suspected by the West of wanting to eventually seek nuclear weapons were several Islamic countries, most recently Saudi Arabia, Egypt under previous governments and, of course, Iran. Libya too had attempted to build the bomb but had been stopped by joint United States and NATO action (see Chapter Eight).

ISIS reckons that the security situation which has faced South Korea and Taiwan, both of which had active nuclear weapons programs in the past, will continue to raise concerns in Washington that they might decide to seek nuclear capability in the future. A new worry is Japan, which feels increasing pressure and threats from North Korea's nuclear weapons. The intentions of both Syria and Algeria in this regard were, for a long time also suspect, but to date their nuclear weapons programmes appear to be dormant or abandoned.

There have been a number of countries that launched or considered launching nuclear programmes that essentially ended by the time that the Nuclear Non-Proliferation Treaty (NPT) was brought into effect in 1970. These were Australia, Egypt and Sweden. Programmes that ended after 1970 included Argentina, Brazil, Romania, South Africa, Spain, Switzerland, and the former Yugoslavia. Of the nine countries that successfully built nuclear weapons, all but Pakistan started before that watershed year.

ISIS stresses that while there is no evidence of an Argentinean nuclear weapons programme, suspicions remain that one actually did exist. Similarly, Spain, which laboured under a powerful military dictatorship, developed unsafeguarded nuclear facilities during the 1960s and 1970s and American officials declared in the late 1980s that they suspected Madrid had nuclear weapons ambitions or a programme. With Spain's 'transparent' democracy now firmly in place, that intent dissipated.

Three other countries listed by ISIS with nuclear capability in the past are Belarus, Kazakhstan and Ukraine, all of which inherited nuclear weapons after the breakup of the Soviet Union but are now non-nuclear weapons states and party to the Non-Proliferation Treaty. Nigeria and Indonesia are occasionally named as countries that had nuclear weapons intentions, but these claims have never been substantiated, Albright disclosed. There are other sources that suggest that the Abuja government might still be harbouring this intent but with the collapse of oil prices, the possibility is now remote.

It is interesting that the one country that actively pursued a vigorous nuclear weapons programme until it was halted by Desert Storm was Iraq. Details of how Iraq went about this were given to ISIS by various sources including Dr Mahdi Obeidy, the former head of Iraq's gas centrifuge programme and Dr Hamza, the most senior Iraqi nuclear scientist to have defected to the US in the 1990s. Although Hamza provided many useful details about the pre-1991 Iraqi nuclear weapons programme in which he personally participated, his views on what may have happened after 1991 have been discredited (see Chapter Fifteen). What we do know is that Iraq used a broad range of assets to acquire the kind of information needed to build the bomb, categorized in three broad areas:

Iraqi intelligence efforts were run by the Mukhabarat, military procurement bodies like the MIMI intelligence agencies as well as Iraqi delegations and envoys from other branches of government. These efforts were directly linked to Iraqi student networks in America run by the Mukhabarat and which provided Iraq with access to libraries at many United States universities and laboratories. At the University of Wisconsin, for example, an Iraqi agent posing as a student in 1984, gained access to library holdings where he photocopied more than 300 documents. Hamza said in an interview with ISIS personnel that:

'… the University (of Wisconsin) had a good, out of the way library that would not have too much security and was less conspicuous than going to somewhere like MIT or the Library of Congress. The agent had a friend who was a student there, so he used that student's ID, went to the library and started copying all kinds of documents related to nuclear research.'

These asides – and a lot else – came from David Albright – who has spent a career highlighting the kind of illegal proliferation I deal with between these covers. Indeed, he dedicated his book *Peddling Peril: How the Secret Nuclear Trade Arms America's Enemies*, published by The Free Press in the United States and Britain in 2010 to '…all those who strive for a world free of nuclear weapons and terror.' Go through some of his writings and he makes consistent warnings about the terror that faces the world – this generation and the next, if there is to be a 'next'.

Albright has stated numerous times that with the global spread of technology and rapid growth of international trade, people involved with smuggling nuclear assets are finding it easier to ply their dangerous trade, 'much more today than, say, a decade ago'. He added that 'this involves both acquiring those materials and equipment as it is to learn how to manufacture the bomb.' Over the next several years, 'many countries in dangerous regions of the world, along with terrorist organisations are expected to pursue nuclear weapons and the ability of governments to detect and stop this perilous trade remains limited…'

Taken in whichever context you chose, these prospects are terrifying, he said, and went on: 'finding new ways to thwart these efforts is absolutely critical.

# Glossary of Nuclear and Related Terms and Phrases

Ｗith grateful thanks to various International Atomic Energy Agency publications as well as excerpts from the glossary of *Plutonium and Highly Enriched Uranium 1996* by David Albright, Frans Berkhout and William Walker: Stockholm International Peace Research Institute (SIPRI) and Oxford University Press, 1997.

**AEA:** Egypt's Atomic Energy Authority

**AEB**: Atomic Energy Board

**AEC:** Atomic Energy Corporation (South Africa) successor to the Atomic Energy Board (AEB).

**AEOI**: Atomic Energy Organisation of Iran.

**AI:** Amnesty International.

**Al-Kibar:** Purported Syrian nuclear planted linked to North Korea and destroyed in an Israeli Air Force raid (See Chapter Seven)

**Atomic bomb:** A nuclear device whose energy comes from the fission of uranium or plutonium.

**amu**: atomic mass units

**ANC**: African National Congress (South Africa)

**Armscor**: Armaments Corporation of South Africa

**AWE**: Atomic Weapons Establishment (United Kingdom)

**AWRE**: Atomic Weapons Research Establishment (UK)

**AVLIS**: Atomic Vapour Laser Isotope Separation.

**Beryllium:** A toxic metal possessing a low neutron absorption cross section and a high melting point, which can be used in nuclear reactors as a moderator or reflector.

**BNFL**: British Nuclear Fuels

**BW**: Biological Weapons.

**BWC**: The Biological Weapons Convention.

**CANDU:** Canadian Deuterium–Uranium Reactor. The most widely used type of heavy-water power reactor. The CANDU reactor employs natural uranium as a fuel and heavy water as a coolant.

**Cascade:** A connected series of enrichment machines, materials from one being passed to another for further enrichment.

**CCI**: Correctness and completeness investigation iro South Africa's nuclear weapons programme

**CEA**: *Commissariat á l'Énergie Atomique* (France)

**Centrifuge**: A machine used in a uranium-enrichment process which separates gaseous isotopes by rotating them rapidly in a spinning tube, thereby subjecting them to centrifugal forces.

**CEP**: Circular Error Probable (in relation to missile-strike accuracy).

**Chembio technology**: Chemical and biological warfare technology.

**Chemical enrichment**: A technique for enriching uranium which depends on a slight tendency of uranium-235 ($^{235}$U) and uranium-238 ($^{238}$U) to concentrate in different molecules when uranium compounds are continuously brought into contact

**CIA**: Central Intelligence Agency.

**CNS**: Council for Nuclear Safety

**Core**: Central portion of a nuclear reactor, containing the fuel elements and usually the moderator.

**Covert Nuclear Trade Analysis Unit**: An IAEA security body which has about half a dozen specialists looking for evidence of deals by organisations such as the A.Q. Khan network.

**CSA**: Comprehensive Safeguards Agreement

**CSIR**: Council for Scientific and Industrial Research

**CTBT**: The Comprehensive Nuclear Test Ban Treaty.

**Critical mass**: The minimum mass required to sustain a chain reaction.

**CU**: controlled unit

**Curie**: A measure of radioactivity based on the observed decay rate of approximately one gram of radium. The Curie was named in honour of Pierre and Marie Curie, pioneers in the study of radiation. One curie of radio-active material will have 37 billion atomic transformations (disintegrations) in one second.

**CW**: Chemical weapons.

**CWC**: Chemical Weapons Convention

**Depleted uranium**: Uranium with a smaller percentage of uranium-235 than the 0.7 per cent found in natural uranium.

**DIA**: The Defence Intelligence Agency.

**DoE**: The Department of Energy (United States) formerly Atomic Energy Commission.

**Elint**: Electronic Intelligence (See **Humint**).

**EMIS**: electromagnetic isotope separation

**Euratom**: The European Atomic Energy Commission.

**EW:** Electronic warfare.

**FAS**: Federation of American Scientists

**'Fat Man':** —The atomic implosion-type fission bomb dropped by the Americans at Nagasaki on August 9, 1945. This is one of the nuclear concepts being assessed but not yet worked on by the Iranians (also see **'Little Boy'**).

**Fatwa:** A formal legal opinion by a religious leader or *mojtahed* on a matter of legal law (as in the decree against the life of Salman Rushdie).

**FBIS:** The Foreign Broadcast Information Service.

**FBR:** Fast Breeder Reactor.

**Fertile material:** Material composed of atoms, which readily absorb neutrons to produce fissionable materials. One such element is uranium-238, which becomes plotonium-239 ($^{239}$Pu) after it absorbs a neutron.

**Fissile Material**: Weapons-useable material such as uranium-235 ($^{235}$U) or plutonium-239.

**Fission:** Weapons which derive their destructive power from the fission or splitting of atomic nuclei.

**Fissile material:** Material composed of atoms which split when irradiated by slow or 'thermal' neutrons. The most common examples of fissile materials are $^{235}$U and $^{239}$Pu.

**FMCT**: Fissile Material Cut-off Treaty

**FSU:** The Former Soviet Union.

**FTO:** Foreign Terrorist Organisation.

**Fusion:** A different type of nuclear reaction from the fission process which involves the fusion of the nuclei of isotopes of light atoms such as hydrogen: thus hydrogen bombs. Development of the H-bomb was impossible before the perfection of A-bombs, as this is the trigger of any thermonuclear device.

**Gas-centrifuge process:** See **Centrifuge**.

**Gaseous diffusion:** A method of isotope separation based on the fact that gas atoms or molecules with different masses will diffuse through a porous barrier (or membrane) at different rates. This method is used to separate uranium-235 from uranium-238.

**GCHQ**: Government Communication Headquarters (United Kingdom)

**GRU:** Main Intelligence Directorate (Former Soviet Union and Russian Federation)

**GW:** Gigawatts.

**GWh**: gigawatt hour

**HANE:** High-altitude nuclear explosion.

**Heavy water:** Water that contains significantly more than the natural proportion (1 in 6 500) of heavy hydrogen (deuterium) atoms to ordinary hydrogen atoms.

**Heavy-Water Reactor:** A reactor which uses heavy water as its moderator and natural uranium as fuel (see **CANDU**).

**HEU**: Highly enriched uranium or weapons-grade material in which the percentage of uranium-235 nuclei has been increased from the natural level of 0.7 per cent to some level greater than 20 per cent, usually around 90 per cent.

**HINW**: Humanitarian Impact of Nuclear Weapons

**HTGR**: high temperature gas-cooled reactor

**Humint**: Human intelligence gathered by field operatives or agents, as opposed to **Sigint** (signal intelligence) or **Elint** (electronic intelligence).

**IAEA**: International Atomic Energy Agency, a UN body, headquartered in Vienna

**IAF**: Israeli Air Force.

**ICBM**: Intercontinental Ballistic Missile

**INFCIRC**: Information circular (IAEA)

**IDF**: Israeli Defence Force.

**IDR**: Jane's *International Defence Review.*

**IONDS**: Integrated Operational Nuclear Detection System

**IS**: Islamic State

**ISI**: Inter-Service Intelligence (Pakistan)

**ISIS**: Institute for Science and International Security (Washington).

**JDW**: *Jane's Defence Weekly.*

**JIR**: *Jane's Intelligence Review.*

**Kiloton (kT)**: The energy-level of a nuclear explosion equivalent to an explosion of 1,000 tons of TNT.

**KRL**: Khan Research Laboratories (Pakistan)

**Laser enrichment**: An experimental process of uranium enrichment in which lasers are used to separate uranium isotopes.

**LEO**: Low earth orbit (of satellites).

**LEU**: Low-enriched uranium in which the percentage of uranium-235 nuclei has been enriched from the natural level of 0.7 per cent to up to 20 per cent.

**Li**: Lithium

**'Little Boy'**: Gun-type fission bomb dropped on Hiroshima by the Americans on August 6, 1945. All six South African atom bombs were gun-type. Iran is following this path, among others (also see **'Fat Man'**).

**LNG**: Liquefied natural gas.

**LRBM**: Long range ballistic missile.

**MAD**: Mutually assured destruction – a term that originated in the Cold War

**MEIB**: Middle East Intelligence Bulletin.

**MIRV**: Multiple Independently Targetable Re-Entry Vehicle

**MLIS**: Molecular Laser Isotope Separation.

**Moderator**: A component (usually water, heavy water or graphite) of some nuclear reactor types which slows neutrons, thereby increasing their chances of fissioning fertile material.

**MRBM:** Medium range ballistic missile.

**Mt**: megaton

**MTCR:** The Missile Technology Control Regime.

**MW:** Megawatt.

**MWth:** Megawatt-thermal (usually reactor).

**NATO**: North Atlantic Treaty Organisation

**NECSA**: Nuclear Energy Corporation of South Africa

**NGL:** Natural gas liquids.

**NGO:** Non-Governmental Organisation.

**NIDR**: National Institute for Defence Research

**NIS**: National Intelligence Service (South Africa)

**NNWS**: Non Nuclear Weapons States

**NPT:** The Nuclear Non-Proliferation Treaty (Treaty on the Non-Proliferation of Nuclear Weapons).

**NSA**: National Security Agency

**NSG:** The Nuclear Suppliers Group.

**NUMEC:** The Nuclear Materials and Equipment Corporation.

**NWS**: Nuclear Weapons States

**OPCW**: Organisation for the Prohibition of Chemical Weapons

**OPEC:** The Organisation of Petroleum-Exporting Countries responsible for coordinating oil policies of major producer countries.

**Osiraq:** A French-built 40MWth nuclear materials test reactor destroyed in air strike by the Israeli Air Force in June 1981.

**P-1**: An earlier, less-advanced centrifuge design of European origin.

**P-2**: A more advanced centrifuge design now being used by in the Pakistani nuclear programme, examples of which have been found, without good reason, at Iranian nuclear establishments.

**PAEC**: Pakistan Atomic Energy Commission

**PFEP:** A pilot fuel-enrichment plant.

**PNE**: Peaceful nuclear explosion

**Po-210** (Polonium-210): An intensely radio-active alpha-emitting radio-isotope which can be used not only for certain civilian applications (such as RTGs - in effect, nuclear batteries) but also, in conjunction with beryllium, for military purposes, specifically as a neutron initiator in some designs of nuclear weapons. This is the same substance used to murder Russian dissident and former KGB operative Alexander Litvinenko in London

**Proliferation Security Initiative:** A Washington-inspired security measure that seeks to intercept illicit nuclear trade at sea or in the air.

$^{239}$**Pu**: Plutonium (also Plutonium-239): a fissile isotope generated artificially when uranium-238, through irradiation (as in a reactor), captures an extra neutron. It is one of the two fissile materials which have been extensively used for the core of nuclear weapons, the other being $^{235}U$ (a small amount of nuclear explosives has been made with uranium-233).

**Radioactivity:** The spontaneous disintegration of an unstable atomic nucleus resulting in the emission of sub-atomic particles.

**RDD:** Radiological dispersal devices (radiological bombs involving radio-active matter - otherwise known as dirty bombs).

**RepU:** Reprocessed uranium.

**RTG:** Radio-isotope thermoelectric generator.

**SAC:** Strategic Air Command

**SAGNE:** Standing Advisory Group on Nuclear Energy

**SAGSI:** Standing Advisory Group on Safeguards Implementation

**Sigint:** Signals intelligence (See **Humint**).

**SRBM:** Short-range ballistic missile.

**SSA:** State Security Agency (South Africa)

**SST:** State-sponsored terrorism.

**RME:** Reasonably maximally exposed.

**RMEI:** Reasonably maximally exposed individual.

**RWSF:** Radio-active waste storage facility.

**SAM:** Surface-to-air missile.

**SWU:** A separative work unit, a measure of the effort required in enrichment facility to separate uranium of a given $^{235}U$ content into two fractions, one with a higher percentage and one with a lower percentage.

**Tails:** Sometimes called tailings: The waste stream of an enrichment facility which contains depleted uranium.

**Tcf:** Trillion cubic feet.

**Thermo-nuclear bomb:** Hydrogen bomb.

**Tritium:** The heaviest hydrogen isotope, customarily used to boost the explosive power of atom bombs. While Pakistan claims to have thermo-nuclear capability, the consensus is that it has only fission or atomic bombs, which its scientists boost with tritium to allow for higher explosive yields.

**U:** The scientific symbol for uranium: the radio-active element with 92 as its atomic number.

**UF$_6$:** Uranium hexafluoride, a volatile compound of uranium and fluorine, which, while solid at atmospheric pressure and room temperature can be transformed into a gas by heating. It is the feedstock in the uranium enrichment process.

**UNSCOM:** The United Nations Special Commission (on Iraq).

**UO$_2$:** Uranium Dioxide (purified uranium: the form of natural uranium used in heavy- water reactors.

**URENCO centrifuges:** Gas centrifuges developed by URENCO, a commercial consortium involving Britain, Germany and the Netherlands, to make LEU for nuclear power reactors.

$^{233}$U: A fissile isotope bred in fertile thorium-232.

$^{235}$U: Also U-235: the only naturally occurring fissile isotope.

$^{238}$U: Also U-238: Natural uranium is comprised of about 99.3 per cent of this substance.

$U_3O_8$: Uranium oxide, the most common oxide of uranium found in typical ores.

**$UF_4$:** Uranium tetrafluoride

**$UF_6$:** Uranium hexafluoride

**Weapons-grade material:** Nuclear material of the type most suitable for nuclear weapons.

**WNA:** World Nuclear Association

**Yellowcake:** A concentrate produced during the milling process which contains about 80 per cent uranium oxide ($U_3O_8$). In preparation for uranium enrichment, the yellowcake is converted to uranium hexafluoride gas ($UF_6$).

**Zirconium:** A greyish-white lustrous material which is commonly used in an alloy (zircalloy) to encase fuel rods in nuclear reactors.

# A Nuclear Attack on London's Financial Centre

A battered car, heavily loaded, drives into the heart of London's financial quarter, goes down several streets, doubles back once or twice and eventually draws to a halt. The car sets off again, circles the area and returns to where it halted the first time. Two men emerge, briefly scan the area and return to the vehicle. By now the suspicion of the police who monitor such movement on CCTV – a legacy of the IRA years – is aroused. An order goes out for a car to be sent to the location.

Finally, the police car approaches the street where it is parked, but just as officers approach, an enormous explosion follows. Both the driver and his passenger – as well as the vehicle – are blown apart. Bodies of dead and injured caught in the blast which has shattered the facades of adjacent buildings lie in the street, some of them dismembered and others covered in blood.

The sound of the bomb going off is followed by the noise of human screams and shortly afterwards by the distant wail of sirens. A dark cloud of smoke is spotted by a security guard who emerged from his building immediately after the explosion, and as he told the police shortly afterwards, there was very little left of the wrecked vehicle and the area around was mired with the choking dust of rubble.

With all this chaos, something far deadlier than the explosive material has been released into the atmosphere, all the more sinister because it is invisible to the naked eye. As emergency service vehicles and personnel arrive at the scene, a plume of radiation reaches up to the sky. More radiation spreads unseen through the streets, contaminating everything in its path.

Those in the immediate vicinity of the blast are quickly exposed to this lethal cloud and will not have long to live, perhaps no more than a few days. Others, on the periphery – and not in the direct line of the explosion – will survive longer, but are almost certain to eventually to succumb to some kind of illness linked to radiation exposure, cancer especially, as was the case with many of the survivors of the atom bomb blasts of Hiroshima and Nagasaki.

The shadow of this act of terror will hang over many people who were in the area for years to come, just as happened with those unfortunate enough to be living near the scene of the Chernobyl disaster in the Soviet Union in 1986.

Moreover, apart from the human cost, the outrage will exact a terrible price in terms of economic dislocation, public fears and a crippling national bill for decontamination of a wide area. It is a price we may soon have to pay, if threats from Islamic terrorists become a reality.

What we already know from past experience is that this scenario could be enacted by disaffected groups of Jihadists who have nothing but contempt for human life. The majority are also implacably opposed to everything represented by Western Society, and more often than not in recent times, in their own countries.

For several years, al-Qaeda has warned that it has been developing its own form of what it terms in its regular propaganda despatches a 'Deathly Weapon', details of which remain secret to all but a chosen few in the top hierarchy of this Islamic movement. Western intelligence agencies that have studied al-Qaeda leadership, methodology and long-term aims are convinced that these radical forces have been aiming at developing a so-called 'Dirty Bomb', a device officially termed an RDD or Radiological Dispersal Device.

It is not a simple weapon, for it requires considerable skill and technical expertise to properly construct. There is also the threat that those building it will themselves be contaminated by radioactivity, but to the Jihadis responsible that is of no consequence for this is a task that glorifies the Will of Allah. The RDD bomb is built in such a way that ideally, to cause serious damage, it packs highly radioactive material around a powerful conventional explosive. When detonated, not only are deaths caused by blast, but more disturbingly, the radioactive material is scattered in deadly layers across a fairly large area.

Precisely because the 'Dirty Bomb' – with the requisite radioactive components – is potentially lethal, al-Qaeda has long been obsessed with trying to master its intricacies, at the same time recognising the upheaval it would cause. Indeed, al-Qaeda's former leader Osama bin Laden once claimed that his followers had several 'Dirty Bombs' hidden somewhere in the West, which he declared, would be detonated 'when the opportune moment arrives'. That threat is credible, as I know from research into global terrorism while doing work for Britain's Jane's Information Group – today IHS Jane's – over many years.

Almost twenty years ago, I predicted that that the jihadists would attempt to blow up the Twin Towers in New York, for no better reason than the two structures were such a potent symbol of western power. The accuracy of that forecast caused me an awful lot of trouble with the American security authorities in the aftermath of 9/11 because I was living in the United States at the time, in Washington State.

As a consequence of my comments – which were made 'off the cuff' to several friends in New York City – FBI Special Agents would drive down from Seattle the four or five hours it would take to reach my home in Chinook at the mouth of the Columbia River to discuss the matter. Obviously, they were not altogether happy with my reasoning because I was visited several times. The FBI agents who interrogated me demanded to know how I was aware that the Twin Towers in Lower Manhattan would be targeted by terrorists. Naturally I did not *know* ahead of the attack, I told them, it was pure speculation, but it certainly made very good sense since the Twin Towers were such an obvious target.

Al–Qaeda's chiefs – those fanatics like the present leader Ayman al-Zawahiri, an eye surgeon who helped found the Egyptian militant group Islamic Jihad, and others who inherited the mantle from Osama bin Laden – have talked often enough of possessing a conventional nuclear weapon, like an atom bomb, which, should it become a reality, would be terrifying. I believe that while talking is easy, building the bomb is doubtful for the simple reason that these terror groups have neither sufficient fissile material to construct such a device, nor the technological capability. With time, that could eventually change. The best chance these people have of acquiring nuclear weaponry would be if the state of Pakistan went into complete meltdown and, in the ensuring chaos, rogue elements in the Pakistani security machine might allow them access to the country's nuclear arsenal. In truth, a far more immediate danger comes from a 'Dirty Bomb' or RDD. The scenario of such an explosion on Britain's streets is real, as recent evidence demonstrates.

In March 2017, the UK's most senior counter-terrorism police officer, Assistant Commissioner Mike Rowley, told the BBC that his people had averted thirteen potential terror attacks since June 2013. He added that there were 500 live counter-terror investigations on the go in Britain at any one time. My own sources have indicated that some of these involve RDDs, though obviously the authorities remain unspecific about the nature and extent of threats curbed. What is significant here is that already in 2003 – more than a decade earlier – British troops captured documents in the Afghan city of Herat that indicated that al-Qaeda had successfully built a prototype model for such a device. They also uncovered documents which suggested that their cadres were instructing its operatives how to use it. Similarly, in an article published by my old friend Bill Broad in the *New York Times* on 29 April 2001 under the title 'Document Reveals 1987 Bomb Test by Iraq', he disclosed that Iraq under Saddam Hussein reportedly tested a one-ton Radiological Dispersal Device, as he phrased it, 'to assess its military usefulness.'

Thereafter, the arrest in Britain in 2004 of the Islamic activist Dhiren Barot provided a wealth of information about al-Qaeda's long-term plans for its operations in Western countries. Again, little emerged from these sessions because both MI5 and MI6 have always been secretive about what they know and how they go about their work. The convicted terrorist Barot has an interesting background. Born in India but brought up in London, he converted from Hinduism to Islam at the age of twenty and subsequently became a deeply committed Jihadi. He carried out intensive reconnaissance and technical research for al-Qaeda in Pakistan and the United States. After his arrest in Britain, it emerged that he had drawn up a series of plans for attacks on major financial institutions in London using limousines packed with radioactive 'Dirty Bombs', on which the introduction to this chapter is based. At one of his legal hearings, the Court of Appeal declared that if Barot's 'businesslike' schemes had been successful, they would have caused carnage 'on a colossal and unprecedented scale'. Barot's life sentence – passed in 2006 – has not diminished the threat.

The former Security Minister and former naval chief Lord West said at the time that the risk of an attack on Britain from a 'Dirty Bomb' was real, and could be made by terrorists using a small craft to enter one of the numerous ports along our coast. As Lord West pointed out, it is almost impossible to maintain complete surveillance of all coastal movements, since hundreds of thousands of boats arrive in Britain every year. Indeed, Islamic terrorists who perpetrated the notorious wave of lethal attacks on the Indian city of Mumbai in November 2008, killing 154 people, arrived at their targets in the Indian port using speedboats from Pakistan.

The horrendous reality of Radiological Dispersal Devices has also been revealed by the activities of several anti-Russian Islamic terrorist groups in Chechnya whose members have close ideological links to al-Qaeda. 'Chetnicks' were identified as fighting alongside ISIS forces in both Syria and Iraq in 2016 and 2017 and indeed, very likely before that. They have also been active with the terror group al-Qaeda in the Islamic Maghreb (AQIM), where French forces – for several years now – have been battling insurgent fighters in Mali, Chad, the Cameroons, Burkina Faso, the Ivory Coast and elsewhere. It says a lot that AQIM has close links with Nigerian-based Jihadis linked to Boko Haram, a terror group that specialises in abducting schoolgirls and sending children – some as young as five – into densely populated market towns to die as suicide bombers.

It is Islamic terror links in the former Soviet Union that has a special significance for everybody in the West, and for good reason. In Russia, during the late 1990s, a device containing a quantity of deadly radioactive caesium-137 was placed in a Moscow park by a group of militants from Chechnya, then under the leadership of Shamil Basayev. The bomb was never detonated because someone tipped off the media, but the event did make news at the time because it was an extremely narrow scrape.

There were at least two other attempts by the terrorists to explode 'Dirty Bombs', one in Argun, a town near Grozny, the capital of Chechnya. That attack failed because the radioactive core material – apparently taken from a local nuclear storage facility and then attached to a land mine – was so noxious that the two militants who put it all together were incapacitated by radiation before they could detonate the bomb; one of them subsequently died from radiation poisoning. Russian intelligence subsequently concluded that, had the bomb gone off, it would have caused devastation across a large area of the city and would almost certainly have taken at least a year to decontaminate affected suburbs and streets.

That much we know. On the periphery of this illegal activity, we are also aware that a large measure of criminal Russian involvement – and the theft of inadequately protected radioactive material from the Soviet era – is central to the deadliness of the threat. The collapse of Soviet Union in the 1990s provided unprecedented opportunities to acquire the kind of radioactive components vital to make a RDD. Radioactive material, such as caesium-137 or cobalt-60 has many benign uses in modern society, such as the sterilisation of medical equipment, radiotherapy for hospital patients, the provision of gauges in industry and in the use of thermo-electrical generators. Within the European Union alone, it is reckoned there are 500,000 sealed radiation sources. However, beneficial purposes apart, such material in the wrong hands can be lethal, for a chunk of radiated metal can be easily be ground down to form the dust that will cause havoc if released into the atmosphere.

There are estimated to be about 10,000 sources designed for radiotherapy, each of them containing 1,000 pellets of cobalt-60. Each pellet has enough radioactivity to put somebody over his or her annual safety limit within just two minutes. Even more disturbing is the possibility that some radioactive sources might already have reached the terrorists. According to Vienna's International Atomic Energy Authority (IAEA), there were 1,562 recorded incidents where nuclear material was lost or stolen between 1993 and 2008, with two-thirds never recovered. In a similar vein, between 1992 and 2007, twenty-five kilograms of highly enriched uranium was seized from smugglers around the world. In one incident, typical of the modus operandi of quite a number of nuclear smugglers, more than twenty radiation sources were reported to have been stolen from the Krakatau steel company in Indonesia, where Muslims form the majority of the population and Islamic militancy is on the rise. Only three have ever been recovered.

The impact of events in the former Soviet Union immediately after the political break-up is even more chilling. Following the collapse of communism in the Soviet Union, there was a very distinct and sudden weakening in security and social order, almost throughout Russia. Radiation sources were often left vulnerable to opportunistic theft. Some of this strategic material was poorly stored, leading to quantities of radioactive material – which included nuclear fuel cores from Soviet-era submarines being decommissioned in the Kola Peninsula in Russia's extreme north – being illegally removed and traded on a lucrative black market. The growth of criminal activities in the former Soviet underworld clearly helped to foster these illicit activities, with gangsters apparently indifferent to the ultimate use to which the radioactive material might be put. Financial gain was the prime motive in just about every case uncovered over the years. In one bizarre event, to which Russian media gave prominence, a woman employed at the naval base of Bolshoi Kamen was caught trying to sell a four-kilogram piece of radiated metal for £33,000 or roughly US$40,000. She had kept it in a lock-up garage wrapped in newspaper, and sometimes carried it around in a shopping bag, even though the substance was 2,500 times above safe radiation levels.

Thefts from Russian nuclear plants, nuclear-powered submarines, machinery for turbines and thermo-reactors have also been worryingly common. One of the most disturbing aspects of this threat, throughout, has been the decommissioning of submarines at Kola, near Murmansk. Western intelligence sources point to nuclear fuel cells which were used to power these undersea craft and are extremely radioactive. Hundreds of these cells had been left unguarded in the submarine dockyard, sometimes left unattended on the dockside and clearly a health threat to those working there. Ground up into a volatile powder, this would be ideal for making a 'Dirty Bomb'.

Specifically, that nuclear threat facing every one of us in the West is not something that emerged only recently. It was underscored two decades ago by Dame Stella Rimington, the retired director general of the British Security Service (MI5) in a global assessment of future security problems. Ms Rimington declared in her farewell speech from MI5 that there were then more than thirty countries dabbling in illegal nuclear research. Twenty years later, that activity continues unabated.

More recently, the British Government has rightly appealed for vigilance in the wake of a considerably increased amount of activity on the part of al-Qaeda especially in Syria and Iraq. Concurrently, British security forces have an excellent record in foiling Islamist plots, notably helped by vastly improved intelligence capabilities. There has been another measure introduced which could be invaluable in the fight against a clandestine nuclear-related threat. Unbeknown to the public, all major roads in Britain (as well as most of Europe and North America) have been equipped with sensors that are geared to inform security forces if an unusual amount of radiation is in transit. But even with such steps in place, the system is not foolproof. It only takes one terrorist cell to break through these barriers, as the London bombings of 7/7 proved. The young people involved in those attacks were using conventional explosives and the damage they caused was stupendous. Imagine a similar situation compounded by a RDD.

It is also a reality that an al-Qaeda backed operation might be able to bring in such a radiological device by using rural roads or, as Lord West warned, by navigating the numerous waterways and shorelines of Britain. The Thames estuary, for instance, is an obvious route into the heart of the capital, while other great ports like Southampton, Glasgow and Liverpool are just as vulnerable. If the terrorists did set off a Radiological Dispersal Device, the fall-out would be disastrous. Depending on the amount of conventional explosive, there would be a significant death toll from the immediate blast; the Irish republicans proved how devastating that might be.

At Omagh in 1998, there were twenty-eight people killed instantly by a 300 kilogram conventional bomb planted by IRA dissidents in the high street. Had this been a RDD, the release of radiation would have been even more serious, especially in terms of disruption and long-term health. The insidious nature of radiation poisoning, as we have seen with Chernobyl, is that people in the vicinity could develop cancer for decades to come. Meanwhile, the task of combating the lingering physical effects of radiation would obviously be enormous. The area for miles around the bomb blast would have to be quarantined, something that would cause near-meltdown in the City of London. More saliently, staff – and here we are talking about hundreds of thousands of people who commute to the city every day – would not be allowed back into their offices to retrieve their belongings. All office equipment, furniture, and computers would have to be carefully removed and disposed and entire stretches of roads ripped up and re-laid. The facades, windows and roofs of many buildings would have to be replaced. Drains and sewers throughout the area could not be used for fear of spreading contamination. Indeed, if a 'Dirty Bomb' went off in central London, it is likely that the tides would carry the radioactivity in the water right up to Kingston or even Windsor.

And then, once the area has finally been decontaminated – a process that could take years if the level of radioactivity is particularly high – who will take the government at its word that the city is now 'safe'? More pertinent, having suffered such a disaster, would you allow your wife or husband, son or daughter to work there? In such a scenario, everyday life in the capital would inexorably grind to a halt and the financial costs would run into billions, which is exactly why the RDD is such a powerful draw for al-Qaeda's anarchists.

For all that, the West has had a series of symbolic triumphs over the Islamic terrorists in recent years, but, as Gerry Adams once notoriously commented when talking about his IRA, 'they haven't gone away'.

# Chapter 1

# Nuclear Terror – What is it All About?

*'The Islamist threat and especially the ambition of a British Hindu convert to Islam, Dhiren Barot, to explode a dirty nuclear bomb in Britain is sobering by contrast. 'For the time we do not have the contacts to enable us to purchase such items,' Barot wrote before his arrest. That was [several] years ago. And they say the Islamist threat is exaggerated…'*

*Christopher Andrew in his book Defence of the Realm: The Official History of MI5[1]*

Alargely-unrecorded but significant nuclear-related event took place in Syria shortly after midnight on the night of 6 September 2007, when the Israeli Air Force launched a bombing raid on a purported Syrian nuclear facility. The installation lay near the northern Syrian provincial town of Deir ez-Zur, whose name translates as 'Monastery in the Forest'. A little more than thirty kilometres away, in a vast, lifeless region characterised by rugged mountains and inaccessible valleys and almost within sight of the great Euphrates River lies al-Kibar, an obscure rural settlement in the desert. Involved in the strike were five or six aircraft from Israel's 69th Squadron, all F-15Is. The operation included the clandestine insertion some hours before of an Israeli Shaldag air force commando group. Their role was to direct laser beams onto the target to provide bearings for the approaching jets.

Deir ez-Zur (or al-Kibar as it was subsequently referred to in Western news reports and as we go to press, adjacent to one of the few main operational centres still run by the ISIS terror group in Syria) was a not very well camouflaged military installation, in part because it was situated fairly close to the Iraqi border and clearly, Damascus did not want to draw attention to what was going on there. What did emerge after the air strike was that it had been the site of a significant joint nuclear effort involving the governments of Syria and North Korea. Apart from a bridge across the nearby river, a large, square multi-storeyed building was in the process of being erected. It was what was inside this box-shaped building that caused the aerial strike.

What subsequently came to light from various sources, including those of a Syrian scientist who defected to the West, was the intent for Syria to construct a North Korean-built reactor designed for producing plutonium that would almost certainly have led this Arab state eventually to produce atom bombs. What was also revealed was that the nuclear facility was identical to North Korea's five megawatt-electric reactor built years before at Yongbyon, in the north-east of that remote Asian peninsula. Moreover, while the North Korean reactor was constructed almost entirely above ground, there were some indications that this Syrian counterpart – in spite of the box-like structure that was flattened by the Israeli jets – would be largely underground.

The Israeli attack on al-Kibar was not entirely unexpected. As details started to emerge of both the reactor programme and North Korean involvement, it was axiomatic that Jerusalem would never have tolerated their largest northern neighbour becoming nuclear-proficient. The West was already aware that Syria possessed one of the most advanced chemical warfare programmes in the region and that many of the hundreds of Scud missiles deployed along the Israeli frontier were tipped with sarin and VX nerve gasses. To allow this threat to expand exponentially and include a nuclear option was, in the eyes of the Israelis, simply not on.

In a sense, the nuclear imbroglio with Damascus might almost have been regarded as a corollary of Israel's current nuclear impasse with Iran, the only difference being that Syria straddles the Jewish State's northern border which includes the Golan Heights, currently dominated by Israel's military forces. Consequently, when the attack happened, it was a surgical cut-and-thrust strike that, from take-off to arriving back to the Ramat David Air Force Base in Northern Israel, lasted perhaps two hours. The American-built Israeli Air Force F-15Is spent less than two minutes over the target area and did what they had been tasked to do before heading home, mission accomplished. What was notable about it all was that the Israeli bombers chose a circuitous route for the onslaught. They entered Syrian air space by flying over Turkey, a detail subsequently released by CNN when it was disclosed that jettisoned IAF F15I fuel tanks had been found on Turkish soil.

Broadly speaking, those are the facts. It was what took place afterwards that makes this event intriguing. Following the attack – one of the biggest Israeli air strikes on Syria for years – nothing about the event emerged from Damascus. Not a word; there was neither an acknowledgement nor a denial that an attack had taken place, or even a protest that the 'hated Zionists' had bombed Syria. In fact, said a senior government official in Damascus once reports started to circulate on the Internet, absolutely nothing untoward had taken place overnight anywhere in the country.

A Syrian official did end up confirming that Israeli warplanes had actually entered its air space, but said that 'they dropped bombs on an empty area while our air defences were firing heavily at them'. He did disclose that local residents said they heard the sound of several planes flying above the target area. There was no mention of a bombing raid. Not a word, even though before and after satellite photos of the al-Kibar target tell a totally different story.

For its part, almost as if the entire process had been rehearsed, Jerusalem was not exactly forthcoming either. The media spokesman for the IDF in Jerusalem denied a Syrian news agency report about Israeli Air Force activity over Syria. Israel Radio was more direct: 'This event never happened,' the broadcast declared, quoting an unidentified Israeli Air Force spokesman. Only fractionally more forthright, Syrian officials said later in the day that its defences had forced the attackers to drop ammunition over deserted areas and turn back

A week later, Israel still maintained its official blackout amid privately circulated reports that the mysterious attack targeted weapons financed by its arch-foe Iran. Citing anonymous Israeli sources, the Arab Israeli newspaper, *Assennara*, declared that the jets 'bombed in northern Syria a Syrian-Iranian missile base financed by Iran'. It went on to say that 'it appears that the base was completely destroyed'.

North Korea had its own take on matters, especially since subsequent reports spoke of some Asians involved with the project having been killed. Following a question from the (state controlled) Korean Central News Agency, a senior functionary in Pyongyang declared that 'this is a very dangerous provocation little short of wantonly violating the sovereignty of Syria and seriously harassing the regional peace and security'. A short while later, a North Korean spokesperson denied that it was in any way involved in the transfer of nuclear-related technology, though he was not able to explain why the Syrian 5 MW reactor was an identical version of Yongbyon's 5 MW reactor...

All these developments were followed by several comments in Washington from the US State Department. Addressing the Daily Press Briefing on 11 September 2007, Sean McCormack, then Spokesman, was asked to confirm whether Israel's Air Force had carried out a strike in Syria. 'No,' he answered, without hesitation: 'I think you should talk to the Syrian Government or the Israeli Government about that.' On asking whether the Israeli Government informed the United States of any operation, the questioner was cut short by McCormack when he suggested that 'any questions about this story you can talk to the Israeli Government. OK, good. We're done. (Laughter) Ah, there you are...'

A totally independent source maintained that the damage inflicted on Syria's secret nuclear facility at al-Kibar actually came from afar. As a regular contributor to the New York-based WABC's John Batchelor programme, I was called for comment by the host and as backdrop, his version of these events offered the most interesting disclosures of all. According to Batchelor, the bombs were delivered by American Air Force B-52s that had taken off many hours before from the USAF base at Diego Garcia in the Central Indian Ocean. They were dropped from extreme altitude, but more to the point, intimated John Batchelor, his source was not only in the top echelons of the Pentagon, but his disclosures had always passed muster in the past.

I deal with Syria – and the attack on al-Kibar – together with a lot more detail in Chapter Seven.

Of more recent vintage, at the December 2016 meeting of the International Atomic Energy Agency (IAEA), its director-general Yukiya Amano told member states:

'Terrorists and criminals will try to exploit any vulnerability in the global nuclear security system. Any country, in any part of the world, could find itself used as a transit point.'

Amano's predecessor, Hans Blix, said during a conversation when he visited the United Nations:

'There is a risk of dirty bombs…and not only caesium; you have cobalt, and you have other radioactive substances that are used industrially and in hospitals and can be stolen.'

In addition, the consensus around nuclear weapons non-proliferation is waning. Writing in *Foreign Affairs*, the United Sates' Council on Foreign Relations

Weapons of Mass Destruction Symbols

president, Richard Haass, explained that part of the problem facing the international community in preventing illegal nuclear propagation is what he referred to as 'the existence of non-state actors'. Other issues that make things difficult are a breakdown in the traditional post-Second World War assumptions of sovereignty and conflict, and a lack of appetite for preventative military action, even in the case of a dangerous nuclear-equipped rogue state such as North Korea.

The Treaty on the Non-Proliferation of Nuclear Weapons – a United Nations founded body, more commonly referred to as the NPT – some say, has become a leaky boat taking on water, with rogue states using their nuclear prowess without consequences. The international community might have learned its lesson with the notorious nuclear smuggler Abdul Qadeer Kahn, the creator of the Pakistani nuclear programme, someone who we see a lot of in several later chapters. This is the same man who admitted to selling nuclear bomb technology to North Korea, Libya, and Iran. Indeed, as the director general of the IAEA stressed, a cash-strapped or isolated nation, such as North Korea under Kim Jong-un, poses more of a risk for selling technology or nuclear material than a potential for a self-annihilating use of a weapon in an attack.

Former American President Barack Obama made the point at the Nuclear Summit in 2016. 2,000 tons of nuclear materials are stored around the world, he declared. They are vulnerable to theft and to being transported across national borders. This created the risk of ISIS or other extremists getting nuclear material, which remains, 'one of the greatest threats to global security.' Along similar lines, the IAEA warned in November 2016 that Iran had notified it that highly radioactive material was missing from its Bushehr nuclear power plant, including a supply of iridium-192, an unstable isotope that can be used to manufacture dirty bombs. The material was later recovered, but the event underscored the need for security, particularly at facilities with advanced nuclear technology. Another case of missing material came in February of that year when Baghdad reported to the IAEA that radioactive material was stolen from a storage facility near the city of Basra.

According to the IAEA's Incident and Trafficking Database (ITDB), which records illicit trafficking involving nuclear and radioactive material outside of regulatory control, as of January 2016, participating nations had reported a total of 2,889 confirmed incidents of unauthorized possession and related criminal activities, reported theft or loss, and other activities and events. The number of incidents reached a peak in the early 1990s; since 2009, the ITDB has received reports of scrap metal shipments contaminated with enriched uranium, an issue of concern, according to the IAEA.

The IAEA has reported recent attempted cyber attacks on two nuclear facilities. The first attempt occurred as an ISIS plan, uncovered in 2016, to target a Belgian nuclear facility. Two men linked to the Brussels attacks recorded ten hours of secret surveillance video of a top Belgian nuclear scientist, likely hoping to use his security clearance to try to obtain radioactive material. Amano would not say where the second cyber attack occurred, but suggested that threats against nuclear facilities are more difficult and, therefore, more infrequent than smuggling. The threat of smuggling, including of highly enriched uranium is real: 'Anything they can get their hands on, they will steal.'

Of note is the fact that several nuclear-related treaties have come into effect in recent years, including the 2016 Amendment to the Convention on the Physical Protection of Nuclear Material (CPPNM), which covers the physical protection of nuclear materials in international transport. This includes protection of nuclear material and of nuclear facilities against acts of sabotage, all of which has a bearing on developments further towards the east when the international community entered a daunting phase in nuclear brinkmanship on an October morning in 2006. That was when North Korea – one of the last of the old-world Marxist dictatorships – tested its first atomic bomb, or so many believed.

There are several tentative indications which suggest that it is not impossible that North Korea – for some years already in a close mutually-beneficial working relationship with both Pakistan and Iran – might have detonated an earlier test bomb at about the same time that Islamabad exploded its first five atom bombs in the late 1990s. What was significant about North Korea's 2006 tests was that in its actions, Pyongyang opened a very distinct and intractable path for other states to do the same, Iran especially.

Western intelligence agencies estimate that at the present time there are dozens of countries that hope to achieve some kind of nuclear expertise. This does not necessarily encompass building the bomb, but in the long term it very well could, especially if these nations – Japan for instance – perceive themselves to be militarily threatened. This tally includes some countries that are of Islamic persuasion: Egypt, Saudi Arabia, Syria, Algeria, several others like Indonesia and Kazakhstan as well as a few on the periphery – like Indonesia and Nigeria – all of whom are known to have expressed interest in achieving some kind of nuclear parity.

While West Africa's Nigeria seems an unlikely candidate for building the bomb, or even a decent-sized nuclear power station, it apparently understands very well the clout that it might achieve with its massive oil revenues. A large proportion of this nation's 200 million people are living – or existing, rather – under severe hardscrabble conditions. Yet, while Nigeria cannot even properly manage a commercial airline (more than half of the 600-something world-wide fatalities on commercial airlines in recent years were in Nigeria) it recently paid China hundreds of millions of dollars to launch NIGCOMSAT-1, a communications satellite that was included on board of one of Beijing's Long March 3-B rockets. Contrast that with a recent report from Human Rights Watch – easily accessed on that organization's website – which declares that the majority of the country's schools and medical facilities – hospitals included – are in an appalling mess. There are thousands of schools without such basics as blackboards and desks, or even pencils and paper for the students. Yet the official line out of Abuja, given in a BBC report on May 15, 2007 was that 'the launch … is part of a drive to enhance rural access to technology and the Internet' and, whatever the following is supposed to suggest, 'boost Nigeria's and Africa's knowledge economy'. The country's fat cats meanwhile are having a field day, siphoning off billions of dollars to overseas bank accounts. Now there are some voices within that country's political hierarchy that want the bomb.

Historically, the appeal of nuclear prowess has motivated quite a few nations in the past, including an Iraq while still under Saddam Hussein[2] as well as the present-day leaders of Iran. For a start, the Saudis – a largely Sunni Islamic nation – are aghast that a Shi'ite Iran might beat them to the punch. One aspect of these developments that has been addressed by none of these authorities, is that if any nation wishes to acquire nuclear weapons, it could do no better than to look at how South Africa managed it.

Working in the kind of secrecy that stymied even British and American scrutiny, South Africa produced six atom bombs, with a seventh nearing completion by the time the white government under President F.W. de Klerk pulled the plug and decided to hand over power to the country's majority black African population headed by the venerable Nelson Mandela.

A lot of what took place at nuclear facilities like Pelindaba and Valindaba – both on the outskirts of Pretoria – and at various plants in the Cape where South Africa, in close cooperation with the Israelis, was constructing several versions of an advanced missile delivery system for more compact nuclear devices, has been fogged by the political transition that brought the African National Congress to power in 1994. Some of it is in the public domain, while much is not, since state secrecy has always been a South African hallmark.

The same applies to Israel. It was only very recently made public that Britain helped Israel to obtain its nuclear bomb half a century ago by selling the Jewish State twenty tons of heavy water. This was disclosed by *The Times* in December 2007 under the heading 'Information released under the British Freedom of Information Act'. France and the United States were also involved, but curiously, nobody can be certain whether this was straightforward collusion between governments, or more likely, industrial espionage involving Jewish scientists working at European and American nuclear establishments.

One of the arguments used by the maverick Pakistani scientist A.Q. Khan – who stole nuclear secrets while working in Europe – was conclusive; if his Jewish counterparts could get away with it, said Khan after he had returned to Islamabad, then why couldn't he?

Studies made by American specialists like David Albright of Washington's Institute for Science and International Security (ISIS) and Professor Helen E. Purkitt, Professor of Political Science at the US Naval Academy and a Research Associate for the Centre for Technology and International Security at the National Defence University, have shown that South Africa, despite an internationally-imposed arms embargo, had managed to reach a remarkable level of sophistication with its nuclear weapons and medium–to-long range ballistic missile (M/LRBM) programmes. In a foreword to *Those Who Had the Power - South Africa: An Unofficial Nuclear Weapons History*[3], Professor Helen Purkitt made the point that what went on under a stringent mantle of security in South Africa in the 1960s, 1970s and 1980s – until the nuclear programme was finally halted and the bombs scrapped under American, British and IAEA auspices – offers a plethora of fascinating revelations to anybody interested in contemporary nuclear proliferation trends.

'The analysis provides valuable insights about how a government can secretly develop, test and store an array of sophisticated nuclear strategic and tactical weapons underground,' reckons Purkitt. She goes on to say that the alternative history of South Africa's former weapons programme 'provides invaluable clues and indicators

Terrorist potential use of nuclear materials

of whom, among the three dozen plus nation-states in the world today capable of developing nuclear weapons and long-range delivery systems are pursuing covert programmes.' The study includes details of how South Africa developed alternative bombs like fuel air explosions (which have been used in recent conflict situations in Angola, and, very nearly, in the civil war in Sierra Leone).[4] '[It also] offers [some] interesting insights about possible weapons and delivery systems that terrorist networks [like al-Qaeda] are likely to attempt to obtain in the future.'

Islamic fundamentalists – and al-Qaeda comptrollers in particular – are known to have a vested interest in acquiring nuclear know-how for their purposes. Apposite here might be a series of lectures posted on to an international al-Qaeda Jihadi website between October 2005 and January 2006 titled *Nuclear Preparation Encyclopaedia*. The material that appeared under the above title was translated from its original Arabic by Stephen Ulph, British Arabist and erstwhile colleague of mine at Britain's Jane's Information Group. An authority on this kind of religious alienation, Ulph – who went on to become a Senior Fellow (Terrorism Programs) at the Jamestown Foundation and visiting lecturer at West Point – has since prepared a White Paper on the subject for the United States Select Committee on Intelligence[5].

The Islamic weapons of mass destruction 'encyclopaedia' that Ulph was working on appears at first glance to be a multi-chapter collection compiled and posted by an Islamist who called himself *Layth al-Islam* (Lion of Islam). He claimed to have been 'studying nuclear physics for two years on various scientific and Jihadi websites'. This posting (Lesson No 13), he declared, was 'a present to the Emir [Captain] of the Mujahedeen Sheikh Osama bin Laden … God bless him, for the Jihad in the path of God,' of which a literal translation can be seen below. The aim of the exercise, he continued, was 'to empower the Jihadi community with knowledge of nuclear weapons.'

On closer examination, the posting was composed largely of a series of historical surveys of nuclear technology, including some detailed and not-so-detailed explanations of nuclear experiments. There was mention of important nuclear pioneers, such as Enrico Fermi and included diagrams and sketches said to be of early nuclear research and detailed explanations of nuclear Gun-Type and Implosion devices. Some sketches purported to detail the make-up of nuclear weapons, critical masses, and the amount of fissile and other materials used in their construction and while much of it was sketchy or inaccurate, the objective was clear; this insurgent movement is demonstrably eager to acquire prowess.

A second posting, revealed a somewhat better understanding of nuclear technology. Unlike previous nuclear 'lectures' on al-Qaeda websites that were amateurish, void of scientific knowledge, and poorly written, subsequent versions included detailed information concerning the technical operation and composition of an atom bomb. More importantly, they would include sketches and diagrams of nuclear weapon designs, actual measurements of warheads and amounts of necessary fissile material that would be needed to build the bomb.

While it is difficult to assess accuracy, the postings do not provide any would-be Jihadi with a step-by-step blueprint for its manufacture. There was nothing that compared even remotely with the detailed nuclear warhead design given to Libya by the disgraced Pakistani nuclear scientist A.Q. Khan. However, certain steps are outlined for extraction of radium and the possible assembly of a 'radium bomb', which the author erroneously claims can yield a nuclear explosion, but which amounted to a RDD.

One British authority on the subject made the point that much of the information presented was actually readily available in open sources, 'but [*Layth al-Islam*] appears to be the first al-Qaeda sympathizer to collect this information and translate it into Arabic'. He added that its release was aimed at increasing the scientific awareness and building the knowledge base of the Jihadi community. As its author declared: 'I believe that the strategic balance of power on the battlefield will not change for the Mujahedeen without correct scientific progress ...'

While some might construe these words as harsh, they certainly point to what might take place sometime in the future when this movement – never wanting for funds from its principal backers which included the Saudis in the past – manages to recruit specialists who could take them all the way. What has not been lost on Western strategists is that while he still strode tall throughout parts of Asia and much of the Middle East, A.Q. Khan was responsible for several Pakistani nuclear physicists visiting Osama bin Laden at his Afghan hideout. Nobody knows what was discussed. Nor is Islamabad in any way forthcoming; in fact, they reject the charge. What is certain is that neither the weather nor the political climate in the Hindu Kush featured strongly.

A very literal translation of the opening page of al-Qaeda's Internet-dispersed 'Lesson 13' – one of dozens – reads as follows:

COURSE IN NUCLEAR PREPARATION FOR
MUJAHADEEN.
The Jihadi Nuclear Bomb
And
The methods of nuclear fission

**Part One**

## *THE JIHADI NUCLEAR BOMB*

In homage to the Commander of the Mujahedeen Sheikh Usama bin Laden (whom God preserve), for the sake of the Jihad in God's path

> *In the name of Allah the Gracious the Merciful,*
> *There is no enmity other than to the Oppressors*
> *A prayer and a greeting upon the Faithful Envoy*
> *Muhammad ibn Abdallah on Him and his Family*
> *and Companions, and those that have rendered*
> *Him support to the Day of Judgement*

(Qur'ānic quote) Surah XLVII (Muhammad), 4.

> *'Now when ye meet in battle those who disbelieve, then it is smiting of the necks until, when ye have routed them, then making fast of bonds; and afterward either grace or ransom till the war lay down its burdens. That (is the ordinance). And if Allah willed He could have punished them (without you) but (thus it is ordained) that He may try some of you by means of others. And those who are slain in the way of Allah, He rendereth not their actions vain.'* (Pickthall translation)

> *After [our affirming our] Reliance upon God:*
> *O Lord I am innocent of all those that kill Muslims unjustly*
> *O Lord thou are Knower of the Unseen and of Things Secret, Glory be to Thee – O Lord accept us among the number of the Mujahedeen and the Martyrs.*

There are forty-nine pages that follow this introduction to the document.

On what might be regarded as a more optimistic note, the West was only recently made aware of the roles of rogue Russian scientists who engaged in illegal nuclear proliferation programmes immediately after the collapse of the Soviet Union. A number of these disclosures came from President Putin, first to Bush and then Obama, in which the Russian leader gave his American counterparts the names of nuclear scientists known to have been recruited by al-Qaeda. That much became clear in a report by American journalist Bill Gertz[6], who also quotes Alexander Lebed, a former Russian national security advisor who went on record by stating that Russia 'could not account' for about eighty portable nuclear weapons, a claim later denied by Moscow.

Of more immediate concern to both Moscow and Washington is another kind of nuclear threat about which much is being made in intelligence circles these days; the prospect of terrorist groups – and al-Qaeda in particular – deploying 'Dirty Bombs'. The consequences of any such action – and it is only a question of time before it actually happens – is of enormous importance to those responsible for security in both the East and the West. Indeed, the detonation of an RDD in the short term in cities such as London, Moscow or New York is a far more likely prospect that any terror group fielding a conventional nuclear device, at least for now. Radiological Dispersal Devices fit the most significant threat picture for the West in the not-too-distant future, not only because al-Qaeda has shown interest in developing these weapons, but because they are relatively simple to make. Documents captured in Afghanistan by Coalition Forces after the Taliban had been overrun in Central Asia during 2001 point directly towards that probability. Indeed, there are several authorities, among them Dr Nic von Wielligh, formerly an advisor to the Director General of the International Atomic Energy Agency (IAEA) and a member of Dr ElBaradei's Standing Advisory Group on Safeguards Implementation, who maintain that this might be the first course chosen by international insurgents in their bid to make some kind of impact. Interviewed at his Pretoria home, Dr von Wielligh told me that the likeliest and possibly most damaging terror option in the short term might be the detonation of a radiological bomb in a major Western city. It could be exploded in a crowded civilian area in any American city, he explained. The good doctor is well versed in such topics. He served on an international panel to review the IAEA's Major Programme on (nuclear) Safeguards in 2003. On a more personal level, he must also be credited with help he gave me in addressing many technical issues in *Allah's Bomb*[7].

Dr von Wielligh – with the help of his daughter – has recently written the definitive work on South Africa's nuclear weapons programme. Published in South Africa in 2015, this hefty work is titled *The Bomb: South Africa's Nuclear Program* and comes with the blessings of Vienna's International Atomic Energy Agency[8].

The 'Dirty Bomb' threat abated since I last spoke to Dr von Wielligh. Concerns about RDDs intensified following revelations that senior al-Qaeda official Abu Zubaydah told his captors that his movement was interested in producing these devices 'in some quantity' and his followers knew how to do it. Adding to these concerns was the arrest of the alleged al-Qaeda operative Jose Padilla in Chicago in May 2002. He was on a 'scouting mission' for an al-Qaeda operation that planned to attack the United States with an RDD.

Clearly, Radiological Dispersal Devices are somewhere near the top list of priorities with several radical groups. That, too, is one of disclosures made in George Tenet's book *At the Centre of the Storm* where he deals with the years he spent as head of the Central Intelligence Agency[9]. This former intelligence director made the point that, apart from thwarting an attempt to release cyanide in the New York Subway and somebody trying to murder Presidential aspirant Al Gore with a Russian-built Sagger anti-tank missile during a trip to Saudi Arabia, al-Qaeda several times made serious moves to buy atom bombs from Pakistani scientists, efforts which we now know were linked to the disgraced nuclear proliferator A.Q. Khan. These issues are all dealt with later, including the hugely successful nuclear weapons website launched by these Jihadists. In one chilling assertion, Tenet reveals that there was good evidence in 2001 to suggest that a small nuclear bomb might have been smuggled onto American soil.

Clearly, the United States takes the lead in monitoring worldwide the development, deployment, proliferation or use of weapons of mass destruction within the international community. Indeed, weapons of mass destruction top the agenda of all fourteen American intelligence gathering organizations for the simple reason that, almost without exception, those clandestinely involved regard the US as 'Enemy Number One'. For this reason, little of what happens within Britain's security domain is not closely examined by American specialists, for very good reason.

A well-placed American security leak in January 2010 disclosed that of all the Western countries hosting radical Islamic cadres, Britain was the most vulnerable. A report in the *Daily Telegraph*[10] was headlined 'British Al-Qaeda Hub is Biggest in West' and recalled that two years before, the head of the United Kingdom's internal security service, MI5, Jonathan Evans, had disclosed that his people were aware of roughly 2,000 radicalized Muslims in Britain 'who might be involved in terrorism plots.' It was not lost on anybody that many recent attempts to destroy American passenger aircraft emanated from the British Isles, included the botched attempt by an al-Qaeda recruit from Nigeria who tried to blow up an American Airlines airliner over Detroit on Christmas Day 2009. The man responsible, Umar Farouk Abdulmutallan, had been a student in London between 2005 and 2008 and subsequently went to Yemen to 'learn a few tricks'.

Before Abdulmutallan, there was Richard Reid. In 2001, this radicalized Briton intended bringing down an American plane flying from London to Miami by unsuccessfully attempting to detonate a bomb hidden in his shoe. That was followed by the most concerted terror effort of all when seven aircraft bound for the United States from Heathrow were targeted with liquid explosives – nitro-glycerine – which is one of the reasons why airline passengers are no longer permitted to take drinks onboard when flying. Thereafter, a pair of medical doctors – again, both of the Muslim faith – were involved in a failed airline bombing attack at Glasgow Airport. These are all incidents in the public domain. In truth, there are other attacks that were foiled, the details of which remain sealed. Unquestionably, there will be more attempts at international dislocation by Jihadi forces; it is only a question of where and when.

Britain's most serious attack took place in 2005 when a group of Islamic zealots killed more than fifty people in a spate of transport bombings. Though not as extensive as subsequent mass-scale attacks that targeted Madrid's metro rail system – or the eighty-four people murdered by a rampaging truck driven by an Islamic lunatic in Nice – it was a serious wake-up call for the embattled island state. It is also no secret that these attacks could have happened in Manhattan. Indeed, following close links between Britain's MI6 and Washington during 2009, exactly such an al-Qaeda-backed terrorist effort aimed at the New York transit system was averted when a bunch of Islamic perpetrators were arrested. At the time of going to press some of those involved were still awaiting trial. What Washington found significant was that almost all of Britain's convicted terrorists were 'home-grown'. Questioned about some of these youthful London bombers afterwards, friends and neighbours referred to them as 'ordinary lads from ordinary homes'. Yet somehow, they became utterly alienated from the society that had nurtured them from birth.

The question here is two-fold. First, how did that all happen? Or rather, how *could* it possibly happen to a local bunch of lads? Second, the United States has several million Muslims, the majority originally from Middle Eastern countries. Like their British counterparts, young American Islamists have assimilated well within their communities. With few exceptions – though in recent years some dissidents have emerged from the woodwork – the majority are American and proud of it. There are many people of Islamic faith serving in the government, both State and Federal. Judging from the casualty lists published when US Forces were still fighting in Afghanistan, there are many serving in the United States Armed Forces.

Why, then, the question must be asked, might these people change their allegiance and become enemies of the state in the countries in which they were born? Stephen Ulph has some very distinct views of his own on these and related matters, many quite disconcerting. For a start, it is his contention that the Islamic World is undergoing a massive and unopposed revolution to establish its 'ideal' future mindset and worldview. Moreover, he reckons, this is not something that is going to end any time soon. This Holy War – 'for that is what it really is', Ulph forcibly declared when we spoke in his London apartment – 'is going to last for a very long time … centuries, perhaps.' Jihadis, he declared, are blending propaganda and education with very thorough indoctrination procedures to shape the means of this indoctrination better and faster than the West is able to oppose it. The Internet is their ideal open access distribution medium, and, as he says, 'they have at least a decade head-start on us'. He maintains that the whole process is 'nothing less than a comprehensive re-education programme of books, treatises, encyclopaedias and fatwas, meticulously constructed to undermine, re-orient and radicalize.'

It is also why ordinary young Islamic people in the West are persuaded to give up everything and commit suicide in dreadful acts of terror like those that have beset Europe and which are waiting to happen in Britain and the United States. He then poses the exact same question that he asked a Senate Committee he addressed. 'If the mujahedeen are investing so much in all this, why then aren't we?'

*Chapter 2*

# Early Days of Chasing the Bomb

*'I have sworn upon the altar of God eternal hostility against
every form of tyranny over the minds of men.'*

*Thomas Jefferson, 1800*

Much of the information in this chapter comes by courtesy of the
Federation of American Scientists, with whom I have been honoured
to work closely for many years. The development of nuclear weapons
over more than seventy years is well documented. One of the most incisive
publications on the subject remains Richard Rhodes's brilliant Pulitzer Prize
winning *The Making of the Atomic Bomb* (Simon & Schuster, New York, 1986).
It is a seminal effort and while largely technical and historical, it gripped me from
the start. Thank you Richard! Reprinted several times, that work is way ahead
of anything on the subject. In fact, the comments of my dear departed friend
Dr Jonathan Tucker of the Monterey Institute of International Studies when we
discussed Richard Rhodes's work were simple and direct; 'it is such an incredibly
complex story, yet it has been handled almost like an adventure story … lots of
drama … keeps you on the edge, which is unusual for a scientific work.'

Adventure it certainly is, because Rhodes manages to encapsulate all the
important elements of developing the bomb, breathing a gusty life into the
major players in a way I doubt has been done before with anybody handling
issues as esoteric as these. In the process, he dealt with the major powers and
their acquisition of nuclear weapons, one by one. But these below are my takes
on the countries and not his, though I doubt he would disagree.

## The United States of America

What we do know about America's role is that the expatriate Hungarian scientist,
Leo Szilard, fearing that Nazi Germany might become the first country to
actually construct such an explosive device, tried to warn the Americans. With

# "Trinity and Beyond"

## Chronology of First Five Nations With Nuclear Weapons

**1945 July 16**       **U.S.** → U.S. explodes the world's first atomic bomb, the 'Trinity Test', at Alamogordo, New Mexico.

**1949 August 29**       **U.S.S.R.** →Soviet Union detonates its first atomic bomb, 'Joe 1', at Semipalatinsk  in Kazakhstan. It's a copy of the Fat Man bomb and had a yield of 21 kilotons.

**1952 October 3**       **UK** → First British atomic bomb, 'Hurricane', was tested at Monte Bello Islands, Australia, with a yield of 25 kilotons.

**1960 February 13**     **FRANCE** → First French nuclear test occurs at Reganne, Algeria, in the Sahara Desert. 'Gerboise Bleue' had a yield of 60-70 kilotons.

-------------------------------------------------

**1964 October 16**   **CHINA** → China explodes its first atomic bomb at the Lop Nor test site on the northeastern edge of the Tarim Basin in the XinJiang Province. It was an uranium 235 implosion fission device named '596' and had a yield of 22 kilotons.

Chrononolgy of first five nuclear powers

time running out, he was frustrated by his failure to interest either the US Army or Navy in his line of thought and, by implication, the dangers linked to developing an atomic bomb. Together with fellow expatriate Hungarians Eugene Wigner and Edward Teller, Szilard eventually expressed their concerns in a letter to President FDR Roosevelt, signed by Albert Einstein, the great man himself. It was dated 2 August 1939. The industrialist Alexander Sachs, a newly acquired friend who had access to the President, delivered the letter (together with a memorandum from Szilard) a little more than two months later. During a second meeting with Sachs the day after he got it, the President told his secretary, General Edwin M. (Pa) Watson, that 'this requires action'.

How to actually achieve a nuclear. explosion would be postulated by a young Berkeley physicist Robert Oppenheimer in a National Academy of Sciences (NAS) report, which, he suggested, was by 'bringing quickly together a sufficient mass of the element 235-Uranium'. A team of chemists at Berkeley subsequently headed up by Glenn Seaborg identified another fissile material – element 94 – early in 1941, which, a year later, would be named Plutonium by Seaborg. All this, and much besides is recorded by Rhodes and it makes for some of his most compelling chapters.

In June 1942, Roosevelt went on to order an all-out effort to build the bomb. He placed the huge construction projects that this would require under the authority of the US Army Corps of Engineers. An associate body was established with its headquarters in the borough of Manhattan, New York City, which was why the project assumed the name 'Manhattan Project'. US Army Colonel Leslie Groves was chosen to command it.[1] In a separate research project in Chicago, it took six more months for Italian national Enrico Fermi – one of the great minds of the last century – to achieve the world's first self-sustaining chain reaction. The way was now finally clear for a large-scale effort to produce plutonium ($^{239}$Pu).

Oppenheimer, who had been involved with nuclear fission since 1939 – and who had proved himself a born leader of this dynamic task force – had by then already been asked by Groves to head up a still-to-be established laboratory. In order to maintain an elaborate shroud of secrecy it was decided to concentrate weapons physics research and design at this one laboratory. Oppenheimer suggested to Groves that a suitable site (aptly code-named Site Y) might be found in New Mexico, where the Los Alamos Ranch School was situated.

Work was started in April 1943 on the application of both Uranium-235[2] and Plutonium-239. This method was dubbed 'Gun' devices or weapons. In contrast, a plutonium gun weapon called 'Thin Man' was shelved when it was found in 1944 that high neutron emissions could possibly cause the weapon to pre-detonate. Work continued on 'Little Boy', a more modest uranium gun-type weapon. While success with the latter appeared to be assured, the efficacy of the implosion device remained uncertain. The scientists involved decided nevertheless that it should be tested before being operationally deployed and selected for this was a site in the Jornada Del Muerto region of the Alamogordo Bombing Range, New Mexico. That historic event – the first detonation of a nuclear device - will be forever known as Trinity. It involved the world's first atom bomb, colloquially termed 'Gadget'.

On the morning of 16 July 1945, the world entered a totally new and uncertain age when the tower-mounted bomb exploded. Its thirteen-plus pounds of $^{239}$Pu (fractionally more than six kilograms) yielded an explosion equivalent to about 21,000 tons of TNT, though somebody else talks about 15,000 tons. Either way, that was one mighty explosion and it was to kill an awful lot of people. 'Little Boy' or Unit L11 was deployed operationally on August 6, 1945. Its 140 lbs (63.5 kgs) of high enriched $^{235}$U (80 to 85 percent) obliterated large parts of the city of Hiroshima with an explosion in the magnitude of roughly fifteen Kilotons (Kt).

It was the first time that nuclear weapons had been used against fellow members of the human race and also not the last. Going by what is taking place east of Suez and on the Korean Peninsula today, that is certainly not the end of it.

## The Union of Soviet Socialist Republics

The Soviet Union, having emerged in 1945 from the most destructive war in its thousand-year history with Nazi Germany, had a fairly good idea of what had been taking place at Los Alamos over the previous two years. But what Moscow lacked were specifics. When the news of nuclear fission first reached the Soviet Union – whether through a letter from Frédéric Joliot-Curie to Abram Fedorovich Ioffe, or by the arrival of scientific journals from the West – it was to cause a good deal of speculation among Soviet physicists. Certainly, they were familiar what was going on because there had been an enormous amount of speculation.

In the summer of 1939, during a seminar held at the Leningrad Physico-Technical Institute, Yuli Khariton and Yakov Zeldovich emphasized the importance of fission by stating as an example that a single atomic bomb would be able to destroy Moscow. The audience was stunned and several people present asked why work had not yet started on something similar in the Soviet Union. While the Kremlin was made aware – through a multiple succession of spy networks of British and American efforts to build the bomb – serious work on a 'Motherland Weapon' only started after the war had ended. Intelligence that came from both UK and US-based sources, ended up saving the Soviets at least two years of research and development. During this period, crucial information on the implosion device would arrive from the American-based Klaus Fuchs and David Greenglass. It supplemented work already done, with the first trace quantities of plutonium having been chemically separated at Igor Kurchatov's Laboratory Two in Moscow in October 1944.

Meantime, Stalin directed his Gulag-master and intelligence chief Lavrenti Beria to oversee the bomb effort. In a meeting, mid-August 1945 with Boris Vannikov, the People's Commissar of Munitions, and leading physicist Igor Kurchatov, Stalin laid squarely on the table what has since become known as his momentous 'Single Demand': 'Provide us with a nuclear weapons in the shortest possible time!' he told those present. Moscow's State Defence Committee set up shortly afterwards was named 'Special Committee on the Atomic Bomb' and chaired by Beria. The Soviet bomb programme was given the code-name 'Operation Borodino' and its scientific director was Kurchatov.

A production reactor – the F-1 (Physics 1) – was built in 1946 in the grounds of Laboratory 2 and went critical at 1800 hours on Christmas Day that year with Kurchatov at the controls. What emerged only afterwards was that it was a carbon-copy of the US Hanford 305 reactor, details of which Soviet spies had also smuggled out of the United States. The test site for detonating the first Soviet nuclear weapon had already been selected in 1947 in Kazakhstan, almost 200 kilometres north-west of the city of Semipalatinsk. The area was subsequently code-named Semipalatinsk-21, also referred to as the Poligon and the device was dubbed Josef-1 or Joe-1, after you-know-who. Having been secured to the top of a tower, it was finally tested on 29 August 1949. The blast, code-named Pervaya Molniya (First Lightning), had a yield of ~20Kt. The designation decided on for the Soviet 'Fat Man' – a carbon copy of its US namesake – was RDS-1.

## Great Britain

Quietly and without fuss, Britain was also forging ahead with its nuclear weapons programme. Originally, George Thomson, a professor of physics at the Imperial College in London had already in 1939 sought to focus British attention on the inherent military potential of the bomb. Thomson was alerted to the incipient danger of what was viewed as a potential revolutionary new weapon when he saw a letter by Joliot, von Halban, and Kowarski published in the 22 April 1939 issue of *Nature*, revealing that 3.5 secondary neutrons were released per fission. He consequently contacted General Hastings Ismay, Secretary of the Committee of Imperial Defence, who in turn involved Sir Henry Tizard, Chairman of the Committee on the Scientific Survey of Air Defence (better known as the Tizard Committee). But Tizard was not convinced and little came of Thomson's initiative.

By the early 1940s, the prospect of Britain developing nuclear weapons was not even a matter of consideration. This approach – or lack of it – was abruptly changed by two refugee scientists, Otto Frisch and Rudolf Peierls at the University of Birmingham. They wrote a three-page technical memorandum titled 'On the Construction of a "Superbomb"; based on a nuclear chain reaction in uranium'. The outcome – as well as a general report written by them – would forever change the face of warfare. The memo only reached Tizard in March of that year, through the good offices of Mark Oliphant – later Professor Sir Marcus Oliphant – an eminent Australian scientist and humanitarian who played a central role in developing the atom bomb.

The Frisch-Peierls Memorandum – as it came to be known – immediately raised interest at government level. The document not only explained theoretically how to build a nuclear device, but dealt fairly accurately with its potential devastating use. The two scientists estimated that a fast fission explosion could be achieved with as little as a couple of pounds (plus or minus a single kilogram) of pure Uranium-235. That was followed by the establishment of the Maud Committee, which decided that a bomb could be made from as little as twenty-two pounds (10kg) of $^{235}U$.

Then the unexpected happened. After approving the report, the Maud Committee was disbanded. Those involved were aghast: this was far too serious a matter to ignore, it was felt in scientific circles, which was probably why details surrounding the report eventually reached Prime Minister Winston Churchill that August. Following the advice of Lord Cherwell, his influential personal scientific advisor, he wrote to his Chiefs of Staff and indicated that he was very much in favour of such work being carried forward. It was, and the records also show that work 'was pursued at all speed.' Not to have done so, in the face of a possible Nazi bomb, Churchill wrote to one of his critics, would have been foolish.

Expecting at least some help from their American cousins, the British were disappointed that nothing was forthcoming. For its part, Washington remained tight-lipped about what it was doing in the nuclear field and the prospect of a direct appeal by Churchill to Roosevelt was considered. The situation needed to be redressed, it was agreed. On 25 May 1943, during a visit to the White House, Churchill managed to elicit a promise from Roosevelt for a sweeping exchange of information. Roosevelt's instruction in this regard was telegraphed to Vannevar Bush in London two months later (after a suitable period of repentance and subsequent procrastination), directing him to 'renew' the complete exchange of information with London.

Plans for building Britain's own atom bomb were laid even as war raged. The decision-making process started in Washington in May 1944, and what emerged was a recommendation that a post-war programme be launched that would enable the country to produce a militarily significant number of bombs (a total of ten was mooted). It was to be done within the shortest possible time, was the gist of it. But the war was to end and a new government elected in Britain before anything tangible resulted. It was only on 8 January 1947 that a committee of six members of government – known as Gen 163 – met at 10 Downing Street and decided that Britain should have the bomb.

This decision was influenced by three considerations. First, the Cold War era had become a reality and almost overnight the Soviets had emerged as a serious threat to all Western interests. Second, Britain was to be given the capability to independently deter the Soviet Union should Moscow develop the bomb. Third involved the influence as well as the prestige that seemed to accrue from the possession of nuclear weapons. Britain's Atomic Energy Committee was established in February 1947.

Britain's bomb-building project was obliquely referred to as 'High Explosives Research' (HER) and the first official indication of such a programme emerged in May 1948, when Minister of Defence A.V. Alexander indicated as much in the House of Commons in reply to a question.

Responsible for designing Britain's first atom bomb was the scientist William Penny who initially worked out of the Armament Research Establishment, Kent. Research was also handled at Woolwich Arsenal, a military firing range at Shoeburyness and at Foulness Island – where warhead explosive assemblies were later tested. Weapons electronics production work was established at Woolwich Common, while environmental testing of the explosive assemblies was carried out at Oxfordness in Suffolk. Security and cooperation considerations eventually convinced the British to concentrate work at a single *locale*, much as the Americans did at Los Alamos, with the result that the Atomic Weapons Research Establishment (AWRE) was established at Aldermaston in Berkshire, in April 1950. Development of Britain's Mark 1 atom bomb proceeded with close cooperation between the scientific community involved and the Royal Air Force.

In the end, an August 1952 deadline was set for completion of the core and was then only met with the help of some Canadian plutonium. That device contained about fifteen pounds of $^{239}$Pu and incorporated a polonium (and presumably beryllium) initiator with a uranium tamper. The British closely followed the design of the original United States' 'Fat Man', although their device would sport a more sophisticated core. Since a nuclear device could not be tested on the British mainland itself, Attlee opened secret negotiations with Australian Premier Robert Menzies late in 1950 to use the Monte Bello Islands – off the northwest coast of Australia – as a testing base. Formal sanction was granted by Canberra the following year.

The non-nuclear assembly of the first British device was dispatched to Monte Bello via Cape Town aboard the frigate HMS *Plym* in June 1952. Its plutonium core arrived three months later aboard a Sunderland flying boat, after a three-day flight. Encased in a watertight caisson beneath the *Plym*, then anchored off Trimouille Island, Monte Bello, the event termed 'Hurricane' took place at midnight on 3 October 1952. The yield of this first British atom bomb was a respectable twenty-five kilotons.

## France

Like Britain, France took longer to complete the initial stages of its nuclear weapons programme, but in the end, achieved similar results. The event, known as *Gerboise Bleue*, took place on top of a tower at the Reggane Proving Grounds in the Tanezrouft desert, French Algeria and yielded an explosion in the order of 60-79Kt. The bomb was a plutonium-fuelled, implosion-assembly nuclear device and was referred to in Paris as Type A.

This was also the first 'indigenous' bomb to be detonated by a country joining this exclusive club that was not a carbon or near copy of the US 'Fat Man' (as was the Soviet RDS-1 and Britain's 'Hurricane' device). But it took a while to get there, and the original April 1939 letter by Joliot-Curie, von Halban, and Kowarski played a significant role. That document concluded that it was uranium's rare $^{235}U$ isotope which fissioned and made a chain reaction possible – even in natural uranium. The significance of this observation may be deduced from three secret patents which Joliot-Curie registered a month later, two concerning the production of energy – and a third concerning explosives.

Joliot-Curie had already in 1935 recognised the possibility of achieving an 'explosive nuclear chain reaction'. For their part, Halban and Kowarski eventually ended up in Canada as part of the British contribution to the US Manhattan Project, as would three Frenchmen – Pierre Auger, Jules Guèron, and Bertrand Goldschmidt.  These five scientists were leading physicists in pre-Vichy France. When General Charles de Gaulle – leader of the Free French – visited Ottawa in July 1944, Guèron went on to inform him about the atom bomb and its potential impact on international politics. It was actually the first such communication to reach any Frenchman of notable political stature.

Sadly, the presence of French scientists in the Manhattan Project also contributed towards the sometimes-strained relations between Britain and America in this sphere of activity. Washington was concerned that secret information would be passed back to France. Indeed, the last thing that the US wanted was a fourth nuclear partner (that is, after the UK and Canada), which, it was felt at the time, could usurp its perceived leadership role in the nuclear monopoly.

The French thought otherwise. After the war, Paris set about the task of building a nuclear infrastructure of its own. The first act of this new chapter was a decree on 18 October 1945 by General Charles de Gaulle that established a French nuclear energy agency, called *Commissariat à l'Énergie Atomique* (CEA). Raoul Dautry was appointed its Administrator-General and Joliot-Curie its High Commissioner. With the exception of Halban, all the leading French physicists who had contributed towards the Manhattan Project returned to France within a year. Although none were formally released from their wartime pledges of secrecy, it would be simplistic to accept that they would withhold details of such important research once they were again on home ground. While the Saclay Nuclear Research Centre near Versailles was being established, the CEA took over an old fortress on the outskirts of Paris – the Fort de Châtillon – where France's first nuclear reactor was erected.

The year 1948 became a milestone for French nuclear aspirations. Uranium was discovered near Limoges, while the first French reactor, called EL-1 or ZOE (Zero power, uranium oxide fuel, and *eau lourde* – heavy water – moderated), built under the direction of Kowarski went critical in December. The first milligram-quantity of French plutonium was extracted in November 1949 at a lab-scale facility at Le Bouchet, using a technique developed by Bertrand Goldschmidt. The following year occurred an event of perhaps greater significance when, during a meeting held at the Saclay, Goldschmidt successfully argued in favour of plutonium producing power-reactors as opposed to research-reactors.

It was only in 1952 that the French military started taking an active interest in nuclear weapons, when a small group of Army officers under the direction of Colonel Charles Ailleret, of the *Commandement des armes speciales* began preliminary studies on the requirements for a nuclear weapon detonation. Like so many other historical reversals, it took the war in French Indo China to create an awareness of the possibility of a French atom bomb. That sentiment surfaced in parliamentary and military circles after the disastrous defeat of the French Army at Dien Bien Phu, Indochina in May 1954.

Another factor had been the failure of French Premier Pierre Mendès-France to interest the United States and the Soviet Union in a policy of nuclear disarmament. Meantime – as in the Middle East today – there were Frenchmen who had not been made aware of the difference in status between the nuclear 'Haves' and 'Have-Nots'. It was Mendès-France who called a cabinet-level, inter-ministerial meeting to discuss the issue shortly afterwards, which was when he asked about the time frame. He demanded two answers: the amount of time required to develop a home-built nuclear device and second, the feasibility of France constructing its own nuclear-powered submarine (an SSN). Two days later, General Albert Buchalet agreed to head up a secret nuclear weapons unit within the CEA, named BEG, the *Bureau d'Éudes Générales.*

By now, May 1956, BEG had expanded sufficiently for it to be transformed into a department – the *Départment de techniques nouvelles* (DTN). The issue was not yet a fait accompli as there were powerful political elements in the country's government opposed to France going nuclear. But that, too, was short-lived because the Suez Canal crisis – referred to as the Suez fiasco by the media – happened shortly afterwards.

On 26 July 1956, Egyptian President Nasser did what the European powers regarded as 'unthinkable' and nationalized the Suez Canal. It was Egypt's waterway, the Egyptian leader declared to his nation in a radio broadcast 'and the time has come to reassert Egyptian sovereignty'. In other words, in Cairo's eyes, foreign ownership of a major Egyptian strategic asset was no longer acceptable.

To redress this situation Israel, Britain, and France, decided to resort to military force. A Franco-British landing that took place on 5 November at Port Said followed an Israeli attack six days before. Ostensibly, British and French forces were there to 'pacify' the situation. In fact, it was nothing of the kind; Paris and London wanted their canal back. Issues were compounded when Soviet Premier Nikolai Bulganin condemned these actions with a 'barely veiled...threat to use nuclear missiles to end the fight...' The war in Egypt ended as suddenly as it had begun, with both countries in disgrace.

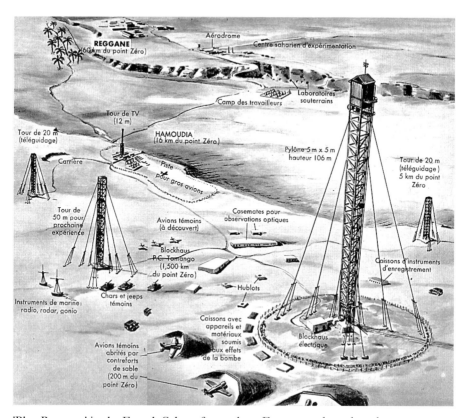

'Plan Reggane' in the French Sahara from where France conducted nuclear tests

At that stage, to the chagrin of the French leadership, a decision still had to be taken at government level whether or not to acquire nuclear weapons. Abandoned by its friends and allies, the humiliation and impotence of both Paris and London were visible enough for all to see. An immediate consequence was a new protocol signed only weeks later between the CEA and the French Armed Forces. It covered both research on all aspects of a nuclear explosive device as well as acquiring adequate quantities of plutonium for this purpose. Further, the French military was charged with the preparations for testing an atom bomb.

## The People's Republic of China

The Chinese Communist Party was presumably aware of the American Manhattan Project from its inception in 1942, thanks in part to members and sympathisers within the Soviet intelligence gathering apparatus in the West such as 'Sonia' (Ursala Hamburger). It certainly knew that the US project was on track by 1944. Ironically, while Mao Zedong was initially dismissive of the atom bomb (he described it as a 'Paper Tiger' during an interview in 1946), Kang Sheng, his spymaster, was at the same time running a campaign to lure home expatriate Chinese scientists who had received training in Western technology. Some of these specialists might have been involved in nuclear weapons and missile projects.

It should be mentioned that while the Sino-Soviet Treaty of Friendship, Alliance and Mutual Assistance of 1950 served to provide the PRC with an implied nuclear umbrella, this did not prevent US threats to use the bomb during the Korean War (1950/53) and, not very long thereafter, the Taiwan Strait Crisis (1954/55).

An early result of these developments took place early 1955 during an enlarged meeting of revolutionary China's Central Secretariat, presided over by Mao and held in Zhongnanhai – the political and state centre in the Forbidden City. It was resolved that the People's Republic would have its own 'Manhattan Project' which would be referred to as Project 02. Because of the perceived urgency, it was also determined to enlist Soviet help. Between January 1955 and September 1958, six accords were eventually signed between the two countries, the most important pertaining to the delivery of a prototype Soviet atom bomb. Agreements followed for the provision of a nuclear reactor and a cyclotron as well as a joint survey for uranium in the PRC.

Prudent, as always, Mao did not put all his trust in Moscow. China went ahead and followed a supplementary, indigenous, route to the bomb. Besides the Soviets, unofficial help allegedly also came by way of the Joliot-Curies in late 1949 when they assisted Qian Sanqiang, one of their former students, to purchase the PRC's first nuclear instruments in Europe. That was followed by Iréne Joliot-Curie giving Yang Chengzong ten grams of radium salt in October 1951. More assistance might have come from Dr Bruno Pontecorvo, an Italian Jew. Pontecorvo had worked in Canada for the Anglo-Canadian team that was contributing towards the Manhattan Project from 1943 onwards. He followed that with a stint in the UK at the Harwell nuclear research centre. Then, to the surprise of many of his colleagues, he defected to the Soviet Union with his family in October 1950.

With the benefit of hindsight, America's initial reticence to get more parties involved in its earlier phases of nuclear research was obviously well founded. Soviet advisors, equipment, and data started to arrive in China in 1958. Unfortunately, so too did Mao's catastrophic Great Leap Forward, which resulted in social, political, commercial and industrial havoc throughout the country. It would go on to adversely affect China's nuclear programme. In a bid to stop the rot and possibly reverse this trend with regard to the country's defence, China's Central Committee approved several ad hoc commissions to allow work to go on without interruption. The PRC's nuclear path was further spelt out by the Central Military Commission during a conference held in 1958 and chaired by the Great Leader himself. This event produced 'The Guidelines for Developing Nuclear Weapons', the most revealing of these being the development of both fissile and thermo-nuclear warheads as well as a clutch of long-range delivery missiles. It was stressed that it would enjoy precedence over the country's reconstruction. That June – the month during which the country's Soviet-supplied reactor and cyclotron started operating – Mao said that China would acquire nuclear weapons within ten years. He was proved right.

Things were not going so well on the international front however. China's new-found intimacy with the Soviets would not see out the decade. Differences were not only ideological; Khrushchev and Mao had very different perceptions about the consequences of a nuclear war. Characteristically, Beijing said very little but it was already aware that the Soviet Union had secretly decided to renege on its undertaking to supply a prototype bomb; a letter dated 20 June 1959, formally notified the Peoples Republic of China of this decision.

For all that, work on the bomb went ahead. The Chinese were not only fast-tracking the highly enriched uranium route, but also working on a plutonium core. In 1958, they started planning for their first plutonium producing reactor. This was situated in Jiuquan Prefecture, Gansu Province. A Soviet-designed, graphite-moderated natural-uranium light water reactor (LWR) was adapted for this purpose and work on site commenced in February 1960.

The 'Three Hard Years' of 1960/62 followed, coupled to social unrest and food shortages, all bound to affect the nuclear programme. Although plant construction and equipment installation at the uranium enrichment site was about complete by the end of 1961, it was nowhere near operational. The Lanzhou Gaseous Diffusion Plant now became a 'national crusade'.

Late in 1962, Mao's Second Ministry directed that $^{235}$U production be brought forward to the beginning of 1964, which was when a youthful Lanzhou scientist, Wang Chengxiao proposed a revised production plan that would enable the original schedule to be constrained by six months. Thus, in January 1964 the first highly enriched uranium was produced. As was noted afterwards in some of Mao's papers, the 'national crusade' – as it was phrased – had paid off.

What was only discovered years later was that Beijing – like Pakistan, Iraq, Iran and North Korea afterwards – benefited immensely from details gleaned from open publications in the West.[3] Open source material which had been unclassified – prematurely, as we now know – such as the so-called Smyth Report, *Effects of Atomic Weapons* by Glasstone and Dolan, Jungk's *Brighter Than a Thousand Suns*, and Groves' *Now It Can Be Told* – all played edifying roles. Not only was the implosion-technique revealed in these documents, but also the manner in which the objective might be achieved, viz. by the use of spherically arranged high explosive 'lenses'. This information had a vital place in enabling the Chinese to work out theoretical designs of their own.

Soviet advisors also unwittingly contributed to what the Chinese were up to when they left behind important scraps of paper. Among other technical information, these provided their former protégés with vital design details for the all-important implosion 'lenses' ultimately used in detonating the bomb. More aid came from clues garnered from Soviet and US test sites. The Chinese collected debris from the periphery and carefully analysed everything for anything useful that might point to how the job needed to be tackled.

Nuclear weapons design in China meanwhile was being handled under the auspices of the Ninth Bureau, which had been initiated at the transitional Beijing Nuclear Weapons Research Institute in the late 1950s. Bureau head Li Jue was fortunate in having the services of three senior nuclear scientists, Wang Ganchang, Peng Huanwu, and Guo Yonghuai, who had been assigned to the Northwest Nuclear Weapons Research and Design Academy (Ninth Academy), then temporarily still quartered at the Beijing Institute. While most of the credit for designing the country's first bomb went to this trio, the 'father' of the Chinese bomb was to be Deng Jiaxian who notably held a PhD from an American university and made some very substantial contributions to the bomb's theoretical design.

Very early on, China had to make a decision and its first nuclear explosive device was named '596' a not-so-subtle reminder of Khrushchev's June 1959 action when he reneged on the delivery of a prototype bomb to the PRC. Early in 1961 China had to make a final decision about what type of nuclear device it would produce and in what quantity. First, came the A-1, an implosion device. The A-2, in contrast, was Gun-Type. Although the A-1 device headed the charge, it is interesting that work on the A-2 was never abandoned – obviously as a backup should A-1 fail.

After approximately thirty months of work, and some 1,000 test shots, the design was perfected by September 1962. A year later, Deng and three groups of theorists under his leadership completed the draft design of the device at the Beijing Institute. In November 1963, another important milestone was reached when a hydrodynamic test was carried out using a half-sized model of the explosive package.

The Nuclear Component Manufacturing Plant, also at Jiuquan, began machining the first HEU 'ball' into a bomb core at the end of April 1964. Appropriate to this communist state, it completed the task on May Day 1964. Final assembly of '596', which weighed 1,550kg, including some 900kg of high explosives and more than 24 detonators, took only seventy two hours. The first atom bomb was completed three months later, and finally detonated at the Lop Nor (also referred to as Lop Nur) Nuclear Weapons Test Base in China's far western Gobi Desert on the morning of 16 October 1964.

The People's Republic of China formally became the world's fifth official nuclear power.

## Chapter 3

# Three Countries That Secretly Built the Bomb: Israel, India and Pakistan

Though hardly a major power, Israel has been the dominant force in the Middle East for many decades. Strategically, it warrants a lot of attention.

Unlike the major powers, it has always been Israeli policy neither to admit nor deny that it possesses the bomb, though the first inkling in 1960 that the fledgling Jewish State had acquired nuclear weapons came in a small article in *Time*[1]. That was when the news magazine stated that 'a non-Communist state had made 'an atomic development'. Three days later the *Daily Express* confirmed that country to be Israel and a day later, the *New York Times* said that France had been assisting it to achieve these aims. The die was cast.

That Israel has a substantial nuclear arsenal is no longer a secret. The issue has become the focus of grievances within the Islamic World and is raised whenever Washington is seen to object to Third World aspirations at acquiring nuclear expertise. No such criticism is directed by the Americans at Israel's nuclear weapons programme, nor has it ever been. Jerusalem has never been brought to account for creating what is arguably the third or fourth largest nuclear arsenal on the planet. Indeed, there are some who maintain that Israel now has more H-Bombs than Britain. *The Bulletin of the Atomic Scientists* estimated that the Israeli nuclear arsenal ranged from between seventy-five to roughly 200 weapons[2]. These comprised bombs, missile warheads and possibly non-strategic (tactical) weapons, it reported. Similarly, the Federation of American Scientists observed in one of its reports[3] that 'based on the plausible upper and lower bounds of operating practices at the Dimona Reactor, Israel could have produced enough HEU and plutonium for at least 100 nuclear weapons, but probably not significantly more than 200 weapons.'

The jailed Israeli nuclear dissident Mordechai Vanunu revealed that the figure was somewhere between 100 and 200 fission bombs and that the tally included a number of fusion weapons. By February 1997 – according to a report in *Jane's Intelligence Review* – the stockpile had been upped to '400 deliverable thermonuclear and nuclear weapons.' The bottom line here is that cumulatively, Israel probably possesses a nuclear potential equivalent to several hundred Hiroshima-type atom bombs, more than that held by either Britain or France, plus an unknown number of H-bombs.

What is notable is that for two generations this activity has been hidden behind an impenetrable cloak of secrecy. Some nuclear physicists involved in the early days of Israel's nuclear weapons programme were Jewish scientists who had worked on the Manhattan Project; many talented Jewish scientists immigrated to Palestine after the Second World War. Still more arrived on *aliya* from countries that already hosted large Jewish communities and included Britain, Australia, South Africa, Argentina and elsewhere. For these and other reasons, Israel's belligerent neighbours today perfectly understand the implications of what has been termed by some as Israel's capacity for 'ultimate retaliation'.

Efraim, former director the head of the country's National Security Council and erstwhile chief of Mossad made that perfectly clear when he declared that any kind of 'mega-terror attack' on his people 'would open options for retaliation that hitherto were unacceptable to public opinion.' The threat came at the turn of the New Millennium and was specifically directed at Syria, after Damascus was accused of deploying a large number of its SCUD-C missiles along its southern frontier with Israel, the majority tipped with sarin and VX nerve gases. More recently, there is conclusive evidence that Syrian forces have used sarin against rebel dissidents in Aleppo, an issue raised several times within the United Nations. What is clear from numerous sources – several of them intentionally leaked by the Israeli Government to create a 'fear factor' among its adversaries – is that nuclear ambiguity fostered by the Jerusalem Government appears to have served its purpose, certainly well enough to have prevented another Arab-Israeli war.

Israel, in the words of Nicholas Valry, who published 'Israel's Silent Gamble with the Bomb' declared that 'Israel [has] used their existence to guarantee a continuing supply of American conventional weapons, a policy [that is] likely to continue[4]'.

More recently, the Jewish Homeland has moved from producing basic fission weapons to fielding American 175mm and 203mm self-propelled artillery pieces capable of firing nuclear shells and manufacturing low-yield neutron bombs. Some evidence has been published in the West that it has 'Micronukes' as well as 'Tinynukes', both of which would be useful for attacking point targets and other tactical or barrier (mining) uses. The word in Jerusalem is that 'Tinynukes', are said to be deployed on the Golan to prevent attack by the Syrians, as happened in 1973. However, a repetition of this is unlikely, due to Israel's state-of-the-art electronic and optical surveillance systems such as satellites. It is ironic indeed that the Germans, of all nations, gave Israel one of its most powerful potential striking mediums by providing three Dolphin-class Type 800 submarines built by Emden's Thyssen Nordseewerke and Howaldtswerke-Deutsche Werft in Kiel[5]. As with the nuclear programme, the security blanket drawn over these craft has been almost impossible to penetrate.

Meantime, Jerusalem embarked on a programme of creating an additional strike capability with nuclear cruise missiles which effectively provides Israel with a capacity that could change the arms race in the Middle East, especially if it operates within Iranian territorial waters in the Arabian Gulf.

Israel began investigating the nuclear field a year after the country emerged from the first of the Arab wars. With French support, it secretly began building a nuclear reactor and reprocessing plant in the late 1950s; support from Paris was seminal to the Israeli nuclear programme, and in many ways, it was mutually beneficial. The Israeli Atomic Energy Commission, working under the Machon Program and in association with the Department of Isotope Research at the Weizmann Institute, developed a means of extracting uranium from raw phosphate recovered in the Negev desert as well as a new technique to produce indigenous heavy water. Julius Bergmann, then chief of research at the Israeli Defence Ministry and Prime Minister Ben Gurion's scientific advisor, sold both patents to France's *Commissariat à l'énergie atomique* for 60 million francs. Israeli scientists also helped construct the G-1 plutonium production reactor and UP-1 reprocessing plant at Marcoule. France and Israel came to develop close relations in many nuclear disciplines and were the only foreign scientists allowed to roam 'at will' at that principal nuclear facility. Israeli scientists were also present at atmospheric tests in the Sahara in the 1960s, all under the auspices of the *Centre Saharien d'Expérimentations Militaires* (Military Experiments Saharan Centre).

Very early on, a number of Israeli physics graduate students were sent to study abroad, including one who went to the University of Chicago and worked for a while under Enrico Fermi, who had overseen the world's first artificial and self-sustaining nuclear chain reaction. Others included Harry Lipkin, born in the United States, who emigrated to Israel in 1950 and spent a year at Saclay in France studying reactor physics in 1953. Another was Amos de Shalit who had originally studied at MIT.

According to the noted polymath Jeremy Bernstein, who had himself visited Israel in the spring of 1960 while travelling with future Nobel Prize winner Murray Gell-Mann, David Ben Gurion was already thinking of a 'nuclear deterrent' after Israel had achieved victory in the War of Independence in 1948. Accompanied by the former prime minister's daughter, Renana Leshem, a biologist, Bernstein, in the company of Murray Gell-Mann, visited Ben Gurion at his home at the desert kibbutz of Sdeh Boker. In an attempt to rationalize the old man's thinking in these early days, Bernstein explained:

'After the experience of the Holocaust [Ben Gurion] had no faith in security guarantees by external powers. He imagined a scenario where there might be a concerted attack by Israel's neighbours that might destroy much of the country before anyone could or would provide help.'

At the time, there were very few Israeli nuclear physicists and no infrastructure for this kind of thing, not to mention money, but Ben Gurion:

'… was not an individual who was easily discouraged,' declared Bernstein. 'He had as allies the chemist David Bergmann who organized the scientific effort and above all Shimon Peres, the *eminence grise* who was responsible for all practical negotiations…it was Peres who ultimately made the arrangements with the French [by the late 1950s the Israelis had put together a group of nuclear physicists] about as good as any.'

They then had to decide what kind of nuclear weapon they were to build.

There are really only two options he explains. One can try to build a bomb whose explosive fissile material is uranium (as the South Africans did) or one can go the plutonium (or Implosion) route. As Bernstein notes, either choice presents technical challenges. 'If uranium is chosen, then one has to deal with enrichment.' The uranium comes from a mine that has less than one percent of the fissile isotope uranium-235. The rest is uranium-238, which is not suitable for a weapon. Thus, the two isotopes must be separated to the degree that a product is produced that contains about ninety percent uranium-235.

The other option left to the Israelis was plutonium and was the one on which they eventually settled. To this end, deals were signed with France, which was why, Bernstein says, if you had visited Dimona in those days, you would have found several hundred people on the site speaking French. The French Saint Gobain chemical company was brought in to build a facility for separating the plutonium that had been created in the uranium fuel rods from the actual fuel rods themselves.

'This is a non-trivial matter. The French had supplied all the uranium used initially and some sort of understanding had been reached that the irradiated fuel rods would be sent back to France. The Israelis kept referring to this when they had difficulty with people like President Kennedy. In fact, it seems that one shipment of fuel rods was sent to France and a small amount of plutonium returned to Israel.

'But then, as soon as they got their own reprocessing plant to work, they did their own reprocessing and kept the plutonium… Ben Gurion and Peres during the beginning of the program, kept all these arrangements to themselves.'

In fact, observes Bernstein, there was never a national debate as to whether or not Israel was to have a nuclear weapons programme, and the existence of Dimona was not revealed to the Israeli people until December 1960, in a speech by Ben Gurion in which he insisted that the reactor was being built for purely scientific purposes. On other occasions, he said that the power from the reactor would be used to desalinate sea water. 'All this deception might have continued indefinitely had it not been for Mordechai Vanunu,' was Bernstein's view. 'And that is another story…'

Though the Israeli Government has never been prepared to comment, it is believed to have begun full scale production of nuclear weapons following the 1967 Six-Day War, although it may have had bomb parts earlier[6]. A CIA report from early 1967 stated that Israel had the materials to construct a bomb in six to eight weeks and according to the Federation of American Scientists, some authors suggested that Israel had two crude bombs ready for use during the war. American journalist Seymour Hersh maintained that everything was ready for production at this time save an official order to do so, but even this is conjecture as no official figures have ever been released, even whether the Jewish State has the bomb or not. Hersh stated that it is widely believed that the words 'Never Again', in English and Hebrew, were welded onto the first warhead.

It has only recently emerged that Britain also played a part in bringing the Israeli nuclear weapons programme to fruition. Top secret British documents obtained by the British Broadcast Corporation's *Newsnight* in 2005 disclosed that the British government allowed hundreds of secret shipments of restricted materials to the Jewish State in the two decades after its founding.

'These included specialist chemicals for reprocessing and samples of fissile material – uranium-235 in 1959, and plutonium in 1966, as well as highly enriched lithium-6 which is used to boost fission bombs and fuel hydrogen bombs. The investigation also showed that Britain shipped 20 tons of [Norwegian] heavy water directly to Israel in 1959 and 1960 to start up the Dimona reactor.'

The transaction was made through a Norwegian front company called Noratom which took a two percent commission on the transaction. Britain was challenged about the heavy water deal by the IAEA after these details came to light and British Foreign Minister Kim Howells claimed this was a sale to Norway.

But a former British intelligence officer who investigated the deal at the time confirmed that this was really a sale to Israel and the Noratom contract was just a charade. The Foreign Office finally admitted in March 2006 that Britain knew the destination was Israel all along. For its part, Jerusalem admitted running the Dimona reactor with Norway's heavy water since the early 1960s.

Israel began full scale production of nuclear weapons following the 1967 Six-Day War, although some pundits accept that it might already have subversively acquired almost all the bomb parts, the majority from France and illegally from the United States through 'amenable' Jewish contacts and businessmen in that country. Again, nobody really knows for sure. Even today, as Jeremy Bernstein points out, Israel might have 100 nuclear weapons. 'It might also have 400.'

Once Israel's programme was on track, it reportedly even conducted underground nuclear tests on domestic soil, though no seismic signature proof has ever been forthcoming. Nor, if it happened, are we aware of the yield. The West German Army magazine *Wehrtechnik* claimed in its June 1976 issue that the first such underground tests in the Negev took place in 1963. Other reports mention a nuclear test at Al-Naqab, also in the Negev, on 2 November 1966[7]. The government was again accused of doing so near Eilat on 28 May 1998 by a member of its own Knesset. Egyptian scientists made similar charges immediately afterwards, both of which were denied by the Israeli deputy defence minister.

South Africa entered the picture with the supply, under specific international restrictions, of 500 tons of uranium concentrates from the mid-1960s on condition that it be used only for peaceful purposes. South African staff attached to its own nuclear authority visited Israel annually to monitor its use. But not long afterwards Israel indicated a need for more plutonium for its nuclear weapons and the stockpiled supply would almost certainly have kept its needs at the Dimona nuclear establishment going for at least a decade. By then, Jerusalem had again approached Pretoria for an additional 100 tons of uranium concentrate and in the end the South Africans, themselves under severe international pressure because of its apartheid policies and, more saliently, in need of technological assistance in its own weapons programmes, acceded to the request. In exchange, the South Africans received thirty grams of tritium which were intended eventually to boost their atom bombs but never used. Additionally, more agreements were signed between the two states and ties to several defence-related projects enhanced. Israel was to go on to play a major role in assisting South Africa to build a medium range intercontinental ballistic missile (MRIBM) based largely on its own Jericho ICMB programme.

What is certain is that early on in its nuclear programme Israel devoted a lot of effort to producing lithium-deuteride, a greyish, stable, solid compound of lithium and deuterium. Without getting into the intricacies of these incredibly complex disciplines, Bernstein explains that when a mixture of tritium and deuterium is subjected to the kinds of temperatures and pressures that a nuclear device can produce, the end result is that the yield of the bomb is substantially increased; in the argot, 'boosted fission weapons'. This is a reaction that is also used in hydrogen bombs. Hence, says Bernstein, 'When a country with a nuclear weapons programme has a facility for making lithium deuteride, one knows that they are in the business of making advanced weapons.' The Iranians have a facility for producing heavy water and hence deuterium, he adds. 'Whether they are trying to produce lithium deuteride, I do not know'.

That Israel tested nuclear weapons in the South Indian Ocean on 22 September 1979, at a time when Israel was still distinctly cosy with South Africa's apartheid regime, has come to the fore of late. South Africa's Deputy Foreign Minister Aziz Pahad was later quoted in the Israeli daily *Ha'aretz* as saying that there 'was definitely a nuclear test'. He also confirmed that the bomb was South African. An Israeli reporter added that:

> 'this was the first time an official spokesman of the Pretoria Government had actually admitted that the flash was the result of a nuclear test [though not necessarily a South African bomb]. The statement contradicts declarations by his predecessors that South Africa never ever conducted such tests.'

Then, to obfuscate matters, Pahad backtracked, claiming afterwards that he had never made the statement attributed to him. His press secretary told the *Albuquerque Journal* of 11 July 1997 that the deputy minister 'did not admit' that a nuclear test took place. Instead, she insisted that he had been quoted out of context. More significant is the fact that three nuclear blasts were specifically mentioned and the circumstances confirmed by the US Embassy in Pretoria. American writer Seymour Hersh, in his analysis of the issue was even more forthright. Referring to a brilliant 'nuclear explosion-type' flash picked up by the US Vela satellite, the blast was the third test of a neutron bomb, he explained. Others believe it was a conventional bomb (or bombs). 'The first two were hidden in clouds to fool the satellite and the third was an accident – the weather cleared.'

## India: South Asian Nuclear Power

The cornerstone of India's nuclear was encapsulated in June 1946 by Pandit Jawaharlal Nehru, the man who was soon to become India's first prime minister.

Taking cognizance of what happen little more than a year before in Japan, he declared:

> 'as long as the world is constituted as it is, every country will have to devise and use the latest devices for its protection. I have no doubt India will develop her scientific researches and I hope Indian scientists will use the atomic force for constructive purposes. But if India is threatened, she will inevitably try to defend herself by all means at her disposal.'

Having clandestinely initiated its nuclear programme in 1967, it took seven years for New Delhi to test its first atom bombs, which it did in May 1974. Since then India conducted a series of tests. The first A–Bomb test, rather inappropriately called 'Smiling Buddha', took place on 18 May 1974. New Delhi claims that the first Hydrogen Bomb or thermonuclear test was held four years later, though there is some dispute as to whether an H–Bomb was detonated or possibly a tritium-boosted A–Bomb. The single largest yield test was Operation Shakti, an underground detonation in the semi–desert western Indian state of Rajasthan in 1998. This purported to be a thermonuclear bomb, and again, the yield was in dispute. One FAS estimate puts it at between twenty and sixty kilotons.

Though India releases little or no information about its nuclear weapons, the country is variously estimated to have between forty-eight and eighty nuclear weapons, even though it is said to have produced enough weapons-grade plutonium for more than a hundred[8]. Clearly, the country has extensive civil and military nuclear programmes. That includes almost a dozen nuclear reactors, uranium mines and milling sites as well as uranium enrichment, fuel fabrication and heavy water production facilities. As a consequence, India's nuclear research capabilities are extensive and rated among the most advanced in Asia. Additionally, it has significant radiological, chemical and biological warfare capabilities.

For all this – and the fact that India is a member of the International Atomic Energy Agency (and has several of its reactors subject to IAEA safeguards) – the country is not a signatory to either the Nuclear Non-Proliferation Treaty (NPT) or the Comprehensive Test Ban Treaty (CTBT). It acceded to the Partial Test Ban Treaty in October 1963, though its last nuclear test, followed by Pakistan, was in 1998. More pertinently, India has a declared nuclear 'No–First–Use Policy' and is in the process of developing a nuclear doctrine based on 'credible minimum deterrence.' In August 1999, the Indian government released a draft of the doctrine, which asserts that nuclear weapons are solely for deterrence and that India will pursue a policy of 'retaliation only'. The document also maintains that India 'will not be the first to initiate a nuclear strike, but will respond with punitive retaliation should deterrence fail' and that the decisions to authorize the use of nuclear weapons would be made by the Prime Minister or his 'designated successor(s)."

Washington's Federation of American Scientists has listed an assessment of India's nuclear potential:

- In 2005, it was estimated that India had between forty and fifty warheads.
- In November 2008, the *Bulletin of the Atomic Scientists* estimated that India has about seventy assembled nuclear warheads, with about fifty of them fully operational[9].
- A report by David Albright, published by the Institute for Science and International Security in 2000, estimated that by the end of 1999, India had 310 kilograms (almost 700 pounds) of weapon grade plutonium, enough for sixty-five nuclear weapons. He also believed that India had 4,200kg (more than four tons) of reactor grade plutonium which would be enough to build 1,000 nuclear weapons. By the end of 2004, he estimated that India had 445kg of weapon grade plutonium which is enough for around eighty-five nuclear weapons, considering that five kg (eleven pounds) of plutonium is required for each weapon. India has the capability of fielding the third largest nuclear arsenal in the world after Russia and the United States[10].
- Former R&AW official JK Sinha, claimed that India is capable of producing 130 kilograms of weapon grade plutonium from six 'unsafeguarded' reactors not included in the nuclear deal between India and the United States.

The Federation of American Scientists website makes the interesting point that in August 2008, the IAEA approved a safeguards agreement with India under which the former will gradually gain access to India's civilian nuclear reactors. A month later, the Nuclear Suppliers Group granted India a waiver allowing it to access civilian nuclear technology and fuel from other countries and the implementation of this waiver makes India the only known country with nuclear weapons which is not a party to the NPT but is still allowed to carry out nuclear commerce with the rest of the world.

Since the implementation of the NSG waiver, India has signed nuclear deals with several countries including France, United States, Mongolia, Namibia, and Kazakhstan while the framework for similar deals with Canada and United Kingdom, at the time of writing, in the offing. More recently, in October 2009, there were reports out of New Delhi that, following a deterioration in India's relations with Pakistan, the country's nuclear establishment had come out strongly in favour of resuming nuclear tests. Initial reports suggested that Prime Minister Manmohan Singh had been vigorous in resisting these efforts, pointing out to his critics that should India go ahead, the United States would be bound by a 2008 agreement to cut off all sales of nuclear fuel and technology. 'That would be a huge setback to India's plans to expand its nuclear power generation and its economy,' he told Parliament.

Another fear voiced at the time was that should India initiate nuclear tests again, Pakistan would almost certainly follow suit. 'That would raise tensions between the two long-time rivals, and it would further distract Islamabad and its generals from the far more important battle against the Taliban and other extremists inside their country and along their border with Afghanistan,' said one commentator.

Among the most comprehensive reports on India's nuclear programmes has appeared under the banner of Washington's ISIS, in particular a report[11] written by David Albright and Susan Basu titled 'India's Gas Centrifuge Enrichment Program: Growing Capacity for Military Purposes'. They record that since the 1970s, India has pursued gas centrifuges to enrich uranium:

'The Indian Department of Atomic Energy (DAE) commissioned India's main enrichment plant, codenamed the Rare Materials Project (RMP), around 1990. In addition to a gas centrifuge facility, this site, located [a short distance] from Mysore, may also contain a uranium hexafluoride production facility.

'By 1997, after several years of difficulty, India seems to have achieved a technical breakthrough at RMP. Although India has experienced difficulties in building centrifuges, it now appears to be competent at constructing centrifuges comparable to those common in Europe in the 1970s.

'Our conclusion is that India is currently operating between 2,000 and 3,000 centrifuges at the RMP. The DAE is currently attempting to expand the number of centrifuges at RMP by 3,000, increasing RMP's capacity by at least 15,000 separative work units (SWU) per year, a common measure of the output of a uranium enrichment plant and more than double its current output. Further expansions in capacity are expected.'

Albright and Basu make the point that as a result of its recently acquired ability to import LEU, India can now devote the enrichment capacity of RMP to highly enriched uranium for military applications:

'India would most likely use the HEU for fuel in submarine reactors and in thermonuclear weapons. The production of thermonuclear weapons may lead India to conduct additional underground nuclear tests as it seeks to make more deliverable, reliable, and efficient weapons.'

The authors state that India has several political and technical motivations for making low and highly enriched uranium. Interviews with senior Indian officials show that they felt pressure to match Pakistan's accomplishments with gas centrifuges. More importantly, Indian officials have expressed interest in having an indigenous source of enriched uranium for domestic research and power reactors, thermonuclear weapons, and naval reactors.

Also dealt with is India's interest in naval reactors for submarines, which, state the two authors, goes back decades.

'More recently, it has concentrated on operating a naval propulsion prototype reactor near Kalpakkam and launching an indigenous nuclear-powered submarine that will use a miniaturized version of this reactor. The naval reactor programme, codenamed the Advanced Technology Vessel (ATV), is surrounded by secrecy. BARC is reported to be responsible for building the reactor, and military organizations and associated contractors are responsible for building everything else in the submarine.'

On thermonuclear weapons, the authors maintain that India has depended principally on plutonium.

'However, highly enriched uranium is desirable for thermonuclear weapons. Indian officials have stated that the 1998 full-scale nuclear tests included a thermonuclear device. In 2000, Dr. Anil Kakodkar, then Director of BARC, told [The Indian Newspaper] *The Nation* that

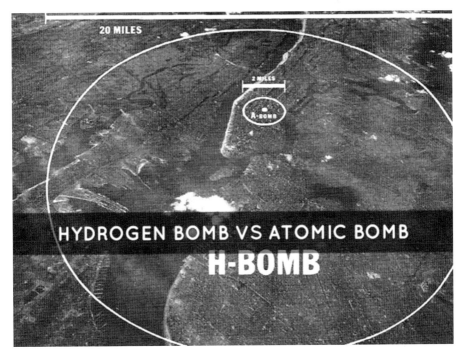

Destructive Power - Hydrogen Bomb vs the Atom Bomb

a thermonuclear device was tested at a relatively low yield, less than 45 kilotons, because of the proximity of a nearby village. He added that India could design a thermonuclear device of a higher yield. These discussions imply that India uses the RMP to make HEU for its thermonuclear weapons[12].'

India's Strategic Nuclear Command was formally established in 2003 and the joint services SNC is the custodian of all of India's nuclear weapons, missiles and assets. It is also responsible for executing all aspects of India's nuclear policy. The only body authorized to order a nuclear strike against another offending strike is the civil leadership, in the form of the CCS (Cabinet Committee on Security): In effect, declared one report, 'it is the Prime Minister who has his finger on the button.'

## Pakistan's Nuclear Weapons: Controversial, Contentious and Perennially At Risk

One of the recurrent nightmares which haunts the major powers is the possibility of the Pakistan Government being overrun by a group of Islamic Jihadis. Were that to happen, multiple prognoses suggest, Islamabad's nuclear arsenal – or part of it – might end up in the wrong hands. This scenario continues to be of serious concern to strategists on both sides of the Atlantic. Following former President Pervez Musharraf being forced to stand down and an insurrection in the Taliban mould overwhelming much of the northern regions of the country adjoining Afghanistan, some Pakistani-Watchers have questioned the ability of the Pakistan armed forces to counter large scale, long-term insurrection.

Rebel forces involved in recent disturbances were both Pakistani tribal and foreign and included a solid Arab and Chechen component. The violence that resulted was, by many accounts, vigorous, committed and extremely well planned. During this phase, and shortly before, there were times when the insurgency was almost within striking distance of Islamabad, at one stage less than 200 kilometres from the capital. There were also several attempts to strike at one or more of the depots where Pakistan is known to store its nuclear arsenal. The Pakistan Army was ultimately able to match force with force and a projected catastrophe, if there ever was one, was averted. Sources within the US Embassy in Islamabad said at the time that the revolt was more serious than some gave credit for, but in the end, preponderant government response prevailed.

At the same time, the adversary – Pakistan's Taliban forces – had learned a lot from what has been going on militarily to the immediate north of the mountainous frontier. Dissident political Imams have shown to be not averse to pulling back their assets and go into hiding in order to fight another day.

A similar scenario emerged in Afghanistan after the Coalition invasion of 2002. Eight years later, that conflict entered a protracted phase that cost far more lives than either the United States or Britain bargained for, especially when you consider that they originally believed they were up against a bunch of ill-trained, semi-literate guerrillas. One of the catch phrases said to have come from Mullah Omar, who led Afghanistan's rebel army for many years, was that 'they [the Americans] have all the watches but we have the time'.

Consequently, while substantially diminished, the threat factor in Pakistan remains a constant. More saliently, having shown that they were able to make substantial military gains against a largely inefficient and corrupt Pakistani Army, the rebels will almost certainly strike again, this time at a time and a place of their making. Western intelligence agencies in Pakistan are on record as stating that there will be further efforts for subversives to gain access to sensitive security areas. If that happens, one needs to ask, what will be the result if there is a complete breakdown of the political process in Pakistan? This was something the late Benazir Bhutto warned about before she was assassinated, in all probability at the hands of the same people she railed about.

It is interesting too, that during her first mandate, Mrs Bhutto – well aware of the subversive role of Pakistan's ISI, the country's secret intelligence service – ordered that no Pakistani nuclear scientist was to leave the country without her written permission[13]. That followed numerous cross-border visits by Pakistani nuclear scientists, not only to meet with Osama bin Laden and his lieutenants in Afghanistan prior to the Coalition invasion, but also to other assignations that included Iran, Libya, Egypt, China, Saudi Arabia and elsewhere.

One needs to accept that previous efforts to gain access to sensitive nuclear-related facilities in Pakistan were all well-planned and coordinated attacks. Some included men in uniform with valid security passes. Most worrying was the involvement of Pakistan Air Force engineers associated with the Air Weapon Complex (AWC) of Pakistan, a leading organization in the field of air-delivered weapons and systems. More important, that happened despite its personnel being subjected to vigorous and intrusive background checks. Yet, some members of this radical group had been deeply penetrated by al-Qaeda, to the extent that there were officers within the ranks prepared to sacrifice their lives for this Islamic fundamentalist cause.

At the start of the second decade of this century, preliminary estimates put Pakistan's arsenal at about sixty nuclear weapons, a situation that still holds. At this stage, Islamabad does not have a thermonuclear capability, though a number of its A-Bombs are tritium-boosted, which would substantially enhance their yields. Most telling is the fact that Pakistan's nuclear weapons programme, like North Korea's yesterday and Iran's today, went forward in the loudly proclaimed name of peace. The three countries have always been vigorous in their denials that in acquiring an advanced measure of nuclear expertise, there might be anything remotely military in intent. In late 2017, Tehran boldly insists that it is eager to use its nuclear assets only to generate power, even though Iran boasts among the world's largest carbon fuel deposits and certainly the biggest natural gas reserves on the globe.

At the start of it all, a succession of wars with India – four in all, so far – originally caused Pakistan to go nuclear. Of them all, the most serious was the conflict in December 1971, when New Delhi's forces intervened in what was then known as East Pakistan, today independent Bangladesh. After a defeat that was described by the media as 'crushing', Pakistan's military leadership retreated from the political battlefield and civilian rule was re-established. The new leader, and President, was Zulfiqar Ali Bhutto, whose daughter was eventually to succeed him as Pakistan's first female Head of State. Formal decision to proceed with nuclear weapons construction was taken in January 1972 during a meeting called by Bhutto and held in Multan, in the Punjab. It was an historic event with some of the scientists who had been invited travelling from Europe and America to attend. From that historic 'Shura' would emerge two of the three men who would play a crucial role in the country's nuclear weapons project, Munir Ahmed Khan, who was eventually appointed chairman of the Pakistani Atomic Energy Commission (PAEC) - and no relative of Abdul Qadeer Khan – and S.A. Butt, the man who would head up Pakistan's worldwide purchasing network, much of it covert. For funds, Saudi Arabia and Libya stepped up to the plate.

Pakistan's first attempts were to follow the plutonium route. In 1974, it contracted a French firm to design and act as the principal engineering contractor for the construction of a reprocessing plant at Chasma, south-east of the capital, Islamabad. Named the Kundian Nuclear Complex (KNC-2), the facility immediately became a subject of interest to Washington, which pressured France to abandon the contract. As with most lucrative export orders, the Elysees Palace responded warily and it took the French three years to halt supplies of components. Still more American pressure followed, with France terminating the project the following year. It was China that came to Pakistan's rescue, in part because of close ties that had meanwhile been fostered between Moscow and New Delhi. In search of allies, it was to be expected that Islamabad would gravitate to the next major nuclear power and clearly, Beijing welcomed the overtures. Mao Zedong personally welcomed Prime Minister Ali Bhutto on the first of several state visits.

In documents released by the *Sunday Times* as well as the *Washington Post* in 2009[14], it was disclosed that China gave Pakistan enough weapons-grade uranium to make two A-Bombs in 1982. The information came from British writer Simon Henderson, formerly with the *Financial Times* who went on to become a senior fellow at the Washington Institute for Near East Policy. Over several years, he maintained a useful contact with the Pakistan nuclear proliferator A.Q. Khan. Along with the uranium, he disclosed, came a blueprint for a simple nuclear weapon that *Washington Post* journalists R. Jeffrey Smith and Joby Warrick maintain had already been tested. There is evidence that some of this information was subsequently passed on to both Iran and Libya, though Khan disputes this, as we would expect him to do; this matter is dealt with in some detail in Chapter Eight. What he does not argue about is that from the start, he had been involved in enriching uranium with the single objective of using it to develop nuclear weapons.

With France out of the equation, the relatively easy route to the bomb had been denied and Pakistan's most obvious alternative was uranium isotope separation which was where Dr A.Q. Khan emerged. An expatriate Pakistani and professionally a European-trained metallurgist, Khan had been working for the Physical Dynamics Research Laboratory (FDO) in Amsterdam since 1972. He had managed to gain access to highly classified ultracentrifuge uranium enrichment technology pertaining to the URENCO enrichment plant at Almelo, Holland and clandestinely told his government so. By late 1975 he apparently had all that he required to duplicate the technology he had been accessing and returned home. Commented one contemporary historian: 'if Zulfikar Ali Bhutto was the father of the Pakistani A-bomb, then A.Q. Khan was its midwife'.

Back home again, a crash programme to construct an enrichment plant followed at a location that would become synonymous with Pakistan's nuclear weapon efforts, namely Kahuta, a tiny village near Islamabad. This is where Khan established his Engineering Research Laboratory – to be renamed the A.Q. Khan Research Laboratories – or KRL – in 1981. Butt's purchasing organization meantime was at work furtively acquiring many of the components for this mammoth undertaking[15].

Pakistan's uranium enrichment initiative entered the record books as Project 706 and was made autonomous from the PAEC in 1976. A crucial stage of the project was passed in June 1978, when the principle was successfully tested for the first time. An entire plant for converting uranium into uranium hexafluoride feedstock for Kahuta had been smuggled into Pakistan from China between 1977 and 1980, where it was assembled and put into operation at Dera Ghazi Khan. Matters were eased by the fact that the country was able to mine its own uranium, at Baghalchar (Dera Ghazi Khan), and afterwards at Qabul Khel; together, the two mines produce enough ore to supply all of Kahuta's needs. The plant entered its full-functioning phase in the early 1980s, with China reportedly supplying expertise and also hexafluoride feedstock. In February 1984, A.Q. Khan stated that Kahuta had produced its first enriched uranium.

It was about then that reports of a second enrichment facility emerged in Washington. This was finally pinpointed in the mid-1990s, first at Golra Sharif, and later at Wah (at the so-called Gadwal facilities), though for a long time actual confirmation remained elusive. Besides uranium enrichment, Pakistan never abandoned its plutonium efforts. Consequently, it was not surprising that work began in the mid-1980s on a 40-70MWt unsafeguarded research reactor, once more with Chinese help. This reactor was completed at Khushab and its two principal stages commissioned in March 1996 and April 1998.

Khushab is apparently able to generate sufficient fissile material for a couple of bombs a year. Notably, the 'New Labs' reprocessing facility at the Pakistan Institute of Nuclear Science and Technology (PINSTECH) had already been 'hot-tested' in the late 1980s. By then, unsafeguarded heavy water production fell under Multan, Karachi, and to a lesser extent, Khushab. A tritium purification and storage plant – first test-operated in 1987 – is located at a heavily guarded paramilitary site about 150 kilometres south of Rawalpindi.

In late May 1998, Pakistan responded to India's nuclear tests by conducting a small number of nuclear explosions over two days[16]. Seismic measurements of the 28 and 30 May tests suggest that the yields were between nine and twelve kilotons and five kilotons, respectively – lower than what the Pakistani government claimed. Pakistan's first nuclear warheads used an implosion design with a solid core of HEU rather than plutonium, likely requiring fifteen to twenty kilograms of HEU per warhead[17].

A number of subsequent developments suggested that Pakistan was preparing to increase and enhance its nuclear capabilities. It has built a second heavy water reactor at the Khushab site which is likely to more than double its plutonium production, together with a new chemical separation facility at Chashma, home to the country's 300 MW Chasnupp-1 reactor. According to *The Bulletin of the Atomic Scientists*, the reactors provide the Pakistani military with several options: fabricating weapons that use plutonium cores; mixing plutonium with HEU to make composite cores; or using tritium to 'boost' the warheads' yield (loading the reactors' targets with lithium-6 will produce tritium)[18]. Additionally, reports ISIS, Pakistan appears to have expanded its plutonium separation capability at the New Labs section of the Pakistan Institute of Science and Technology (PINSTECH) near Rawalpindi.

'A series of commercial satellite images from February 2002 through September 2006 show the construction of what appears to be a second plutonium separation plant adjacent to the original one (suggesting that Pakistan is increasing its plutonium separation capacity in anticipation of an increased supply of spent fuel from new heavy water reactors). The plutonium separated from the spent fuel is usable in nuclear weapons. [19]

'Between 2000 and 2002, Pakistan began constructing a second plutonium production reactor at its Khushab nuclear site. In approximately mid-2006, Pakistan began constructing a third plutonium production reactor at the site.'

With construction of the second reactor completed, building a third reactor followed soon afterwards. ISIS assessed that this on-going expansion of

Pakistan's plutonium production programme was in all probability linked to a strategic decision by Pakistan to develop a new generation of thermonuclear weapons and smaller, lighter and more powerful plutonium-based weapons. Also, ISIS noted that Pakistan would likely need to expand its plutonium separation capacity in order to handle the extra spent fuel from the new reactors.

A more recent development, according to a US Congressional Report is the implementation by the Islamabad government of Second Strike Capability, which, it is claimed, addresses issues linked to an envisaged nuclear attack by India. Pakistan has built hard and deeply buried storage and launch facilities to this end. It was also confirmed that it had built Soviet-style road-mobile missiles, state-of-the-art air defences around strategic sites as well as a variety of other concealment measures. Additionally, there are hard and deeply buried storage and launch facilities to retain a second-strike capability in case of a nuclear war. In 1998, the report declared, Pakistan had 'at least six secret locations', and since then 'it is believed the country may have developed many more such sites.'

Seymour Hersh provided us with a fascinating if incomplete glimpse into what was going in these departments in an article he wrote for the *New Yorker* in November 2009[20]. Interviewed in London, former President Musharraf told him that following the 9/11 attacks, his government had held extensive discussions with the Bush Administration about measures taken to protect the country's nuclear pile. Musharraf said that Pakistan had constructed a huge tunnel system for the transport and storage of nuclear weaponry. 'The tunnels are so deep that a nuclear attack will not touch them' and would also make it impossible for the Americans intelligence community to monitor the movements of nuclear components by satellite.' Hersh added:

'Safeguards have been built into the system. Pakistan nuclear doctrine calls for the warheads (containing an enriched radioactive core) and their triggers (sophisticated devices containing highly explosive lenses, detonators and krytrons) to be separately stored from each other and from their delivery systems (missiles or aircraft). The goal is to ensure that one can launch a warhead – in the heat of a showdown with India, for example – without pausing to put it together.'

Final authority to do so rested with Pakistan's ten-member National Command Authority, with the Chairman – by statute, the president – casting the deciding vote. Yet, for all this, the United States still has to admit that it does not know where all of Pakistan's nuclear sites are located, since government officials there have continued to rebuff and deflect American requests for details[21].

In terms of delivery systems, Pakistan lags behind India by a considerable margin: the bulk of its nuclear arsenal remains aircraft deliverable. Though various missile systems have been produced locally or are in development with several successful test firings noted by Western authorities, the Pakistan Air Force relies heavily on the nuclear delivery role of the American-manufactured F-16, although other aircraft, such as the Mirage V or the Chinese produced A-5, could be employed in this role. Forty aircraft in different variants of the F-16 were delivered from 1983 onwards, but further purchases were suspended in 1988 because of the Pressler Amendment, which forbids United States military aid to suspected nuclear weapons states. Curiously, this restriction does not apply to Israel.

According to the *Bulletin of the American Scientists*:

'Pakistan's 1998 nuclear tests deepened US opposition to delivering the aircraft, but attempts to enlist Pakistan as an ally against the Taliban in Afghanistan prompted President George W Bush to waive the Pressler Amendment on 22 September 2001, so that the aircraft could be delivered[22].

'The F-16 has a refuelled range of more than 1,600 kilometres (1,000 miles), still more if drop tanks are fitted. It can carry up to 5,450 kilograms externally on one under-fuse centre-line pylon and six under-wing stations. Each aircraft can each carry up to two B-61 nuclear bombs, but Pakistan's F-16s most likely carry a single bomb on the centre-line pylon because its weapons are probably heavier than the B-61.'

Pakistan has devoted a substantial part of its defence budget to developing several types of missiles, the majority capable of delivering a nuclear warhead. These include the short-range Ghaznavi (Hatf-3) and Shaheen-1 (Hatf-4), the medium-range Ghauri (Hatf-5) while a fourth missile, Shaheen-2 (Hatf-6) remained under development for more than a decade.

The Ghaznavi entered service in 2004. The solid-fuelled, single-stage missile – since further enhanced with the help of South African scientists who were enticed with generous offers after Nelson Mandela took power[23] – can deliver a half-ton payload to approximately 400 kilometres and was derived from the Chinese M-11 missile, of which approximately thirty were delivered to Pakistan in the early 1990s.

Pakistan's Shaheen-1 ('Eagle'), in contrast, is a reverse-engineered M-9 missile originally supplied by China. The solid-fuelled, single-stage missile has been in service since 2003 and can strike targets to almost 500 kilometres with a payload of up to a ton. Islamabad claims that its two-stage Shaheen-2 medium-range ballistic missile, unveiled in 2000 – but still under development – has a range of roughly 2,500 kilometres and can carry a payload of a ton. The more advanced Shaheen-2 was test-launched in February 2007, over a distance of 2,000 kilometres. Pakistan is also in the process developing a range of cruise missile that American intelligence estimates claim may be nuclear-capable.

*Chapter 4*

# The Bomb and Those Who Seek to Acquire Nuclear Expertise

*'There are no 'legal' rules and regulations in the dense field intelligence, espionage and collection...it seems only logical that the more you know, the safer you are and the greater the chance that you will get things right...'*

*Efraim Halevy, head of Mossad, Israel's intelligence service from 1998 to 2002 in 'By Invitation': The Economist, London, 31 July 2004*

'There are thirty-five or forty countries believed to be capable in the long term of manufacturing nuclear weapons,' said Dr Mohamed ElBaradei, the Egyptian head of the International Atomic Energy Agency (IAEA) said shortly before he retired late 2009. He was quoted by the French newspaper *Le Monde* after he had been interviewed a short while before. Following the usual preliminaries, which included an overview of the international situation, Dr ElBaradei stressed the need to reinforce and update the current status of the Nuclear Non-Proliferation Treaty (NPT). These, he declared forcibly, had not kept pace with recent international developments.

Though this event took place a few years ago, what he said remains valid, including the fact that nobody had been able to halt Iran pursuing a clandestine nuclear weapons programme for two decades. It was advanced enough for the Tehran Government to have developed its own uranium enrichment plant that would ultimately produce enough fissile material to arm atom bombs. With time, compelling evidence emerged that several other countries had been implicated in the Iranian programme, either by supplying equipment or technical know-how. Among them were Pakistan and North Korea. That was followed by news that scientists in Pakistan had been selling nuclear secrets to North Korea and, possibly, Libya.

A *New York Times* report on 4 January 2004 disclosed that Pakistani leaders 'who, for years, had denied that their scientists at the country's secret A.Q. Khan

Research Laboratories were peddling advanced nuclear technology' were doing exactly that. The paper went on to say that the Islamabad Government 'must have been averting its eyes from a most conspicuous piece of evidence: the laboratory's own sales brochure. For several years that document was quietly circulated to aspiring nuclear weapons states and a network of nuclear middlemen around the world.'

The third notable event on Dr ElBaradei's watch was the revelation that Libya not only aspired to nuclear weapons parity but had also gone some distance towards trying to achieve that objective. That became clear after a ship carrying thousands of centrifuges capable of developing weapons-grade uranium (a key process in the building of an atomic bomb) was intercepted on its way to Tripoli in 2003. The German freighter, en route from Dubai, was diverted to Taranto, southern Italy, shortly after it passed through the Suez Canal. Intelligence agents boarded it and seized the centrifuges, the design of which were said to have been stolen from URENCO, the European nuclear consortium. It was this interception that forced the Libyan leader to 'come clean' with his WMD programmes.

How advanced was the Libyan nuclear programme? According to the IAEA, Libya's nuclear programme was years away from producing a nuclear weapon as the important pieces of equipment were now largely dismantled and stored in boxes. British and American officials who made secret visits to Libya's weapons laboratories before that happened countered that statement with one of their own. They declared that the now deceased Colonel Gadaffi was 'well on his way' to making a nuclear bomb. If they are right said *The New York Times*, Libya posed a far more serious threat than that detected by UN inspection teams. 'We saw uranium enrichment going ahead,' said one senior diplomat with knowledge of the Anglo-American inspections. 'We were satisfied that they were in the process of developing a weapon … Libya was third on our list of concern after North Korea and Iran.'

While London and Washington had been aware for some years that Gadaffi was dabbling in chemical and biological weapons, nobody suspected that this nation of desert Bedouins had anything like the nuclear ambitions uncovered, for no other reason than that Libya lacks that kind of technological ability. It was the view of Joseph Cirincione, director of the Non-Proliferation Project at the Carnegie Endowment of Peace that the know-how must have come from elsewhere – Pakistan, Iraq, or possibly Iran.

Nor can South Africa be ruled out. At the behest of Pretoria's ANC Government, an extensive chemical and biological warfare facility was established in Libya in the mid-1990s. A serving member of the South African National Defence Force is alleged to have handled that work. It is notable that this man has never been convicted of any crime, even though some of his efforts contravened a major international non-proliferation treaty to which South

Africa remains a signatory. The question is whether Pretoria might have had some kind of nuclear interest in Libya as well, obviously curtailed when Colonel Gadaffi was murdered in 2011.

Unfortunately that is not the end of the story. In October 2014, Libya asked for foreign assistance to transport its 850 tonnes stockpile of precursor

## Enrichment Processes

A. Gas Diffusion Process

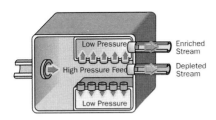

B. Gas Centrifuge Process

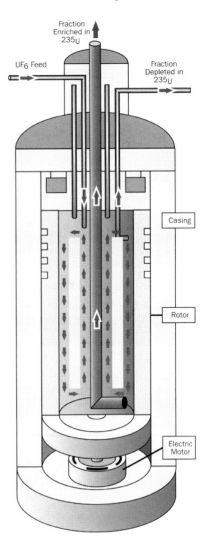

The gaseous diffusion process uses molecular diffusion to separate a gas from a two-gas mixture. The isotopic separation is accomplished by diffusing uranium, which has been combined with fluorine to form uranium hexafluoride ($UF_6$) gas, through a porous membrane (barrier) and using the different molecular velocities of the two isotopes to achieve separation.

The gas centrifuge process uses a large number of rotating cylinders in series and parallel configurations. Gas is introduced and rotated at high speed, concentrating the component of higher molecular weight towards the outer wall of the cylinder and the lower molecular weight component toward the center. The enriched and the depleted gas are removed by scoops.

Gas centrifuge enrichment process

chemicals for making nerve gas out of Libya for destruction. Four months later, in February 2015, Libyan military sources told media that unidentified armed men have captured large amounts of the country's chemical weapons, including mustard gas and sarin nerve agent. It was a total disaster and the ramifications are still likely to surface, possibly in the hands of one of the Jihadi groups like al-Qaeda or Islamic State. Still more serious is the fact that nobody knows where this material that remains on the threat alert list of almost every country on the globe is now lodged.

Sam Nunn, the former senator and co-chairman of the Nuclear Threat Initiative made a number of interesting comments with regard to nuclear proliferation while he served the nation in Washington, especially with regard to irregular forces hostile to the United States.

'If a ten-kiloton nuclear device goes off in Midtown Manhattan on a typical work day, it could kill more than half a million people,' he told a group of specialists. It was plausible yield 'for a crude terrorist bomb'. What he did not tell those listening was that such a device would require about twenty kilograms of highly enriched uranium, HEU in the argot. If the fissile material of choice was plutonium, it would be considerably less; four or five kilograms would do just nicely. He added that only about a quarter to a third of the almost 500 nuclear reactors currently active or in the process of construction was secured in a manner that might accord to American Department of Energy standards. Most countries, Russia especially, regarded DoE strictures as too demanding, too expensive and too labour intensive. As chairman of the board of trustees at the Centre for Strategic and International Studies, Senator Nunn added the rider that most of us appear to have forgotten the 'devastating, world-changing impact' of a nuclear attack that might be launched by terrorists.

The eminent legislator is not alone in voicing these misgivings which could ultimately affect every single person on the globe. There is a disturbing passage in George Tenet's book *At the Centre of the Storm*[1] that seems to have eluded most commentators. The former head of the Central Intelligence Agency said he was puzzled that the al-Qaeda terror group had not followed up their actions of 9/11 by sending 'suicide bombers that would easily be able to cause chaos in half a dozen American shopping malls on any given day.'

Tenet's inference was clear: this kind of disaster is going to happen in the United States in the not too distant future; it is only a question of where, when, and what kind of weapons might be deployed, was his educated view. Elsewhere in his book, Mr Tenet tells us that when former President George W. Bush addressed his Russian counterpart about missing nukes towards the end of his tenure, President Putin admitted that he could not account for all of Moscow's nuclear weapons at a time when al-Qaeda had made efforts to buy three former Soviet nuclear devices on Russia's black market. That was when Mr. Putin disclosed details about an organization *Umma Tameer-e-Nau* – which we now know was indirectly linked to Pakistan's Inter-Service Intelligence (ISI) – and which included local scientists involved with the Taliban and al-Qaeda in an attempt to develop nuclear weapons. Unconfirmed reports have since indicated that there are at least three atom bombs filched from former Soviet Union nuclear arsenals, an issue that gave rise to what the media termed a 'Mini-Nuke Conspiracy'. The fact is that it is not only the United States that is at threat and those dispensing terror are likely to employ any means available.

Similar warnings have come from several individuals who have been involved with nuclear terrorism in all its forms for many decades, especially from Vienna's International Atomic Energy Agency (IAEA), widely known as the world's 'Atoms for Peace' organisation within the United Nations. One of the most important of the world bodies, it came into being in 1953, during President Eisenhower's tenure and its declared purpose is threefold: nuclear verification and security; safety; and technology transfer.

In an interview given shortly before he retired in 2009 to Julian Borger, at the time diplomatic editor of Britain's *Guardian* newspaper, Dr ElBaradei issued a stern warning when he declared that the number of potential nuclear weapons states could more than double in a few years 'unless the major powers took radical steps towards disarmament.' The threat of proliferation was particularly grave in the Middle East, he said, a region that he described as a 'ticking bomb'.[2] As the outgoing IAEA director general who was awarded the Nobel Peace Prize for his efforts in Iraq – he remained at the helm of this United Nations nuclear monitoring body for almost a dozen years – and was obliged during this time to tackle nuclear and related issues in several countries to the east of Suez. One of his last tasks was voicing serious misgiving about several nuclear imbroglios that faced the IAEA in Syria, not least that with North Korean help. It was while he was still in office that the Damascus government was found to be engaged in building one or more nuclear reactors not covered by NPT provisions or safeguards.

Dr ElBaradei told Borger that almost from the start of taking office he was hampered by a series of historical issues, some of which dated back almost four decades in the period that the nuclear Non-Proliferation Treaty (NPT) had found regional expression. Initially, only three 'nuclear nations' were involved: the United States; the Soviet Union; and Britain with France and China in train. But then Israel, India, Pakistan and South Africa followed in short order, all having illegally entered the nuclear race and ignoring basic NPT precepts. With North Korea detonating its first atom bombs late in 2006, the IAEA head declared that:

'the system is [now] in danger of collapse, with an abrupt spread in nuclear weapons technology ... we still live in a world where, if you have nuclear weapons, you are buying power: you are buying insurance against attack. That is not lost on those who do *not* have nuclear weapons, particularly in [conflict] regions.'

He suggested that the next wave of proliferation would involve 'virtual nuclear weapons states', who can produce plutonium or highly enriched uranium and possess the know-how to make warheads, but who stop just short of assembling a weapon. They would therefore remain technically compliant with the NPT while being within a couple of months of deploying and using a nuclear weapon. It is worth mentioning that most of the commercial nuclear power reactors operating or under construction in the world today require uranium 'enriched' in the U-235 isotope for their fuel.

It did not take long for some of these projections to reach fruition. Word has since reached the West that North Korea has further expanded its nuclear proliferation interests. Apart from assisting Syria to build the al-Kibar nuclear reactor, it worked clandestinely with the government of Myanmar – formerly Burma – to build one of its own, which would ultimately produce enough plutonium to fuel an atom bomb. Under normal circumstances, this kind of scientific collaboration within the international community is quite acceptable. Relationships between both countries are amicable and the venture would be transparent, with the IAEA playing its customary observer role. But with North Korea and Myanmar, arguably the world's two most xenophobic countries at the time, the situation was not only dangerous, but complex in the extreme. For a start, both states when all this was taking place had a zero human rights tolerance potential and both were ruled from the barrel of a gun. Moreover, neither country tolerated any form of freedom of speech, nor the kind of free and fair elections that most of us in the civilized world take for granted. Things in Myanmar have changed, but not North Korea. There, as we have been made aware, state-sponsored terror remains the norm while political opponents are either imprisoned – some for life – or murdered.

On Syria, Dr David Kay, a senior research fellow at Washington's Potomac Institute and, for a while, a weapons inspector with the United Nations in Iraq, declared that North Korea's involvement in the Arab World remains a cause for concern.

'This is what the Syrian case points to. States can, on their own, secretly make arrangements to acquire at least portions of a nuclear weapons production cycle … countries in the Middle East that procure nuclear weapons would be at the top of my list of concerns … Myanmar, on [its] own, with [its] indigenous technical capacity to produce either plutonium or highly enriched uranium, it's not something that would keep me awake at night. They simply don't have it. But this illicit network, government sanctioned and black market certainly means that if they desire it, there may be a real possibility of their gaining it.'

There have been other developments which have been worrying. In an interview posted on several Jihadi websites[3], al-Qaeda's leader in Yemen claimed that the organization actually 'possessed some nuclear weapons,' though this could just as easily be radioactive material that could be used to manufacture 'Dirty Bombs'. He vowed to attack the United States as well as Western interests 'to compel them to withdraw their forces from the region'. According to the interview, the then leader of al-Qaeda in Yemen, a 33-year-old Arab, Nasir Abdul Kareem al-Wahayshi (aka Abu Basir), was Osama bin Laden's secretary until he was arrested by Iran and extradited to Yemen in February 2002. Al-Wahayshi has been a fugitive since he escaped from a Yemeni prison in 2006. Shortly afterwards, Dr. Ayman al-Zawahiri, Osama bin Laden's deputy, commended al-Wahayshi and named him the Amir of Mujahedeen in Yemen. Since then, there has been a growing unity between al-Qaeda's Saudi and Yemeni affiliates and the mainstream al-Qaeda group along the Pakistan/Afghanistan border region. Led by an Amir, a deputy Amir, and a military and Shura council, the Saudi and Yemeni affiliates have linked forces and operate today as al-Qaeda in the Arabian Peninsula.

Following the bombing of the American warship the USS *Cole* in Aden harbour in 2000 where seventeen American servicemen and women were killed and forty injured – coupled to a variety of terror acts in the south-western corner of the Arabian Peninsula, – the West reacted accordingly. Ties were fostered with Djibouti, a former French colony on the Red Sea and a US Special Forces base was established at the former headquarters of the French Foreign Legion in that predominantly Islamic country. Many of the missile strikes against al-Qaeda targets from drones were launched in Djibouti. Similarly, of the dozen-odd NATO countries currently involved in anti-piracy operations off Africa's Horn, the majority are also tasked with monitoring Yemeni developments. Clearly, this has become a priority issue since most of the weapons that reached Somalia in the past were shipped either from Aden or other ports in the peninsula. Alarm has also been expressed about al-Qaeda possibly using Mogadishu and its environs as a potential gathering point for nuclear assets, such as those that might feasibly be used in Radiological Dispersal Devices.

Israel takes a keen interest in developments in the region, though its intelligence efforts tend to be concentrated on its nearest neighbours as well as Iran. Mossad (the word means 'Institute' in Hebrew) was founded in 1949, shortly after the creation of the Israeli state and is still the last great intelligence service to operate mainly on human intelligence, or in the lingo, HUMINT. Yet there have been some significant gaps; even with the largest intelligence infrastructure in a region half the size of Western Europe, the Israelis spectacularly failed to detect the Iraqi build-up to the invasion of Kuwait.

Faced with domestic terror threats that have already claimed scores of lives, Britain remains active in the Near East and for good reason. One only has to look at recent events in England to understand why. On April 30, 2009, four British nationals – all males with Pakistani family links – were sentenced to life in London's Old Bailey for conspiring with al-Qaeda to set off a series of explosions. Jurors in the year-long trial heard of plans to target a shopping centre, nightclub and the gas network with a giant fertilizer bomb. A fifth man had already been sent down.

The convicted men were 34-year-old Abdul Aziz Jalil, Junade Feroze 31, Mohammed Zia Ul Haq, 28, and the youngest of the bunch, 23-year-old Omar Abdul Rehman. All admitted that they had conspired with Dhiren Barot, who had earlier been sentenced to life in prison for planning attacks on targets in the United States and Britain. Barot, who was 34 years old at the time, originally pleaded guilty to plotting to bomb several American targets that included hotels and train stations. Almost all of Britain's convicted terrorists are, as the phrase goes, 'Home Grown'. Questioned about London's transport bombers, friends and neighbours referred to them as 'ordinary lads from ordinary homes'. Yet somehow, they had become utterly alienated from the society that had nurtured them from birth. The question that needs an answer is how did all that happen?

Peter Clarke, Britain's top counterterrorism police officer disclosed at the time that his nation had survived a 'prolonged multinational assault' from al-Qaeda and that its supporters had 'established an inexorable trend toward more ambitious and more destructive attack planning. These efforts might ultimately include such pernicious weapons as nuclear-linked RDDs. Speaking at the Policy Exchange, a private policy research group, the talk offered a distinctive insight to 'Britain's secret intelligence service countermeasures in recent years.' Clarke drew attention to the complexities of confronting what he called 'networks within networks, connections within connections and links between individuals that cross local, national and international boundaries'. Interestingly, he reached the same conclusions as George Tenet: 'The only sensible assumption is that we shall be attacked again,' Clarke declared, adding that how and when all this would happen was another matter.

When asked whether the pattern would be similar to the London transport attacks of July 2005, when fifty-two commuters were killed and 700 injured, he was not prepared to comment. Nor did he have anything to say about whether there would be a repeat of attempted al-Qaeda attacks on Heathrow and Gatwick, two of Europe's largest airports. At the time, he said, there were about 100 terrorism suspects awaiting trial in Britain, almost of all of which pointed to young British Muslims travelling to Pakistan for military training before returning home to plot attacks.

In this regard, Britain does not stand alone. In recent years there have been persistent reports from Minneapolis of a number of young Somalis who had disappeared from their homes and turned up in the Horn of Africa. At least one of these youngsters has since been killed in a terror attack, and information divulged from several reliable sources maintains that the majority had undergone military training in al-Qaeda camps in this vast East African state that has been ungovernable for decades.

In this context was Dame Eliza Manningham-Buller, former head of the MI5, Britain's domestic security body – roughly equivalent to the FBI in the United States. She disclosed that she knew of at least thirty terror plots that threatened Britain at the present time. She also revealed that her people were keeping something like 1,600 individuals under surveillance. Some of these plots were serious. 'Tomorrow's threat may, I suggest, include the use of chemicals, bacteriological agents, radioactive materials and even nuclear technology.' It was her view that current terror threats in the West will last at least another generation and that the majority were linked to al-Qaeda.

More recently, Britain's Fourth Estate disclosed that the hunt was on for eighteen suspected suicide bombers who had recently returned from Asia and that among targets listed were London's underground system, where it was feared chemical agents would be dispersed. All of those involved were attached to a fundamentalist Jihadi group that calls itself Al-Qaeda of England. Al-Qaeda leaders in Iraq also put out the word – it first surfaced in a leaked intelligence report – that they were planning the first 'large-scale' terrorist attacks on Britain and other western targets with the help of supporters in Iran. One operative had said he was planning an attack on 'a par with Hiroshima and Nagasaki' in an attempt to 'shake the Roman throne', a distinct reference to the West.

Still further afield, India is constantly raising fears about Pakistan, its restive, nuclear-active neighbour. India's Prime Minister, Manmohan Singh, told President Obama on a visit to Washington that it was not inconceivable that nuclear sites in one or more of Pakistan's frontier province are 'already partly' in the hands of Islamic extremists. That claim was made under the headline 'Singh Warns Obama: Pakistan is Lost' in *Debka*, a journal said to have close ties with Israeli intelligence. The Indian prime minister apparently named several Pakistani nuclear sites in areas that were Taliban-Qaida strongholds and suggested that they were already 'partly in the hands of Muslim extremists'. A sub-heading to the story read: 'India gets ready for a Taliban-ruled nuclear neighbour.'

Robert Windrem, a visiting scholar with the Centre for Law and Security in New York University and an expert on South Asia nuclear issues tended to confirm this view, stating in an interview that Pakistan had 'a much worse record of proliferation and security breaches than any other country in the world.' The news report went on:

'Windrem, a former producer with NBC whose book *Critical Mass* was among the first to red-flag Islamabad's proliferation record going back to the 1980s: it referred to recent reports and satellite images showing Pakistan building two large new plutonium production reactors in Khushab, which experts say could lead to improvements in the quantity and quality of the country's nuclear arsenal.'

Windrem reckoned that the reactors had nothing to do with 'power-production'. 'They are weapons-specific, and are being built with resources whose diversion is enabled by the billions of dollars the US is giving to Pakistan as aid.' He also pointed out that Khushab's former director Sultan Bashiruddin Mahmood had met with Osama bin Laden and his deputy, Ayman al-Zawahiri, and offered a nuclear weapons tutorial around an Afghanistan campfire, as attested by the former CIA Director George Tenet in his memoir:

'Yet successive US administrations had adopted an attitude of benign neglect towards Pakistan's nuclear programme and its expansion at a time the country was in growing ferment and under siege within from Islamic extremists.'

Many of these events foreshadow future developments in the United States after al-Qaeda theoretically manages to shift its focus from executing terror from Europe to America. While nothing is firm, the most obvious question that needs to be asked is what is likely to be their targets?

As some security analysts have suggested, it might be a mall or a sports stadium, or possibly one of the nation's subway systems. Such an attack could cause huge casualties if a nuclear-related RDD or chemical or biological agents were to be employed. Several motorway tunnels – including those in New York as well as the twenty-six-kilometre undersea tunnel along US13 between Cape Charles and the Norfolk and Virginia Beach area – have been mooted as targets by fundamentalist Islamic operatives. Again, a 'Dirty Bomb' would be the medium, enough to permanently destroy these vital motorway links. Several bridges have also been mentioned. These include several prominent structures around San Francisco, as well as the bridge across the Columbia River that straddles Oregon and Washington. This structure is tall enough to allow passage by the US Navy's largest aircraft carriers. Portland, roughly 100 miles upstream is the busiest motor vehicle shipping port in the world, almost all this movement coming across the Pacific.

Because of the variety of radioactive sensors already deployed in all major American (and Western) cities, as well as along all significant trunk roads, al-Qaeda's immediate option would still be of a conventional explosive nature. The terror group has had several spectacular successes. These include:

- The 2008 terror attacks in Mumbai, India. Ten Pakistani men associated with the terror group *Lashkar-e-Tayyiba* stormed buildings in Mumbai, killing 164 people. Nine of the gunmen were killed during the attacks, one survived. Mohammed Ajmal Kasab, the lone surviving gunman, was executed in India in November 2012.
- The attack on Madrid's metro rail system 11 March 2004, by Moroccan-based al-Qaeda cadres that killed almost 200 people and wounded more than 2,000.
- The London transport bombings of 7 July 2005. Almost to a man, these bombers – the majority of whom were young British-born nationals – had undergone clandestine military training with al-Qaeda in Pakistan.
- Before that, in August 1998 – while I was on assignment in East Africa – there were the bombings of two American embassies. More than 200 people died in the Nairobi attack and eleven more in a concurrent bombing in Dar es Salaam, capital of Tanzania. Somalia, it later emerged had a hand in both acts of terror.
- Jihadi elements out of Somalia tried to bring down an Israeli passenger jet at Mombasa Airport in November 2002. They used missiles that were shown later to have been smuggled out of Iraq.
- There have been several attempts to blow up Saudi Arabian oil installations. These resulted in security operations that nabbed more than 200 terror operatives in the Kingdom. While early reports are sketchy, some of those involved spent months learning to fly. Which raises another issue; where exactly were these people taught to fly?
- It is worth mentioning that there have been at least three attempts at detonating 'Dirty Bombs' in Russia and were all the work of Chechnyan dissidents. In the second attempt, one of the 'Chetnick' operatives called a Moscow newspaper and told a reporter about the bomb as well as its location. The device was dealt with by Russian security forces. The third RDD bomb included radioactive waste from an industrial site near Grozny, the capital of Chechnya. It too, was discovered in time and neutralized. More specific details are to be found in Chapter Six.

What is significant about these events is that rebel 'Chetnicks' not only maintain powerful links with al-Qaeda's leadership in several Asian and Near Eastern regions, but these Russian insurgents can today be found fighting alongside similarly-minded Islamic Jihadists in Afghanistan and Iraq. Some snipers ranged against U.S. Forces during the war against Islamic State were from Chechnya and characterized by one Coalition intelligence source as 'pretty good…both brave and resourceful'.

## Chapter 5

# An Israeli Army Major Smuggles Nuclear-Related Devices for Pakistan's Atom Bomb Programme

*'To understand A.Q. Khan, you have to understand ego, greed, nationalism and Islamic identity.'*

*David E. Sanger of the New York Times*

Number 109, Ocean View Drive in Cape Town's Sea Point suburb is a choice address in South Africa. Stand on the balcony of this garden-laced mansion and on a good day you can easily scan fifty kilometres or more out to sea. Not for nothing that this tree-lined enclave on the road between Green Point and Camps Bay is referred to by some as 'Millionaires Row'. When the weather's right, the vista from these lower slopes of Cape Town's famous Signal Hill allows a gulls-eye view of Robben Island, where former President Nelson Mandela was held in close custody for a substantial part of the twenty seven years that he was imprisoned by the old apartheid regime. Until recently, this Ocean View address was also the home and offices of Top-Cape Technologies (Pty) Ltd., owned by a fifty-one-year-old Hungarian-born Israeli citizen Asher Karni. An enterprising fellow, he made major in the Israeli Defence Force before emigrating to the shores of the South Atlantic.

To start with, Karni was regarded by those who knew him as the model citizen. Moreover, he was thoroughly at home in one of the largest Jewish communities in the Southern Hemisphere. He and his wife were respected members of Sea Point's Beit Midrash congregation where he taught Torah. Occasionally he would stand in for Rabbi Jonathan Altman when there was need. In an article published after his arrest in the United States, the Israeli newspaper *Ha'aretz* said that Karni spent his first few years in South Africa with *Bnei Akiva* where he acted as a mentor to Jewish youth. In fact, the report read, he encouraged many of them to do their *aliya* in the Promised Land. To almost everyone with whom Asher Karni came into contact, this was one upstanding *mensch*. Finally, he resigned his religious obligations and joined a local electrical company, Eagle Technology, owned and run by a prominent Jewish couple Alan and Diana Bearman, together with their son Nathan.

On the face of it, the firm's Greenmarket Square outlet – while competing with a huge Afrocentric open-air market on the cobblestones outside – sold everyday items like electrical appliances, coffee machines and the like. But its real interests lay in sophisticated security-linked electronic items. In fact, Eagle Technology made good money during the apartheid years importing sensitive high-tech equipment which found a ready application within the country's security establishment. Frankly, with a black government in power and many of the country's ills being blamed on racism, this is not something you talk about in South Africa today.

Being ex-military, Karni was almost made for the job. He understood what was required and this he did well and he and the company prospered. While working with Eagle Technology, he brought in business from all over the world. At his peak, he was easily earning $10,000 a month, which, going by South African standards where even earning $1,000 a month is good money, he was bringing in a fortune. So it comes as a bit of a surprise to learn that, for all his new-found wealth and good intentions, Karni began doing a bit of moonlighting on the side as a smuggler. Again, he took the obvious route and concentrated on high technology goods, only these were nuclear-related and intended for Pakistan's atom bomb programme. Among items he secretly dealt with were spark-gap triggers, esoteric technological instruments that have a variety of functions and which can be used in nuclear weapons, specifically for detonation purposes. He ordered sixty-six from an American firm – part of a larger consignment of 200 – and took delivery in Cape Town. The triggers were then forwarded to a Pakistani businessman, Humayun Khan, who, as an intermediary, used a Dubai address. One needs to explain that spark-gap triggers are very unusual for just anybody to acquire. They are rated – apart from actual uranium and other radioactive materials – among the most tightly-restricted items in the world, listed number 2,641 on the 'Control List'. In fact, the Bureau of Industry and Security of the US Department of Commerce categorized them as what is known in the trade as 'dual use' items; these might have either a civilian or a military use. Because of their civilian application – they are used in machines for pulverizing kidney stones – it is quite legal to sell them to South Africa, but certainly not to Pakistan, North Korea or Iran, all countries suspected of using them in their nuclear weapons programmes. If they want them – even one – shippers must request an export license.

In the 1990s, when the Iraqi Health Ministry requested small numbers of the devices for use in several hospitals, Vienna's International Atomic Energy Agency (IAEA) confirmed their proper use, sometimes an exhaustive but thorough job.

'The only way for the Iraqis to get a new trigger,' said Mark Gwozdecky, an IAEA spokesman, 'was to send back the one they had been using and which needed to be replaced.' The surveillance system worked, he said, and the agency was confident that none were diverted for non-medical purposes.

Humayun Khan, though not related to A.Q. Khan – the name is as common in Pakistan as Smith might be in London – was one of a host of shadowy figures working out of Pakistan in illegal nuclear proliferation enterprises. Though he will deny that he had anything to do with his namesake, others involved with A.Q. Khan who have since agreed to talk said there were scores of such people involved in the illicit trade. One British operative told the BBC's security consultant Gordon Corera that some were even competing against each other; they would bid for the same contracts, deal with the same clients and often surreptitiously manipulate prices.

The fact that Humayun Khan was involved in that kind of work points pretty conclusively to his ties to the illegal network. He was described by one source as an Islamabad businessman with close ties to Pakistan's military and who had been linked by American government officials to militant Islamic groups, some suspected of arming fighters in the Kashmiri conflict. Also, the spark-gap triggers were not a one-off job; Karni was linked to his Pakistani bosses for a very long time and though the Americans admit to nothing, this was one job among many. Once he had been nabbed, it took the authorities months to go through all his documents, which included information held on several computer hard drives. Karni was a key element in this game, which could be why, in his customs declaration to his American counterpart, he declared that the triggers were to be used in equipment installed in Johannesburg's Chris Hani/Baragwanath Hospital. In a subsequent investigation the doctor responsible for dealing with such matters admitted that he might use a couple of them a year; it would take a lifetime to use up all sixty-six spark-gap triggers that Karni had ordered.

The gravity of Asher Karni's actions was underscored by a more recent visit to South Africa by retired Major-General M.K. Paul, controller of the National Institute for Advanced Studies in Bangalore, India. General Paul told those present at the South African Institute of International Affairs at Witwatersrand University (now, the University of Johannesburg) that Karni's actions had 'upset the delicate nuclear balance in south Asia between India and Pakistan.' While a lot of what took place between Karni and his Pakistani counterparts did emerge at the time of his sentencing – revealed by US Attorney Kenneth L. Wainstein in the American capital on 5 August 2005 – a lot more of what Karni had to tell the FBI remains sealed. Corey Hinderstein, formerly at the Institute for Science and International Security told me when we last met at her

Washington office that she had seen the file and confirmed that only essentials were made public. In fact, without being specific, she disclosed that there was much more and, possibly true to form for this was no hero, Karni revealed all, which was why he got only thirty month's in jail.

The background makes for an epic tale. US Attorney Wainstein told the presiding judge in Washington DC that in August 2002, Khan approached Karni and asked him to help acquire certain models of oscilloscopes manufactured by an Oregon company, Tektronix, Inc. What Khan did not disclose was that the models he asked for could be used for testing in the development of nuclear weapons and missile delivery systems. For that reason, said Wainstein, the US Department of Commerce required licenses for their export to certain countries, Pakistan included. Khan did ease the passage of events a little by telling Karni that he was an authorized distributor for Tektronix in Pakistan which, it has since transpired, he was. At that stage, Karni had already set up Top-Cape Technology at his Ocean View address, through which he came to channel all his business. On the trigger request, he told Khan he would help, even though the Pakistani warned him that they were subject to American export controls. Notably, Karni was cautioned not to disclose the ultimate destination of the goods *to anybody*.

After several false leads, Karni eventually got hold of one of the Tektronix controlled oscilloscopes in March 2003 from a firm in Plainview, New York. The company was directed to send it to Cape Town and Karni re-exported it to Khan in Pakistan, the deal taking place without requisite licenses. Two additional oscilloscopes were bought five months later and again, were diverted to Khan. For much of the rest of the year, the two men worked to fill a $1.3 million order for the spark-gap triggers that eventually resulted in Karni's arrest. Khan told him that they were for a third party in Pakistan.

The spark gaps that Khan sought were manufactured by Perkin Elmer Optoelectronics of Salem, Massachusetts. Because of the sensitive nature of the deal, Karni first made inquiries of Perkin Elmer's French sales representative. It took a little while but eventually he was quoted a price. At the same time, he was told that he would need to certify that the product would remain in South Africa and, more importantly, that they would not be used for nuclear purposes.

Karni forwarded this information to Khan and because of the sensitivity of the deal; he initially declined to continue. But Khan was an assertive type and he prevailed. Anyway, the money was quite remarkable, even by Karni's standards; it would have earned him millions. Court documents from Washington detail the rest of the story:

'In July 2003, an anonymous source [in Cape Town] informed agents of the Office of Export Enforcement of the Department of Commerce and

Immigration and Customs Enforcement of the Department of Homeland Security that Karni was in the process of using a broker in Secaucus, New Jersey, to obtain 200 Perkin Elmer triggered spark gaps for ultimate shipment to Pakistan through South Africa. The agents approached Perkin Elmer, which agreed to cooperate in the investigation but to render [them] inoperable.'

Three months afterwards, US agents were able to track the first instalment of sixty-six triggered spark gaps to Top-Cape in South Africa and then on to Pakistan through the United Arab Emirates.

One of the people who helped get Asher Karni arrested was Cape Town attorney Michael Bagraim, a fellow Jew. More importantly, when the rumpus started, Bagraim was chairperson of the South African Jewish Board of Deputies, a powerful position in a country with such a large Jewish population; he was its chief spokesman for anything affecting the community, parliament included. Following Karni's arrest and sentencing in the United States, Bagraim told a Cape Town newspaper that he believed that possibly Karni did not understand the enormity of what he was doing:

'But then again, being Jewish possibly made it worse ... if he really sold nuclear material as he is accused of doing, then he deserved what he got ... He might have been unwitting, but even so it is a hard lesson to others not to deal in weapons of mass destruction. If this conviction stops someone like that, then I applaud it.'

Getting involved with Pakistani nuclear middlemen was probably the worst mistake of Asher Karni's life. It was not his last. Despite earlier visits to his premises in Cape Town by investigators, he blundered badly when he flew to the US on a skiing holiday with his wife and daughters. The authorities grabbed him at Denver International Airport.

Britain's Jane's Information group has given a good deal of coverage to the Pakistani weapons of mass destruction imbroglio in recent years, particularly since its own forces remain active in a number of military theatres in the Middle East and further afield. One of its flagship publications, *Jane's Intelligence Review* – for which I wrote for some years – went further[1]. Andrew Koch, *JIR*'s former Washington-based correspondent, published a report on events relating to the A.Q. Khan network on 1 July 2006 that included the fact that the hugely publicized smuggling operation, though declared moribund by Islamabad, just is not so, this in spite of the fact that three years before, the world was told by President George W Bush that the Khan network had been neutralized.

Koch made a number of prescient observations including the reality that the Khan network and its middlemen successfully used:

'the conveniences of the time. [This involved] front companies in pliant jurisdictions, flexible communications and travel, swiftness and anonymity of international finance. Most of the participants – particularly in Europe and South Africa – were market savvy rather than geopolitically inspired, and the culprits used loopholes in the new global marketplace to sidestep international restrictions that were often too cumbersome or unwieldy to keep up with changing tactics.'

Although the arrests of A.Q. Khan, his Sri Lankan deputy Buhary Seyed Abu Tahir and several other senior members of their network eliminated a major source of nuclear weapons-related goods for would-be proliferators, it did not end the trade in nuclear wares. In fact, says Koch, recent evidence suggested that part of the Khan network continues to flourish. One senior international investigator told *Jane's*, 'There is no reason to believe this is the whole story,' a comment which Koch says sums up a widely held view regarding known information on the enterprise to date. He also made the point that parts of the organization still remain to be uncovered. Moreover, Koch tells us, this includes individuals who are more senior in Khan's illegal establishment than first thought.

He goes on:

'Recent clues that have been uncovered by law enforcement officials, international nuclear inspectors and intelligence operatives, support this contention. One major piece of evidence was that Iranian agents and to a lesser degree, Pakistani ones, have attempted numerous illicit nuclear-related purchases since 2003, suggesting that such a reconfiguration of suppliers is occurring and that atomic goods continue to be available for those with the means and desire to buy them.'

While these new suppliers cannot provide the kind of 'one-stop-shopping' that Khan offered, and are insufficient by themselves for moving a nuclear weapons programme very far forward, they point to the likelihood that some tentacles of the system have yet to be discovered.

Key points mentioned by Koch include:

• Iranian and, to a lesser degree, Pakistani agents have attempted numerous illicit nuclear-related purchases since 2003

- Tehran has been seeking material from European and Russian firms and included some of the Khan middlemen in the process
- Heightened procurement activity by Pakistani agents has occurred since at least 2004

What is interesting about Khan's network is that he did not keep it 'home grown'. He ran the full international gamut in recruiting people who might be useful. Some were exceptionally well-placed to fulfil their role for which each one of them was handsomely paid. They recruited anybody who might be useful, including, as we have seen, a former major in the Israeli Defence Force. Among others were a handful of British, Malaysians, Swiss, Indians, South Africans and Sri Lankans, together with the inevitable bunch of Germans. Which makes one wonder why so many of these otherwise respectable Northern Europeans so often get themselves involved in illegal nuclear smuggling operations. Some were arrested after Saddam Hussein's nuclear operations were destroyed following Gulf War 1[2]. Still more were named in reports which detail South African and Brazilian quests for the bomb.

Of the more prominent Germans in the operation there was Gotthard Lerch who has been described as the 'main contractor' for Khan's principal operating officer, Buhary Syed Abu Tahir. Lerch was eventually brought to trial in Germany and charged with illegally helping to build vital parts of a uranium enrichment plant in South Africa destined for Libya. There was also Heinz Mebus, who was to become an important link in filling Tehran's 'wanted lists' and was actually involved in the first centrifuge transfers to Iran in the 1980s. Another German was the technician Gerhard Wisser who owned Krisch Engineering at Vanderbijlpark near Johannesburg, the same firm hired by Khan to build parts for the illegal Libyan uranium plant. Otto Heilingbrunner was yet another German and an associate of Lerch.

Among other Europeans linked to Khan was his long-time associate Swiss national Urs Tinner, fingered as the man who, until 2003, was responsible for the production of centrifuge parts in Malaysia. Bold to a fault – stupid, say some – Urs Tinner also recruited his father Frederich, together with his brother Marco, into this nefarious network. Over lengthy periods, all three men were linked to illegal nuclear operations in Libya and Iran. Frederich specialty as president of the Swiss firm CETEC, was to act as a procuring agent for many of the European components needed by Khan. It was an ideal setup, the Swiss being accepted by most as squeaky clean when it comes to moral issues.

Then a British father and son combination in Peter and Paul Griffin became implicated. Peter Griffin actually designed Gadhaffi's 'Machine Shop 1001' which involved acquiring high tech equipment from several European countries. Much of this stuff was transhipped to Libya through Dubai where Griffin Jnr. ran Gulf Technical Industries, a convenient arrangement since Khan himself spent a lot of time in the Gulf state.

Top of Khan's external network was the Indian-born Mohammed Farook (also spelt Farouq) who had the ultimate say in most things in which the group was involved. Like his nephew, Tahir, he too was based in Dubai, where both men were linked to a company called SMB Computers. That company, together with several others linked to A.Q. Khan seemed to 'vaporize' after the Libyan link to Khan had been pinpointed. That came shortly after the German ship *BBC China* was seized by a NATO-led naval task force after it had entered the Mediterranean (See Chapter Eight).

At first glance, it seems just a little absurd that a single individual – a disgraced Pakistani metallurgist who ran the world's most successful nuclear smuggling operation – might have strategically turned the world on its head with his underworld role in acquiring material for weapons of mass destruction. Granted, Khan did not work alone. There is little doubt that his government was very much in on the act; how else, since they were dealing with what later emerged as 'billions of dollars'? The cold truth is that North Korea became the ninth country to detonate a nuclear weapon as one of the consequences of A.Q. Khan's actions. By all accounts, Iran was part of the same equation. That, in turn, has triggered a nuclear race in the Middle East.

In late October 2006, Vienna's International Atomic Energy Agency disclosed that apart from other countries interested in acquiring nuclear parity, among the half-dozen Arab states in the hunt were Egypt, Saudi Arabia, Syria and Algeria. It is worth a mention that all four countries at one time or another had surreptitiously dabbled in things nuclear, though none would admit as much today. By November 2017, the Saudis were at it again.

If nothing else, Abdul Qadeer Khan has led a charmed life. Though in disgrace and said to be ailing, he enjoys the status of a nationally acclaimed hero in Pakistan, even if he was not born there. His parents slipped across the border from India after the subdivision of the sub-continent that was both bloody and traumatic; they had originally come from Bophal. In fact, it affected young Khan so much that for the rest of his life he could never utter the word 'Hindu' or 'Hindi' without embellishing it with a curse.

As one of his biographers pointed out, a good deal of what Khan did in making Pakistan proficient in the nuclear domain was achieved with one eye on similar events across the border to his immediate east. For all their travails – his father became a headmaster of a local school – the Khan family quickly managed to pick up the pieces in their new environment and the illustrious Abdul Qadeer, having been sent abroad to study, in 1972, got himself a doctorate in metallurgical engineering from the Catholic University of Leuven in Belgium. Within months he had started work at a research laboratory which was linked to Ultra Centrifuge Nederland (UCN). Some of that work involved classified research into the URENCO uranium enriching project. It was not long before

Khan was allowed access to URENCO's advanced UCN enrichment facility in Holland to familiarize himself with the complexities of centrifuge operations.

As a metallurgist, it was to be expected that he would be involved in this phase of production; special steels was his forté, especially where they were linked to strengthening metal centrifuge components. Officially, Khan was not cleared to visit the facility, but what emerged after he had left the country was that he did so many times, with or without the consent of his employers. Meantime, he met and married Hendrina, a South African-born Dutch girl and they set about raising a family.

The date 18 May 1974 changed everything for the still-youthful Pakistani when India conducted its first nuclear test. A press release issued by the New Delhi government referred to it as 'a peaceful nuclear explosion'. It is not all that surprising therefore that four months later, Khan wrote a personal note to the Pakistan Prime Minister Zulfikar Ali Bhutto, delivered to the office of the President by a personal friend. He had unusual scientific services and expertise to offer his beloved country, was the thrust of it. Alarmed at India's nuclear progress – and having been involved in several wars with their more preponderant neighbour – Pakistan had meanwhile initiated a nuclear programme of its own. By mid-1975, Islamabad acquired the basics for an enrichment programme from European agents and it was all legitimate.

A.Q. Khan's timely letter to his prime minister obviously had the required effect and to the consternation of his Dutch bosses, Khan started taking an inordinate amount of interest in nuclear-related projects that were not part of his domain. That was only a few years after he had graduated and already this youthful scientist was making waves. The matter was compounded by the detailed questions he liked to ask, many of them dealing with issues regarded by European governments as classified; there was pressure put on his bosses to move him to less sensitive projects.

Khan must have been aware that he was being watched, which was probably why he suddenly left Holland in December 1975. In the family baggage was a batch of classified URENCO blueprints together with lists of European suppliers, many of whom he would be contacting in the years ahead. A lot more such information had already been passed onto Pakistani intelligence agents operating out of their embassy in The Hague. There is no doubt that A.Q. Khan was one sharp fellow. Back home, as his former bosses in Holland discovered shortly afterwards, the still-youthful Khan began immediate work on developing an indigenous uranium enrichment capability, Pakistan's first, and in his view, a possibly a long-term counter to India's military dominance. By now, others had discovered his duplicity and not long afterwards, the Netherlands government took its first steps to indict Abdul Qadeer Khan for criminal espionage. The only problem was that the bird had flown.

After he had left Holland, Khan formally told his company that though he had intended to return to his old job, he had problems at home and decided to stay in Pakistan. It is interesting too, that though Khan visited Europe often in later years and there were warrants out for his arrest, it was CIA Headquarters at Langley that prevented its European counterparts from arresting him; the CIA wanted to keep track of his movements, they maintained.

Back in Pakistan, A.Q. Khan spent almost all his time working in centrifuge-related projects within the confines of the country's Atomic Energy Commission (PAEC), headed by a namesake Munir Ahmad Khan. It was not an easy relationship because it soon became clear that the two men were suspicious of each other and that led to dissention and a series of confrontations which became public. In a bid to stabilize a situation that was to have an impact on Pakistan's nuclear weapons programme that was both strategic and critical, the upshot came when Khan was given autonomy and control over Pakistani uranium enrichment programmes from July 1976 onwards. He founded his own company, Engineering Research Laboratory (ERL) at Kahuta, about an hour's drive out of the capital. The rival PAEC meantime went ahead with programmes of its own, related to both nuclear power and nuclear weapons.

Khan's uranium-enrichment programme was based largely upon developing an indigenous gas-centrifuge system which he dubbed Pak-1. In fact, there was nothing new about it; it was little more than a modification of URENCO's first generation design. Nor was it something that came easily. He had difficulty in the early days producing aluminium rotors which would pass a rigorous 'spin' to which all centrifuges are subjected to ascertain whether they are able to maintain the extreme speeds needed to 'spin off' uranium-235. It was only in the 1990s that Khan was able to develop his more advanced Pak-2, a modification of URENCO's second-generation design, which had steel rotors. He continued with research that would later contribute toward Pakistan's first generation of nuclear weapons. But this labour – and that of others involved in similar projects – had already attracted attention from the West. In 1979 Islamabad was cut off from all US financial and military support.

That impasse was short-lived, however, thanks to the Soviet Union. Following Moscow's invasion of Afghanistan, Washington had no option but to re-establish friendly ties to the embattled country's nearest neighbour. In fact, for the duration of the Afghan War, Pakistan played a seminal role in channelling aid and equipment to a variety of mujahedeen factions fighting in the mountainous north. The situation was consolidated after President Reagan was elected in 1980.

On the domestic front in the early 1980s, there was more progress. Khan – having initiated strong contacts through his government with a variety of countries, China included – managed to acquire the plans for Beijing's first atom bomb that was tested at Lop Nor fifteen years before. The event made the man and he was showered with plaudits. From then on, there would be no looking back. Nobody is certain exactly when Khan and his entourage decided to make money on the side by selling some of the nuclear secrets he had stolen or subsequently had a hand in developing. Word has it that about the time that the Soviets were driven out of Afghanistan, he was quietly approached by an Arab state, purportedly Saudi Arabia, perhaps even Syria, with requests for nuclear assistance. By then, we are told by Michael Laufer, who compiled an A.Q. Khan Chronology[4] that Khan's early successes with the Pakistani uranium enrichment programme were 'followed by the more advanced design and technologies of the P-2 centrifuge, an adapted version of the German G-2 that can spin twice as fast as the previous P-1 design.' Says Laufer, Khan was left with an excess inventory of P-1 components and he began to purchase additional P-2 components that he would ultimately export through many of the same channels he had used to import centrifuge components. Notably, he adds, 'Khan makes nuclear sales in this period to Iran and offers technologies to Iraq and possibly others.' That was followed by a secret nuclear deal signed by Pakistan and Iran and the provision for groups of Iranians to study nuclear-related sciences at Pakistani institutions, something that certainly did not please Washington and led to a good deal of friction. Relations between the two Islamic states were good enough for Khan to visit the Iranian nuclear facility at Bushehr on the Gulf several times in the late 1980s.

In 1987, Laufer reckons, Khan is believed to have made a centrifuge deal with Iran to help build a cascade of 50,000 P-1 centrifuges. He adds that Tehran may also have received centrifuge drawings through the offices of an unknown foreign intermediary around this time. His firm, KRL:

> 'begins to publish publicly available technical papers that outline some of the more advanced design features Khan has developed. The papers include information that would normally be classified in [the West] and show that KRL is competent in many aspects of centrifuge design and operation. The papers also include specifications for centrifuges with maraging steel that can spin faster than earlier aluminium designs. 'Later, in 1991, KRL publishes details on how to etch grooves around the bottom bearing to incorporate lubricants. These technical developments are important for Khan's P-2 centrifuges.'

Almost exactly a decade later, on 11 May 1998, India detonated five devices in nuclear tests that included at least one thermonuclear – or hydrogen – bomb. Pakistan responded less than three weeks afterwards with its own first of six tests and became the eighth country in the world to possess nuclear weapons.

Abdul Qadeer Khan was hailed by one and all in Pakistan as national hero. This is the man, some of his countrymen maintain – taking a distinctly unsubtle swipe at what is regarded by many of his fellow countrymen as unwarranted Western opprobrium – who can do no wrong.

In an interview with Elizabeth Dougherty, *The Atlantic's* William Langewiesche sheds some light on how this all came about.[5] His comments are interesting because he met many of the players and also went to Pakistan to do field research. His view is that Khan succeeded where others did not because he was so very aggressive:

'He was very effective. He was a great organizer and manager. People say he's a great scientist and a brilliant scientist. But it wasn't science that mattered, it was management. He was highly energetic and had an unlimited budget. That helped, but had it not been for him it would have been someone else.'

As he explains, there were many different reasons for it. The Pakistani military, which runs the Pakistani army and Musharraf, says Langewiesche:

'... does not want the real story to come out because it will definitely implicate them. There's just no question about that. They don't want Khan's export activity to be explored fully out of political self-preservation ... It's important to realize that the United States, unlike Pakistan, is a very large and complex country politically. Pakistan has a lot of people, but it's actually a very small country because the great majority of people are extremely poor and basically don't count politically. Pakistan is a dictatorship with very small elite running it as if it's a small country...'

*Chapter 6*

# Al-Qaeda's Obsession with 'Dirty Bombs'

*'On the day the Islamic State overran the Iraqi city of Mosul in 2014, it laid claim to one of the greatest weapons bonanzas ever to fall to a terrorist group; a large metropolis dotted with military bases and garrisons stocked with guns, bombs, rockets and even battle tanks. But the most fearsome weapon in Mosul on that day was never used by the terrorists. Only now is it becoming clear what happened to it. Locked away in a storage room on a Mosul college campus were two caches of cobalt-60, a metallic substance with lethally high levels of radiation. When contained within the heavy shielding of a radiotherapy machine, cobalt-60 is used to kill cancer cells. In terrorists' hands, it is the core ingredient of a Dirty Bomb, a weapon that could be used to spread radiation and panic.*

*'How ISIS Nearly Stumbled on the Ingredients for a "Dirty Bomb"'*
*Joby Warrick and Loveday Morris,*
*Washington Post 22 July 2017'*

What we now know is that intelligence agencies in the West attempted to monitor the situation with regard to the radioactive material in Mosul from the start. Things were difficult because of the acute security situation in regions controlled by Islamic State. Matters were not helped by IS boasts that that they had access to radioactive material, the inference being that they could now build radiological dispersal devices – more commonly referred to as 'Dirty Bombs'. But nothing more was heard. Instead, the terror movement turned its attention to chemical weapons such as nerve and mustard gasses as well as - claimed by some sources but never verified - biological weapons.

We are now also aware that prior to the final onslaught on Mosul, military commanders in the field were apprised of the potential radiological threat so that when their men eventually overran the college campus they would be aware of what lay behind the heavy cladding that shielded the storage room where the cobalt machines were kept.

As Warrick and Morris reported, 'they were still there, exactly as they were when the Islamic State seized the campus in 2014. The cobalt apparently had never been touched.' Had the Cobalt-60 been accessed by Islamic State, one observer familiar with the situation volunteered, 'Islamic State would have had enough radiated material to build dozens of RDDs.' He suggested that among those most relieved were the Russians, especially since there were so many rebels from Chechnya with the ranks of IS. For almost three years they had to access enough Cobalt-60 to kill hundreds of people, maybe thousands. But they never went near the stuff. Another source believed that for all their technical expertise with modern weapons, Islamic State specialists were stymied by the thick cladding surrounding the radioactive source. Simply put, 'they didn't know to dismantle it without exposing themselves to the lethal radiation that lay behind.'

Among the most consistent debates along the corridors of power in Washington, Whitehall and the Kremlin is whether nuclear, chemical or biological weapons will be the first to be used in upgraded weapons of mass destruction (WMD) onslaughts by Islamic zealots. This activity dates back quite a while as William J. Broad wrote in the *New York Times* on 29 April 2001, under the heading 'Document Reveals 1987 Bomb Test by Iraq.' As things stand at present, say some of pundits within the security establishments of several Western nations, an enhanced form of the 'Dirty Bomb' – has the edge. Clearly, other options cannot be ignored and nor are they.

It is interesting that the United States investigated radiation weapons in the 1940s and 1950s for possible wartime use, but the concept was finally canned. One reason given at the time was that its deployment would have been regarded by the civilized world as barbaric, not that conventional nuclear weapons are any less so. What sets the RDD apart from weapons used by other dissident political groupings is that al-Qaeda has shown an unusual and historic interest in these weapons. Taking a cue from among the staunchest of al-Qaeda's allies, anti-Russian Chechen dissidents, also of Islamic persuasion, have tried several times to detonate RDDs in recent years.

In 1995, a 'Dirty Bomb' containing highly radioactive caesium-137, Cobalt-60 and possibly strontium-90 was secreted in Moscow's Izmailovskiy Park by a group of Chechen militants under the command of Shamil Basayev. The device was never detonated because somebody in the group tipped off the media. What subsequently emerged was that the RDD was intended as a warning that these Southern Caucasus's rebels had the wherewithal to cause serious damage. Moreover, they declared, if their hand was forced by the Kremlin's intransigence, they would go ahead and use it. Having been involved in an attack that killed scores of children at a school not long before, this desperate band of dissidents clearly meant what they said. There was apparently another attempt in or around Moscow afterward, but neither detail nor confirmation about that effort was ever made public.

Pamela Falk, writing in *Foreign Affairs* in an article titled 'The Dirty Bomb Threat, Too Dangerous to Do Nothing' (published in 4 April 2017) disclosed that in one investigation in Chisinau, Moldova, samples of uranium-235 and caesium-135 were seized by police when a smuggler offered an informant posing as a buyer for Islamic State enough caesium to contaminate several city blocks for $2.5 million.

She goes on:

'An in-depth investigation into dirty bombs by the Associated Press revealed four other attempts by criminal networks to traffic radioactive materials through Moldova. Last spring, in a New York federal court, another perpetrator, this time a Colombian national, was convicted for obtaining enriched uranium with the purpose of supplying a South American–based terrorist group with a dirty bomb to attack US military personnel or a US embassy. What investigators from INTERPOL, the International Atomic Energy Agency and various national intelligence agencies have found is that radioactive materials that can be used in a dirty bomb are the new illicit trade of choice.'

Also pertinent are comments made by the present incumbent of the office of the IAEA, when director-general Yukiya Amano told member states in December 2016 that 'terrorists and criminals will try to exploit any vulnerability in the global nuclear security system. Any country, in any part of the world, could find itself used as a transit point.' The implications of all these disclosures are staggering and without question, more will be forthcoming almost in the immediate future.

In the broader context, we need go no further than a comment made by Christopher Andrew in his book *Defence of the Realm* released in London in 2009[1].

Writing under the alias of Esa al-Hindi in a book titled *The Army of Madinah in Kashmir* (Madinah, or more commonly Medina, refers to the second holiest site in Islam) Dhiren Barot declared that one way to counter what he referred to as 'Western interference in Muslim lands' would be to conduct large-scale attacks that might include these same radiological materials that he suggested would be highly radioactive. 'And they say the Islamist threat is exaggerated…' declared Andrew in a rare display of scepticism.

Elsewhere in the United States, we had al-Qaeda operative Jose Padilla (aka as Abdulla al-Muhajir) arrested in Chicago in May 2002 while on a scouting mission for an al-Qaeda operation to attack the city with an RDD. He was subsequently tried, found guilty and is currently serving a prison sentence. He is on record as saying that the knowledge exists for the use of Caesium-137. Even better, said a linked source, al-Qaeda seriously considered using spent fuel cells from dismantled former Soviet Union nuclear submarines currently being taken apart in Russia's far northern Kola Peninsula. Though the damage would possibly not be as severe as might be caused by using Caesium-137, it would still be substantial if dissipated by a 'Dirty Bomb'.

It might also be recalled that not long before that, CNN's David Ensor reported that a hand-drawn diagram of an RDD bomb was uncovered in a Taliban or al-Qaeda facility in the mountains south of Kabul during the early stages of the Afghanistan invasion. It was actually found by one of their journalists and very clearly depicted an RDD design together with a variety of technical comments. A sequel to that event followed, with George Tenet, former CIA chief telling Congress before he retired that United States security forces had uncovered rudimentary diagrams of nuclear weapons in a suspected al-Qaeda house in Kabul.

It is only in recent years that we have been able to observe al-Qaeda's particular interest in matters nuclear from fairly up close. We have also seen the organization's 'Nuclear Briefs', some of which appeared on websites in the form of lessons or lectures. There has been a constant flow of intelligence emanating from both the Middle East and Central Asia with regard to Osama bin Laden's original intention to use weapons of mass destruction against the West. In America's case, the idea was – and still is – to smuggle a bomb or possibly even pathogens such as anthrax or something equally deadly onto American soil. The most common scenario suggested would be to get it across the Mexican border in the southwest, or possibly secreted in a shipping container through a major US port.

A typical example of this kind of activity – without delivery details – was research completed by the same convicted British terrorist Dhiren Barot mentioned earlier. Robert Wesley elaborates on the activities of this man in an edition of Washington's Jamestown Foundation's *Terrorism Focus*[2]:

'Barot initially conceptualized the decision to incorporate radioactive materials into his attack scenarios much in the same way as one would decide between attaching nails or ball bearings to a pipe bomb (i.e. as an after-thought). He quickly discovered that radioactive materials had enough potential to be addressed as a primary weapon rather than simply as a secondary consideration.

'Barot's surprisingly detailed research unsettlingly reveals just how accessible and instructive the relevant literature is concerning radioactive materials and their potential for malicious use. For example, Barot was able to obtain numerous public documents concerning the potential effects of RDDs, including employment scenarios. The literature available greatly assisted Barot's investigation of the core obstacles that would need to be overcome for a successful [radiological] operation. 'Another significant consideration is that Barot approached targeting selection and methods of attack for radiological weapons based on, among other things, the simplicity of the plan and availability of resources. This is in line with the traditional practice and advice of al-Qaeda operatives and strategists. Correspondingly, he recommended that acquisition of radioactive sources should be based on ease of access rather than the hazardous effects of the source. The inference was that high activity sources (usually the most harmful) were also the most difficult to secure access to, and thus were to be in most cases avoided in favour of less radioactive, yet more accessible sources.'

Cumulatively, these threats are regarded as akin to a terror wake-up call, not only by Russia's FSB security services, but by Washington and London as well.

A Congressional Research Service (CRS) Report for the United States Congress on Radiological Dispersal Devices at about the same time all this was going down went some distance towards focusing public attention on efforts to counter the use of this weapon[3]: It declared that a RDD attack 'might cause casualties, economic damage, and, potentially, public panic,' though it also suggested that experts might disagree on the likely magnitude of each of these effects. The impact of an RDD attack it said, 'would depend on many variables, such as meteorological conditions, type and amount of radiological material, duration of exposure, and method of dispersal.'

In a sense, consequently, radiological dispersal devices might be referred to as weapons of mass disruption, rather than of destruction.

The report goes on: 'both the threat posed by terrorist RDD use and the magnitude of impact are matters of some contention. Some experts believe that terrorists could, without great difficulty, obtain radioactive material and construct an RDD. Others assert that radiation sources intense enough to cause casualties in an RDD attack would be injurious to the terrorists during acquisition and use. Most experts agree that few casualties would be likely to directly result, generally only among those close to the device, but many disagree on how attractive an RDD would be to a terrorist.

'Some assert that the inherent difficulties of handling radioactive material combined with few direct casualties make RDDs less likely terrorist weapons. Other experts claim that terrorists recognize the potential economic and psychological effects of such a weapon and are thus more highly value RDDs as terror weapons.'

The argument about terrorists falling victim to their own destructive device is viewed by some as superfluous, or, as one authority suggested to me, do those who compile these reports not read the daily newspapers? More to the point, Islamic zealots have proved many times in recent years that no matter what the risk – radiation sickness or otherwise – they would be happy to die for the cause in order to achieve their objectives. Suicide bombers are as much a feature of today's fundamentalist Islamic world as their five-times-a-day call to prayer.

A number of the more prominent authorities who helped in compiling this work agree that indeed, the threat is viable. These include Dr Nic von Wielligh who for some years was associated with Vienna's IAEA. He was advisor to the Director General and a member of its Standing Advisory Group on Safeguards Implementation. Another source consulted was Dr Mike Foley, a geologist who has made a career in specializing in nuclear-related issues and somebody with whom the author communicated.

Based at Washington's Pacific Northwest National Laboratory, Dr Foley hosted me on one of several fact-finding missions for Jane's *International Defence Review* as well as *Jane's Islamic Affairs Analyst*. From there, I reported on measures being taken in countering the overland movement of potentially harmful radioactive materials that might have been stolen from source or been smuggled. Dr Foley's simple warning was that weapons-radioactive materials 'could be used in terror acts as pollutants rather than as fissionables'. Why this matter is not being addressed, he suggested, was because the effort needed would be immense. It would also be expensive, extremely so, he declared and explained:

'All countries would need to expand coverage to everything including radon waste storage sites, medical waste and the rest...there is an incredible amount of radioactive waste about...not all of it safeguarded and in the Former Soviet Union, very badly'.

Of significant concern in this regard are the burgeoning numbers of incidents that involve internationally-linked nuclear smugglers. According to the IAEA, they are increasing exponentially by the year. Prior to his retirement as head of the IAEA in December 2009, Dr Mohamed ElBaradei disclosed that the Vienna-based UN watchdog organisation was aware of hundreds of cases of nuclear smuggling each year, much of it linked to uranium or plutonium. On the downside, the IAEA conceded that the success rate, such as it was, tended to be limited to about one in ten or twelve incidents that actually came to light, never mind those never uncovered. Simply put, for every smuggling case we know about, there are another dozen or more not detected. In almost every case listed, people of Islamic or Middle East extraction are listed as receiving parties.

It is worth mentioning that IAEA investigators believe that those involved from former Eastern bloc countries are rarely ideologically motivated. Rather, they are interested only in the money and it is of little concern to many of them whether cities or people are contaminated by deadly radiation. 'The fear, essentially, is that the criminals may have no qualms about selling to Jihadist groups,' read the IAEA report. Al-Qaeda's Abu Hamza al-Muhajir actually called for Muslim scientists to join the organization and experiment with radioactive devices for use against coalition troops. The IAEA statement also disclosed that captured al Qaeda leaders confessed to the CIA – 'under duress' – that at one stage they had attempted to smuggle a radioactive device into the US. This kind of report, released years later, is always worrying.

A report in Britain's *New Scientist* spelt some of it out in its issue of June 2004, which included details of another IAEA report:

'There are … tens of thousands of large radiation sources used by industry such as gauges, sterilizers and metal irradiators.'

That was followed by the IAEA expressing particular concern about the security of hundreds of thermo-generators made in Russia and the West, in which heat produced by radioactive decay drives a generator to provide power in remote areas. The IAEA's smuggling figures did not include radiation sources that had simply gone missing. 'An average of one a day is reported to the US Nuclear Regulatory Commission as lost, stolen or abandoned,' it read. 'In Tbilisi, Georgia, a taxi driver, Tedo Makeria was stopped by police in May 2003 and found to be carrying lead-lined boxes containing strontium-90 and caesium-137. In Belarus customs officials seized twenty-six radioactive cargoes between 1996 and 2003, six of them from Russia,' the IAEA disclosed.

Which brings us to what a Radiological Dispersal Device or 'Dirty Bomb' is all about. In the simplest terms, these devices are intended to disperse radiation. In a large RDD blast within the confines of a city, there would obviously be a number of casualties, including people exposed to the actual blast who would succumb to the effects of the chemical explosion, as would be the case with a conventional bomb and the shrapnel that it disperses. While the radiation effect which follows the detonation is secondary, it is important to accept that when human tissue is exposed to radiation, energy is absorbed which could lead to a variety of harmful consequences and associated symptoms. At the same time, the number of casualties would not be nearly as many as some authorities like to predict: a major bomb in downtown Chicago or Berlin would result in hundreds rather than thousands of casualties, of which only a limited number would die. The reality is that radiation can either have deterministic (acute) or stochastic (probabilistic) effects.

Acute effects occur after high doses are delivered in a relatively short period and manifest typically within days. Stochastic effects typically occur after low doses of radiation are assimilated but will only manifest in years or decades after exposure and then probably as a form of cancer. With the victims of the Hiroshima and Nagasaki blasts, there were people still dying a generation or two after the attack. Even when persons are exposed to high radiation, such as the 'Blue Flash' chain reaction incident associated with a plutonium criticality accident, it will not lead to immediate death.

The scientist who experienced the first 'Blue Flash' at Los Alamos walked across unaided to the hospital where he died four weeks later. One of the facility's security guards standing three or four metres away suffered no lasting injury. Using the same plutonium set-up, another person involved in the Manhattan Program created a second criticality accident about nine months later and he died after about a week. Death due to radiation, consequently, is seldom immediate. In both these incidents, with enough reflection provided, chain reactions were generated; the plutonium actually went critical, releasing prodigious amounts of radiation.

A chain reaction in a solution of, say, enriched uranium salts in water is even more deadly. Whereas one needs scores of pounds of metal to go critical, about 200 grams of HEU salts in water can quickly become critical. Many criticality accidents in laboratories in which people subsequently died, took place in solution systems during processing. None of these examples pertain to RDDs; it would be impossible to link the kind of laboratory experiments involved in 'Blue Flash' accidents to anything even vaguely resembling 'Dirty Bombs.'

Ideally, the radioactive material used in a 'Dirty Bomb' terror attack should be something that might be dispersed by the initial explosion: most likely in the form of a powder, the finer the better. Solid and highly active spent fuel ceramic uranium oxide pellets would need to be crushed or remotely ground. Similarly, uranium metal/zirconium fuel plates would have to be remotely mechanically powdered to be of use. Dispersing whole ceramic uranium oxide pellets by an explosive will make clean-up much easier as the contamination will mostly be contained within the pellets. Using spent uranium-zirconium metal fuel would probably result in some shrapnel, but the contamination would also be localised and therefore not difficult to clean up. Spent fuel elements are consequently unlikely candidates for a RDD.

The radioactive material in a RDD would most probably come from medical therapeutic sources (such as Caesium-137 and Cobalt-60) or from industrial radiographic equipment (in which case it would probably be Cobalt-60). There are many documented cases where obsolete equipment that involves such sources have ended up in scrap heaps and were subsequently melted down and incorporated in steel, rendering the metal radioactive. This has happened where entire structures have had to be torn down as a consequence. There was also a case where about 100 grams of Caesium-137 in a therapeutic device – from an abandoned clinic in Goiânia, Brazil – was scavenged and the glowing caesium salt sold to curious buyers. That incident resulted in the death of four people. Under normal circumstances, Cs-137 is extracted in small quantities during the reprocessing of spent fuel and must be remotely handled in so-called 'Hot Cells'. Moreover, Cs-137 is a strong emitter of penetrating gamma rays (similar to X-rays). No glove or surgical mask will provide protection. Terrorists with little regard for their own longevity or the deaths of others, as we have already seen, will undoubtedly freely handle this material without protection from the emanating deadly radiation, and they too will die within a comparatively short time.

One nuclear scientist who was prepared to offer advice on the subject, suggested that rather than go through the complicated and hazardous steps to specially prepare spent fuel in a suitable form for a RDD, it would be easier to visit a scrap yard with a wheelbarrow and search for a discarded, shielded source in a developing country where regulatory oversight is weak or non-existent. Alternatively, he said, one could steal industrial sources in their protective containers. It is accepted in the West that such industrial and medical sources disappear at an alarming rate all over the world. He recalls at least one case where a container with a medical isotope was stolen from the freight section at Johannesburg International Airport.

Another possible scenario would be to get hold of the waste left after the reprocessing of spent fuel. This will not contain plutonium (this is extracted in the reprocessing process together with any unused uranium) but more likely, produce lots of unwanted fission products. Because it is regarded as waste it is only protected for its hazardous properties and not for any intrinsic value. Spent fuel reprocessing plants are little more than large industrial plants that use special materials and can be found in France, the UK, Japan and Russia, he declared.

On the important matter of exposure to radioactivity, it is important to accept that each one of us is exposed to a combination of cosmic radiation, terrestrial radiation (due to soil and rock) and radiation in the air we breathe and the food and liquids we ingest. The exposure depends on many factors but typically, it is about two to six mSv in one year. A dose above 7000 mSv is absolutely lethal within three to five days, for example, as in the case of those in immediate vicinity of the Chernobyl reactor, immediately after the blast. Above 4500 mSv, there will be a fifty percent mortality rate, in spite of treatment. Exposures between 1000 – 2000 mSv will strongly affect the blood count, but would be lethal only in rare cases. For exposures from 500 – 1000 mSv, recovery would probably take a few months for an otherwise healthy person. Obviously the very young and very old are always the most vulnerable. This helps explain why a typical Western reactor accident, such as at Three Mile Island in the United States could cause an exposure of 0.1 mSv/h at a distance of roughly twenty miles.

As a consequence, the scientific community has come up with a basic rule of thumb: a roughly acceptable radiation level that has been set for the public is five mSv per year. For radiation workers who work in nuclear facilities and suchlike, it is fifty mSv. In the extremely rare event of a serious reactor accident such as the one at Chernobyl, the immediate nuclear damage to humans comes from the pressure wave and heat radiation. Direct radiation in such a case occurs from between two and three kilometres and the initial dose rate within about eight kilometres miles to about 140 kilometres would typically be about 1000 – 3000 mSv/h. What is important is that by decreasing the length of the exposure (minutes or hours), by sheltering, for example, the dose absorbed by an individual can be minimised. The emergency helpers at Chernobyl died not so much of the high levels of radiation, but through their prolonged exposure to it.

To measure the total disintegration rate of a sample, in other words, to determine its actual activity in bequerels, is quite a procedure. A Geiger counter will indicate whether the material is very active. What is of immediate concern is whether the radiation doses encountered by the population are abnormally high; these will be measured in mSv or mrem (the latter in the United States since they still use the old system).

In the event of an actual nuclear attack, for instance, on a city like Tehran, the scenario would terrifyingly different. For a start, it would probably involve one or more thermonuclear devices, or what we commonly refer to as hydrogen bombs. These have yields that are potentially scores of times greater than any A-Bomb ever detonated. The consequent damage would be vast, indescribably so. So would be the casualties. As one scientific report speculated, the contamination released into the air in the form of radionuclides would spread over a large area, and thousands of Iranians who live nearby would be dying immediately. In addition, possibly many hundreds of thousands – possibly even a million souls in a city of ten or fifteen million people – would subsequently succumb. Because northerly winds blow in that region of the Gulf almost throughout most of the year, the authors of the above report concluded that, 'most definitely Bahrain, Qatar and the UAE will be 'almost as heavily affected' by radionuclides.'

While reports in the mainstream media regarding the possible use of RDDs by terror groups have been sparse, an exception was a report by Frank Gardner, security correspondent to the BBC who covered the issue in some detail from Chicago[4]. His story was broadcast in August 2007 and made the point that the authorities in Britain and the US were in the process of preparing for the possibility that a radiological dirty bomb would be detonated by terrorists sometime in the future. Gardner disclosed that the matter was being taken seriously enough in Britain for pagers to have already been issued to some ambulance drivers to detect personal radiation exposure. He told listeners that the authorities had developed a number of novel ways of mitigating the likely effects of RDDs, with the principle of minimizing the effect on human lives:

'At the United States' Argonne National Laboratories, hidden behind a guarded perimeter, scientists in white protective suits burst out of a van and prepared to spray a fine liquid plastic on to the surface of a wall. It is an exercise. The wall has not really been contaminated and the world has yet to experience a dirty bomb for real. But emergency planners are now training for when terrorists might one day detonate a RDD. Left unchecked, its after-effects could contaminate whole streets.

'The two issues you have with a dirty bomb release are the spread of the contamination and also the contamination of the public as well as first emergency responders. Ideally, you'd have a fleet of vehicles on the ground that would be supplied with our coating, and have the spray equipment to disperse it over a large area.

'You'd also have aircraft to spray it on the top of the plume to lock it down to the surface. And the whole purpose of this being to lock it down into a solid form such that when the first responders come back in by foot or by vehicle, there's no recontamination.'

One of the problems with radioactive contamination is you cannot see it, which was why so many emergency workers fell ill at Chernobyl in 1986; they did not realize how seriously they were being radiated, in many cases with fatal consequences. Scientists in America have been working on ways to detect radiation immediately and under a bilateral deal, they are sharing their findings with Britain. One of the more portable devices is the commercially available Sirad Personal Dosimeter, as explained by Gladys Klemic from the US Department of Homeland Security. It would be carried like an ID card, she told Gardiner:

'In situations where there are high levels of radiation, its central rectangle would darken and a blue square could be used as a reference to establish radiation levels. If emergency responders arrive at an RDD blast with the device, they can quickly check whether there is exposure to radiation.'

Then, said Gardiner, there was the Argonne super gel, a highly absorbent substance which is sprayed onto a contaminated building. It is designed to tackle the most dangerous radioactive materials that might have penetrated deep into the concrete:

'It literally sucks out the radioactive particles then removes them with a wet vacuum before they are disposed of as radioactive waste. In theory, that means a building can be decontaminated in days instead of waiting weeks or even demolishing it altogether.

'But herein lies the catch: until terrorists actually detonate a dirty bomb, the funding for dealing with such an attack is limited. Some equipment is now being distributed – in both the US and Britain – but privately scientists question whether it will really be enough to cope with a full-scale radiological disaster.'

Clearing up after an RDD attack will always be a monumental task. Even with appropriate chemical action, decontaminating after an RDD has been detonated it will take an inordinately long time to counter the effects of serious radiation. Also, the entire area would have to be quarantined, certainly for many months and, depending on both the nature of radioactive material employed and quantity, possibly for years. Were it to happen outside the Bank of England in London, for instance, the level of radiation would be the ultimate deciding factor. Not only buildings, but the entire grid of roads and sidewalks would need to be ripped up and once the all clear is given, re-laid. Contaminated debris would be dealt with in the appropriate manner, in itself a formidable task on a relatively small group of islands that comprise the United Kingdom. It is axiomatic that costs would run into billions.

For the workers involved, coming onto the job and going off again after a shift would be a time consuming and enervating business that would involve constant checks as well as appropriate screening. It would include what is referred to in the trade as 'full wet decontamination' which would take place at the end of the working day. Workers who enter hazardous areas would need to be protected by the same kind of 'space suits' that are used by staff who work in laboratories that specialize in such things, such as at the United States Army Medical Research Institute of Infectious Diseases (USAMRIID) at Fort Detrick in Maryland.

There are other considerations like official hot zones as opposed to random hot zones, as well as ground shine and cloud shine, which, for now, we will leave to the specialists. Overall, it is an extremely complex and multifaceted matter.

Structures within a specific radius of this new blast spot (or ground zero, the latter an appellation that originated in the Japanese nuclear blasts and not what occurred on 9/11), would be dealt with piecemeal and critical distances dictated solely by the levels of radiation emitted. The danger area could easily extend a kilometre or more from where the initial detonation took place, especially if the amount of explosives employed by the terror group is vast. To a lesser or greater extent, each building would have its facade and roof removed. Surrounding plaster would be stripped down to the core. That would be followed by the entire area washed again and again by chemical decontaminants, an issue compounded by the fact that the wash-off would filter into drains and the sewage system and would eventually affect areas further afield.

The Thames would obviously become contaminated by radioactivity because some of the off-flow would almost certainly enter the river. The permutations for disaster are endless and exactly the same scenario would hold for New York where the Hudson River and East Coast tides would shift the threat along the shores along the entire Manhattan and adjacent coastlines all the way to New Jersey, Long Island and beyond.

There are no short cuts in this business, for the simple reason that radiation detectors do not lie. Simply put, the affected area would be quarantined until it is safe. Nobody goes anywhere near the place until a host of monitors indicate that the threat factor is as close to zero as to be of no consequence. Meantime, there would be total prohibition on anybody not specifically involved in the clean-up process entering the blast area and the stricture would be immediate. Even animals and their droppings would be affected. Any creature that may be capable of setting off Geiger counters would be affected. That includes rats, mice, stray and domestic cats as well as dogs, all of which would have to be tracked.

In this regard, a *New York Times* report mentioned a government contractor at Hanford nuclear reservation in Washington State who, in a recent systematic clean-up, mapped radioactive rabbit faeces with detectors mounted on a helicopter flying 15 metres over the desert scrub. 'An onboard computer used GPS technology to record each location so workers could return later to scoop up the droppings for disposal as low-level radioactive waste,' it stated.

An immediate consequence would be that a vital part of the city would be isolated, with resultant disruption of commerce, banking, the normal day-to-day movement of people, as well as tourism especially. Nothing would be a greater deterrent to overseas visitors travelling to London than the prospect of being contaminated. And even after a successful clean-up, a real or imagined threat perception would have the stultifying effect of keeping visitors well away from the British Isles.

Washington's Federation of American Scientists succinctly analysed this problem. As detailed by its website, the FAS reached three principle conclusions[5]:

- Radiological attacks constitute a credible threat. Radioactive materials that could be used for such attacks are stored in thousands of facilities around the US, many of which may not be adequately protected against theft by determined

terrorists. Some of this material could be easily dispersed in urban areas by using conventional explosives or by other methods.
- While radiological attacks would result in some deaths, they would not result in the hundreds of thousands of fatalities that could be caused by a crude nuclear weapon. Attacks could contaminate large urban areas with radiation levels that exceed EPA health and toxic material guidelines.
- Materials that could easily be lost or stolen from US research institutions and commercial sites could contaminate tens of city blocks at a level that would require prompt evacuation and create terror in large communities even if radiation casualties were low. Areas as large as tens of square miles could be contaminated at levels that exceed recommended civilian exposure limits. Since there are often no effective ways to decontaminate buildings that have been exposed at these levels, demolition may be the only practical solution. If such an event were to take place in a city like New York, it would result in losses of potentially trillions of dollars.

An analysis conducted by Michael Levi, Director of the Strategic Security Program at the Federation of American Scientists and by Dr Robert Nelson of Princeton University and FAS, made the following comments:

'Materials are radioactive if their atomic nuclei (or centres) spontaneously disintegrate (or decay) with high-energy fragments of this disintegration flying off into the environment. Several kinds of particles can so be emitted, and are collectively referred to as radiation. Some materials decay quickly, making them sources of intense radiation, but their rapid decay rate means that they do not stay radioactive for long periods of time.

'Other materials serve as a weaker source of radiation because they decay slowly. Slow rates of decay mean, however, that a source may remain dangerous for very long periods. Half of the atoms in a sample of Cobalt-60 will, for example, disintegrate over a five-year period, but it takes 430 years for half of the atoms in a sample of Americium-241 to decay.'

Gamma rays, it was stated, posed two types of health risks: intense sources of gamma rays can cause immediate tissue damage and lead to acute radiation poisoning. Fatalities can result from very high doses:

'Long-term exposure to low levels of gamma rays can also be harmful because it can cause genetic mutations leading to cancer. Triggering cancer is largely a matter of chance: the more radiation you're exposed to, the more often the dice are rolled. The risk is never zero since we are all constantly being bombarded by large amounts of gamma radiation produced by cosmic rays, which reach us from distant stars.

'Alpha particles emitted by plutonium, americium and other elements also pose health risks. Although these particles cannot penetrate clothing or skin, they are harmful if emitted by inhaled materials. If plutonium is in the environment in particles small enough to be inhaled, contaminated particles can lodge in the lung for extended periods. Inside the lung, the alpha particles produced by plutonium can damage lung tissue and lead to long-term cancers[6].'

## Chapter 7

# Case Study: Syria's Efforts to 'Go Nuclear'

*In the spring of 2004, the American National Security
Agency detected a suspiciously high number of telephone calls
between Syria and North Korea, with a noticeably busy line of
communication between the North Korean capital Pyongyang
and an obscure site in the northern Syrian Desert called al-
Kibar. The NSA dossier was sent to the Israeli military's
'8200', responsible for radio reconnaissance with antennas on
hills near Tel Aviv. Al-Kibar, as they say in intelligence jargon,
had become 'flagged'.*

*The Story of Operation Orchard by
Erich Follath and Holger Stark.*[1]

The main highway that threads north out of Tel Aviv towards Metullah,
a small town straddling Israel's frontier with Lebanon, covers ground
that encompasses much ancient Middle East history. Apart from the
port of Haifa and various archaeological Tells, you are likely to pass through
Megiddo which, the Bible tells us, is to be the site of Armageddon, the ultimate
battle between good and evil. Along this route, just south of Haifa, is Ramat
David, one of the Jewish State's major tactical air bases. It was there, shortly
before midnight on 5 September 2007, that orders were given to a small
squadron of Israeli Air Force F-15Is to launch 'Operation Orchard'. The place
to be targeted was referred to simply as al-Kibar.

Affectionately referred to as *Raam* by their pilots – the Hebrew word for
thunder – the F-15Is were fitted with a variety of missiles as well as 500-pound and
half-ton bombs. It was significant at the time that the Israeli pilots were primed
not only for one of the biggest air strikes deep into the interior of a neighbouring
state for some years, but the raid had been a long time coming. More saliently, it
had the sanction of Washington's defence planners because to reach their objective
the jets initially had to overfly Turkish airspace. Included in the operation was

an Israeli Air Force ELINT: an electronic intelligence gathering aircraft, though it is likely that some American assets might have been involved. It is also possible that Jerusalem conveyed all the relevant information directly to senior members of the Bush Administration without it first being vetted by American intelligence agencies. This process, known as 'Stove-piping,' literally overwhelmed Washington's intelligence-gathering processes before the war in Iraq.

While there was no comment initially from Jerusalem about the attack, we do know that some hours prior to the jets going in, an Israeli Shaldag air force commando group had been inserted, their job once on the ground in Syria being to direct laser beams onto the target for the pilots. Some reports talk of Hi-Altitude-Low Opening (HILO) parachute drops, but nothing has ever been confirmed. Once over 'enemy' airspace, the squadron headed deep into Syria's desert interior to a region that lies adjacent to both the Iraqi and Turkish frontiers. Because of an earlier precision strike that destroyed one of the largest Syrian radar installations in the region which lay not far from the country's northern border with Turkey, its removal eased the possibility of being detected. Once over target, each of the IAF F-15Is used their onboard computers to make a single pass over al-Kibar, dropped their bombs and headed home.

As soon as it was established that all the Israeli jets had returned intact and the prime minister Ehud Olmert informed that the target had been eliminated, he called his opposite number in Turkey and briefly explained the situation. He added that additional information would be sent early the following day. He also requested that the Turkish premier advise President Bashar al-Assad in Damascus that the raid was aimed solely at what was termed 'a nuclear facility'. Adding insult to injury, the Israeli Premier asked that the Syrian leader be advised that Jerusalem was 'still interested in making peace' with Damascus. Interestingly, Olmert cautioned that his government would say nothing about the strike if Damascus would agree to do the same.

It says a lot that there was no protest about the attack forthcoming from Ankara, for the rather obvious reason that the Turks would hardly have been enthralled at the prospect of a nuclear-armed Syria straddling their southern borders. There was no protest from the United States either, though Washington was already onboard with the details, not surprising since the US had recalled its envoy from Damascus after Rafiq Hariri, Lebanon's former prime minister had been assassinated in a bomb attack blamed on Syria. This remarkably low-key approach to what was later regarded by the intelligence community as one of the most successful tactical strikes in recent times, was in sharp contrast to Jerusalem's earlier efforts at hitting at strategic targets in the Arab World, more specifically when the Israeli Air Force destroyed Saddam Hussein's Osiraq nuclear reactor near Baghdad in 1981.

In that attack – also involving American aircraft and including a squadron of Phantom F-4s – the Israeli government made no secret of its delight at destroying one of the largest nuclear reactors then nearing completion in the Arab World. They not only released scores of reconnaissance photographs which pointedly displayed the extent of damage, but allowed their pilots to be widely interviewed, something that had rarely happened before within the extremely security-conscious Israel military establishment.

In contrast, events following the strike on al-Kibar were different. At daybreak, the morning after the attack, there was not a single report in the Israeli media of what had taken place. Then, as rumours started to circulate and local and international correspondents began to press the IDF Spokesman's Office in Jerusalem for answers, the reply was the same each time: 'No comment'. Similar events took place in Syria. Hours after the attack, government spokespersons in Damascus maintained not only that nothing untoward had happened, but that no Syrian establishment had been targeted either by Israeli aircraft or any other aircraft. When the Syrian Liaison Office was eventually obliged to concede that Israeli aircraft had entered Syrian airspace, they said there had been no damage inflicted and that the IAF jets had been driven off after harmlessly disposing of their ammunition.

Only eighteen months later did President al-Assad enter the fray when he declared in an interview with the German magazine *Der Spiegel* that al-Kibar was not a nuclear plant, 'but rather a conventional military installation'. He insisted that the Syrian Air Force could have struck back. 'But should we really allow ourselves to be provoked into a war? Then we would have walked into an Israeli trap,' was his off-the-cuff retort.

Today, more than a decade after the event, the name al-Kibar has entered the historical lexicon of notable military successes. Yet the international community still knows very little about Syria's putative nuclear weapons programme, except that, for a while, such a programme was actually on the cards. More recent events – with the subsequent discovery of radioactive particles at two or three other locations in this Arab state – might suggest that the nuclear agenda was not as moribund as first believed. We are aware, for instance, of an unclassified 2004 report by the Deputy Director of National Intelligence for Analysis that declared that A.Q. Khan visited Damascus in a bid to entice the Syrian government to acquire 'nuclear technology and hardware.' The report expressed concern 'that expertise or technology could have been transferred, and probably was', in much the same way that he had more successfully visited other countries in the region that included Libya, Iran, Saudi Arabia and Egypt.

Press reports circulated at about the same time that Khan had actually visited Syria on several occasions and also met with senior Syrian officials in Iran.

While Syria remains schtum about it all, even today, President Bashar al-Assad actually acknowledged in a 2007 interview with an Austrian newspaper that he had received a letter from Khan in 2001. At the same time, he consistently maintained that the Pakistani maverick had been rebuffed because, as he declared, 'it might have been another Israeli ploy.' There is no reason to doubt the man because just about everything about al-Kibar was linked to North Korea and not to Pakistan.

It was in 2004 – according to an American news report – that Israel's security services first learned that Damascus was engaged in a project that suspiciously resembled a clandestine nuclear operation. It went on:

'[The Israelis] proceeded to either place a mole inside the plant or convince a worker to provide the Jewish State with intelligence. Through this source, Israel obtained important video footage as well as photographs that provided evidence that al-Kibar was indeed a nuclear facility (with a large cylindrical structure, a pumping station and the rest).'

At that point, according to the *Jerusalem Post*, Israel approached Washington and the Americans began to closely examine satellite coordinates for the site. The US also 'helped Israel pinpoint possible 'drop sites',' with both countries discussing the possibility of the United States handling the strike; American officials even examined options for doing so. Eventually, said the *Jerusalem Post*, the US President conveyed the message 'that [it] preferred not to attack.' In fact, Secretary of State Condoleezza Rice and Defence Secretary Robert Gates made some effort to convince Israel that to confront the Syrian Government in dialogue was a much stronger option than taking any kind of military action.

Meantime, according to a report written by Noah Klieger, Israeli commandos from the *Sayeret Matkal* reconnaissance unit covertly raided the suspected Syrian nuclear facility in mid-August 2007 and brought back nuclear material to Israel. [2] Thereafter, two helicopters ferried a dozen commandos to the site – probably dressed in Syrian uniforms – in order to get photographic evidence as well as soil samples which, after analysis revealed traces of nuclear activity.

Whatever else might emerge from Washington about events that took place at al-Kibar in September 2007, the fact that North Korea was involved in a nuclear weapons-related project half a world away from its own extremely limited sphere of influence was of critical interest to the United States Government. While early reports were sketchy, it gradually emerged that not only was a nuclear reactor being built at al-Kibar, but that it bore a striking resemblance to North Korea's reactor in Yongbyon. This was confirmed by David Albright and Paul Brannan of ISIS in April 2008. [3] While their conclusions are dealt with in detail below, it is worth mentioning that specifically, they 'measured the footprint of the Yongbyon reactor building and compared it to that of the suspected reactor building in Syria and found them to be approximately the same'. Moreover, prior to Syria's construction of al-Kibar, the Yongbyon model was the only one of its type built in almost four decades.

Video footage from inside the Syrian facility has also been described as 'very, very damning' by a nuclear weapons specialist who spoke to the *Washington Post*. Those visuals demonstrated that al-Kibar's core design was the same as the Yongbyon reactor, 'including a virtually identical configuration and number of holes for fuel rods.' The final piece of information to emerge is that the video material acquired also shows North Korean personnel on the site.

Interestingly, in a subsequent report, London's *Daily Telegraph*, citing anonymous sources, reported that in December 2006, a top Syrian official (according to one article, the head of the Atomic Energy Commission of Syria, Ibrahim Othman) arrived in London under a false name.[4]

'The Mossad had detected a booking for the official in a London hotel and dispatched at least ten undercover agents to London. The agents were split into three teams: one group sent to Heathrow Airport to identify the official as he arrived, a second to book into his hotel, and a third to monitor his movements as well as visitors. Some of the operatives were from the Kidon Division which specializes in assassinations, as well as the Neviot Division, which deals with breaking into homes, embassies, and hotel rooms to install bugging devices.

'On the first day of his visit, he was followed to the Syrian embassy and then went shopping. Kidon operatives closely followed him, while Neviot operatives broke into his hotel room and found his laptop. A computer expert then installed software that allowed the Mossad to monitor his activities on the computer.

'When this material was examined at Mossad headquarters, officials found blueprints and hundreds of pictures of the al-Kibar facility in various stages of construction, and correspondence. One photograph showed North Korean nuclear official Chon Chibu meeting with Ibrahim Othman, Syria's atomic energy agency director. Though the Mossad had originally planned to kill the official in London, it was decided to spare his life following the discovery.

Subsequent investigations have revealed that key materials for al-Kibar were smuggled from China and possibly Europe into Syria by Namchongang Trading, a North Korean firm, which raises an issue linked to similar nuclear developments in Iran, a close ally of Syria. Why did the Israeli Army not go straight in and eliminate the target?

An immediate reason was certainly linked to the IDF having taken a series of heavy knocks during the previous year's invasion of the predominantly Hezbollah-controlled regions of Southern Lebanon. What should have been a series of surgical strikes against a fundamentalist Iranian-backed guerrilla movement that was intended to last only weeks went badly amiss from the start.

Israeli soldiers did not match the vigorous levels of discipline, planning or, in many instances, the naked aggression displayed by the foot soldiers of the Party of God. The IDF, it seemed, in fighting a close quarter ground war with a seasoned guerrilla force appeared to be totally out of its depth. To cap it, many young IDF conscripts had been inadequately trained for the rigors of a vicious counter-insurgency campaign that quickly reversed itself when the hunters became the hunted. Some Jewish boys went to war with their cell phones, compromising both themselves and their colleagues. Also, much of the equipment fielded in this limited-venture campaign was simply not up to the standard that most Israelis had historically come to accept. Questions also emerged about the competence of some Israeli field commanders, several of whom were subsequently exposed as having fudged their records for promotional purposes.

With the benefit of hindsight, it is clear today that Hezbollah had the measure of the Israeli Army from the start. While Israeli warplanes enjoyed air superiority throughout and destroyed huge swathes of Lebanese assets in the south – that included residential parts of cities, power houses, bridges, roads and the rest, as well as most of Shi'ite-controlled Southern Beirut – Jerusalem's human toll was unacceptably high. As a consequence, it might be argued, an Israeli military strike deep into Syria might have gone some way to redressing some of these wrongs and prove that the IDF was the original force it had always been vaunted to be. But it did not. Indeed, Christopher Pang, head of the Middle East and North Africa programme at the Royal United Services Institute in London, told the Associated Press, 'In terms of deterrence, the effect was clear by invading Syrian airspace, by showing that Israel is not only able, but willing to still launch strikes against Syrian targets.' All of which raises the other notable issue; was al-Kibar actually intended to become an illegal nuclear establishment?

This debate lasted a while and had numerous components, not least that Vienna's International Atomic Energy Agency was outspoken in its denials that the Syrians had transgressed the provisions of the nuclear Non Proliferation Treaty (NPT). The then head of the IAEA, Dr Mohamed ElBaradei vigorously expressed his frustration when he declared before the world body that 'if a country has any information about a nuclear activity in another country, it should inform the IAEA and not bomb first and ask questions later'. He added a short while later that 'our experts who have carefully analysed the satellite imagery say it is unlikely that this building was a nuclear facility.'

That was followed soon afterwards by an unfortunate lapse of judgment on the part of Joseph Cirincione, for some time the director for nuclear policy at the Centre for American Progress, a Washington DC think tank:

'Syria does not have the technical, industrial, or financial ability to support a nuclear-weapons program. I've been following this issue for fifteen years, and every once in a while a suspicion arises and we investigate and there's nothing.'

Without waiting for the results of some of the more intrusive investigations then taking place, Dr Cirincione declared publicly that 'there was and is no nuclear-weapons threat from Syria. This is all political'. He went on to castigate the press corps for its handling of the story. 'I think some of our best journalists were used,' he said. Before and after satellite photographs of the al-Kibar site to be found elsewhere in this book totally contradicts that thesis.

David Albright, always cautious in such matters, was more guarded in his approach, though he did make the point that Israel did not have much faith in the international arms-control community:

'I can understand the Israeli point of view, given the history with Iran and Algeria. Both nations had nuclear-weapons programs and, after being caught cheating, declared their reactors to be civil reactors, for peacetime use. The international groups like the UN and the IAEA never shut them down.'

Enter Seymour Hersh who, like Dr Cirincione, launched an intensive investigation of his own months after the attack and in the process visited both Israel and Syria and spoke to scores of individuals on the fringe of it. In a report titled 'Annals of National Security: A Strike in the Dark: What did Israel bomb in Syria?' published by the *New Yorker* on 11 February 2008 (or little more than four months after the raid) Hersh's report was inconclusive. In fact, he took the more controversial approach that Israel might have blundered, saying:

'One top foreign-ministry official in Damascus told me that the target "was an old military building that had been abandoned by the Syrian military" years ago. But a senior Syrian intelligence general gave me a different account.

'"What they targeted was a building used for fertilizer and water pumps," he said, "part of a government effort to revitalize farming. There is a large city— Deir ez-Zur—fifty kilometres away. Why would Syria put nuclear material near a city?"'

'I interviewed the intelligence general again on my second visit to Damascus, and he reiterated that the targeted building was "at no time a military facility".'

Meantime, as we now know, subsequent on-site investigations proved all these prognostications to be hopelessly inaccurate. The IAEA did eventually discover traces of uranium at the reactor site that were not included in Syria's declared inventory, exactly as the Israelis had done when they clandestinely sent their own specialists in. Not to be outdone, Damascus declared that the uranium came from Israeli missiles used to destroy the al-Kibar reactor in September 2007.

The presence of uranium particles was detected at a second site near Damascus, the Miniature Neutron Source Reactor. Syria said that came from the accumulation of samples and reference materials used in neutron activation analysis, but this time the IAEA was not buying either of the two explanations and pressed Damascus for more answers. Vienna demanded to know the origins of that uranium. The agency also ran its own tests and the word that emerged was that Damascus was not telling the truth.

An interesting report also emerged from the Cairo paper *Al Ahram*, which reported that after Syria 'granted IAEA inspectors access to the al-Kibar site, where they took environmental samples (while denying them access to three other sites), Damascus suspended cooperation with the IAEA saying, 'it was awaiting the results of the samples'. The *Al Ahram* report also disclosed that Syria had gone to great lengths after the bombing strike to 'sanitize' everything in and around al-Kibar and went on, 'Despite all that Damascus had done to scrub the site, IAEA soil samples revealed "a significant number of natural uranium particles" that were "anthropogenic": that is, produced by human action rather than being already present in the environment. Since then, Syria has refused to respond to IAEA requests for additional information.'

In order to properly understand the level of obfuscation with regard to the illegal acquisition of weapons of mass destruction in recent years, one needs to examine some of the related issues linked to Iraq, prior to Gulf War 1. Not to be confused with the subsequent Gulf War 2 invasion by Coalition Forces, much of what was uncovered under the headings of nuclear, chemical and biological warfare are all within the public domain and easily accessible on the United Nations UNSCOM website, or for those eager to pursue an easier route, a simple Google search under these headings will provide a trove of material.

What is often set aside in some of the recriminations that followed the lack of anything concrete in the WMD domain after the *Second* Iraqi invasion, is that lethal assets uncovered the first time round in Iraq led some pundits to believe that Saddam Hussein might have been at it again after Coalition Forces withdrew. A similar case history now exists for Iran, which has always claimed that its pursuit of a nuclear programme was strictly for peaceful purposes.

Recent disclosures of huge centrifuge programmes at secret locations, with still more subterfuge linked to other nuclear research programmes have caused to international community to examine Iranian issues a good deal more intrusively than in the past and exactly the same analogy would have applied to al-Kibar had the Israeli not destroyed it in a bombing raid in September 2007.

## Syria's Covert Al Kibar Nuclear Reactor

## Extracted from an Intelligence Briefing: Washington, April 24, 2008

What became apparent immediate after the raid on the al-Kibar facility was that Syria was in the process of building a gas-cooled, graphite-moderated reactor that was nearing operational capability in August 2007.

Brought into full production, the reactor would have been capable of producing plutonium for nuclear weapons, was not configured to produce electricity and was ill-suited for research.

The reactor was destroyed before it was loaded with nuclear fuel or operated. [United States intelligence] is convinced, based on a variety of information, that North Korea assisted Syria's covert nuclear activities, both before and after the reactor was destroyed.

## Only North Korea has built this kind of reactor in past decades.

Features of the facility and its location indicate that Syria attempted to maintain its secrecy. Moreover, Syria moved quickly to cover up its covert nuclear activities by demolishing and burying the reactor building and by removing incriminating equipment. These actions were intended to forestall identification of reactor debris by international inspectors and are inconsistent with peaceful nuclear intentions.

### Syria/North Korea Nuclear Connections

- Senior North Koreans from the Yongbyon nuclear complex made multiple visits to Syria before construction of the al-Kibar reactor began in 2001
- In 2002, North Korean officials were procuring equipment for an undisclosed site in Syria. North Korea that same year sought a gas-cooled reactor component we believe was intended for the Syrian site
- A North Korean nuclear organization and Syrian officials involved in the covert nuclear programme reportedly were involved in a cargo transfer from North Korea to probably al-Kibar in 2006
- North Korean nuclear officials were located in the region of the reactor both early and late in 2007. Our information shows that North Korean advisors also probably assisted with damage assessment efforts after the reactor was destroyed
- A high level North Korean delegation travelled to Syria shortly after the reactor was destroyed and met with officials associated with Syria's covert nuclear programme

None of these events were lost on Israel. Citizens in the Jewish State have been building expensive nuclear shelters in their back yards for years, a not-altogether defensive move since, almost daily, Israeli media features Iran going nuclear. There have been hundreds, possibly thousands of nuclear shelters built over the years and companies like Ahim Torati, a local firm producing parts for 'Atomic Shelters' is booming. Even Shari Arison, Israel's wealthiest woman – estimated to be worth close to $3 billion – has made vigorous preparations for what one newspaper termed 'her personal Armageddon'. She has had two sophisticated structures erected, both underground, and her facility includes bedrooms, bathrooms, studies and store spaces – all of which are linked to rather elaborate decontaminating systems where occupants would be able to sit out a month or more of hostilities and consequential nuclear fallout.

Some of the prefabs being built are reckoned to be strong enough to withstand all but a direct hit from an atom bomb and while the scenario is distinctly 'doomsday', these precautionary measures have merit, especially since the Tehran Government – and especially its *Majlis* (Iran's Parliament) – make routine pronouncements about wiping Israel off the map. More recent reports indicate that even the country's leaders are taking appropriate steps. The Israeli newspaper *Yediot Ahronot* claimed in December 2007 that workers at the Prime Minister's official Jerusalem residence were thickening walls, digging, and installing air purification equipment capable of countering chemical agents. Others suggested it was a measure against a nuclear onslaught. Regardless, the message is clear.

## Chapter 8

# Libya's Attempt to Build the A-Bomb

*A report from International Atomic Energy Agency fills in some key missing details about Libya's now-dismantled nuclear weapons program, while acknowledging that holes remain in the account. Additionally, Tripoli has disclosed that some materials it ordered from foreign sources remain unaccounted for, prompting concerns in Washington that third parties may have acquired them.*

*Paul Kerr: IAEA – Questions Remain About Libya[1]*

There was a period, early in the New Millennium, while I was still writing for various Jane's publications, including *Jane's Islamic Affairs Analyst*, when intermittent reports kept coming through about Libya possibly being involved with nuclear weapons. To most of us, the idea was preposterous. As I expressed it at the time to Stephen Ulph, the London-based editor of *IAA*, the Libyans – their Bedouin tribal folk especially – were a lot better known for goat or camel herding on the fringes of the Sahara Desert than anything hi-tech. It was that much more surprising consequently, when former Israeli Premier Ariel Sharon told his Knesset about eighteen months before the story finally broke that he believed that Muammar Gadaffi's Libya might be the first Arab country to go nuclear.

Overnight, we started taking notice. Suddenly the concept was not as outlandish as we first believed. If Israel's Mossad reckoned that Gadaffi was trying to build the bomb, people listened. That was followed in October 2003 by a NATO naval task force seizing a German-flagged 6,440-ton freighter, the *BBC China*. That happened shortly after the vessel had transited the Suez Canal into the Mediterranean. Once onboard, a group of inspectors, including several from Vienna's IAEA, discovered a shipment of containers that included equipment that could be used to build the bomb. As things started to unravel, it was clear that the Israelis had been involved from the start. So too, had Pakistan's maverick nuclear smuggler A.Q. Khan.

The material, though transhipped in Dubai by a local firm TUT Shipping, included sophisticated second-generation P-2 centrifuges that could be used to enrich uranium. All had originally come from Karachi. There were further surprises, when a complete industrial assembly linked to uranium enrichment was seized by the South African Police only days before it was due to be shipped out of the country through Maputo, in the neighbouring country of Mozambique. Built by a commercial engineering firm near Johannesburg and loaded into eleven containers, the consignment was listed on shipping documents as a 'water purifying plant'. The shipment was to have been taken onboard an unnamed freighter headed for Dubai.

In the words of George Tenet, the former CIA director, intercepting the *BBC China* was not only 'an operation superbly planned and perfectly executed,' it was the result of many years of undercover work in Pakistan, the United Arab Emirates, Malaysia, Turkey, Germany, South Africa and elsewhere.

In Malaysia meantime, following another American tip-off, the police arrested Mr B.S.A. Tahir, A.Q. Khan's chief lieutenant for several years. His activities were investigated by Malaysian authorities, which elicited a claim from Tahir that, together with the seized components on board, was a consignment sent to Libya by Gunas Jireh, a Turkish national who supplied aluminium casting and dynamos to the Tripoli Government[2].

The *BBC China*, built in 2000 and originally named *Beluga Superstition*, was owned by Bremen-headquartered Beluga Superstition Shipping Ltd, part of Beluga Shipping GmbH. It had been chartered to a neighbouring Bremen company called BBC Chartering and Logistic, but something about its itinerary or movements must have alerted Western intelligence agencies because the ship was on the radar even before it arrived at Dubai to pick up what is often referred to in the trade as a 'mixed cargo'. Once seized and under NATO command, the ship was escorted to Italy where it took intelligence agents just two hours to identify and discreetly unload five large containers. The ship was then allowed to proceed to Libya and other North African destinations. As one of the ship's owners commented, 'it was all very orderly, and civilized and apparently done well away from public gaze.'

What was not mentioned until five months later was that the containers were marked 'used machine parts'. When subsequently opened by American, British and German intelligence agents – in conjunction with International Atomic Energy Agency officials – a shipload of centrifuge parts manufactured in Malaysia by the Khan network were uncovered. Accounts which surfaced later suggested that the *BBC China* had onboard a veritable trove of equipment that could ultimately be used for making the bomb.

Shortly afterwards, when accosted about the cargo, Libyan officials back in Tripoli admitted they had been dabbling in nuclear research, Though nobody in Washington, London, Vienna or anywhere else are prepared to go on record and detail the discussions that followed, we do know that only after this the recalcitrant Libyan leader had been warned that if he did not 'come clean' on the issue, he and his nation would have to accept the consequences. On the advice of his son, Saif al-Islam, the colonel did not prevaricate, which was probably just as well.

Meantime, an IAEA official was handed a stack of documents in the very same way they had been received – stuffed into two shopping bags from Good Look Tailors in Islamabad. With that, Gadaffi, on the advice of his son, acquiesced and a number of Libyan facilities were thrown open for inspection. The IAEA took a while to go public on what was uncovered, though the United Nations nuclear body did concede that there were 'some substantial surprises' in store for their team.

'It was a revelation to see how much material was being shifted from one country to the other,' an IAEA inspector said after inspecting several facilities, expressing astonishment at the extent of the black-market network. What emerged, it was explained, 'was the existence of a shadowy network of middlemen involved in nuclear-related matters who tend to circumvent national export controls. These measures were supposed to control the movement of weapons of mass destruction. What I encountered in Libya proved that these controls are simply not working.'

According to former *New York Times* correspondent Judith Miller, who scoured these reports, 'the designs were for a bomb that could, if "properly" unleashed, devastate a city. The plans had apparently arrived in Libya more than two years before through a nuclear proliferation racket that spanned at least nine countries on three continents'.[3]

If they are right, said the *New York Times*, Libya posed a far more serious threat than that detected by UN inspection teams. What was of real concern to pundits in London, Washington and Vienna was that it was obvious to all that on its own, Libya, could not have been able to grapple with all the intricacies linked to advanced nuclear physics. Ultra-centrifugation for obtaining uranium-235, for instance, cannot be done simply by putting natural uranium through the centrifuges.

As one source indicated:

'it requires the complete mastery over the front end of the nuclear fuel cycle, beginning at uranium mining and refining, production of uranium ore, conversion of ore into uranium dioxide $UO_2$ (which is used to make nuclear fuel for natural uranium reactors like Pakistan's Khushab and KANUPP), conversion of $UO_2$ into uranium tetrafluoride $UF_4$ and then into the feedstock for enrichment ($UF_6$).'

There are a lot more disciplines besides, including the complete mastery of fluorine chemistry and production of highly toxic and corrosive hydrofluoric acid and other fluorine compounds required.

Among other questions raised as a consequence was who was helping Muammar Gadaffi to overcome these hurdles? In a 'Restricted Distribution' report by the Director General of the IAEA and titled 'Implementation of the NPT Safeguards Agreement in the Socialist People's Libyan Arab Jamahiriya' (GOV/2008/39), dated 12 September 2008, countries involved with the Libyan quest to manufacture nuclear weapons included Germany, Italy, Japan, Liechtenstein, Malaysia, Pakistan, Republic of Korea, Singapore, South Africa, Spain, Switzerland, Turkey and the United Arab Emirates. Obviously, few of these states were knowingly involved, or rather, it was some of their citizens – usually at the behest of A.Q. Khan – that got clandestinely involved.

Elsewhere, the Director General's report stated that between 1978 and 1981, Libya imported a total of 2,263 tons of uranium ore from Niger. In the mid-1980s, Libya, with the support of a Brazilian company also carried out uranium explorations in the interior of the country. Further, Paragraph 15 of the report tells us that Libya acquired from a Belgian entity in 1982 'a basic design for a uranium ore concentration and conversion facility, which was planned to be located in the Sabha region, but never built'.

In terms of its Safeguards Agreement, declared the IAEA, Libya failed to report the following:

- The import of $UF_6$ in 1985, 2000 and 2001, and its subsequent storage
- The import of other uranium compounds in 1985 and 2002, and their subsequent storage
- Activities involving the conversion of uranium ore concentrate (UOC) into uranium oxides, $UF_4$ and uranium metal, and the disposition of the nuclear material and resulting wastes
- The fabrication and irradiation of uranium targets, and their subsequent processing, including the separation of a small amount of plutonium
- Timely design information for a pilot centrifuge facility
- Timely design information for the Uranium Conversion Facility (UCF), and the locations where uranium conversion experiments had been carried out and nuclear material stored, and
- Timely design information for hot cells associated with the IRT research reactor at Tajura

What is interesting about all these developments is that the report traces Libyan nuclear activity all the way back to 1973, when the Libya's Atomic Energy Establishment (AEE) was set up with a view to 'building Libya's capabilities and infrastructure in nuclear sciences and technologies'. On the face of it, everything was above-board and, in answer to questions, the responsible Libyan ministry declared that the motive was entirely peaceful and linked to an envisioned domestic nuclear power station 'similar to those already in operation in some European countries.' That was followed in January 1981 with the creation of the Libyan Secretariat of Atomic Energy (SAE) and the Tajura Nuclear Research Centre (TNRC), since renamed, rather prosaically, the Renewable Energies and Water Desalination Research Centre or REWDRC. It was the view of Joseph Cirincione, at that stage director of the Non-Proliferation Project at the Carnegie Endowment of Peace that this expertise must have come from elsewhere.

It is my contention that another country that cannot be ruled out is South Africa. At the behest of Pretoria's ANC Government, an extensive chemical and biological warfare facility was established in Libya in the mid-1990s, *after* Nelson Mandela had taken over in Africa's most industrialized country. The question that now begged was whether Pretoria might also have had some kind of nuclear interest in Libya? Not only was Nelson Mandela's African National Congress – the ANC – staunchly communist, its national trade union structure COSATU continues to remain doggedly belligerent, as well as being outspokenly anti-American. Almost three decades after former President de Klerk abdicated white authority at the southern tip of Africa, that situation still holds. We are also aware that following Mandela taking over, he often visited Libya, sometimes two or three times a year. I was able to speak to one of the pilots, a veteran of the South African Air Force, who regularly flew him there onboard a South African registered Falcon 900, complete with a pair of air hostesses to cater for passenger in-flight needs. All flights were coordinated by SAAF Command in Pretoria and listed as secret. Also, there was zero input from European Air Traffic and Navigation (ATN) Control.

Mandela and his entourage – usually five or six people – declared the pilot, would on arrival at Tripoli be whisked away by a string of security personnel while the aircrew would be taken to a local hotel to await the call to return to South Africa. It was the same routine each time, the former SAAF colonel explained. 'You did the job and you didn't ask any questions. Nor were you supposed to see who else was onboard,' he told me. It is notable that other South Africans were also concerned about the South African Libyan connection, which with Mandela in power had become decidedly cosy.[4]

Dr Niël, then director-general of the country's National Intelligence Service (NI) is quoted at the time as saying that if South Africa's nuclear weapons capability had been handed over to Mandela's African National Congress, 'it would have very serious and negative implications for South

Africa's international relations, its [new] constitutional status and indeed, its legitimacy as a state.' He said too, that this was an important reason for South Africa dismantling its nuclear arsenal and that he was 'worried about these weapons ending up in the hands of the ANC, particularly as Mandela and Gadaffi were so close.'

What was immediately clear to both the IAEA and to the West is that the centrifuges on their way to Libya originated in Pakistan. As one observer noted, in other nations, such sales would be strictly controlled. But, he said, Pakistan has always marched to the beat of its own drum[5]. Pakistan has been fingered as a major player in the illegal nuclear business. Following the *BBC China* incident, numerous authorities disclosed that as investigators continued to unravel the intricacies of North Korean, Iranian and then the Libyan nuclear projects, Pakistan – and those it empowered with knowledge and technology – was furiously busy selling this technology on its own.

*The Times* reported:

'That country has been identified as the intellectual and trading hub of a loose network of hidden nuclear proliferators. The network is global, stretching from Germany to Dubai and from China to South Asia. It involves many middlemen and suppliers. But what is striking about a string of recent disclosures, experts say, is how many roads appear to lead back to the Khan Research Laboratories in Kahuta where Pakistan's own bomb was developed[6].

'In 2002 the United States was surprised to discover how North Korea had turned to the Khan laboratory for an alternative way to manufacture nuclear fuel, after the reactors and reprocessing facilities it had relied on for years were 'frozen' under a now shattered agreement with the Clinton administration.'

Which brings us again to the industrial plant manufactured by Krisch Engineering near Johannesburg and paid for by Libya, all of it handled at the behest of A.Q. Khan.

What came out after the containers had been seized by the South African Police was that Johan Meyer, the owner of Tradefin, a local company associated with Krisch Engineering and with links to a clique of German nuclear proliferators, was arrested on suspicion of manufacturing restricted centrifuge parts and equipment for the Libyan nuclear weapons programme. It also emerged that neither the project nor the subsequent investigation were simple matters: they spanned years and cost millions. Subsequent disclosures showed that there were a number of people involved who were very well aware that the project was nuclear-related and, more important, that it was intended for Libya, one of the arch revolutionary states of the modern period. Moreover, Meyer had himself been involved in South Africa's original clandestine nuclear programme, so he knew the score. It was perhaps no accident there that the Libyan dictator and both the first and second South African presidents in the post-apartheid period – Nelson Mandela and Thabo Mbeki – had become house friends.

Following the initial disclosures, Pretoria said they knew nothing about it, but obviously, government ignorance is no excuse. Too many people in South Africa – a state that in its day had one of the most intrusive intelligence organizations on the continent – were in the know. Also, huge amounts of money arrived directly from Libya, peculiar in an era with so many significant money-laundering stop-gaps. The cash was arriving in tranches of millions of dollars at a time from a bank in the Libyan capital: a multi-coloured flag if there ever was one.

More disturbing, the Krisch project was not the only one that was South African built; others had preceded it and had been ferreted out of the country to Pakistan. Unusual, say some observers, never mind the fact that people talk. Then, when American authorities, as a matter of some urgency asked the South Africans to look into what was going on at Krisch Engineering in December 2003, it took until September 2004 – a full nine months – for them to do so, and that, in itself, says a lot. Dr Nic von Wielligh was brought in as a consultant to monitor South African Government interests.

What has subsequently been pieced together, as court records show, is that apart from Meyer, two foreign nationals with permanent South African residency status were 'implicated in the manufacture of products meant to enrich uranium – and facilitate its supply to Libya'. These were Daniel Geiges, a Swiss citizen and a director of Krisch Engineering and Gerhard Wisser, also German and the firm's managing director. Additionally, Wisser arranged for two Libyans to come to South Africa and inspect the completed project. Brought to court the first time, the State showed that some of these individuals were linked to the Nuclear Energy Corporation of South Africa (NECSA), a government body, as well as to the A.Q. Khan network.

NECSA was the same government body that disputed that anything untoward had taken place when eight men armed with automatic weapons (AK-47s) hit the Pelindaba nuclear plant outside Pretoria (See Chapter Thirteen). Wisser, it has since transpired, had a long history of involvement with Khan. Shortly after the illegal South African shipment had been seized, a Swiss national, Urs Tinner, was nabbed in Germany for complicity. That was followed by the arrest of another German, regarded as pivotal to the operation and here things start to get interesting.

In the 1970s and early 1980s, according to David Albright and Corey Hinderstein, that German national was Gotthard Lerch, the 'main contractor' for Khan;s principal operating officer, employed by Leybold Heraeus, a German company that developed and produced vacuum products and technology. Before undergoing significant internal reform in the early 1990s, Leybold Heraeus and its sister companies had been major suppliers to many secret nuclear weapons programmes, including those in Iraq, Iran, South Africa, and Pakistan. In this instance, Leybold Heraeus – where Lerch worked – supplied a prototype valve which was 'clandestinely exported' to South Africa. When asked about it, a spokesperson for Leybold refused to comment, saying that the company was cooperating with what he referred to as 'relevant institutions'.

A South African weekly paper, the *Mail & Guardian,* laid it on the line in a comprehensive exposé on the subterfuge. It showed that Meyer had turned state witness early on and 'blown the whistle' on his associates. It also emerged that Krisch Engineering – and specifically Wisser and Geiges – had worked on the apartheid nuclear weapons programme. Also disclosed was the fact that Geiges had approached Meyer 'in the late 1980s' to manufacture part of a nuclear enrichment plant, ordered by 'a client' of Krisch Engineering. It was built at his South African factory and exported. Meyer, said the *Mail & Guardian*, had subsequently established that the client was Pakistan, though we still do not know what it was that was manufactured.

There were other deals, some of them involving Pakistan's arch enemy India. The South African Police charge sheet claims: 'In the late 1980s and early 1990s, [Wisser] commissioned one of his employees to produce equipment designed for a $UF_6$ [the processed uranium ready for enrichment] application. This was all subsequently smuggled out to India.'

The most ambitious project was yet to come, one that implicated all the major players. In July 1999, says the charge sheet, Wisser travelled to Dubai for technical discussions with Lerch and others. Later that year Geiges – by now drawn into the project by Wisser – approached Meyer to help. Most of the manufacturing was to be done at Meyer's company Tradefin. In the Gulf, the South African participants had met A.Q. Khan's chief money man, Bughari Seyed Abu Tahir who was subsequently arrested in Malaysia, where, coincidentally, he had arranged for the materiel found on the *BBC China* to be engineered by a company co-owned by the Malaysian prime minister's son.

Meanwhile, Meyer opened a Swiss bank account. When asked about it, Wisser claimed that Meyer received $6 million for what he maintained was 'only a water purification plant'. Personally, he admitted to receiving a commission of about a million US dollars, though the German magazine *Der Spiegel* reports that German investigators believe he received up to ten times as much. Also spelt out were details of what had come off the production line. This included all the equipment to service a cascade of 5,832 centrifuges, the machines central to nuclear enrichment. Additionally, there were units made to feed uranium hexafluoride gas into the centrifuges and extract the enriched product and waste as well as piping used to connect the centrifuges and a variety of control, regulating and monitoring systems.

The specialized centrifuge cylinders would also have been manufactured at Tradefin. Controlled manufacturing machinery was illicitly shipped to South Africa for this, but was shipped back to Dubai after that part of the project was abandoned. Wisser allegedly arranged for Tahir to be informed that the machine was on its way back in the following words, 'The gift has been dispatched with DHL'. The machine was eventually recovered in Libya by US investigators.

When plans were made to export the plant through Mozambique, a fake contract for what was termed 'high purification water treatment plants' and supposedly destined for Jordan was drawn up and signed by 'Professor Tahir'. But then the *BBC China* was stopped in Italy and the Libyan nuclear programme abandoned. Wisser destroyed evidence at Krisch Engineering and travelled to Dubai for further instructions. From there, he sent a frantic SMS to Meyer: 'The bird must be destroyed, feathers and all … They have fed us to the dogs.' Meyer did not comply. The 'bird' – the better part of a nuclear enrichment plant ordered by Libya, we now know – survived intact.

This was by no means the first time that Muammar Gadaffi had been trying to make his mark among the fifty-odd countries that today comprise the African Union. His attempts at destabilizing his neighbours, as well as several states further afield, had met with little success. Several times he tried to invade

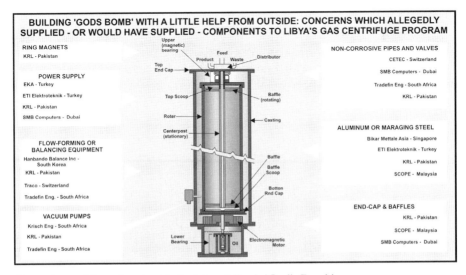

Countries and firms involved in building Libya's 'God's Bomb'

Chad, the huge, impoverished desert state to Libya's immediate south but his forces were invariably rebuffed, usually with the help of the French. The same happened with the always-volatile Sudan, constantly in the news these days with news about Darfur. At one stage Gadaffi had a hand in trying to foment revolution in oil-rich Nigeria, which today supplies North America with about a fifth of its crude oil[7].

On Chad, Gadaffi even hired a bunch of American mercenaries to fly an aircraft to the outskirts of Ndjamena, the capital. Dana Drenkowski – an American veteran of 200 US Air Force combat missions in Vietnam and until recent today a California district attorney – was hired for the job in the 1970s for what at the time was a relatively fat fee of $12,000. What should have been an easy eight weeks of work went sour when some of the tribal leaders involved in the insurrection turned against their leader. Dana and his friends managed to escape, and then only by a whisker. In fact, they were lucky to get their plane off the ground.

The group managed to fly to Sabha, one of Libya's notorious terrorist training camps in the Sahara where they shared quarters with revolutionaries from just about everywhere, including cadres from the Japanese Red Army, members of the long-defunct Baader-Meinhof gang as well as a bunch of IRA malcontents. The full story of Dana Drenkowski's adventures while serving as a mercenary in Libya is covered by the author's book War Dog, published by Casemate in the United States.

## Chapter 9

# North Korea's Nuclear Weapons Programme: A Third World Template for the Future

Barely a day goes by without news about North Korea appearing in the newspapers of the world. It has been like this for an inordinately long time.

The headlines demanded a lot more attention on Sunday 3 September 2017, when North Korea did what was regarded by many nuclear physicists as among the most unlikely events of the seventy year nuclear epoch: it detonated its first thermonuclear bomb, or more commonly in the kind of language everybody understands: hydrogen or H-bomb. For a small, bankrupt nation with few industries and even fewer friends, this was a remarkable and frightening achievement, especially since 'Dear Leader' Kim Jong-un promised to unleash later and more advance versions of this weapon of mass destruction on his enemies, most notably South Korea and the United States of America.

Details about the nuclear test are vague, except that the explosion took place at the test site at Punggye-ri in North Korea's mountainous northeast and, as that country's news agencies had boasted in previous weeks, the H-bomb had been miniaturised so that it could be fitted into one of Kim Jong-un's intercontinental ballistic missiles, another astonishing development.

A day later, more news about the blast emerged, much of it from an army of intelligence officials linked to a dozen countries that had been monitoring North Korean nuclear developments over the years.

The latest nuclear test was estimated to have a yield of as high as 120 kilotons—about ten times the power of the North's previous test and roughly five times that of the atomic bomb that the U.S. dropped on Nagasaki, Japan, in 1945. Also, the blast triggered an initial magnitude 6.3 earthquake whose reverberations were felt in China. That was followed by a magnitude 4.1 temblor that scientists believe was caused by the structural collapse of a series of tunnels that the West was aware had been constructed around the test site.

The rest, by the time this book reaches the shelves, will be history and sadly, the event does not augur well. Indeed, as one notable authority in the Pentagon declared only hours after the blast, 'this is the sort of thing that could result in the entire North Korea ending up looking like a parking lot.'

Tough words, but then these are tough times...

우리의 최고존엄을 감히 모독하고 그에 손을 대려는자들은

무서운 징벌을 면치 못할것이다!

North Korean wall posters depicting victorious battles against Western forces

During the years that it took North Korea to develop the bomb, Pyongyang crossed virtually every red line possible. Through a myriad of outright lies, prevarications, half-truths, last-minute ultimatums and the rest, it pulled off the classic weapons of mass destruction coup. Beyond the usual ineffectual protests there was little real reaction from the West; the late Kim Jong-il simply played along and in doing so, gained both time and the kind of impetus needed to achieve results.

His son, the unstable and brutal Kim Jong-un, follows this unsavoury tradition, only he has added a few macabre touches of his own, like orchestrating his intelligence services to murder his brother Kim Jong-nam in February 2017 by surreptitiously jabbing him with a needle containing deadly VX nerve gas while waiting at Kuala Lumpur Airport to board a plane for Macau. Kim was dead within twenty minutes. There have been numerous other developments. In January 2017, United States satellite imagery showed that the Democratic People's Republic of Korea (DPRK) had resumed operation of a reactor at its main nuclear site used to produce plutonium for its nuclear weapons programme. That was followed by a report that the Pyongyang regime was in the process of restarting its reactor at Yongbyon. Spent fuel rods had apparently been unloaded for reprocessing to produce additional plutonium for its nuclear weapons stockpile.

North Korea also produces highly enriched uranium for atomic bombs and, added a source linked to the website 38 Degrees North, which provides 'Informed analysis of events in and around North Korea' a project of the US-Korea Institute – under the auspices of the Johns Hopkins School of Advanced International Studies – the country would have sufficient fissile material for approximately twenty bombs at about the time this book goes to print, coupled to the capacity to produce seven more a year, something we deal with in more detail, below. At the same time, a BBC report suggested that North Korea claimed to have successfully 'miniaturised' nuclear warheads. While this has never been independently verified and there is some doubt about its veracity, the intent is clear, these actions obviously linked to the pariah state developing intercontinental ballistic missile which would fire nuclear weapons.

Still more worrying was a report by David E. Sanger and William J. Broad in the *New York Times* on 15 April 2017 that North Korea is now capable of making a nuclear bomb 'every six weeks'. That acceleration in pace, impossible to verify until experts get beyond the limited access to North Korean facilities that ended years ago, they stated, 'explains why President Donald Trump and his aides fear they are running out of time'. The article continued:

'For years, American presidents decided that each incremental improvement in the North's programme – another nuclear test, a new variant of a missile – was worrisome, but not worth a confrontation that could spill into open conflict. Now those step-by-step advances have resulted in North Korean warheads that in a few years could reach Seattle.'

Meantime, the DPRK was threatening more nuclear tests. The three previous atom bomb tests, said Sanger and Broad, 'generated Hiroshima-size explosions'.

In the January/February 2010 issue of *Foreign Affairs*, Graham Allison, the Douglas Dillon Professor of Government of the Belfer Centre for Science and International Affairs at Harvard's Kennedy School of Government, raised an issue that has a critical bearing on nuclear proliferation among Third World countries[1]. What, he asks, are the consequences for the [Non-proliferation Treaty] 'if one of the world's weakest states can violate the rules of the regime with impunity and defy the demands of the strongest states, which are those charged with its enforcement?' In short, Professor Allison addressed one of the most serious issues currently facing the international community and by his own admission, he offers no solution.

More to the point, Dan Yurman, publisher of the nuclear energy blog *Idaho Samizdat*[2], asks the obvious; while nations with nuclear weapons have elaborate mechanisms to prevent a rogue commander from setting one off, what does the chaos inside North Korea's military suggest about this threat? In itself, he indicates, this is a perilous situation with security implications for the entire region. He goes on:

> 'There are actually two threats. The first is the potential for compromise of command and control mechanisms for the nuclear weapons. The second is the loss of material accountability for weapons grade materials/ technology and their diversion for personal profit to third parties outside the country.'

While Professor Allison does not say as much, the ramifications are clear. The international community has been emasculated by a series of cunning feints and ploys, first on the part of North Korea and thereafter, by several other states, including Libya and Syria.

An interesting and related comment that emerged from the White House early 2010 came from President Barack Obama's Director of National Intelligence. In testimony before the United States Congress, Dennis Blair, a top intelligence official, said that North Korea relied on its nuclear weapons programme 'because of a crumbling military that cannot compete with South Korea.' He went on:

> 'We are dealing there with an army that struggles with aging weapons, poorly trained, out-of-shape soldiers, inflexible leaders, corruption, low morale and problems with command and control.'

North Korea, Blair said, had little chance of reversing a huge gap in military capabilities with South Korea: it 'relies on its nuclear programme to deter external attacks on the state and to its regime.'

There is a corollary to this argument that is equally relevant: The DPRK is not a government as we in the West understand civil authority. It is more like a consortium of criminal families at the top, with a small, tightly-integrated power structure that characterizes these types of dictatorships. It is likely that a few hundred people run the whole country. The rest of the population is either in abject servitude, with frequent instances of mass starvation, or in the process of running their own criminal enterprises, customarily with tacit approval of the leadership through payoffs. For the leadership cabal, there is no ideology except self-perpetuation and defence against any intervention from the outside. Like all hardened criminals, these people are sociopaths: that alone suggests that conventional western diplomatic overtures will fail.

The real challenge now is to convince the people behind this cabal that it is in their interest (self-preservation of a vast criminal enterprise) to abandon their nuclear aspirations. Short of any real measure of intervention from China, that is simply not going to happen. China is North Korea's major trading partner. It is consequently in the interests of Beijing to keep the appearance of a North Korean spear pointed at the West, since it affects international relations with the West in multiple dimensions.

Until the obstreperous and distinctly unstable Kim Jong-un took over in North Korea in late 2011, who was actually running the country before that was yet another matter. Ostensibly his father, Kim Jong-il, was in charge, but conflicting reports of ill health, alcoholism and a possible stroke surfaced in later years, giving some credence to the possibility that his sister, the more strident Kim Kyong-hui was actually running the show. Whatever the truth, North Korea has remained a family affair for three generations.

The methodology of the Democratic People's Republic of Korea in developing the bomb over the years was hardly unique. Following the United States, the Soviet Union, Britain and France, China and then India had played similar games in their respective nuclear lead-ups. India followed with a significant nuclear weapons programme of its own and not long afterwards, Pakistan displayed its initial clutch of weapons of mass destruction.

North Korea's nuclear weapons programme, the Federation of American Scientists tells us, dates back to the 1980s. Focusing on practical uses of nuclear energy and the completion of a nuclear weapon development system, initial work was on facilities for uranium fabrication and conversion. Under the guidance of 'Great Leader' as the father of Kim Jong-il is still referred to, North Korea began construction of a 200 MWe nuclear reactor and nuclear reprocessing facilities in Taechon and Yongbyon respectively and conducted high-explosive detonation tests. Kim Il-sung, it will be recalled, was handpicked by Stalin after the Second World War to rule the new Soviet puppet state and it was he that initiated the DPRK's nuclear programme. In 1985, US officials announced for the first time that they had intelligence data proving that a secret nuclear reactor was being built about eighty kilometres north of Pyongyang near the small town of Yongbyon.

China and the West had been aware of what was happening at Yongbyon for about eight years and much of it came from official IAEA reports. In 1985, under international pressure, Pyongyang acceded to the Treaty on the Non-Proliferation of Nuclear Weapons (NPT). However, the DPRK refused to sign a safeguards agreement with the IAEA, an obligation it had as a party to the NPT. That was followed in July 1990 by the *Washington Post* reporting that new satellite photographs indicated a presence in Yongbyon of a structure which could possibly be used to separate plutonium from nuclear fuel.

During this period, the DPRK embraced a variety of disciplines, some Soviet, others Chinese. Then Pakistan entered the chase with A.Q. Khan having offered assistance by exchanging missile technology in return for uranium enriching prowess and second-generation gas centrifuges. These exchanges continued even after Khan had been stopped by his government from smuggling nuclear-related material. In a report published by Britain's *Jane's Intelligence Review*, Andrew Koch, then Jane's Washington correspondent, disclosed that a lot of Khan's nuclear goods had 'gone missing' and some of the transfers had been going on in spite of protestations to the contrary from the Pakistani Government[3].

Koch wrote that explanations for the missing nuclear goods range from another still unknown buyer, to additional shipments to Iran or North Korea. The goods could also have been placed into storage or even destroyed by participants in the network who were scared off after a number of associates were arrested or after they suspected they were being watched by government authorities. Koch disclosed that diplomatic sources said IAEA investigators believed some centrifuge parts such as ring magnets, motor stators and even key rotors may ultimately be found warehoused in some unknown location. It is also possible that intelligence agencies know where they are and have them under observation, waiting to see who shows up to collect.

While full-scale nuclear testing by North Korea had been on the cards for a while, the timing of the first explosion surprised Western intelligence agencies. More than three years before, on 24 April 2003, Pyongyang disclosed to both the Americans and the Chinese at a tripartite meeting in Beijing that they actually possessed the bomb. North Korea also confirmed that it reprocessed spent fuel rods to acquire the plutonium necessary for these weapons and threatened the exportation of nuclear know-how and materials if Washington balked at one-on-one talks on North Korean soil.

As Dan Yurman comments:

'... this is a dirty business which requires extensive and expensive infrastructure and a lot of nitric acid (which produces a poorer grade of plutonium than by other methods). Also, there is a staffing issue. It creates a large waste volume of liquid radioactive material that requires a tank farm to manage it. All these activities and more, raises the issue why satellite photos did not pick up the construction of these facilities when it started?'

For instance, the infrastructure of the now decommissioned Idaho Chemical Processing Plant is easily visible from low earth orbit satellites. Putting it all underground still requires electricity transmission to the site, rail and truck transport as well as procurement of sophisticated equipment and materials. Secrecy throughout has been a paramount consideration in Korea's Upper Peninsula, though this is not difficult in a country as xenophobic as North Korea where any kind of travel more than a few kilometres beyond home requires a permit.

This policy of 'blanket concealment' has been inordinately effective, especially after the Pyongyang Government expelled IAEA inspectors. In fact, so thorough have these restrictions been, that the West is still uncertain whether the Yongbyon reactor is the primary reprocessing facility or even the exact location of a putative uranium enrichment plant that sparked the international security crisis in 2002. At the same time, these are large facilities. Unless North Korea is building them inside mountains, they are difficult to miss from satellites. You need multiple large buildings to move heavy radioactive materials through the nuclear fuel cycle, irradiate the fuel in a reactor and then separate the relatively small amount of $^{239}$Pu from each fuel assembly.

Looking back, the West took a while to grasp both the extent of North Korea's nuclear programme as well as the unusually complicated steps that President Kim Jong-il took to conceal it. We now know that much of what took place occurred underground in some of the most extensive burrowing strategies seen anywhere in the world since Vietnam. Researchers Kongdan Oh and Ralph C. Hassig disclosed in 2000 that North Korea had more than 8,000 below-surface installations that included 500 kilometres of tunnels[4].

What they did not say was that tunnels involved in such large scale industrial activity, have strenuous logistical and physical problems of venting the $CO_2$ and treating and removing service waste at some point from all the people working in such underground sites. Obviously, this would show up at some stage through infra-red detection. It is axiomatic, with North Korea again in the spotlight and having been involved in clandestine nuclear operations as far distant as Libya, Syria, the Yemen and more recently Myanmar (Burma), these facilities would have been substantially increased.

Meantime, Pyongyang capitalized successfully on the carefully crafted ambiguity that surrounds its nuclear programmes, its public pronouncements about it being about self-defence, coupled to a reticent West, inordinately fearful of initiating a catastrophic war that would involve South Korea and result in casualties that might be counted in seven digits. In his thoughtful assessment of the situation, Victor Cha maintains that North Korea not only capitalized on the ambiguity of developing the bomb, but also the manner that Pyongyang has fostered uncertainty about its motives. Clearly, the incipient threat of nuclear war in the region had to play a significant role in the West's strategic calculus.

Cha depicted North Korea's nuclear motives as a clear measure intended to prevent attack from its two most active traditional enemies, South Korea, in concert with its most powerful ally, the United States. Metaphorically, he described the WMD programme first as a shield for protection, second as a sword intended for aggressive or revisionist purposes, then as a badge of prestige and most importantly, to provide multi-lateral leverage in negotiations.

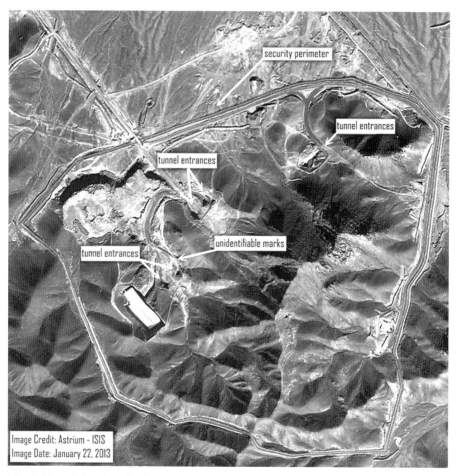

North Korea's Fordow Fuel Enrichmen Plant (Source ISIS)

Certainly, the biggest problem facing the West today is the series of stop-start agreements reached with North Korea. An accord would be achieved and then at a whim, the country's leader – first the late Kim Il-sung, followed by his son – would abrogate agreements and make fresh demands. A similar pattern can be seen today with Iran, with the North Koreans no less intrusive in their machinations. As with Tehran, they were buying time with the credible appearance of developing nuclear-tipped ICBMs.

At one of the first of several agreements in the mid-1990s, the DPRK agreed to freeze and eventually dismantle its existing suspect nuclear programme, including the 50 MW and 200 MW graphite-moderated reactors under construction, as well as its existing 5 MW reactor and nuclear fuel reprocessing facility (thought to be of RBMK Russian design).

In return, states the Federation of American Scientists:

'Pyongyang would be provided with alternative energy, initially in the form of heavy oil, and eventually two proliferation-resistant light water reactors (LWR). The two 1,000 MW light-water nuclear reactors would be safer and would produce much less plutonium, in order to help boost the supply of electricity in the North, which is now in a critical shortage. The agreement also included gradual improvement of relations between the US and North Korea, and committed the DPRK to engage in South–North dialogue.

'A few weeks after the signing of the Agreed Framework, President Kim loosened restrictions on South Korean firms desiring to pursue business opportunities with the North. Although North Korea continued to refuse official overtures by the South, economic contacts appeared to be expanding gradually.'

A close examination by the IAEA of the radioactive isotope content in the nuclear waste surreptitiously recovered revealed that North Korea had extracted dozens of kilograms of plutonium. North Korea was supposed to have produced 0.9 grams of plutonium per megawatt every day over a four-year period from 1987 to 1991. Multiplied by 365 days over four years and by 30 megawatts comes to thirty-nine kilograms (85 pounds) of weapons-grade $^{239}$Pu. The actual number is probably lower due to outages for maintenance and other down time of the reactor.

The IAEA agreed with this assessment. It wrote:

'When the yearly operation ratio is presumed to be 60 percent, the actual amount was estimated at 60 percent of thirty-nine kilograms or some twenty-and-a-half kilograms (roughly fifty pounds). 'Since the twenty-kiloton standard nuclear warhead has eight kilograms of critical mass, this amounts to a mass of material of nuclear fission out of which about three small nuclear warheads could be extracted … 'Estimates vary of both the amount of plutonium in North Korea's possession and number of nuclear weapons that could be manufactured from the material. South Korean, Japanese, and Russian intelligence estimates of the amount of plutonium separated, for example, are reported to be higher by seven to twenty-two kilograms, sixteen to twenty four kilograms, and twenty kilograms respectively, than the reported US estimate of about twelve kilograms (or about twenty six pounds).'

At least two of the estimates are said to be based on the assumption that North Korea removed fuel rods from the 5-MW(e) reactor and subsequently reprocessed the fuel during slowdowns in the reactor's operations in 1990 and 1991. The variations in the estimates about the number of weapons that could be produced from the material at the time depended on a variety of factors, including assumptions about North Korea's reprocessing capabilities – advanced technology yields more material – and the amount of plutonium it takes to make a nuclear weapon. Until January 1994, the Department of Energy (DoE) estimated that eight kilograms (seventeen pounds) would be needed to make a small nuclear weapon. Thus, the United States' estimate of twelve kilograms could result in one to two bombs. In January 1994, however, DoE reduced the estimate of the amount of plutonium needed to four kilograms (almost nine pounds), or enough to make up to three bombs if the US estimate is used and up to six bombs if the other estimates were used.

There has been much controversy as to why North Korea took the nuclear road it did. Grandstanding was obviously a part of it. So was being totally overshadowed economically by its southern neighbour. One source maintains that a successful American programme of nuclear psychological warfare against the People's Republic during the Korean War years 1950/3 probably kindled the first interest. Regardless, in 1964 the North Korea established the Yongbyon Nuclear Research Centre and it would become the cradle of its nuclear activities, 'peaceful' as well as otherwise.

The next step was procuring a small (800kW-4MWt) HEU-fuelled IRT-2M research reactor, as well as a 0.1MWt critical assembly, from the Soviet Union the following year. The ITR reactor went critical in 1967. Its weapons intentions, probably never in doubt, came with an unconfirmed report that suggested that DPRK nuclear scientists had been present at China's first nuclear test in October 1964. Eleven years later, North Korea was separating small quantities of plutonium from Soviet-supplied irradiated fuel. They used 'hot cells' at a radiochemical laboratory built at Pyongyang with Soviet assistance.

Its next, and most notable weapons pointer, occurred in 1980 when Pyongyang started construction on a 5MW MAGNOX-type experimental power reactor at Yongbyon, this time without foreign assistance, though Charles Vick, a Senior Fellow at globalecurity.org, suggests that the reactor might be termed 5MWt (thermal) instead of 5MWe (electrical), conceding too that one can probably argue both ways. The uranium and graphite required for this endeavour was mined and purified indigenously. Though locally built, it was certainly based on foreign designs, such as the British Calder Hall MAGNOX reactor, a Canadian heavy water research reactor as well as the French G1 power/plutonium production reactor. The facility went online in January 1986 and started operating at full power in October 1987. It is capable of producing approximately fifteen pounds of weapons grade plutonium a year.

Meanwhile, despite huge internal problems that included failed harvests and starvation on an almost biblical scale, the DPRK continued to co-operate with likeminded countries such as Romania and East Germany (before unification) as well as Czechoslovakia, and Cuba. Technology, expertise, equipment, material and training from advanced countries such as the then Federal Republic of Germany, Japan, France, the Former Soviet Union, and the People's Republic of China, were readily accepted. It is interesting that Pyongyang did not discriminate between potential nuclear beneficiaries, whether they were ideologically friendly or hostile.

Two countries stand out above all others in North Korea's push to acquire a nuclear capability; Pakistan and Iran.

Pakistan reportedly forged nuclear (and missile) contacts with the DPRK between 1985 and 1988. An agreement which was said to have been signed in January 1989 with Tehran may have covered nuclear development as well as the development of nuclear warheads for missiles. One particular area of activity pertaining to this agreement appears to have been the development of plutonium-fuelled warheads, using clandestinely-acquired Chinese technology and sub-systems.

In 1989, the 5MW reactor was shut down for several months, followed by 'low power runs' in 1990 and 1991. It is not impossible that the North Koreans might have used the breaks to unload fuel, allowing Pyongyang to amass between fifteen and thirty pounds of plutonium.

That was followed by the completion, in 1992, of North Korea's first, rudimentary, implosion device. When the reactor was shut down for refuelling in April 1994, it was estimated that the 8,000 spent fuel rods might have contained as much as seventy pounds of weapons grade $^{239}$Pu. Analysis of DPRK-separated plutonium by the IAEA in 1992 indicated that indeed, reprocessing had taken place four times during the preceding three years and as was expected, the revelation caused a furore. North Korea threatened to withdraw from the NPT, not that it made much difference whether it was a member or not anyway.

Washington 'saved the day' with the so-called 'Agreed Framework', signed in October 1994. For its part, the DPRK undertook to freeze its plutonium production programme and to eventually dismantle its existing nuclear facilities. In exchange, Washington provided fuel oil, economic co-operation and the construction of two modern light-water nuclear power plants. At the end of it, North Korea abrogated the agreement; it accepted all that had been offered but did not follow through on its obligations. Clearly, the agreement had almost no effect on North Korea's ultimate nuclear goal.

Enter Pakistan, or more accurately, the nuclear proliferator A.Q. Khan. Pakistan's lack of funds – coupled with a desire for missile technology that fringed on desperation in the face of what was regarded as an aggressive India – was the motive. From 1994 onwards, North Korea received large numbers of P-1 and P-2 centrifuges. Also passed along were drawings, sketches, technical data and even depleted uranium hexafluoride gas, courtesy of the Khan 'network'. This could mean that the Pakistan enrichment process was inefficient and that there was enough $^{235}$U in the tails to be worth shipping to North Korea. It also handily solved a waste disposition problem for the Islamabad Government. In turn Pakistan got the No-Dong-A missiles it sought and thus was born the Ghauri-II missile, as it was rebranded.

Although Khan later publicly 'confessed' these nuclear transgressions – again offering nothing explanatory – he was pardoned by President Musharraf. In retrospect, it is certain that such transfers could never have taken place without the knowledge of the Pakistani government. Flights between Islamabad and Pyongyang were almost weekly, many of them involving Pakistani Air Force C-130s; huge cargoes moved in both directions. One needs to question whether Beijing was aware of these transfers – through its airspace and all – which would clearly imply an element of complicity.

The scale of North Korea's uranium enrichment programme is vast, at least for a backward Third World state. Washington has identified at least three sites where suspected enrichment tests were conducted. These are the Academy of Sciences near Pyongyang, together with sites in the Hagap region and Yehong-dong.

In November 2002, North Korea restarted its 5MW reactor and resumed reprocessing plutonium, for what were termed 'peaceful nuclear activities'. During a visit of an American delegation to the DPRK in January 2004 a government spokesman told the group that all 8,000 spent fuel rods in the Radiochemical Laboratory at the facility at Yongbyon had been reprocessed. Also disclosed was

Kim Jong-un with the prototype of his North Korean H-Bomb

that it had been achieved in a single continuous process: it was begun mid-January 2003 and completed five months later, no small achievement.

One of the world's foremost authorities in nuclear proliferation is Dr Siegfried S. Hecker, a senior fellow and affiliated faculty member at Stanford University's Centre for International Security and Cooperation and the Freeman Spogli Institute for International Studies. He is also a research professor in the Department of Management Science and Engineering at Stanford and director emeritus of the Los Alamos National Laboratory, where he served as director from 1986 to 1997 and as senior fellow until July 2005. In the website 38 Degrees North, this eminent physicist attempted to master two related issues in answer to a question raised after the September 2016 detonation of another nuclear device by the Pyongyang regime.

The first was what to make of the latest nuclear test of the Democratic People's Republic of Korea? Also at issue was how many nuclear warheads can the DPRK produce? And finally, can North Korea produce lighter, smaller warheads and as claimed by the DPRK Nuclear Weapons Institute, ones that have been 'standardised to be able to be mounted on its ballistic missiles' of which there have been many test firings in the past year?

The article which followed, dated 12 September 2016 is both balanced and prescient, as is so much of this scientist's work. He also provides us with an insight to a rather arcane environment on the far side of the world to which he obviously has some access and his revelations are fascinating. I quote several extracts:

'On September 9, 2016, seismic stations around the world picked up the unmistakable signals of another North Korean underground nuclear test in the vicinity of Punggye-ri. The technical details about the test will be sorted out over the next few weeks, but the political message is already loud and clear: North Korea will continue to expand its dangerous nuclear arsenal so long as Washington stays on its current path.

'Preliminary indications are that the test registered at 5.2 to 5.3 on the Richter scale, which translates to an explosion yield of approximately 15 to 20 kilotons, possibly twice the magnitude of the largest previous test. It appears to have been conducted in the same network of tunnels as the last three tests, just buried deeper into the mountain. This was the fifth known North Korean nuclear explosion; the second this year, and the third since Kim Jong-un took over the country's leadership in December 2011.

'Unlike previous announcements, such as the claim of having detonated a hydrogen bomb in January 2016, the current statement can no longer be dismissed. This time, the North Korean News Agency reported the following from the country's Nuclear Weapons Institute:

'The **standardization of the nuclear warhead** will enable the DPRK **to produce at will and as many as it wants a variety of smaller, lighter and diversified nuclear warheads** of higher strike power with a firm hold on the technology for producing and using **various fissile materials.** This has definitely put on a higher level the DPRK's technology of **mounting nuclear warheads on ballistic rockets.**[5]

'This statement brings up some fundamental questions, including the seminal issue of how many nuclear warheads can the DPRK produce?

'North Korea's capacity to produce plutonium remains limited to six kilograms, or approximately one bomb's worth, per year. We estimate that it may have a stockpile of thirty-two to fifty four kilograms (roughly six to eight bombs' worth) of plutonium now. Whereas plutonium production can be estimated reasonably accurately because of tell-tale signals resulting from reactor operation, production of highly enriched uranium (HEU) remains highly uncertain.

'However, based on what I saw at the Yongbyon centrifuge facility during my last visit in November 2010, the expanded footprint of the facility since, and our probabilistic estimates of how much it could make in covert facilities,[6] it is possible that the DPRK could add 150 kg of HEU (roughly six bombs' worth) to a current stockpile of perhaps 300 to 400 kg.[7]

'In other words, a stockpile of sufficient fissile material for approximately twenty bombs by the end of this year and a capacity of adding approximately seven per year makes the DPRK claim sound plausible.'

Which brings us to the second issue: Can the DPRK produce lighter, smaller warheads and as claimed by the DPRK Nuclear Weapons Institute, ones that have been 'standardized to be able to be mounted on its ballistic missiles'? As Dr Hecker declares, with two successful nuclear tests the previous year the international community must assume that the DPRK has designed and demonstrated nuclear warheads that can be mounted on some of its short-range and perhaps medium-range missiles. He goes on:

'Its ability to field an ICBM fitted with a nuclear warhead capable of reaching the United States is still a long way off – perhaps five to ten years, but likely doable if the programme is unconstrained.

'As much as a doomsday nuclear shot at the United States worries Americans, it is not what I consider to be the primary threat from Pyongyang's unrelenting drive to more bombs and better bombs. At a minimum, the current state of the North's nuclear arsenal is an effective deterrent to potential hostile external intervention. It has reinforced Kim Jong-un's legitimacy as leader of what the North considers a beleaguered nation.

'The current situation is very different from what my Stanford colleagues and I encountered during our November 2006 visit a few weeks after the North's first nuclear test. At each of our stops – the Ministry of Foreign Affairs, the Department of Atomic Energy, and the military – we found their pronouncements of having achieved a deterrent against the United States to ring hollow.

'Nevertheless, Kim Jong-il [North Korea's previous leader and father of Kim Jong-un] appeared sufficiently confident of the state's security that he accepted the Bush administration's change of heart and new willingness to find a diplomatic solution.

'The years 2007 and 2008 marked significant diplomatic progress, which resulted in a rollback of operations at the Yongbyon nuclear complex, the return of international inspectors, and the presence of an American technical team. However, in the summer of 2008, the Bush administration pulled back followed by a similar response by the North in August.

'By the time our Stanford team visited Pyongyang in February 2009, we were told that times had changed – the North was going to launch a long-range rocket and that matters would get much worse. And, so they did. The launch was followed by UN condemnation and Pyongyang's expulsion of the international inspectors and American team. Then in May, the North conducted its second nuclear test, which, unlike the first, appeared successful. Seoul and Washington apparently rebuffed Pyongyang's overtures in the summer of 2009 to get back on a diplomatic track and the DPRK was off and running on a determined path for more and better bombs, combined with greatly increasing its missile threat.

'The death of diplomacy, namely the Obama administration's retreat to "strategic patience" and the demise of the Six Party Talks, opened the door to an unrelenting expansion of the North's nuclear weapons programme, as best as one can tell, unconstrained by international opprobrium and escalating sanctions.'

Dr Hecker concludes with the question: 'So, what to do?' As he says, the latest nuclear [and missile] tests demonstrate conclusively that attempting to sanction the DPRK into submission and waiting for China to exert leverage over Pyongyang's nuclear programme do not work. He goes on:

'Increasing sanctions and adding missile defences in South Korea to that mix will also not suffice and make China even less likely to cooperate. What is missing is diplomacy as much as Washington may find it repugnant to deal with the Kim regime.'

Western media is very much aware of the potential North Korea missile and nuclear threat

## Chapter 10

# South Africa Builds Six Atom Bombs

O ne of the urban legends which has been doing the rounds just about forever is that any good university with an advanced scientific faculty would, with solid application, be able to build the bomb. That is nonsense. If it were so easy just about everybody would be doing it, especially if those involved could master some of the arcane disciplines that include things as abstruse as spherical coordinates, a necessary adjunct to nuclear weaponization. Also, constructing the bomb requires a substantial industrial and scientific base…

South Africa's nuclear history had its origins in the Manhattan Project in Los Alamos during the Second World War. Though not all that long in coming, once the programme was put into motion, Pretoria's scientists went through a series of similar transition phases which were both baffling and difficult. It is interesting too that its roots went back to long before the South African nuclear initiative became a reality. The first word on the military application of nuclear power to reach a South African was communicated to the then Prime Minister Jan Christiaan Smuts in 1944 by Sir John Anderson, who reportedly briefed him on the new weapon being developed in the United States and which had been dubbed the Atomic Bomb.

Anderson followed with a communication to Smuts that requested an investigation into reported deposits of radium and pitchblende both in South Africa and the then former German African colony of South-West Africa (Namibia today). The South African Army had taken the territory in conquest in the First World War and at that stage it was being administered in trust under a League of Nations mandate. One of the curious anomalies of the era was that scientists believed uranium to be a scarce commodity. But it did not take long to establish that the mineral was almost commonplace in South Africa's gold mines; a year after the end of the Second World War, the establishment of a controlling body known as the Uranium Research Committee was approved.

Another South African, Sir Basil Schonland had headed one of Churchill's wartime scientific teams and at one stage during the war was also scientific adviser to Montgomery in England, France and Belgium. With him in the chair, the URC held its first meeting in March 1946. It was decided that Smuts, together with a few highly placed government officials and some senior representatives of the gold-mining industry would exercise initial control over the development and production of uranium. By then the United States was already producing nuclear weapons in quantity and for these it needed uranium, lots of it. It was South Africa's gold mines that initially filled that gap, though earlier supplies had come from the copper mines in Katanga, the southernmost province of the Congo, then still under Belgian control.

This was followed by the Atomic Energy Act of 1948 and the creation of South Africa's Atomic Energy Board or AEB, a controlling body which would oversee the production of, and trade in, uranium. By this time the CSIRO, the forerunner of the Council for Scientific and Industrial Research, was already in existence, founded in 1946, and its Applied Radioactivity Division, which had come into being as part of its National Physical Laboratory. This body was initially linked to some of the early efforts aimed at nuclear research and outside assistance came by way of a November 1950 agreement whereby the Atomic Energy Board would supply uranium to the joint US-United Kingdom Combined Development Agency. Those countries reciprocated by extending technical and financial aid to South Arica to help it to develop its own technology and infrastructure in this field.

From the early 1950s, vast quantities of uranium were exported, principally to the US and Britain. This situation continued until 1966 and 1973 respectively. France too, took some of it, and later Israel got into the act. By then South Africa was dealing not only in uranium but also in thorium, of which likewise, it had vast deposits and which was required by the West. However, this was also a period when a reactionary new government replaced the traditional order in South Africa, one which looked to discarding all civilized norms by legally instituting racial discrimination based solely on colour. It was a retrogressive move and went into effect with a brutal determination that changed the lives of millions of people. The Americans were among the harshest critics of apartheid, but they tended to ignore the reality that South Africa's racial discrimination followed in the tracks of a system then still very much in evidence in many of the southern states of the United States. In this regard, some critics maintain, South Africa simply followed an example set by its most notable mentor.

The political implications of these acts were nonetheless partially deflected by America because the Soviet Union – joined shortly afterwards by Britain – began detonating nuclear test bombs and like the US, were doing so on a breath-taking scale. It was possibly not all that surprising that Pretoria, even then, should have considered the nuclear alternative.

The first hint of intent came during the 1954-1958 period, during the tenure of Prime Minister J. G. Strijdom. The South African *Weekly Mail* newspaper revealed in 1993 that documents dating back to the Strydom era 'show research into the military implications of a nuclear capability…'

In part, a reason for this approach stemmed from the possibility of South Africa using its massive stocks of uranium to develop nuclear energy for power. With more gold mines coming into production – including some of the wealthiest in the country's history – the economy was expanding. Moreover, it was doing so at an astonishing rate. The need for additional electricity supplies suddenly became urgent in a land where droughts were frequent and industrial water supplies often inadequate. In also led to limited potential for hydro-electric power generation, coupled to the prospect of producing heavy water locally on a large scale.

Dr Abraham Johannes 'Ampie' Roux was charged with establishing a formal commission of enquiry to report on the utilization of nuclear energy for these purposes and shortly afterwards, in June 1958, he presented his proposals for a comprehensive nuclear research and development project.

Roux's proposals were far-reaching. They ranged from the mining, extraction, and processing of uranium – and, surprisingly, the possible use of limited nuclear explosions in underground mine-shafts – as well as the use of nuclear fuel. The search for further deposits of thorium also came into focus, as well as the development of extraction and processing methods for reactor materials.

Helen Purkitt, Professor of Political Science at the US Naval Academy and a Research Associate for the Centre for Technology and International Security, wrote in a paper presented at several forums in the US that Roux explicitly noted the links between the peaceful and military applications of nuclear research[1].

After some minor adjustments, the proposed nuclear research and development programme was recommended for implementation. Then a measure of dissent regarding these proposals emerged among the AEB's board of directors, supposedly concerning different legal interpretations of a small phrase contained within the Atomic Energy Act. The precise cause of the objection remains a mystery; Hounam and McQuillan note that the board's expurgated official history, *Chain Reaction*, does not identify the reason[2].

Was it perhaps nothing more serious than an egotistical turf battle, or possibly because of a latent nuclear-weapon potential, all of which must surely have been perfectly clear to those involved? Whatever the case, the cabinet's historic decision ultimately opened the door for the future acquisition of $^{239}$Pu, $^{235}$U, *and* $^{233}$U, and little more than a decade later highly-enriched uranium production would flow from these proposals.

In 1958 the newly founded Atomic Energy Board (AEB) established the first nuclear research curriculum, which included 'research on a power reactor concept appropriate to South Africa'.

At its head was Andries 'Ampie' Roux, who is regarded as the doyen of South Africa's nuclear weapons programme which was to come later. Like his more famous contemporary, heart transplant pioneer Dr Christiaan Barnard, Roux was a country boy by birth and background. He came of solid old South African stock, descended from a group of Huguenot refugees who fled to the Cape of Good Hope in the 1680s to escape anti-Protestant persecution in France, very much as both Britain and the American colonies welcomed respective groups of these religious 'dissidents'.

Roux's branch of the family eventually migrated north-eastwards and settled in the Bethlehem district of what became the Orange Free State and his original intention was to become a farmer like his father. Roux Senior had other ideas: he persuaded his son to go to university instead, where he obtained a bachelor's and then a master's degree in science, followed by a doctorate in mechanical engineering at the Witwatersrand University.

At the end of the Second World War, Ampie Roux became a senior lecturer at the University of Stellenbosch in the Cape Province. From there he joined the CSIRO, forerunner of the Council for Scientific and Industrial Research (CSIR). At this stage, he met Dr Wally Grant, another of his colleagues who eventually went into nuclear work. From there Roux progressed to the Atomic Energy Board, of which he would become chairman in 1967, tasked with planning and formulating South Africa's plans for nuclear research and development.

Dr Wally Grant arrived at the Atomic Energy Board along a different route. Born in difficult economic times, he attended 13 schools in eight years and dropped out of the Johannesburg Technical High School to join the South African Air Force at the end of 1940 as an apprentice in aircraft engines and airframes.

Grant, having got his degree, followed the path of so many young colonial academics in later years who came from Commonwealth countries and elsewhere to spend time at a good British, European or American university to enhance their experience. Indeed, there was a procession of South Africans who received nuclear training in the United States and Europe and, as a consequence, a preponderance of scientists, engineers and technicians at South Africa's Atomic Energy Board who had either studied or qualified abroad.

An interesting sidelight here, and which has a bearing on future developments, was that one of the institute's projects involved using a Rosegard/Wikdahl vortex tube (which has the ability to separate room air into two components, one hot and the other cold) for use in cheap air-conditioning units. One thing led to another, and eventually the relatively humble vortex tube gave birth to the 'Advanced Vortex Tube Process' and the innovating 'Helikon' cascade arrangement which was subsequently used for isotope separation by the Uranium Enrichment Corporation of South Africa Limited (UCOR).

As a postscript, it would appear that Grant never lost his enthusiasm for things aeronautical, nor his pioneering spirit. At the ripe old age of eighty-five he undertook his first parachute jump. In the process he broke a leg, but that did not stop him from routinely calling in at his office.

Wally Grant was the first to acknowledge the value of spending time at British academic establishments by young professional South African, Canadian, Australian, New Zealand and other Commonwealth citizens. The majority were academics who had qualified in their respective professions and wished to enhance their experience work-wise. South Africans scored handsomely.

South Africa's nuclear project, essentially, was composed of three basic facets. The first was research on uranium and other fissile materials, followed by a range of ground-breaking work on radio-isotopes and radiation and finally, a study on the establishment of a power reactor. To house this kind of research, which, with time became expansive, the Atomic Energy Board moved from its suite in a Pretoria office block to secretly purchased farmland to the west of Pretoria. Called Pelindaba (in the Zulu language it means the 'Time for Talking is Over'), this site became the new home of the South African National Nuclear Research Centre.

The amended Atomic Energy Act of 1959 provided for the research, development, and utilization, of nuclear energy. During the 1950s, the South African nuclear industrial base expanded, with new capabilities periodically being added. By 1955 there were sixteen mines that had been authorized to produce uranium, and by then a CSIR-designed cyclotron had also been brought into operation. That was followed by a bilateral agreement with the United States in July 1957, in the terms of which South Africa agreed to buy a 6.66-megawatt Oak Ridge-type nuclear research reactor (up-gradable to 20 and even 30-megawatt/thermal capacity), together with all the nuclear fuel it might need. The agreement also provided for selected South Africans to be trained at United States nuclear and research establishments, which included the Argonne National Laboratories outside Chicago, the Oak Ridge National Laboratory in Tennessee and other venues. When they subsequently returned to South Africa, members of this group were to form the nucleus of an increasingly powerful nuclear bureaucracy.

On the international front, apartheid had not yet taken as much of a grip of the nation's politics as was to follow later. In fact, South Africa's international stock at this time was relatively high, other than in the precincts of the United Nations General Assembly and within the Communist Bloc. Purkitt notes that due to its close political and military links with America and Britain – the two major Western nuclear powers of the time – Pretoria was regarded almost as an appendage of the West[3]. Vast quantities of South African uranium were being used to arm nuclear weapons produced by these countries, and as the Cold War grew hot, it was lost on nobody that Pretoria was proving to be a loyal member of the Western political camp. Consequently, it was not surprising that South Africa became a founding member of the International Atomic Energy Agency in 1957. It was one of the states to draft its statute, which meant that its status as the most advanced nuclear country on the African continent guaranteed it a permanent seat on the IAEA's board of governors.

Then things started to change. On the domestic front, the country held its first controversial all-white election with the ascension to power of Dr H.F. Verwoerd, the man recognized as the architect of apartheid. As National Party leader and prime minister, he was able to shunt a variety of discriminatory measures through Parliament, though it would be a while before the truth of what racial classification meant to people of colour and really began to bite.

That part of South Africa's 'apartheid-era' history has been well documented. What soon becomes clear was the negative effects of intensified racial discrimination on that part of society that was not white, and in particular people who had already climbed partly the way up many professional ladders. Its number included many people of Indian extraction as well as the so-called 'coloured' people. This was South Africa's multi-million-strong community of persons of mixed blood, many dating from a large body of Malay slaves who were shipped to the Cape by the Dutch[4].

Verwoerdian-style institutionalized apartheid led to South Africa being forced out of the Commonwealth of Nations as well as the breaking of many traditional ties with Britain, many of them dating back a century and a half. Pretoria was also forced to vacate its seat on the IAEA's board.

By now, the first rumblings of Southern Africa's regional wars were beginning to be heard, although the only actual clashes were in the Portuguese territories of nearby Angola and Mozambique: the Rhodesian War and the South West African/Namibian Border conflict were still some years away. By the early 1960s the South African government had made the decision to build the bomb. By then too, the southern tip of Africa had already become part of the international nuclear-weapons equation. It was an open secret that the British Government had stored nuclear ordnance in South Africa at a military facility called Kaalpan, near the town of Warrenton, which lay about fifty miles by road from the famous diamond-producing city of Kimberley in the Northern Cape.

A clearer time-frame indication might be obtained by analysing early deployments of British nuclear weapons outside the Home Islands. The first of these were shipped by Royal Navy aircraft carriers in 1960 and sent to the Royal Air Force Akrotiri Air Base in Cyprus in 1961. A year later authorisation was given to deploy British nuclear weapons to Tengah, Singapore. Others were reportedly deployed in Malaya (later Malaysia); it is a fact that nuclear-capable RAF Canberra B-15 light bombers were stationed at Tengah from 1962 onwards, and that heavy Victor and Vulcan strategic bombers started arriving there at intervals from late 1963. It is unlikely that Westminster would have deployed nuclear-capable aircraft to the other side of the globe without also making provision for their primary weapon systems to be available in reasonable proximity.

The bombs stored at Kaalpan could only have been the 20Kt/900kg Red Beard tactical nuclear gravity type, which was first delivered to the Royal Navy in 1959. Before this, the only other British-made nuclear weapons had been some twenty unwieldy 'strategic' Blue Danube bombs which could only be hauled by the RAF's V-bombers, the Valiant, Vulcan and Victor, and possibly a handful of equally unwieldy 'megaton-range' precursors to the Yellow Sun Mark-1, known as Violet Club.

Nor was South Africa the only African country to become an associate member, as it were, of the nuclear club. Kenya soon entered the picture, with Embakasi Airport – today, the Jomo Kenyatta International Airport – used as a transit-point for the movement of British nuclear weapons by air, presumably en route to the Far East. At Pelindaba a short while later, one of the buildings constructed was designed to house the research reactor that had been provided by Washington and which ran on highly enriched weapons-grade uranium, or HEU. The anti-apartheid crusade had not yet taken off and the United States was prepared to supply it on condition that Pretoria signed a safeguards agreement which allowed international inspection of the facility.

The South African government agreed, and in March 1965, SAFARI-I was commissioned. This was the HEU-fuelled, light water-cooled, beryllium-reflected reactor (the facility's rather African-sounding name was actually an acronym for 'South African Fundamental Atomic Research Installation'). Designed and fabricated by the Allis Chalmers Corporation of the United States, it went critical in March 1965 under the vigilant eye of a trilateral safeguards agreement between South Africa, the US and the IAEA.

The country had already revealed its interest in what it termed a 'peaceful' nuclear explosives programme in 1968 in its position regarding the Non-Proliferation Nuclear Weapons Treaty. A year later, the Atomic Energy Board formed an internal group to evaluate the technical and economic aspects of such explosives which might have an application in some of the exceptionally deep South African gold mines, a concept which some mining specialists believe might still be feasible.

That was followed by an address to Parliament in July 1970 by the then Prime Minister John Vorster who revealed that local scientists had developed a uranium enrichment process that he claimed was 'unique in its concept'. He gave no details, saying only that it was a remarkable system that had been developed locally. Throughout his tenure, John Vorster repeatedly emphasized what he termed the 'peaceful intentions' of South Africa's nuclear efforts and at one stage even offered to collaborate with any non-communist country in the exploitation of what was regarded as an unusually efficient scientific process. It is interesting that exactly the same noises about peace and goodwill were made by Pakistan before it detonated five atomic bombs in the late 1990s at a site at the Ras Koh Hills in Chagai, in that country's desolate south-western region and at the present time, similar reassurances are coming from the Iranians as they defy both the United Nations as well as the international community while pursuing an enrichment programme that is already producing weapons-grade uranium[5].

In South Africa, meanwhile, things were proceeding apace. In November 1970, the Uranium Enrichment Corporation of South Africa Limited – UCOR – was established and work commenced on a pilot enrichment facility called the Y-Plant at a site alongside the Atomic Energy Board's research centre at Pelindaba. This one was named Valindaba and in short term, all weaponization work linked to building the bomb was taken over by Armscor, the Armaments Corporation of South Africa. Meanwhile, with the demand for uranium from South Africa's mines remaining constant, the country's Chamber of Mines decided in 1967 to set up its own sales organization. As a result, the Atomic Energy Act of 1948 was repealed and replaced with another which restored it all to private enterprise. The Chamber of Mines also revamped its sales arm and established the Nuclear Fuels Corporation of South Africa, or NUFCOR. During the second half of the 1960s, critically important decisions were taken that would determine the type of fissile material which would ultimately be used in the country's nuclear endeavours.

During October and November 1965, uranium isotope separation had been achieved, and, as Newby-Fraser noted two years later 'the feasibility of the vortex-tube enrichment method had been demonstrated on laboratory scale…'[6] At the same time, work on the Pelinduna concept was proceeding, with an exponential assembly being followed by a critical assembly using four fuel elements of uranium enriched to two percent; the employment of this slightly enriched uranium, instead of natural uranium, enabled the number of fuel elements for the assembly to be reduced from nineteen to four. Renamed SAFARI-2 and also Pelindaba-Zero in place of the original Pelinduna 0/4, the continent's first indigenously designed and constructed reactor went critical in November 1967, its fuel and heavy water also supplied by the United States. It had a power rating of just less than 1 MWt[7].

Plans were then put in place for the construction of the 30MWt prototype Pelinduna-type reactor – also fuelled by slightly-enriched uranium, which would be used to test components for an intended 300MWe power station. During 1967 several initiatives, including Pelinduna had reached the point where the next logical step would be major research and material investment in a weapons programme. To achieve this, some serious modifications would be required for Pelinduna and almost overnight, financial considerations became a factor.

Although South Africa was wealthy by African standards, it simply did not have the resources to pursue all these projects simultaneously. The result was a decision that year to abandon Pelinduna in favour of the more economical light water reactor (LWR) technology, which also implied uranium enrichment. Until then the production of heavy water in South Africa had been a possibility mooted by several of those involved. The existing reactors were to enjoy mixed fortunes; modifications to SAFARI-1's cooling system during 1968 enabled it to operate at a power rating of 20MWt, but work on the nuclear power reactor project was terminated in 1969 and SAFARI-2 was shut down the following year.

Steyn, van der Walt and Van Loggerenberg made the point in their remarkable little book on how South Africa went about constructing their bomb. This was *Armament and Disarmament: South Africa's Nuclear Weapons Experience*, the first to appear after the A.R. Newby-Taylor report, and that part of the work, including that on sodium technology and the reactor physics of the concept, was to continue for several more years[8]. In this privately-printed publication, which ran to only a few hundred copies, the authors explained that reactor physics work in South Africa at the time focussed mainly on the critical facility based on this reactor concept. This was thought necessary to confirm development work on acquired, as well as developed, computer programmes for the reactor-physical design of the reactor.

The decision to build nuclear weapons was taken by Prime Minister John Vorster in 1974, the same year that the Portuguese dictatorship in Lisbon collapsed and which led directly to many independent black states of Africa combining their efforts in a bid to topple the governments, in what was colloquially referred to as 'the White South'. In 1978, the Y-Plant yielded its first enriched uranium and by November the following year, had delivered enough material to produce a fissile core. By then too, the AEB had completed its first device for the core, which included 120 pounds of enriched uranium. Shortly thereafter, the first of South Africa's atomic bombs, complete with 'Gun Type' nuclear warheads came off the production line. Subsequent estimates indicate that the bomb had yields that varied between 15 and about 18 kilotons, or roughly the same size as those that ended the war with Japan more than 30 years before.

There was no question that these early South African nuclear devices were clumsy and over-large, some pundits describing them as 'museum pieces'. But plans were already in hand to build smaller, more manageable weapons which could be mounted on missiles or UAVs. The prospect of eventually producing thermonuclear warheads was also mooted, but none of these projects, nor the building of more sophisticated 'Implosion' bombs, for which property had already been acquired in the Eastern Cape near the mouth of the Gouritz River, ever reached fruition.

## KEY EVENTS IN PRETORIA'S NUCLEAR WEAPONS PROGRAM

| Year | Activity |
|------|----------|
| 1950s and 1960s | Scientific work on the feasibility of peaceful nuclear explosives and support to nuclear power production efforts |
| 1969 | AEB forms group to evaluate technical and economic aspects of nuclear explosives |
| 1970 | AEC releases report identifying wide applications for nuclear explosives |
| 1971 | R&D for gun-type device approved for "peaceful use of nuclear explosives" |
| 1973 | AEC places research priority on gun-type design over implosion and boosted weapon designs |
| 1974 | PM Vorster authorizes funding for work on nuclear device and preparation of test site |
| 1977 | AEC completes assembly of nuclear device (less HEU core) for "cold test" in the Kalahari Desert<br>Soviet Union and United States detect preparations for the nuclear test and pressure South Africa into abandoning the test<br>AEC instructed to miniaturise device; groundwork laid for ARMSCOR to take program lead |
| 1978 | Y-Plant uranium enrichment facility produces first batch of HEU<br>Three-phase strategic guidelines established for nuclear deterrent policy<br>P W Botha "Action Committee" recommends arsenal of seven nuclear weapons and ARMSCOR formally assumes control of program |
| 1979 | "Double-flash" event detected; first device with HEU core produced by AEC. |
| 1982 | First deliverable device produced by ARMSCOR; work continues to improve weapon safety and reliability |
| 1985 | ARMSCOR strategy review expands original three-phase strategy to include specific criteria to transition to next deterrent phase |
| 1987 | First production model produced; total of six weapons built with a seventh under construction at program termination |
| 1988 | ARMSCOR revisits Kalahari nuclear test site and erects a large steel hangar over test shafts and prepares the shafts for a possible nuclear test.<br>Angola, Cuba and South Africa formally agree on Namibia's independence and schedule for Cuban troops to withdraw from Angola |
| 1989 | FW de Klerk elected President and orders weapon production halted |
| 1990 | Y-Plant formally shut down and nuclear weapons dismantlement begins |
| 1991 | South Africa signs the NPT and enters into a comprehensive safeguard agreement |
| 1993 | President de Klerk publicly discloses details of former South African nuclear deterrent program |

Source ISIS, Washington D.C.

What was also clear was that several of these developments fell within the ambit of the Treaty on the Non-Proliferation of Nuclear Weapons, a difficult matter for Pretoria because at the time of its adoption by the United Nations General Assembly in 1968, there had been concern that some of the required disclosures might compromise details of South Africa's gold production and uranium-extraction technology. Another concern surfaced shortly afterward, this time about the need to preserve the secrets of South Africa's uranium-enrichment technology. As a consequence, the government decided that it would not become a signatory to the treaty at that stage, ostensibly because of South Africa's purported interest in 'peaceful nuclear explosives' for the mining industry. Involvement in a possible covert nuclear weapons project was mooted, but never admitted.

With time and considerable effort, other avenues of uranium enrichment would also be investigated. Centrifuges entered the picture from the 1970s until the early 1990s, while molecular and atomic vapour laser isotope separation (MLIS and AVLIS) programmes were launched in the early 1980s.

Michael Montgomery, linked to California's Centre for Investigative Reporting, did his own take on South Africa's nuclear weapons programme on 9 April 2008 following an interview with one of the kingpins involved, Professor Andre Buys. As he stated, Andre Buys 'is a respected scientist and university professor. He's a reserved man. But his voice swells with pride as he recalls assembling a secret nuclear weapons arsenal.' He goes on, quoting Buys directly: 'technically, it was an achievement we were proud of, but we weren't sure whether having a nuclear device was going to be to our advantage or not.'

Montgomery explained that the Buys working group eventually settled on a three-phase strategy that emphasized using the bomb as a deterrent, and diplomatic cudgel, rather than for possible battlefield deployment:

'The first phase was "strategic ambiguity" – neither confirming nor denying the bomb, but holding it in reserve in case of a national emergency. Phase two would have involved privately acknowledging the bomb to western powers like Great Britain and the United States in order to win diplomatic backing in a showdown with the Soviets. The third phase, as planned by Buys' team, would have involved a public demonstration of the bomb such as a detonation over the ocean.'

Today, South Africa plays a big role in the global non-proliferation movement. But nuclear expert David Albright says lessons from the South African bomb programme are not all comforting. Albright told the Chicago Tribune:

'Even though they were complete outcasts, and even though it took them a decade of trial and error, they managed to build weapons of mass destruction with a small, inexpensive and tightly focused program.'

According to Montgomery, estimates for the total cost of the South African nuclear bomb programme range from $500 million to $1 billion (in early 1980s valuation):

'Part of the money, according to Buys, went to an international network of smugglers for technology and know-how not available on the domestic market. But Buys' team wasn't working from scratch. South Africa already had a vibrant civilian nuclear industry built from technology and know-how imported from the West a decade earlier.'

In a blog headed Arms Control Wonk (of which he is the founding publisher) Dr Jeffrey Lewis, director of the East Asia Non-proliferation Program at the James Martin Centre for Non-proliferation Studies at the Middlebury Institute of International Studies at Monterey had a few comments of his own about South Africa's nuclear weapons programme. These were contained in a review of Dr Nic von Wielligh's book *The Bomb* and some of his observations warrant repeating here. For a start, said Dr Lewis:

'South Africa's bomb was much smaller than you think. We've long known that South Africa's nuclear program used highly enriched uranium in a gun-type device, similar to the Little Boy bomb that the United States used to devastate Hiroshima. The common view from the non-governmental community has been that South Africa's bomb was bulky, more of a demonstration object than a deliverable weapon. This owes, in no small part, to the public representations of some South African officials who described it as the sort of thing one might 'kick out of the back of a plane' or as a 'bulky gun-type device that lacked neutron initiators. The dimensions of the device, as provided by Armscor *in public*, were quite rotund – 1.8 by .65 metres.'

He goes on to state that when South Africa began building operational nuclear weapons, those atom bombs were to be delivered by aircraft armed with a television-guided glide bomb called Raptor I and eventually, by a medium-range ballistic missile based on Israel's Jericho-2. Raptor I was also known as the H2 and was further developed to be marketed internationally by South Africa, where it is today known as Raptor II:

'Von Wielligh doesn't come out and say this explicitly. But he does provide the dimensions for South Africa's test devices, narrative information about how South Africa's nuclear weapons were to be delivered and the full text of many formally secret official documents in an appendix to the book. It

Yukiya Amano of Japan, Director General of Vienna's International Atomic Energy Agency. The IAEA is a United Nations body. *(Photo United Nations)*

Illustrative image of centrifuges enriching uranium. *(United States Department of Energy)*

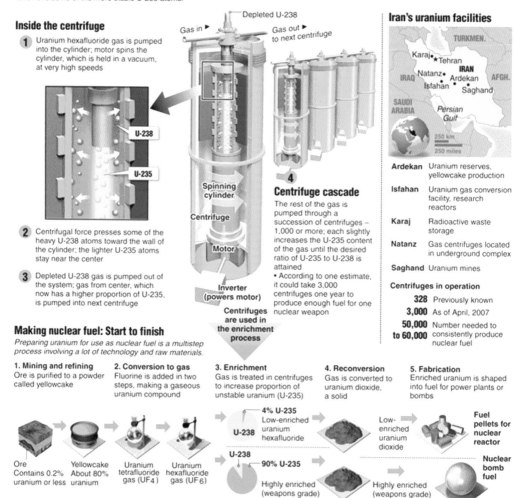

# CENTRIFUGES AND URANIUM ENRICHMENT

Less than 1 percent of naturally occurring uranium is composed of unstable U-235 atoms. To be useful as nuclear fuel, a uranium mass must have a higher percentage of these atoms. Centrifuges, large cylinders that spin rapidly, are used to remove some of the more stable U-238 atoms.

## Inside the centrifuge

1. Uranium hexafluoride gas is pumped into the cylinder; motor spins the cylinder, which is held in a vacuum, at very high speeds

U-238

U-235

2. Centrifugal force presses some of the heavy U-238 atoms toward the wall of the cylinder; the lighter U-235 atoms stay near the center

3. Depleted U-238 gas is pumped out of the system; gas from center, which now has a higher proportion of U-235, is pumped into next centrifuge

Depleted U-238
Gas in ►
Gas out ► to next centrifuge

Spinning cylinder
Centrifuge
Motor
Inverter (powers motor)
Centrifuges are used in the enrichment process

## 4. Centrifuge cascade

The rest of the gas is pumped through a succession of centrifuges – 1,000 or more; each slightly increases the U-235 content of the gas until the desired ratio of U-235 to U-238 is attained

- According to one estimate, it could take 3,000 centrifuges one year to produce enough fuel for one nuclear weapon

## Iran's uranium facilities

TURKMEN.
Karaj • ★ Tehran
IRAN
Natanz • Ardekan
IRAQ
Isfahan • Saghand
AFGH.
SAUDI ARABIA
Persian Gulf
250 km
250 miles

| | |
|---|---|
| Ardekan | Uranium reserves, yellowcake production |
| Isfahan | Uranium gas conversion facility, research reactors |
| Karaj | Radioactive waste storage |
| Natanz | Gas centrifuges located in underground complex |
| Saghand | Uranium mines |

**Centrifuges in operation**

| | |
|---|---|
| 328 | Previously known |
| 3,000 | As of April, 2007 |
| 50,000 to 60,000 | Number needed to consistently produce nuclear fuel |

## Making nuclear fuel: Start to finish

*Preparing uranium for use as nuclear fuel is a multistep process involving a lot of technology and raw materials.*

**1. Mining and refining**
Ore is purified to a powder called yellowcake

**2. Conversion to gas**
Fluorine is added in two steps, making a gaseous uranium compound

**3. Enrichment**
Gas is treated in centrifuges to increase proportion of unstable uranium (U-235)

**4. Reconversion**
Gas is converted to uranium dioxide, a solid

**5. Fabrication**
Enriched uranium is shaped into fuel for power plants or bombs

Ore
Contains 0.2% uranium or less

Yellowcake
About 80% uranium

Uranium tetrafluoride gas (UF4)

Uranium hexafluoride gas (UF6)

U-238

4% U-235
Low-enriched uranium hexafluoride

U-238
90% U-235
Highly enriched (weapons grade) uranium hexafluoride

Low-enriched uranium dioxide

Highly enriched (weapons grade) uranium dioxide

Fuel pellets for nuclear reactor

Nuclear bomb fuel

Source: U.S. Nuclear Regulatory Agency; U.S. Dept. of Energy; USEC Inc.; Uranium Information Center (Australia); Encyclopaedia Britannica; Reuters; CNN; Global Security.org; South Florida Sun-Sentinel; AP

© 2007 MCT

Above: The extremely complex uranium enrichment process used by many nations - past and present - to acquire highly enriched uranium for the core of an atom bomb.
*(Photo sourced to Washington's Institute for Science and International Security – otherwise referred to as 'The good ISIS')*

Chemical, biologal and nuclear weapons of mass destruction symbols.

Scientists inspecting Iraq's first nuclear reactor in Baghdad, supplied by the Soviets, February 1968. *(Photo United States DoE)*

Soviet Scud missile captured in Israeli cross border strike into Syria and partly disassembled at the Hanford Nuclear Facility, Washington State. *(Photo Al J. Venter)*

Secrets of Israel's nuclear arsenal – Front Cover of *The Times*, London which exposed everything.

Map showing route taken during course of the historic June 1981 Israeli air attack of Syria's controversial Osiraq nuclear facility.

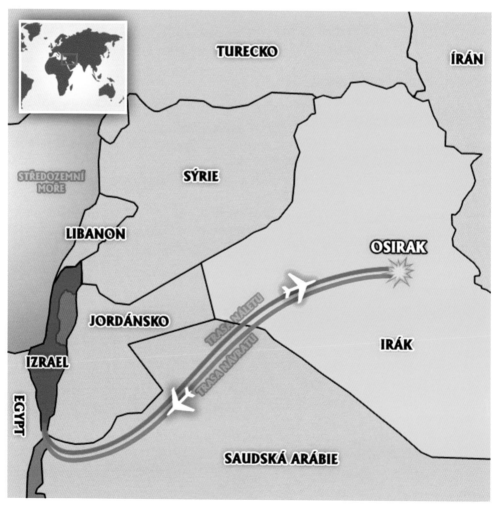

In Tokyo rescue workers take part in a 2008 trial to improve the city's response to a dirty bomb attack. *(Japanese Government photo)*

Timeline of Iraq's 1981 nuclear reactor programme.

# Bombing of Iraqi Reactor (1981)

**Osirak nuclear reactor after Israeli attack**

*"With thanks and appreciation for the outstanding job you did on the Iraqi nuclear program in 1981, which made our job much easier in Desert Storm!"* – inscription on photo of destroyed Osirak reactor given by US Sec. of Defense Cheney to IAF Commander Ivry, who led the strike on Osirak (Jun 1991)

▶ In 1970's, Iraq begins building "Osirak" nuclear reactor with French & Italian support; Israel fails to convince France & Italy to cease their assistance

▶ Mossad bombs reactor structures in France prior to being shipped (Apr 1979) and assassinates Egyptian scientist working on reactor (Jun 1980)

▶ Upon receiving intelligence that reactor would soon become operational, PM Begin orders attack despite considerable opposition within Israeli gov't and IDF

▶ 14 Israeli aircraft fly over Jordanian, Saudi and Iraqi airspace, completely destroy reactor, and return safely to Israel (Jun 7, 1981)

▶ UN Security Council unanimously passes anti-Israel resolution; Thatcher and Reagan administrations strongly condemn Israel

ق - معسكر أشبال الزرقاوي    الدّولة الإسلاميّة في العراق والشّام

Islamic State promised to develop chemical and biological weapons which this terror group would disperse across many Western nations. *(ISIS photo)*

Syrian nuclear installation at al-Kibar prior to the 2005 Israeli air strike.
*(Photo ISIS Washington)*

Satellite view of al-Kibar after the Iraqi nuclear facility built with North Korean help had been levelled by Israeli jets. *(Photo ISIS Washington)*

# DIRTY BOMB OR RADIOLOGICAL DISPERSAL DEVICE

### What is a dirty bomb?

A dirty bomb is a mix of explosives, such as dynamite, and radioactive powder or pellets. It is also known as a radiological dispersal device (RDD).

A dirty bomb cannot create an atomic blast.

RADIOACTIVE MATERIAL

When the bomb explodes, the blast carries radioactive material into the surrounding area.

### What are the dangers from a dirty bomb?

The main danger from a dirty bomb comes from the explosion, not the radiation. The explosion can cause serious injuries and property damage. People nearby could be injured by pieces of radioactive material from the bomb. Only people who are very close to the blast site would be exposed to enough radiation to cause immediate serious illness. However, the radioactive dust and smoke can spread farther away and could be dangerous to health if people breathe in the dust, eat contaminated food, or drink contaminated water. People injured by radioactive pieces or contaminated with radioactive dust will need medical attention.

### What should I do to protect myself?

GET INSIDE

STAY INSIDE

STAY TUNED

U.S. Department of Health and Human Services
Centers for Disease Control and Prevention

http://emergency.cdc.gov/radiation

Details about Radiological Dispersal Devices or Dirty Bombs.

Beale Air Force Base simulation of a terror weapon which could also be an RDD.
*(Photo US Department of Defense)*

Billet of highly enriched uranium recovered from scrap processed at the United States Y-12 National Security Complex.
*(US Government photo)*

Radioactive Cobalt-60 container recovered by authorities at Hueypoxtla near Mexico City after it had been stolen. *(Wiki photo)*

Recent inspection of Iran's nuclear plant by officials of the International Atomic Energy Agency. *(IAEA photo)*

Israeli Air Force F-16D fighter bombers deployed in the raid on Syria's purported nuclear facility at al-Kibar. *(Israeli Air Force photo)*

Internationally recognised radiation symbol.

United States spy satellites unveiled high-resolution images showing the deployment of Russian nuclear-capable ballistic missiles in Syria

2 Iskandar vehicles

Mordechai Vanunu who originally leaked details of the Israeli nuclear weapons programme to the London Times speaks to the media at the Jerusalem Magistrate's Court, 10 September 2015. *(Photo Times of Israel)*

A Mark-28 thermonuclear bomb is unloaded from a USAF B-52H Stratofortress bomber during Exercise Global Shield in 1984. *(US Air Force photo)*

Poland's Poznan law enforcement authorities released this photograph of a canister similar to ones stolen from a Russian nuclear facility and seized at the border.

## Table 2. Radiation Zones and Suggested Activities for Each Zone During the First 12 Hours

| Decision Exposure Rate mR/hr | Radiation Zones mR/hr | Activities | Total Accumulated Stay Time for First 12 Hrs * |
|---|---|---|---|
| Background | Uncontrolled | No restrictions. The best location for Incident Command and decontamination activities. | Unlimited |
| < 10 | Low-Radiation Zone < 10 -100 | If feasible, restrict access to essential individuals. Initial decontamination of first responders should occur near the outer boundary of this area. Uninjured personnel within this zone at the time of the RDD explosion can be directed to proceed directly home to shower if resources do not permit contamination surveying at the scene. (For RDDs containing up to ~1000 Ci, this may be the only zone that exists.) | Full 12 Hours |
| 100 | Medium-Radiation Zone 100-1000 | Restrict access to only authorized personnel. Personal dosimetry should be worn. Serves as a buffer zone/transition area between the high and low radiation zones. People within this zone at the time of the explosion should be surveyed for contamination before being released. (For RDDs up to ~ 10,000 Ci, this may be the highest radiation zone that exists.) | 5 - 12 Hrs (12 Hrs for critical property and lifesaving activities) |
| 1000 | High-Radiation Zone 1000 - <10,000 | Restrict access to authorized personnel with specific critical tasks such as firefighting, medical assistance, rescue, extrication, and other time- sensitive activities. Personal dosimetry should be worn. People within this zone at the time of the explosion should be surveyed for contamination before being released. | 30 minutes – 5 Hours |
| 10,000 | Extreme Caution Zone ≥ 10,000 | This area, located within the high radiation zone, is restricted to the most critical activities, such as lifesaving. Personal dosimetry required, although one monitor for several responders is acceptable if they remain near the person with the monitor. Limit time spent in this area to avoid Acute Radiation Sickness. People within this zone at the time of the explosion must be surveyed for contamination before being released. | Minutes to a few hours |

Radiation zone – Suggested activities for those caught up in such a disaster in the vital first twelve hours after a nuclear strike.

Former Iranian President Mahmoud Ahmadinejad during a visit to the country's ultra secret Natanz nuclear enrichment facility.
*(Photo Washington's Institute for Science and International Security)*

Dismantling of former Soviet nuclear submarine at Russia's northern naval base near Murmansk. Security measures for many years after the collapse of the Soviet Union were lax, resulting in thefts of nuclear fuel cells. *(Photo http://russianforces.org/navy/)*

David Albright, founder and head of Washington's Institute for Science and International Security. *(Photo ISIS)*

South Africa's strategically located atom bomb storage shelters near Pretoria which once held six of these nuclear bombs. *(Photo David Albright)*

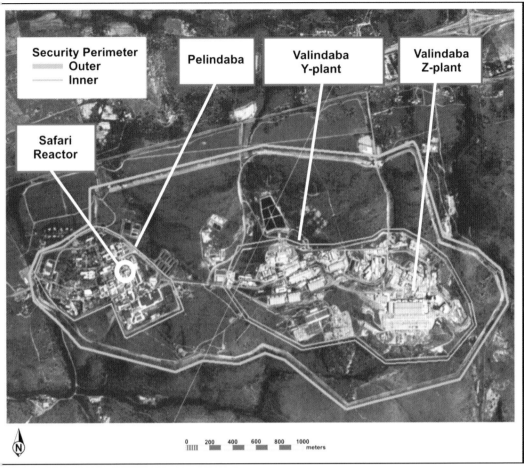

Aerial view of South Africa's nuclear facility at Pelindaba, on the outskirts of Pretoria.
*(Photo David Albright, ISIS)*

Panoramic view of South Africa's nuclear facility at Pelindaba. *(Photo Pierre Lowe Victor)*

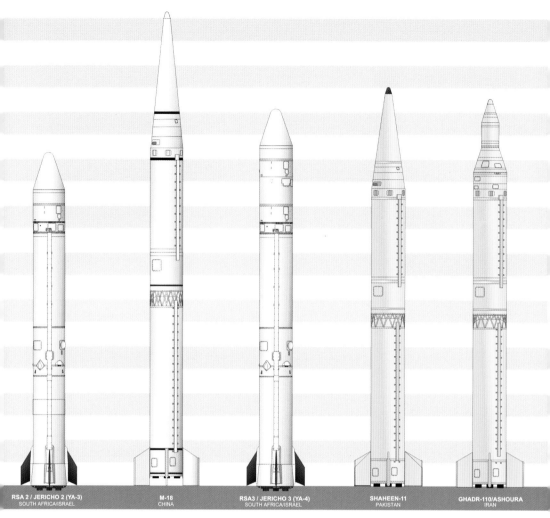

| RSA 2 / JERICHO 2 (YA-3)<br>SOUTH AFRICA/ISRAEL | M-18<br>CHINA | RSA3 / JERICHO 3 (YA-4)<br>SOUTH AFRICA/ISRAEL | SHAHEEN-11<br>PAKISTAN | GHADR-110/ASHOURA<br>IRAN |

Israeli, South African and Iranian medium range intercontinental ballistic missiles compared. Much of what South Africa produced in this field ended up in Iran, courtesy of the African National Congress. *(Graphic courtesy of Charles Vick, formerly senior fellow with GlobalSecurity.org Washington)*

Arab leaders who enthused about acquring nuclear expertise half a century ago - Egypt's President Nasser on the right and Algeria's Boumeiddin far left.

## Third stage AKM.

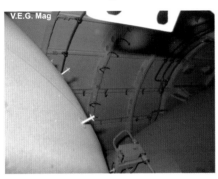

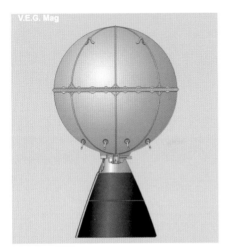

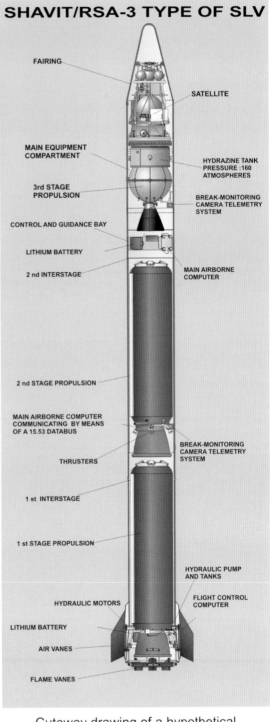

**SHAVIT/RSA-3 TYPE OF SLV**

- FAIRING
- SATELLITE
- MAIN EQUIPMENT COMPARTMENT
- HYDRAZINE TANK PRESSURE :160 ATMOSPHERES
- 3rd STAGE PROPULSION
- BREAK-MONITORING CAMERA TELEMETRY SYSTEM
- CONTROL AND GUIDANCE BAY
- LITHIUM BATTERY
- MAIN AIRBORNE COMPUTER
- 2 nd INTERSTAGE
- 2 nd STAGE PROPULSION
- MAIN AIRBORNE COMPUTER COMMUNICATING BY MEANS OF A 15.53 DATABUS
- BREAK-MONITORING CAMERA TELEMETRY SYSTEM
- THRUSTERS
- 1 st INTERSTAGE
- 1 st STAGE PROPULSION
- HYDRAULIC PUMP AND TANKS
- FLIGHT CONTROL COMPUTER
- HYDRAULIC MOTORS
- LITHIUM BATTERY
- AIR VANES
- FLAME VANES

Cutaway drawing of a hypothetical
Shavit/RSA 3 – type SLV.

Cooperation between Jerusalem and Pretoria during the apartheid era produced this medium range ballistic weapon, named Shavit in Israel and RSA-3 in South Africa.
*(Image sourced to Pierre Lowe Victor)*

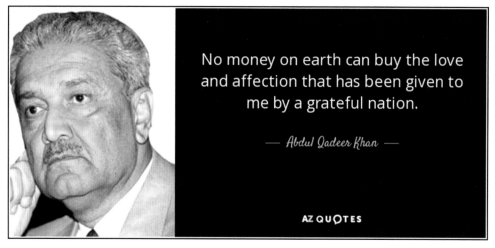

The Pakistani nuclear proliferator A.Q. Khan. The damage he caused to international security is inestimable.

A public poster which depicts North Korea's potential missile threat.

A bunch of nuclear submarines left to rust at Russia's Pavlovskoye Submarine Base.
*(Wiki photo source)*

Libya's dictator Muammar Gaddafi shortly before he was murdered. In his day he aspired to acquire nuclear, chemical as well as biological weapons of war .
*(Source al Anya Libya)*

Military parade through North Korea's capital in 2012 included a range of increasingly sophisticated ballistic missiles. *(Official North Korean Photo)*

Radioactive contamination drill in Japan, a country which takes such matters extremely seriously. *(Japanese Government photo)*

More than 1,300 Syrians – the majority women and children – died in this chemical weapons attack launched by President Assad's warplanes. *(UN photo)*

A chemical weapons installation in Libya – ultimately destroyed by NATO. A lot of this expertise came from South Africa after the ANC took over in Pretoria. *(Photo from NATO HQ)*

Bodies of children killed in a government launched chemical attack on Ghouta, a Syrian town in the north.

Idlib twins, killed in a nerve gas attack in Syria on 4 April 2017, with their father Abdul-Hamid Alyousef.

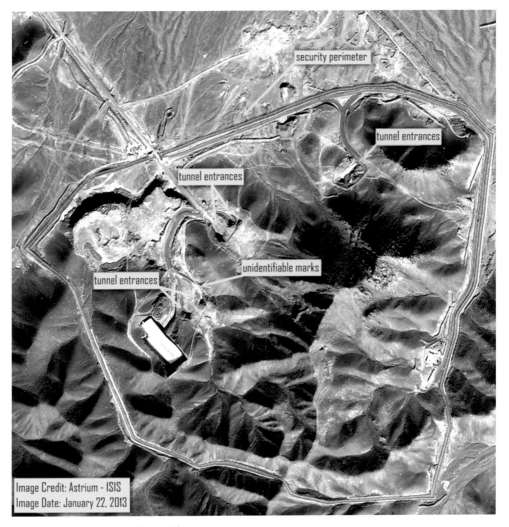

Iran's Fordow Fuel Enrichmen Plant. *ISIS Washington DC*

K-25 Oak Ridge nuclear installation, once the largest building in the world.

One of Saddam Hussein's uranium calutrons, destroyed by the UN after it had been discovered.

Destroyed: Saddam Hussein's Tammuz-2 reactor building located in the centre background next to the narrow smokestack. *Photo courtesy of the IAEA*

took me a little while to put two and two together, but then I realized what he was saying. Since then, I've confirmed that this understanding of von Wielligh's book is correct.'

He explains too that South Africa's Armscor built the country's first operational weapon, code-named Hobo (and later Cabot) in 1982 and that this device also had a yield of six kilotons.

'Armscor then built a series of pre-production and production models under the code-name HAMERKOP. HAMERKOP is an awesome code name. It's a bird – according to a 19th century anthropologist, the locals said that when a HAMERKOP appears overhead and cries, someone has died. I don't know if the lore was reported correctly, but it makes a pretty fine code-name for a nuclear weapon. While Hobo/Cabot was a 'dumb bomb,' the HAMERKOP series were 'smart' television-guided glide bombs...

'I have a sneaking suspicion that the 'H' in H2 is for HAMERKOP. (*Jane's* reported it as "Hammerhead", which is pretty close). It was also referred to as Project Hanto. Ultimately, South Africa built five HAMERKOP devices. Based on public information released by South Africa, a nuclear weapon that could fit inside the H2 glide bomb could be *no more* than 1.67 x 0.38 metres Total mass would be around 600 kg and this device had a yield of twenty kilotons.'

At the time that Pretoria made the decision to abandon its nuclear weapons programme, the South African bomb was already small enough to arm both the H2 and South Africa's ballistic missile under development. And, perhaps not all that surprisingly, some rather significant remnants of this programme showed up on the market for export to places like Pakistan.

*Chapter 11*

# Why South Africa Built the Bomb

*'...the case of South Africa, which developed a relatively
small nuclear weaponization programme, showed the
rudimentary facilities needed to make 'Gun–Type' nuclear
weapons. A terrorist group would need only a subset of these
facilities to accomplish its goals.'*

*David Albright, President of Washington's Institute for
Science and International Security (ISIS)*

It was an open secret for many years towards the end of the last century
that South Africa had built the bomb; six of them. Washington knew that
like Israel, South Africa had a modest nuclear arsenal, though obviously
not nearly as extensive as that of the Jewish State. London was also aware of
these developments, though Britain's Secret Intelligence Service (MI6) was
never able to penetrate the darker domains of South Africa's weapons of mass
destruction programmes before the ANC took over. The United States fared
little better.[1]

Moscow probably knew a lot more about Pretoria's nuclear strides before
the others, because the Soviet Union enjoyed the confidence of Commodore
Dieter Gerhardt. For more than twenty years this extremely well-placed South
African Navy officer of German extraction was a KGB operative and as we were
all to discover afterwards, his tentacles extended well into the inner realms of
the apartheid-orientated military system.

It was to his country's atom bombs that President F.W. de Klerk gave his
immediate attention after he had unceremoniously ousted his predecessor
President P.W. Botha. Within weeks of taking office in the Union Buildings,
he ordered all nuclear weapons work be halted. Concurrently, he advised the
Americans and the British as well as the International Atomic Energy Agency
not only that South Africa had built six atom bombs but that he needed their
help to dismantle them, (See Chapter Twelve).

For the West – as well as for all of Africa – this was a remarkable coup. Not only did it remove from the international strategic equation one of the major Third World nuclear mavericks, but de Klerk also offered all the assistance that might be needed to achieve that aim. Also, he insisted that this be accomplished before he handed power to Nelson Mandela's African National Congress. With close ties to the Former Soviet Union, the objectives of the ANC had always been suspect and once the facts were known, the bomb issue became the subject of much conjecture in the West. Langley felt as strongly as London's Vauxhall Bridge that the nuclear arsenal still in its underground bunker at Kentron Circle on the outskirts of Pretoria be neutralized before one of the Kremlin's most outspoken allies in Africa assumed power at the southern tip of the continent.

One of the more interesting conjectures that was to emerge subsequently is that had Pretoria demanded $10 billion – or possibly two or three times as much – for its nuclear arsenal, together with everything that went with it, the West would have coughed up, and probably done so willingly. Instead, President de Klerk demanded not a penny.

Once the decision had been made, a large party of international scientists, physicists, military and intelligence personnel as well as IAEA weapons inspectors descended on South Africa's nuclear installations; they set to work evaluating that country's nuclear expertise while the weapons were being disassembled. An imposing complex in its day, Pelindaba and its ancillary nuclear sites for many years was the single largest nuclear facility in Africa and in the Southern Hemisphere. Considerable effort went into examining all details related to the South African fissile programme and it took the specialists almost 18 months to reach a consensus that the amount of uranium that Pretoria claimed it had enriched actually tallied – within a few kilos – with what finally emerged in the enrichment process. There were many thousands of details that needed to be corroborated and in the end, they were.

All files, documents, blueprints, diagrams and ancillary data linked to the bomb project were either destroyed by the South Africans (in the presence of IAEA inspectors) or handed over to officials handling the dismantling process: President F.W. de Klerk eventually gave his personal assurance that nothing had been held back. The last thing the new South African political dispensation needed was that one of the proliferating right wing organizations might acquire one of these weapons of mass destruction and possibly use it in a racial terror strike at a later date.

There was a huge amount of good faith at stake, to the extent that both former President de Klerk and the newly-inducted President Nelson Mandela were awarded the Nobel Peace Prize for their joint efforts. Against all odds, these two diverse characters, the one white and in his day, an avowed disciple of apartheid and the other, a committed radical black revolutionary who had been imprisoned for decades brought stability to what was potentially one of the most volatile countries in Africa.

Just about everything went to plan. While the international community came to embrace South Africa as the only country in the world to have voluntarily demolished its nuclear weapons programme, it emerged early in the New Millennium that somewhere in South Africa, somebody had kept back a set of the blueprints which might be used at some future date to build the bomb. Worse, they were in the hands of the new black government, the African National Congress. Because of ongoing security controls in the media relating to everything linked to weapons of mass destruction, very little publicity was given to this disclosure at the time in South Africa. What emerged, followed a meeting arranged by South Africa's KGB-trained Intelligence 'Supremo' Ronnie Kasrils, one of President Thabo Mbeki's top ministers; Mbeki by then had succeeded the venerable Nelson Mandela.

Kasrils, Jewish by birth but vituperatively anti-Israeli, gathered together a bunch of his intelligence operatives who were addressed by Professor Renfrew Christie, dean of research at the University of the Western Cape. South Africa being a virtual one-party state, the head of the country's intelligence services would almost certainly have needed a nod from his boss to have been able to have done that. It came as no surprise then that Christie – an academic who had been jailed by the Apartheid regime – warned of possible future wars in Africa and what astounded everybody at the gathering was that he went on to suggest that the country should again look at possibly building the bomb. The thrust of his argument was that South Africa needed to 'quickly be able to revert to a nuclear weapons state if it became vital to the country's interests'.

The professor noted that South Africa still legally retained a stockpile of weapons grade highly enriched uranium derived from the country's former nuclear weapons programme. He also reminded everyone present that technical knowledge of South Africa's former atomic bombs was available, 'contained on a bunch of CDs held by the ruling ANC government'. 'The presentation was greeted with loud applause from the intelligence community,' reported Cape Town's *Weekend Argus.*

Is it not ironic therefore, that the presentation came as Abdul Minty, South Africa's Special Representative on Disarmament, was busy chairing the fiftieth session of the International Atomic Energy Agency in Vienna? That was followed by the incumbent South African Minister of Minerals and Energy declaring that South Africa strongly supported the Convention on Nuclear Safety. She called on nuclear-weapon states to reaffirm their commitments and undertakings to systematically and progressively eliminate their nuclear weapon arsenals.

As somebody else commented, perhaps a little wryly, *c'est l'Afrique…*

History has never been kind to Africa, especially when the continent has been desecrated by the fanciful whims of others, as was the very human tragedy orchestrated by Belgium's King Leopold in the Congo which he ended up colonizing as his personal fief in the last quarter of the nineteenth century. In the strictest sense, Joseph Conrad's *Heart of Darkness* was certainly no work of fiction. His observations in that book incorporated just about everything he had personally either seen or experienced on a trip up the Congo River and he was appalled by what the Congolese people were subjected to by their European colonial overlords. The brutality he witnessed was often cruel and mindless; people could be executed for real or imagined sedition, or a man's hand sliced off for not paying so-called 'government taxes'.

In the British and French African colonies that came later, the people fared a good deal better, even though there are those that will dispute that the creation of ordered societies in places like the Gold Coast (Ghana today), Senegal, Kenya, the Cameroons or Nigeria – coupled to the inexorable spread of commerce, industry, roads, railways and ports on what until then had been a largely primitive continent - ultimately did more harm than good. In this regard, it is interesting that during British Nigeria's 'Imperial Period' the Northern Region was largely left to govern itself – a legacy of what in its day was termed Lord Lugard's 'Indirect Rule'. Effectively, the Islamic Faith was held in great respect by London and the British never meddled with it. France, too, played a largely paternal role in Equatorial Africa, though the object of these colonial exercises in both London and Paris was clearly for the exploitation of natural resources. This was very much along the lines of China's role on the 'Dark Continent' today, exploiting Africa's enormous natural resources.

Where Africa did suffer serious harm was when France conducted seventeen atmospheric tests in the Sahara in the 1960s, all under the auspices of what was referred to as the *Centre Saharien d'Expérimentations Militaires* (Military Experiments Saharan Centre). The first explosion took place about forty kilometres from the military base of Reggane, the last town on the Tanezrouft Track which heads south across this vast desert region to Mali, almost 700 kilometres from the town of Colomb-Bechar in Algeria. That series of nuclear tests was not inspired or affected by the bloody Algerian insurgency then unfolding along Algeria's Mediterranean Coast, and while these efforts are still regarded as unconscionable, it could have been a lot worse. France conducted more than 200 nuclear tests, the majority in its Pacific theatre of influence.

South Africa's nuclear weapons programme of the 1970s and 1980s was a different story. It sprang from a perceived strategic and tactical necessity, and its aim was not to gather scientific knowledge but to build a clutch of operational nuclear weapons as expeditiously as possible. The objective in building A-Bombs was to counter what was perceived in Pretoria as a serious military threat from surrogate forces linked to the Soviet Union and Cuba and comprising a huge conventional army then actively fighting in Angola. As such, South Africa's nuclear potential, if tactically employed, would almost certainly have resulted in chaos far beyond the frontiers of the African continent itself.

Castigated internationally for their racial policies and subject to a range of arms and economic sanctions, the South Africans nevertheless built their atomic bombs in the comparatively short time of six years, an indication of how difficult it is to prevent an industrialized or even a reasonably well-developed country from arming itself, particularly if it has willing collaborators to help it do so.

What is indisputable is that there was nothing theoretical about South Africa's weapons of mass destruction programmes, chemical and biological included. Pretoria not only built a nuclear arsenal, but towards the end of white rule on the sub-continent, they reached a point where they might have been able to deliver the bombs to any given target within a range of perhaps 3,500 kilometres. This would have been accomplished either with South African Air Force British-built Buccaneer strike aircraft or, as we saw in the previous chapter, by laser-guided smart bombs or even by means of the most sophisticated medium-to-long range ballistic missile project ever undertaken on African soil.

Also nearing completion at the time was an unmanned aerial vehicle the SKUA, which had all the makings of a long-range South African cruise missile and which would have been able to carry a miniaturized version of the bomb. Built by Kentron, one of the better-known arms manufacturers in South Africa, the SKUA survived the ANC takeover and this UAV subsequently went into limited production.

Another who has carefully monitored South African developments over several decades includes David Albright, who is among the most intrusive of research specialists in the West[2]. The Washington-based ISIS website contains numerous entries on South Africa, including some of the first photos of the nuclear bunkers where the bombs were stored. But neither Albright nor any of his opposite numbers at similar think-tanks in the United States and abroad have been able to decide conclusively whether South Africa actually detonated a nuclear device. There are many theories and numerous conjectures but so far, no smoking gun, though I am convinced, despite the views of other, more distant authorities, that none of those devices were ever live-tested.

One person who reached a conclusion of his own was a retired Central Intelligence Agency clandestine service officer named Tyler Drumheller. In 2006, this former Langley operative published a book entitled *On the Brink* which includes details about his South African tour of duty between 1983 and 1985. He wrote[3]:

'We had operational successes, most importantly regarding Pretoria's nuclear capability. My sources collectively provided incontrovertible evidence that the apartheid government had in fact tested a nuclear bomb in the South Atlantic in 1979, and that they had developed a delivery system with assistance from the Israelis.'

This is not altogether surprising, nor is it implausible. Even today, in spite of decades of government mismanagement and corruption on an almost biblical scale under the ANC, South Africa ranks as the most developed country on the continent. More to the point, the country has an abundance of natural resources, uranium included. Indeed, South Africa seems always to have been blessed with a talented and diverse scientific and academic corps, the majority working in tandem with a huge industrial base.

While work on the nuclear programme had already started some years before, issues came to a head at the end of the 1970s when the Rhodesian government finally succumbed and South Africa lost a small but important military ally that had been 'holding the fort' on its northern frontier. Matters were further compounded as the quasi-military social struggle on the domestic front steadily escalated – particularly following widespread unrest in Johannesburg's Soweto black township complex in and after July 1976. This was coupled to a marked expansion of clandestine activities by the banned African National Congress. The government responded with intensified repressive measures, which generated more violence and unrest.

Looming over everything was the recent American military disaster in Vietnam, the effect of which was to foster a determination in governing circles in Pretoria that the same would not be allowed to happen in Southern Africa. It is not surprising, therefore, that a deep-rooted paranoia began to develop about what local political leaders referred to as a 'Total Onslaught' syndrome that involved both external attack and an escalating level of internal subversion, a ghastly prospect which demanded a 'Total Strategy'. Almost inevitably this gave the fillip required for South Africa to develop and build nuclear weapons as quickly as possible. As it happened, common sense did ultimately prevail, though it took quite a few years. Sensing a potential nuclear threat as a consequence of the war in Angola, Washington went to inordinate lengths to neutralize the Angolan threat and bring all the participants to the negotiating table. Former President FW de Klerk's efforts at trying to limit this gathering maelstrom, was transmogrified into the other half of this convoluted anagram.

One of South Africa's major assets has always been its strong pool of independently-minded educated specialists, including business men and women, industrialists, manufacturers, entrepreneurs and of course, a huge body of medical personnel, some of whom can be found in almost any major hospital in the world today. Like their American, Canadian, Australian and New Zealand counterparts, the majority have consistently displayed fine pioneering talents, in part because the country's educational system – for the whites, at least – has always been, as the saying goes, top drawer.[4]

The classical example remains Field-Marshal Jan Christiaan Smuts, a barefoot farmer's son who became one of the leading legal minds of his day and ran British forces ragged in the Second Anglo-Boer War after turning himself into a gifted fighting soldier. Little more than a decade later, he became a leading politician, not only in his own country but internationally. During the First World War of the early twentieth century he temporarily set aside his duties as a cabinet minister to lead operations against the Germans in East Africa before being summoned from the field to serve in the Imperial War Cabinet in London, where, among a host of other tasks, he helped to create the Royal Air Force. By the end of the Second World War, he was a member of Churchill's War Cabinet after which he went on to write the preamble to the Charter of the United Nations (as he had done almost thirty years before with the League of Nations).

Many of his countrymen emulated Smuts' hard-driving passion for excellence, although a lot of them ended up abroad for reasons ranging from political objections over the country's racially-imbued politics to lack of specialist opportunity. A classic example here was Dr Raymond Hoffenburg who left South Africa in the 1960s to settle in Britain through his obdurate opposition to apartheid. For his adopted country, this remarkable academic became an asset of considerable note, ending up a Knight of the Realm and President of the Royal College of Physicians.

An earlier member of South Africa's scientific Diaspora – and also one of the world's nuclear pioneers – was Sir Basil Schonland, who too was knighted and became director of Britain's Atomic Energy Research Establishment at Harwell before going on to become Director of the Research group as well as the newly created British Atomic Energy Authority. He was raised in the small university town of Grahamstown, studied at Cambridge's Gonville and Caius Colleges before joining the British Army during the First World War. By the time hostilities ended, he had been wounded in action at Arras and twice Mentioned in Despatches. His introduction to nuclear research started in his student days at the Cavendish Laboratory, which was among the first to conduct research into the splitting of the atom; as early as 1911 New Zealand-born Sir Ernest

Rutherford had shown that by far the major part of an atom's mass was contained in a very small nucleus at its core. This nucleus was made up of protons, which were surrounded by a web of whirring electrons. On the outbreak of the Second World War, Schonland began working on radar. He returned to England and was recruited by Sir John Cockcroft to be Director of the Army Operational Research Group of the Air Defence Research and Development Establishment at Richmond, Surrey, and in 1944, became Scientific Adviser to General – later Field-Marshal – Bernard Montgomery with the 21st Army Group in Britain, France and Belgium.

The cumulative result of the scientific moving abroad of large numbers of highly qualified South African individuals to gain British, European and American expertise, was that when serious nuclear research started in South Africa – less than two decades after the Second World War – there was no dearth of scientific minds that were extremely well-versed in the most advanced academic disciplines. Consequently, when the South African government tasked its small group of selected specialists to produce the country's first nuclear device, they did so in less than half the time it took Pakistan to accomplish the same goal many years later, and *without* the help of China.

The South African nuclear weapons project was a good deal more sophisticated than some of its critics allow credit for. It was also an example for others to follow, because, as one British observer noted: 'If a relatively small country like South Africa could do it, then so can others.' In David Albright's ISIS postings on the South African nuclear effort, one of these reports written by himself and his former deputy Corey Hinderstein (who has since moved on to become Director of Special Projects, International Program at the Nuclear Threat Initiative) explained that South Africa's first efforts to research and develop 'Gun-Type' nuclear weapons were conducted in a small building under tight security at a propulsion laboratory at the Somchem establishment in the Cape Province.

They go on:

'At that time, Somchem was a military facility involved in the development and manufacture of explosives and propellants. At Somchem, South Africans worked on the mechanical and pyrotechnic subsystems for this relatively simple nuclear device. The team designed a scale model which – with a projectile constructed of non-nuclear material – was tested at this facility near Cape Town in May 1974. It demonstrated that a nuclear explosive was feasible.

'The team working there tested the first full-scale model of the device using a natural uranium projectile in 1976. This proved the mechanical integrity of the design.

'Soon afterward, construction started on a series of buildings in a valley in the south-western section of the Pelindaba nuclear research site to the west of Pretoria. These nondescript facilities were isolated from the main site and while all effort was focused on making 'Gun-Type' devices, some of the scientists also studied the 'Implosion' system of nuclear weapons.'

Together, with a series of photos, Albright and Hinderstein explain that the main weaponization facilities included a pulse reactor for the experimental verification of theoretical computer models in what was generally referred to as Building 5000. In 1979, the reactor was used as a fast critical assembly in an experiment which was to prove the design of the bomb. The adjacent Building 5100 contained the control room, offices, research and development laboratories and facilities for machining uranium metal.

They also elaborate on Building 5200, arguably one of the most interesting structures in the complex. This building housed a critical facility to verify separately the multiplication factors of the two parts of a nuclear explosive device. The bottom line there was that it provided the confidence that South Africa's bomb design would actually work:

'Building 5300 was designed exclusively as a laboratory for high explosives. In the early stage of this nuclear work, small quantities of high explosives were pressed and machined into shapes at this facility. In order to develop a rudimentary, working fissile device, a terrorist group would need fairly sophisticated test facilities like those developed by the South Africans, and also have to acquire a fairly substantial amount of highly enriched uranium to fuel the nuclear explosion.'

At this point it is necessary to explain in the simplest terms what an atom bomb is all about. It is actually quite simple because there are two basic types: the 'Gun Type' on which South Africa hedged its bets and which, as we have seen, was identical to the bomb dubbed 'Little Boy', dropped on Hiroshima. There is also the more complex 'Implosion' weapon used at Nagasaki, named 'Fat Man'.

To be more specific, the first method got its name from the 'gun' barrel ('cannon' in the Soviet idiom), a method advocated by physicists from the start of the atomic age and which works like this:

At one end of the barrel is a sub-critical chunk of $^{235}U$, or uranium-235 – usually referred to as the 'projectile' or 'bullet'. At the other end, as can be seen in the accompanying sketch – is another larger piece of sub-critical $^{235}U$, referred to as the 'target'.

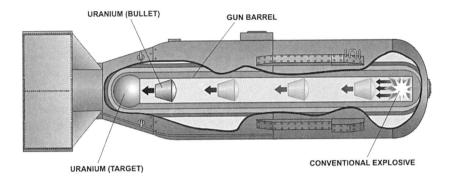

URANIUM (BULLET)        GUN BARREL

URANIUM (TARGET)        CONVENTIONAL EXPLOSIVE

South Africa built six of these atom bombs, similar to 'Little Boy' dropped by the Americans on Hiroshima

The purpose is to bring together or 'assemble' these two pieces of uranium, using a conventional explosive charge to fire the projectile down the barrel into the target in order to form a critical mass. This has to be achieved at exactly the right speed. Too slow and the two pieces will prematurely interact before the complete critical mass is fully 'assembled', a *sine qua non* in order to sustain a chain reaction. Should this take place, it could lead to a pre-detonation and result in a less powerful explosion than planned, something which seems to have bugged several North Korean nuclear tests.

In contrast, if all goes according to plan, the projectile will strike the intended target at the other end of the barrel and break the beryllium-polonium neutron source located in a recess in its centre. A flood of neutrons will then be released, initiating a chain reaction. Materials such as boron or tungsten which surround the target will reflect escaping neutrons back into the now chain-reacting $^{235}U$, in turn increasing the efficiency of the process and at the same time, contain the explosive energy and give it those vital few nano-seconds to build.

A millionth of a second later, when this explosive energy becomes overwhelming, the device will be blown apart by a truly devastating explosion. When the first atom bomb was tested at Trinity in the Nevada Desert in 1945, some of those present said it was 'like watching the sun exploding.' Simple, if you know how.

A modern 'Gun Type' nuclear weapon design requires a fairly large amount of $^{235}U$. Because the principle underscoring this method is uncomplicated, it manages without a neutron source and relies on a passing neutron to initiate the chain reaction.

For a variety of reasons plutonium is not suited to the 'Gun Type' device, which brings us to the second method, namely the 'Implosion Type' of Atom Bomb. The system initially got its name from the way in which it functions; it implodes inwardly rather than outward, as in a normal explosive detonation.

As can be seen from the sketch below, an implosion device is round (thus the appellation 'Fat Man' for the Nagasaki bomb) and can be either large or miniaturized to about the same size as a beach ball. At its core rests a gold-plated mass of material, usually $^{239}U$ or plutonium-239, though uranium-235 can also be used. This material may be shaped as either as a solid or hollow sphere which has at its centre a beryllium-polonium neutron source.

Around the $^{239}Pu$ sphere is a shell which acts as a reflector as well as a tamper and covering this is yet another sphere consisting of aluminium-boron. Its purpose is to exercise a squashing or compressing inward force. Around this globe are a number of block-shaped explosive charges and evenly-spaced detonators. Because of their three-dimensional shape and purpose – which is the shaping and directing inwards of the shock waves that are created by the initial blast – these charges are also referred to in scientific lingo as 'lenses'. Finally, a shell of dural or aluminium covers the entire 'beach ball'.

When all the explosives are simultaneously detonated, the resultant shock wave is forced inwards and causes the aluminium-boron shell to start compressing or imploding. Moments later these forces reach the core of the device, with the neutron source creating huge amounts of neutrons, which start the anticipated chain reaction. The reflector and tamper then functions as described above until the expanding energy can no longer be contained and the bomb is ripped apart by the huge forces generated by an atomic explosion.

The intensity of a modern Implosion nuclear device is dictated largely by the measure of scientific expertise employed. Typically, it can incorporate as little as ten or twelve pounds of plutonium, or even a good deal less for a tactical battlefield nuke that might be fired by a conventional 210mm (Israeli)

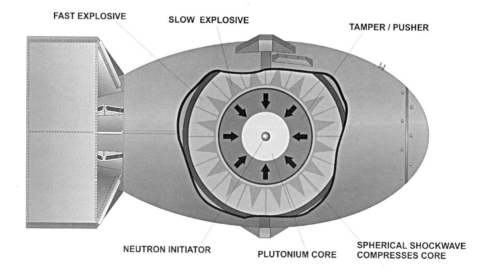

FAST EXPLOSIVE    SLOW EXPLOSIVE    TAMPER / PUSHER

NEUTRON INITIATOR    PLUTONIUM CORE    SPHERICAL SHOCKWAVE COMPRESSES CORE

or 155mm (US and NATO) artillery shell. The same remarks apply to that modern media favourite, the so-called 'suitcase' bomb which contrary to the comments of some sceptics, really does exist.

The path towards nuclear status taken by South Africa in the last quarter of the twentieth century is instructive. In a presentation given in Castiglioncello, Italy in 1995, at the conference called 'Fifty Years After Hiroshima', Dr Waldo Stumpf, the former head of the Atomic Energy Corporation of South Africa presented a paper titled 'South Africa's Nuclear Deterrent Strategy'. Although he was never personally involved with nuclear weapons work, his comments were incisive and provided the kind of overview which, until then, had been lacking.  Dr Stumpf told his fellow delegates that:

'though the Atomic Energy Board was established in 1948 by Act of Parliament and assumed general nuclear research and development activities at its Pelindaba site near Pretoria in 1961, all activities in the early years was based on the peaceful uses of nuclear technology, especially since South Africa was (and still is) a prominent producer of uranium which is a bi-product of its many gold mines. It was to be accepted that attention was given to uranium enrichment technology as a means to mineral beneficiation.'

Not everyone in the field would agree. Research into the military implications of a nuclear capability reportedly was already undertaken by South Africa in the 1950s[5] and according to Dieter Gerhardt, the country began to develop an independent nuclear option in 1964. There is also the statement made in 1960 by Ampie Roux; South Africa, he declared 'is capable of producing a nuclear weapon if it is prepared to isolate the best brains in the country, and give them all the funds they need.'

In his Italian presentation, Dr Stumpf made the point that nuclear weapon design is not a simple matter, and that some of the associated technical problems could be awesomely complex:

'After encouraging laboratory results were achieved in 1969 with an indigenous uranium-enrichment process based on a stationary wall vortex tube, approval was given for the further development of the process on an industrial scale. At the same time the construction of a pilot plant to prove the process was begun.

'This work was undertaken within the newly-created (1970) Uranium Enrichment Corporation on the Valindaba site, which lies immediately adjacent to Pelindaba. Construction of a pilot enrichment plant, which the South Africans called the Y-Plant, went ahead in 1971, and the first stages at the lower end of the cascade (were) commissioned by the end of 1974.'

Full cascade operation was initiated in March 1977, Dr Stumpf recalled, which was about a third of the time it took Pakistan to achieve the same results. 'Due to the long equilibrium time of the plant (the period necessary to establish the full enrichment gradient) the first and relatively small quantity of high enriched uranium hexafluoride ($UF_6$) was withdrawn from the plant only in January 1978' (this substance, a volatile compound of uranium and fluoride, is the feedstock in the uranium enrichment process and ultimately becomes the core of the bomb).

During all of 1978 and most of 1979, more uranium hexafluoride was withdrawn from the plant and converted to highly enriched uranium in its metal form. This material was still of relatively low enrichment (about 80 per cent $^{235}U$); compared with so-called 'weapons-grade' material, which, for bomb purposes is customarily enriched to about 93 percent. Then followed what can only be regarded as a disaster. Dr Stumpf explained that at one stage, the plant had developed what he termed a 'massive catalytic in-process gas reaction between the feedstock and the carrier gas, hydrogen'. This led to work at on the bomb being halted for almost a year.

However, there are those who maintain today that the flow of HEU was never actually interrupted, and that the material produced during those critical nine months of official inactivity was used to fuel one or more atomic bombs which were tested in co-operation (and under great secrecy) with the Israelis in the extreme southern latitudes and subsequently detected by an American Vela nuclear monitoring satellite. It will be recalled that shortly thereafter, in September 1979, there was an international hullabaloo over a distinct 'double flash' detected by a US Vela almost 2,000 kilometres south of Cape Town. The data subsequently recovered appeared to provide strong evidence that the characteristic nuclear 'double flash' was caused by a low-yield nuclear explosion.

In June 1980, the CIA reported to the United States National Security Council that the nuclear test – with a yield of between two and three kilotons – had probably involved Israel and South Africa. In the meantime, US intelligence confirmed it had tracked frequent visits to South Africa by Israeli nuclear scientists, technicians and defence officials in the years preceding the incident, and concluded in a classified report, since released, that 'clandestine arrangements between South Africa and Israel for joint nuclear testing operations might have been negotiated.' Because of its potentially adverse political impact, Washington strove to find a way to avoid calling this event 'an Israeli-South African test'. The publication *The Message* noted that 'an affirmative report might have affected the ongoing negotiations over the creation of Zimbabwe [then Rhodesia] in which South African co-operation was essential. It might also have upset the recently-negotiated Camp David accords between Israel and Egypt[6].' Such speculation received further fuel in

1986 when the 'disgraced' Israeli nuclear technician Mordechai Vanunu said in an interview with the London *Sunday Times* newspaper that it was common knowledge at the Dimona nuclear facility that South African metallurgists, technicians, and scientists were often there on joint technical exchange projects.

The Vela satellite issue remains contentious. Both Israel and South Africa continue to deny that nuclear weapons were tested, even though a member of Nelson Mandela's cabinet told a newspaper shortly after the ANC had taken over that the flashes had indeed been nuclear, though he retracted this statement soon afterwards.

Whatever the truth, it remains Dr Stumpf's view that valuable lessons were learnt from South Africa's brief-but-productive nuclear experience. What he told the delegates at Castiglioncello says much, not only in respect of the South African nuclear weapons programme but also about similar projects likely to follow, including those in North Korea, Iran and elsewhere:

'Although the technology of uranium enrichment and unsophisticated nuclear weapons is of a very high level, it is still within the bounds of a reasonably advanced industrialized country and therefore is not in itself an insurmountable barrier. This is particularly so where the technical goals are relatively modest, as with South Africa's 'Gun-Type' devices without neutron initiators.

'Although the vast Iraqi nuclear weapons programme and the huge financial and human resources it required may leave the impression of a self-limiting constraint, the South African experience proved otherwise.

'While international political isolation might be an instrument to contain individual cases of nuclear proliferation, a point in such an isolation campaign may be reached where it actually becomes counter-productive and really pushes the would-be proliferator towards full proliferation. In the case of South Africa, this point was probably reached by the US government's cut-off of contractual supplies of fuel to the Safari research and Koeberg commercial nuclear reactors, together with punitive financial measures. What little leverage the US had over the South African nuclear project was consequently lost.

'Where proliferation occurs because of a real or perceived political threat, a reversal towards de-proliferation may occur on removal or neutralization of that threat or the perception. This means that international pressure by a superpower from outside the region on a would-be proliferator can be helpful, but only up to a point. In the final instance, regional tensions must be resolved before the cause of non-proliferation can be fully realized. This was the case with South Africa and the premise certainly holds for the Middle East and the Korean peninsula.

'The reversal from a position of nuclear proliferation to a true and permanent status of non-proliferation within the Non-proliferation Treaty (NPT) will probably not be achieved by technical or military/strategic decisions, but rather will require a fundamental political decision by the leader(s) of the country concerned. The 'roll-back' option for a so-called threshold non-nuclear weapon state is not an easy path to follow: the NPT and its instruments were not designed to deal with such an eventuality. The international community should therefore take great care in its application of pressure on the process of normalization where a threshold state already has taken the fundamental decision to embark on this road. South Africa experienced a lot of unnecessary international pressure during the 'completeness investigation' by the IAEA, which, under different circumstances, might even have derailed the process.

'It is difficult for a so-called "threshold state", which has taken the political decision to roll back to then achieve international credibility and acceptance within the NPT. It can be eased considerably, however, by a sustained policy of full openness and transparency with the IAEA. Once more, this is a political decision.'

# Chapter 12

# How South Africa's Nuclear Weapons Programme Took Shape

*The South African nuclear programme was an extreme response to its own 'identity crisis'. Nuclear weapons became a means to achieving a long-term end of a closer affiliation with the West. A South Africa yearning to be identified as a Western nation – and receive guarantees of its security – rationalized the need for a nuclear deterrent.*

*'Out of [South] Africa: Pretoria's Nuclear Weapons Experience' by USAF Lieutenant-Colonel Roy E. Horton III: Occasional Paper No 27, USAF Institute for National Security Studies, August 1999.*

The initial South African nuclear weapons programme – called 'Operation Kerktoring' (the Afrikaans word for 'church tower') – was surprisingly modest in extent and, as might have been expected, enmeshed in secrecy. Workers on some of the more sensitive aspects were restricted to South African nationals who had been born in the country; dual-passport holders were denied access. Security was such that it was only after it all ended that the CIA and Britain's SIS were able to obtain details about what had been taking place in the large building at Kentron Circle, a short drive to the west of Pretoria. It was there, under the auspices of Armscor that the bombs and their weapons-grade uranium cores, enriched to about 93 percent, were manufactured and stored.[1]

Given the country's substantial and active Jewish population, it is hardly surprising that once defence links between Pretoria and Jerusalem began to gel, sooner or later somebody would sound out the Israelis about a possible joint venture in these military-related spheres of activity. South Africa at the time was on a roll, its mines and industries flourishing, while Israel was still struggling to prepare for war against its hostile neighbours, simultaneously absorbing huge numbers of immigrants pouring in from Russia as well as several Middle Eastern countries. Indeed, Jerusalem had a perceived need for the kind of tactical missiles that her scientists were working on at the time and what could be better than a mutually-beneficial cost-sharing arrangement?

It was a strange choice of bed-partners, although not as peculiar as it might appear at first glance. In the 1930s and 1940s thousands of survivors of Adolf Hitler's genocidal campaign against the Jews were made welcome in South Africa, and in 1948 the South African government had given unflinching support for Israel in its independence war, among other things, making it possible for large numbers of South African Jews to go and fight there. One of the founders of the Israeli Air Force was South African. The bond thus created remained strong, although many Israelis – and many South African Jews – strongly disapproved of Pretoria's racial policies.

There was an additional bonding factor; by and large, Israelis and South Africans shared a religious link. As the age-old phrase has it, 'Christians and Jews are people of the Book'. Above all, the issue of national survival by two pariah states in a world in which communist nations – as well as their surrogates – appeared to be advancing on every front remained paramount. As a consequence, the liberal Israeli government 'got into bed' with its South African equivalent, their wildly different ideologies overwhelmed by shared objectives and unusually, the arrangement seemed to work. The products that emerged from this unlikely liaison (largely financed by Pretoria) took their place in both the Israeli and South African defence inventories.

Among the most interesting interchanges of technology involved missiles developed by Israeli and South African scientists. It is instructive that one of the enduring aerospace mysteries that evolved was the rather obvious connection between the Israeli Jericho-2 (YA-3) ballistic missile, its Shavit SLV extrapolation, the South African RSA 3 look-alike of Shavit and the Pakistani Shaheen-II ballistic missile (see illustrations for comparisons). Iran's Ghadr-110 family of launchers also falls within this category, with specifications passed on to Tehran after Nelson Mandela's African National Congress took over the South African government in the early 1990s. Members of the ANC – during lengthy periods spent in exile prior to de Klerk's efforts at rapprochement with Mandela's followers – had fostered close ties with countries like Iran, Cuba, Libya, Vietnam, the PLO, Syria as well as the Soviet Union and these were reinforced once they took over the reins in Pretoria. Clearly, mutual interest in some of the sophisticated weapons systems developed in a South Africa that had maintained close links with an equally embattled Israel was only part of it.

There is some speculation about whether Prime Minister Vorster's announcement that his country was in the process of going nuclear was timed to pre-empt the UN Security Council immediately before it adopted Resolution 282 of 1970, which was concerned with violations of the arms embargo passed against South Africa six years before. This measure had originally called on member states to revoke all licenses and military patents granted to the South African government. The resolution also demanded that no country supply South Africa with material for the manufacture of arms, ammunition, aircraft, naval vessels or other military vehicles: it also prohibited investment or technical assistance for the manufacture of such items.

This measure had a considerable effect on South Africa's efforts to acquire advanced warplanes, naval strike craft and a variety of other weapons, but it did not prevent Pretoria from proceeding with its double-edged nuclear objectives. Ostensibly there was a semi-overt 'peaceful' indigenous acquisition programme which involved the possible commercial use of nuclear explosives in the country's mines, but it was the covert military programme that was of concern beyond the country's borders. While the 'peaceful' track would fully embody the original intent of Project Kerktoring, the military application heralded Israeli involvement on a scale that is still in dispute. The American writer Seymour Hersh noted in his book *The Sampson Option*[2] that Israel and South Africa initiated this link 'in earnest' after the Six-Day War of 1967. French involvement with South Africa at that stage – while certainly possible – remains speculative.

Whatever the case, the fact is that these developments took place during the historical years between 1963/64 and 1968 when several countries – Israel included – were involved in nuclear weapons development of their own and there seems little doubt that the Pretoria-Jerusalem link did have an economic framework, it was also military-orientated; Hersh actually cites a source who claimed that this was indeed so.

Regarding the 'peaceful' track, Professor Helen Purkitt noted that early 'peaceful nuclear explosives' research was encouraged by the West under such programmes as the American 'Plowshare Program', and that considerable amounts of nuclear data and technology were transferred to South Africa under its auspices[3]. According to a subsequently declassified Central Intelligence Agency report at least one South African scientist studied the application of PNEs in the United States.

It would also be naïve to believe that the skills and knowledge South Africans acquired while studying abroad or carrying out nuclear research in American and European universities and research programmes were not applied, where appropriate, to their country's nuclear weapons programme. Indian, Pakistani, Israeli and other nationals did exactly that on their return to their home countries after acquiring the same kind of vital information, and there is no reason to believe that the South Africans were any different.

General H.J. Martin, the South African Army Chief of Staff, was quoted in December 1968 as saying that South Africa was ready to make its own nuclear weapons. He referred to the Warsaw Treaty Organization invasion of Czechoslovakia in August that year and it was his view – and that of his government – that the inability of the West to appropriately react on such occasions was a salutary lesson that could not be ignored. This deplorable episode was neatly sidelined by the United Nations on the pretext that it was a 'domestic' matter within the Soviet Bloc, as had been blazoned by the media as the 'Rape of Hungary', more than a decade earlier and it was perhaps not surprising that South Africa was one of several nations that viewed international impotence in the face of such naked military aggression with alarm.

Martin's comments were also assumed to have referred to the country's developing uranium enrichment programme, the vortex-tube enrichment method having been fully demonstrated on a laboratory scale by the end of 1967. The general's comments were repudiated by the then Minister of Defence, P.W. Botha, but the point had been made, namely that the difference between a peaceful nuclear explosion and a military one narrowed down to one of them having fins at the back. This is not to say that serious consideration was not given to taking the nuclear route as a means of solving some large-scale engineering problems, which might have included blasting with unconventional explosives; a 1970 report identified a wide range of applications for nuclear explosives. Unofficially however, this was nothing more than an administrative exercise to rationalize the acquisition of nuclear weapons under a 'peaceful' guise, in much the same way that Iran today claims it needs to enrich uranium for the purpose of peaceful generation of power, and that from a country with the biggest natural gas reserves on the planet.

Peter Liberman, in a footnote to his paper 'The Rise and Fall of the South African Bomb' observes that a 1970 AEB proposal recommended the development of 'Gun-Type' implosion, boosted fission and thermo-nuclear PNE designs, with paper studies on the last being approved later[4]. As one critical observer saliently pointed out, 'this is an awful lot of firepower for a mere PNE application'.

In order to give South Africa's enrichment plans a bit of muscle, the Pretoria government passed the Uranium Enrichment Act in August 1970, followed three months later by the establishment of the state-run Uranium Enrichment Corporation of South Africa Limited (UCOR), again with Dr Ampie Roux at the helm. The site for the pilot facility, which was linked to the Y-Plant venture, found a home adjacent to Pelindaba. Carey Sublette notes that the primary function of this pilot plant was always the production of HEU for nuclear weapons[5]. It was called Valindaba, another vernacular-derived name made up from 'vala', meaning in Zulu, 'to close' and 'indaba' which suggests a 'tribal council' or 'discussion'.

A uranium-enrichment plant, of course, requires feedstock, which is uranium hexafluoride or $UF_6$. This is a volatile compound of uranium and fluorine, which, while solid at atmospheric pressure and room temperature, can be transformed into a gas by heating. British scientists in the 1960s were instrumental in providing their South African counterparts with enough technology to be able to produce $UF_6$ feedstock on the domestic front, and this ultimately went to a variety of countries, France and Israel included. Milling to produce yellowcake, or $U_3O_8$ – a yellow concentrate which contains about 80 per cent uranium and which has always been much in demand by any country or group desiring to build a bomb – commenced in South Africa in the 1950s, and steps had been taken thereafter to expand capabilities, which was useful since these minerals were bi-products of South Africa's gold mines, then the world's biggest producer of the precious metal.

The process included the establishment of a pilot uranium refinement plant which produced the country's first ingot of refined uranium in 1961. Newby-Fraser notes in his monograph *Chain Reaction*[6], that parallel research covered the conversion of ammonium diuranate into the compounds uranium oxide ($UO_2$), uranium tetrafluoride ($UF_4$), and $UF_6$.

United States Air Force veteran and intelligence specialist Lieutenant-Colonel Roy E. Horton III added come comments of his own on these issues. These were put forward in a study of the South African nuclear saga and appeared in *Occasional Paper #27*, completed for the USAF Institute for National Security Studies in August 1999. Horton felt it was possible that South Africa leap-frogged the testing phases and concentrated on the weaponization and delivery of its nuclear explosive device because it had no other alternative:

'Afrikaners are (by their nature) a contingency-minded people and, as such would probably prefer to have a deliverable nuclear weapon rather than be forced to develop one hastily in the face of a worsening security situation.'

Thus, he maintained, the ebb and flow of the South African nuclear deterrent effort was all the more remarkable, given the small number of personnel involved (roughly 1,000 in total during the course of the entire programme and no more than 300 at any one period). Those actually responsible for key decisions reportedly never numbered more than between six and a dozen individuals. In fact, South Africa's nuclear weapons programme was minuscule compared to that of other states, as can be seen by comparing it with the reported 20,000 or so staff working on the Iraqi bomb prior to the Operation Desert Storm (Gulf War One), detailed in Chapter Fourteen.

On 26 March 1993, the London *Sunday Times* published an interview with a former South African nuclear scientist who was involved in the weapons programme until the mid-1970s. He revealed that while he was at Pelindaba, there were only about thirty scientists actually working on the bomb project.

Horton says:

'The decisions emerged from the synthesis of four basic groups – the scientists, politicians, the military, and technocrats – who shaped the focus and direction of the programme. The scientific zeal and drive of the Atomic Energy Board's "Ampie" Roux and Wally Grant – who headed UCOR (the uranium enrichment plant) … to demonstrate that South Africa could make a nuclear device established the technical foundation for the programme.'

Yet, as Horton observes, their work was not done in isolation from the political leadership, the support of the military on military-to-military co-operation matters and the technocrats responsible for actual weapons production. Finally, he explains, there were the technocrats – the engineers at Armscor. This group exerted a heavy influence over the nuclear programme, he reckoned, particularly during its critical middle stage. Armscor Managing Director Tielman de Waal headed a corporation that not only produced nuclear weapons but also established the capability to mate them with ballistic missiles:

'There are also indications that Armscor was involved in more than just producing munitions – it also worked in developing the nuclear strategy itself. Together, these four groups formed a partnership that conceived, produced, and eventually discarded South Africa's nuclear deterrent.'

But at the end of the day, he maintains, the political leadership exerted the pivotal influence over its progress.

More disclosures come from the modest monograph *South Africa's Nuclear Weapons Programme* by Steyn, van der Walt and van Loggerenberg. All three authors are well-placed to discuss the South African nuclear weapons issues because they were directly involved. Hannes Steyn was linked to the industrial side of the enterprise through Armscor, the Armaments Corporation of South Africa, while Richardt van der Walt was the nuclear specialist, having worked on the weapons programme at Pelindaba. The military component came from Lieutenant-General Jan van Loggerenberg who at one stage headed the South African Air Force and possessed intimate knowledge about how the bombs would ultimately have been delivered to targets; one source claimed that he was actually a member of the planning executive.

Another of the points made was that the responsibility for executing the entire nuclear set-up fell under the control of the Atomic Energy Board's Reactor Development Division. There were nine designated groups, each with its own field of responsibility, namely: the Nuclear Engineering Group; the

Theoretical Reactor Physics Group; the Theoretical Nuclear Physics Group; the Experimental Reactor Physics Group; the Reactor Engineering Group; the Electronic Engineering Group; the Process Metallurgy Group; the Physical Metallurgy Group; and the Nuclear Chemistry Group. Taken together, all these disciplines provide something of an insight to the incredibly complex ground that needs to be covered in building the bomb.

The design office and workshops were located within the Reactor Engineering Group. Actual work on peaceful nuclear explosions hardware was carried out from about 1972 by a small team of Atomic Energy Board personnel, assisted by staff from the National Institute for Defence Research, or NIDR which, in turn, operated under the auspices of the Council for Scientific and Industrial Research (CSIR). As mentioned, such work was initially carried out under tight security in a small building at a propulsion laboratory in Somerset West, called Kentron South. During the early 1970s, this responsibility lay under the control of the NIDR, but it would eventually amalgamate with the nearby Somchem plant, which would itself become part of Armscor during the second half of the decade.

It is interesting that in the early 1970s, this Cape facility played host to the country's first facility dedicated to nuclear explosives. Priority was assigned to the 'Gun-Type' device, rather than implosion and boosted (weapon) designs, with two modified naval guns brought in from Simonstown and used to assist in development. The naval guns were acquired with the help of South African Navy Commodore Dieter Gerhardt, then already providing the Soviets with valuable defence-related information, of which the development of nuclear weapons was only a part.

Two decades after the dismantling of the six South African atom bombs, a number of claims were made about what remains a contentious issue. Even today, South Africa's Official Secrets Act proscribes publishing details about it. One early question pertains to why it was started at all. The second relates to its status as a deterrent.

Speak to some members of South Africa's 'Old Guard' these days and they will tell you that there was never any intention to actually use the bombs. They will argue correctly, that the weapons were never deployed outside their bunkers near Pretoria, or even integrated into the country's military infrastructure. Other claims pertain to the programme's 'modest' technological investment and the fact that foreign assistance was neither requested nor acquired, which, to some extent, is true. Another claim is that no nuclear tests were ever carried out, which raises more questions because there are two schools of thought.

Yet another assertion within the confines of the South African military and political leadership was that nothing advanced was ever manufactured; there was no thermo-nuclear objective on the distant horizon, though land was acquired in the South Cape near Gouritz – not far from Mossel Bay – where a programme involving advanced plutonium research was to have been started. That might ultimately have led to the development of an 'Implosion' type nuclear device like 'Fat Man', the atom bomb dropped on Nagasaki at the end of the Pacific War.

Then came the cost involved. The entire project, according to various authorities, totalled between $500 million and $600 million at the exchange-rate then prevailing; in fact, it was a good deal more, probably three or four times as much, but then South Africa, with its gold, diamonds and the largest platinum reserves in the world as well as gargantuan coal deposits was one of the wealthiest of Third World nations.

Finally, present-day apologists for the nuclear programme like to say that they had always intended dismantling everything when the time came. Perhaps they might have, but in the end, it was international politics that forced South Africa's hand. The Cold War had ended, the Soviet Union was falling apart and nobody cared about controlling the Indian Ocean any more, except possibly India. In a nutshell, South Africa had lost its usefulness. Moreover, a simple numbers game had come into play, the bottom line of which was that in the long term, a few million white South Africans would never have been able to maintain full and final control over a black community that was already six times as large.

In all fairness, most whites had begun to realize this as well, which was one of the reasons why the 1994 transition to President Nelson Mandela taking over the government went as smoothly as it did. It was clear to the younger and more progressive elements of the South African leadership that a black-on-white civil war was imminent. Moreover, the ideological static of the Cold War had evaporated. That allowed basic issues to emerge and there was simply no way the white minority could prevail against such preponderant numbers. Also, this was not an overnight Damascus-like epiphany. Tentative and strictly limited moves toward power-sharing had been in place for some years. The South African Army had gone multi-racial, followed by the police and it was no secret that the government had been discreetly conferring with Nelson Mandela – then still in prison – since the late 1980s.

But the Gordian knot did have to be severed, and that sword was wielded by F.W. de Klerk. It is an interesting comment on general white opinion that when he called a referendum on the question of further negotiations, a substantial majority voted in favour of what he and his lieutenants proposed.

Exactly the same premise might hold for Israel today vis-à-vis the Arab world. The tiny country's plus-minus six million Jews are ranged against roughly 200 million Arabs scattered around in all directions around the frontiers of this nation about as big as New Jersey. Ultimately, it is obvious that something is going to have to give, and in this regard a Middle Eastern de Klerk and an equally receptive Mandela have yet to be identified. Though spokesmen for Jerusalem will argue that there is simply nothing to compare Israel to South Africa, then or now – though former President Jimmy Carter, as expounded in his book *Palestine: Peace Not Apartheid* believes otherwise[7] – the difference was that the government in Pretoria was acutely aware that the price of bringing peace to an embattled Southern African region meant dismantling its atom bomb programme. South Africa had nuclear weapons, but it would remain a pariah state if it kept them, and no kind of realistic headway would be possible.

But all this too, is only part of what really took place. The whole truth remains elusive, and finding it requires the observer to examine all the alternative options *and* with an extremely critical eye. In retrospect, there were several other feasible approaches that might have been possible, because much of what subsequently emerged in the post-apartheid era remains unsubstantiated to a greater or lesser extent. For that one can thank the destruction of millions of official documents before Mandela's followers were allowed anywhere near the Union Buildings, the country's seat of government in Pretoria, not to mention the shredding of minutes of almost all the most important official meetings that took place over many decades. Several analyses have been written about the country's weapons of mass destruction programmes[8] – there were also chemical and biological weapon projects – and a growing body of evidence that suggest that these projects were very much more substantial than had previously been assumed.

The chemical and biological warfare programme known as Project Coast, for instance, is not under discussion here, but it is worth mentioning that it began slowly and grew fast, so that by the time some, but not all, its laboratories were closed down, the South Africans had produced germs and chemicals galore. The industry was vast, to the extent where Pretoria, at least in theory, could have armed its aircraft with WMD payloads that might have included anthrax, smallpox and plague, as well as sarin, VX and tabun nerve gasses, all of which were being produced in South African facilities by early 1989. It is also worth mentioning that some of these pathogens and nerve agents eventually found their way to Muammar Gadaffi's Libya, a not-so-little aberration which took place on the watch of the Libyan leader's good friend Nelson Mandela and not F.W. de Klerk.

## Chapter 13

# The Unanswered 'Hit' on Pelindaba and its Supply of Enriched Uranium

South Africa's Pelindaba Nuclear Research Facility – the primary nuclear establishment on the continent of Africa that produced enough weapons grade uranium to fuel six atom bombs in the 1970s and 1980s – was the setting for an armed raid in 2007 involving two groups of insurgents armed with automatic weapons. The implications remain serious because nobody has come up with answers as to who exactly was responsible, especially since those involved were clearly aiming at Pelindaba's stocks of enriched uranium. For its part, the South African government has been obscurantist throughout, dismissing the incident as little more than minor and that the incident involved criminals. Facts suggest otherwise.

Picture the scenario. One of the biggest nuclear establishments in the Third World comes under a concerted attack by unknown elements that had gone to great lengths to plan the strike. What emerged afterwards was that the onslaught was mounted not only with clear-cut military precision, but evidence of inside collusion is overwhelming. Had there been a powerful, coordinated attack by persons unknown on an American nuclear facility such as the one at Los Alamos, a defence nuclear weapons laboratory in New Mexico or possibly a highly-enriched uranium production facility at Oak Ridge Tennessee, the fall-out would have reverberated around the world. In the United States, the media reaction might almost have been on par with 9/11. *Any* military strike on a high security nuclear installation raises flags, no less so in the Third World where there are powerful revolutionary forces at work, among them organisations such as al-Qaeda and ISIS, both of whom have displayed an inordinate interest in matters nuclear.

Had there been an attack on any other nuclear installation anywhere else in the world, the media would have been inundated with news reports, comment and conjecture. In the United States, the issue would have been raised in Congress. Additionally, security measures would have been increased: possibly tripled or quadrupled, as has taken place with an aviation industry labouring under threats of international terrorism. Exactly the same situation would have held had the target been a nuclear establishment in Britain, France or Germany. Or, for that matter Japan.

More to the point, barely a day goes by without something appearing in the news about Pakistan's nuclear assets, regarded by those familiar with the industry to be under Islamic fundamentalist threat. Islamabad's problems might not be serious at present, but things change, sometimes rapidly, which begs the question: since there was a large amount of weapons grade uranium at risk during the armed attack on Pelindaba – enough to manufacture half-a-dozen A-Bombs or more, why has the international community remained all but mute? More saliently, what makes South Africa's nuclear facilities different from the rest? Could it be that Africa and Africans are immune from criticism? Or, as suggested by WABC radio host John Batchelor in one of his intrusive New York-based talk shows: Is it wise for the international community to ignore the kind of lax security measures that might conceivably result in a terrorist group acquiring enough HEU to make nuclear weapons?

What is interesting is that in response to fears that a terrorist organization might launch an operation to 'liberate' Pelindaba's stock of fissile material (which would conservatively be worth hundreds of millions of dollars on the international black market), the South African Government has repeatedly assured Vienna's International Atomic Energy Agency – as well as all the major nuclear powers – that Pelindaba, very literally, is a 'fortress'. Of critical significance, maintains Idaho's Dan Yurman, is that the reality of the Pelindaba attack demonstrates undeniable evidence of military experience and planning, or as he phrased it in a communication to me: 'a composite signature'. The entire process reflects a professional military presence behind its planning, he suggests[1].

Throughout, Pretoria has maintained that the facility is 'powerfully guarded against any form of outside attack', a comment endorsed by a South African cabinet minister, though he spoke on the condition of anonymity; hardly important, because there are only so many cabinet ministers involved with nuclear issues in South Africa. What he did stress was that the principal role of South Africa's Atomic Energy Corporation was to manufacture nuclear fuel for the reactor at Koeberg power station, to participate in the decommissioning of the discontinued nuclear weapons programme and to perform research to support all these functions. Facilities at the nuclear establishment include, among others, the Safari-1 research reactor (a 20MW swimming pool-sized research reactor which has been under IAEA safeguards since its commissioning in 1965), a hot cell complex, a waste disposal site as well as conversion and fuel fabrication facilities.

For all that, Pretoria's immediate reaction to the onslaught on Pelindaba from Day One was, if anything, duplicitous. The responsible ministry actually denied that the attack had anything to do with nuclear materials. Indeed, it told the American current affairs programme *60 Minutes* 'the intruders wanted to steal laptops or other commercial products at the facility.' Frankly, that is absurd. Also, it suggests a government cover-up, which is not unusual in South Africa today since it rates as one of the most corrupt nations on the globe. Look at the facts. There were at least two groups of attackers – every one of them armed with AK-47 Kalashnikov automatic weapons. They had managed to slice their way through a de-energized 10,000volt electrified fence and in the process, evade banks of security cameras. All this was achieved without them being noticed. That complicated procedure must have taken the best part of half an hour, yet nobody was made aware that an attack was taking place. Pelindaba security officials later said that guards maintaining the site's closed-circuit video television (CCTV) system were asleep and that they had subsequently been either disciplined or sacked.

Meantime, the two squads of intruders penetrated undetected more than a kilometre (three quarters of a mile), according to the ABC report to a control room that monitors such emergencies. What followed was a gunfight between the attackers and Anton Gerber – a member of the Pelindaba staff in charge of the control room. Gerber was seriously wounded but in the confusion the attackers withdrew. Yet for all that activity – the rumpus included shots, shouts, alarms, an alerted reaction force and the rest – it took 24 minutes for the first security unit to arrive where all this was taking place, the same squad, incidentally, that had been specifically delegated to protect Pelindaba from just such an attack.

It also emerged afterwards that at one point, a second team of four intruders were detected by a security patrol inside the site perimeter. The guards opened fire on them, but nobody was reported wounded in the exchange. This intervention may have been crucial in thwarting the intended theft of HEU. The first team, clearly, had the mission of disabling the security centre; the second was to gain access to the storage area and hijack the weapons grade material.

Anton Gerber's heroic battle in countering the efforts of the first team prevented them from spiking the security systems for the HEU storage area. Even if the second group of intruders had reached their intended objective, it would have remained locked out. Officially, the response time that should have followed a break-in is listed as four minutes.

Considering the nature of the attack and a succession of security lapses that followed, the single conjecture most often raised by those who have been sceptical of the answers provided by the South African Government, is that the hit was what some security cognoscenti might refer to as 'an inside job.' As CBS *60 Minutes* concluded in its investigation, 'while the camera operators who missed the gunmen were fired, the investigation is stalled, leaving no clue as to who was behind the assault on Pelindaba or whether their intent was to supply uranium for a nuclear bomb…'

The incident took place on a November evening in 2007. Yet, apart from a handful of cursory notices in some American newspapers, including a report in the *New York Times* posted from South Africa, nobody took much notice. The *Washington Post's* reporter in South Africa, possibly under pressure from the South African government, declined to submit a file to his editors even after the

*New York Times* published its report and it was not until almost a year later that *60 Minutes* devoted a segment to an attack that remains vague and unexplained. This lapse in reporting a critical issue that has immense international ramifications is all but culpable, never mind the security implications.

Dan Yurman provided a time-line to this development. He makes some disturbing observations:

- November 9, 2007 - Pelindaba break-in reported by the South African press, later censored, but not soon enough. Some of the newspaper pages come down along with early government efforts at disinformation. For instance, one of them says that Gerber is reported to be delusional.
- *Pretoria News* reported it was phoned by a man identifying himself as a National Energy Corporation of South Africa (NECSA) legal adviser, saying the newspaper will be breaching the National Keypoints Act by publishing the story. He reportedly claimed that the interview with Gerber was 'unethical' as 'he was under sedation and thus incoherent' when it was conducted.
- Yurman sees their web pages and reports on the basic facts and event on his blog.
- On 13 November 2007 – South African security forces admit there were two teams that broke into the facility. The first was to disable the security systems and the second to steal HEU. Note: Both teams were likely 'expendable' due to possible extended exposure and/or inhalation in powder form 90 percent highly enriched uranium. The South Africa bomb programme reportedly produced enough HEU for six to seven weapons, which, at a minimum would be 25-30 kg per bomb or 150-180 kg (330-400 pounds in total). Four men could carry that weight, but not the lead shielding that stored it to prevent criticality. Some of the apparent logistical requirements for the theft remain a mystery. For instance, he asks, if the intruders were to remove the shielding to lighten the load for transport, do they then set up conditions for a criticality incident in the confines of a truck?
- 14 November 2007 – *New York Times* publishes a report from South Africa which gets some of the facts wrong, but which brings the essential fact about the break-in to world attention. The *Washington Post* correspondent in South Africa, contacted by email, declined to cover the story.
- 20 December 2007 – Miach Zenko, a graduate student at the Belfer Centre, Harvard University, publishes a detailed Op Ed in the *Washington Post*. He gets all the facts right. In Yurman's subsequent telephone interview with Zenko, he expressed impatience with any theory about the break-in that would discount the coordinated nature of the attack, an inside job or the objective, which was the theft of HEU. He does not speculate on who it was that might have been after the fissile material.
- 2 February 2008 – The International Atomic Energy Agency reviews security measures at Pelindaba and pronounces them to be in order.
- A year after the attack, on 23 November 2008, CBS's *60 Minutes* broadcasts a report on the Pelindaba break-in. They get all the facts right but make no progress

in identifying who ordered the attack. Pelindaba officials talk with CBS on camera, including a visit to the 10,000-volt security fence, but decline to respond to questions about whether the attack was an inside job.

- Note that the incident comes four months after NECSA's newly-appointed services general manager Eric Lerata was gunned down in front of his home after returning from a business trip in France. It is believed he was followed from Johannesburg's Oliver Tambo International Airport. Two men were subsequently arrested for stealing his car: they were reportedly driving it at the time of the arrest. Is there a connection between the compromised security systems the night of the attack and his death? With most such incidents in present-day South Africa, the country with the highest murder rate in the world, nothing ever came of the case.

The international reaction to an attempt to penetrate the security of the largest single nuclear facility in Africa and the entire Southern Hemisphere remains astonishing. The matter becomes more complex when it is appreciated that almost without exception, every terrorist or insurgent movement eager to acquire nuclear expertise is vehemently anti-American and axiomatically, anti-West.

Since the Pelindaba 'break-in', there has been a lot of speculation about what actually took place there on the night of 8 November 2007. While much has been published, a good deal of information linked to the attack has been kept secret. Immediately afterwards, Pretoria implemented a legal gagging order which prevented local media from following up on some of the more controversial issues under review. What we do know is that Anton Gerber, the Pelindaba emergency control room station commander, was shot by the intruders after they had entered the facility. His fiancé, Ria Meiring, an operator at the facility, was assaulted by the four men who had managed to penetrate the secure area. Apparently, Gerber should not have been there that night, but he went anyway 'to keep my fiancé company'. There is some evidence to suggest that the attackers were as surprised to find him on duty as he was to discover their presence. Since Gerber was armed, he was able to retaliate, but then hand guns are never a match for automatic weapons. Indeed, as he himself admits, he is extremely lucky to be alive.

Meanwhile, Rob Adam, the chief executive of NECSA, confirmed immediately afterwards that 'four armed, *technically sophisticated* criminals' had entered the nuclear site by cutting the outside fence and slipping through the electric fence. This comment is disingenuous. They could not have cut through the fence unless they knew it was already de-energized. A breach of an electrified fence would have immediately set off security alarms. He also said that the attackers had roamed the premises for about an hour, during which they stole a ladder from a fire engine to gain access to the first floor of the emergency control centre through a window, during which time a computer was stolen and placed on a balcony. Then the men moved to the control room where they attacked Gerber and Meiring before fleeing, leaving the computer behind as the fled the facility. Adam emphasised at the time that it was evident the criminals had prior knowledge of the electronic security systems and while there are some timing inconsistencies in what Adam said, his gist is more or less correct with what happened.

In an earlier report, NECSA disclosed that 'these activities were captured on surveillance cameras, but unfortunately, they were not detected by the operators on duty', after which Rob Adam muddied the water still further by adding a post-script by stating that 'at no time were the emergency control room systems compromised'. He did however confirm that after the control room area had been penetrated, a breach on the opposite boundary fence was discovered by a security guard. Immediately afterwards, a second group of men were spotted and all fled in the ensuing shootout.

Meanwhile, Anton Gerber and Ria Meiring took legal action against their former employers and sued NECSA for damages and loss of income following their ordeal. Papers filed in the Pretoria High Court show that Gerber was claiming for about $110,000 (at ruling foreign currency exchange rates), while Meiring was demanding a bit less. Summonses were issued against NECSA and a security services manager, security shift supervisor as well as the two camera room operators who were on duty and the fact that it took them an inordinately long time to come to their aid. Interviewed by *60 Minutes*, Gerber disclosed that it took the South African Police ten months to interview him.

When the *New York Times* finally got into the story a week after the event, their correspondent Michael Wines confirmed that after the attack, which, incidentally, was 'the most serious on a nuclear installation in recent memory' the South African government was reticent to provide specifics about the attack[2].

Wines wrote:

'Already, the attack is raising questions among advocates and analysts about the wisdom of plans by South Africa and other African states to embrace nuclear energy as a solution to chronic power shortages and the looming problems of climate change … The assault on the Pelindaba nuclear reactor and research centre, one of South Africa's most zealously guarded properties is a severe embarrassment to the government. The eight gunmen escaped cleanly, neither caught by guards nor identified on surveillance cameras.'

Subsequently, after an internal investigation, about which nothing has been made public, the three security guards responsible for monitoring the process at Pelindaba on the night of the entry were fired. They had been asleep in front of the monitors when the two groups broke into Pelindaba and found to be negligent. More to the point, were they asleep or were they paid to look away?

Since then, the Pelindaba attack had become something of an item of discussion in the security industry abroad, so much so that Mike Kantey, the chairperson of the Coalition Against Nuclear Energy in South Africa (CANE), said that it had been developed into a defence safety analysis case study. That was followed by Matthew Bunn of Harvard's Kennedy School of Government, who told *60 Minutes* that if terrorists got hold of the uranium, 'it would not be hard to build a crude atomic bomb'.

Meanwhile, Pretoria has consistently remained on the defensive. Arie van der Bijl, general manager of NECSA told *60 Minutes* that the two attacks on the same night were linked, though he could provide no evidence to the contrary. He was supported by Adam who believed it was a random criminal act and that if these were 'sophisticated terrorists', Gerber would not be alive. Abdul Minty, South Africa's one-time nomination for director-general of the International Atomic Energy Agency (IAEA) reached the same conclusion after a senior South African police official declared that the case was being investigated by the serious and violent crimes unit. There was a clear indication that what took place at Pelindaba was more than a 'mere break-in', said the police officer. Which leads one to speculate how a similar event, had it taken place on American soil, would have turned out.

Since Nelson Mandela's African National Congress took power in South Africa, there have been a number of incidents related either to the country's nuclear facility or to the country's weapons industry. In 1997 for instance, there was an unscheduled visit to Pelindaba, on instructions from the Office of the

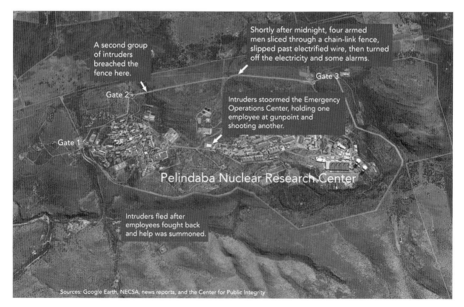

Armed intruder strike on South Africa's Pelindaba nuclear establishment

President in Cape Town, by Reza Amrollahi, Iran's Deputy Minister of Atomic Affairs who presented the then incumbent head at South Africa's nuclear project Dr. Waldo Stumpf with what he referred to as 'a nuclear shopping list'. Specifically, what Amrollahi was asking for was material with which to build an A-Bomb and in the presence of Pik Botha, for a brief time Minister of Mineral and Energy Affairs in Mandela's cabinet. Of course, recounts Stumpf, the Iranian was politely rebuffed; the two South Africans took the defensive the line that the provisions of the Non-Proliferations Treaty simply did not allow either Stumpf or any other member of his staff to comply with such extraordinary demands.

Dr Stumpf told me subsequently that his riposte was along the lines of South Africa having recently signed the NPT and that Pretoria's entire nuclear arsenal had been demolished by the IAEA in concert with Washington and London[3]. The episode was dealt with at length in the September 1997 edition of *Jane's Intelligence Review*. But that did not prevent me from coming under critical attack at ministerial level by members of the Pretoria Government, even though Pik Botha admitted to South Africa's *Mail & Guardian* that he was actually in the office at Pelindaba when the initial Iranian request was made. Notably, the government version was supported by Stumpf, who denied any contact with me. His words were, 'I have never discussed such matters with Al J. Venter.'

What is significant is that Dr Stumpf has since recanted: he has admitted that the meetings with both me and the Iranian Minister Reza Amrollahi took place, though it took him years to do so. His initial duplicity exposed me to serious credibility problems with Britain's Jane's Information group at the time because the South African protest was made at the topmost diplomatic level.

Another event which hardly warranted comment in South Africa's media at the time was the disappearance of drums of fissile waste material from Pelindaba after a winding down of the country's nuclear weapons programme. According to Dr. Ben Sanders of the Program for Promoting Nuclear Non-proliferation, this was a serious matter, but no satisfactory answers were ever forthcoming about the issue from Pretoria.

That was followed by the shipment from Pelindaba of a complete zirconium tube factory to China, also during 1997. Zirconium is a greyish-white lustrous metal commonly used in an alloy form (i.e. Zircalloy) to encase fuel rods in nuclear reactors, and here too there is a Tehran connection, though zirconium tubes can be used with equal efficiency to hold fuel in reactors for commercial and well as military uses. With Iran striving for nuclear self-sufficiency, it would ultimately be in need of zirconium tubes, great numbers. However, under restrictions imposed by the international NSG, Tehran is forbidden from acquiring them from any supplier in the West.

As Tehran was to discover, there was an easy way to overcome this imbroglio. While the Iranians might have taken advantage of their close ties to Moscow and possibly bought such a plant from them, they sought another route. The same year that Dr. Waldo Stumpf recanted on his original story, strong evidence was to emerge that the Iranian government – in complicity with Beijing – tried to secure a surplus zirconium tube factory in South Africa. Moreover, it was to have been accomplished without any of the customary nuclear checks and balances in place.

What we do know is that the packing up and dispatch of a disused zirconium plant at Pelindaba had progressed to the point where it was about to be shipped out of the country without mandatory end-user certificates. Then somebody blew the whistle. The publication *NuclearFuel* is on record as stating in its 19 December 1997 issue that Washington feared the plant might end up in Iran, and for good reason. China had apparently contracted with Tehran to build a zirconium plant at one of its nuclear facilities a short while before and the Pelindaba plant would have been an ideal stop-gap.

The story emerged after a group of about forty Chinese technicians entered South Africa on 'business' visas in August 1997. They spent months at the nuclear establishment preparing the plant for shipment. In fact, it was already packed into a number of reinforced cases when an alert journalist doing a routine story on Pelindaba tipped-off the South African Police that something illicit was taking place there. Only after details surfaced in a South African newspaper did the police raid the place, and promptly arrested all these foreigners for what was termed on the charge sheets as 'illegally working in the country.' Business visas, the police said, did not permit aliens to work in South Africa and certainly, not a large number of Mainland Chinese.

Then followed the first surprise. On the authority of a South African minister, the Chinese contingent was released from custody, even though the Ministry of Home Affairs was explicit that the activity of the group had violated the terms of their stay. The second surprise came when another minister interceded and prevented the Chinese group from being deported. An observation made by a Western diplomat at the time was that the Chinese had gained regular and routine access to an extremely high-security nuclear establishment. Moreover, while this went on for months, nobody questioned their presence. Another source claimed that the group put in ten and twelve-hour shifts, six days a week. Somebody was in a desperate hurry.

What was of concern to those familiar with NPT Accords was that while the original contract for the sale was concluded between South Africa and China in the summer of 1997, almost nothing was made public about the deal. It hadn't even gone through parliament, a pre-requisite for state-owned enterprises. In fact, it only became newsworthy when the so-called Chinese 'Illegals' were arrested.

Had this event not caught the eye of the individual who tipped off the authorities, there might have been nothing to prevent the entire plant from leaving the country. And that would have taken place even though South Africa is a signatory to the Nuclear Suppliers Group, or NSG. According to David Albright, President of Washington's Institute for Science and International

Security, NSG provides clear dual-use guidelines for the export of such equipment. 'It would appear that these were not observed,' he stated. This is pertinent because under SA Government regulations, the Council for Non-proliferation of Weapons of Mass Destruction of the Department of Trade and Industry – an interdepartmental export control body headed by the same Abdul Minty who, for a time, sat on the IAEA Board of Governors in Vienna – should have been informed as a simple matter of procedure.

Since Pelindaba was then and still is a high security government installation, the people in charge of the installation were obviously aware of what was taking place in their own back yard. But nothing was said and one must ask why this was allowed to happen and more saliently, *on whose authority*. Also, such shipments require end-user certificates since a zirconium tube plant is classified as dual-use or nuclear related equipment. The South African Government has always been aware that such transfers cannot take place without official sanction.

At issue here, said *NuclearFuel*, was a facility that had been in use until 1993 to make zirconium tubing for fuel loaded at the two Koeberg nuclear reactors just north of Cape Town. The sequence of events went something like this:

Early in 1997, South Africa's Atomic Energy Commission requested tenders for the sale of the zirconium facility. Brokered in the Channel Islands by a firm calling itself Pacific Development Services, a deal was concluded with the China National Nonferrous Industry Corporation at Shaanzi in north-central China. The price, quoted by Dr. Stumpf, was $4.6 million. Still more peculiar was that subsequent attempts by the media to make contact either with the broker or the listed company failed. This raises another issue: If the deal between the governments of China and South Africa was legitimate, why would anyone have involved an obscure middleman who is not only untraceable, but has yet to come forward to clarify some of the more sensitive issues? Clearly, something is seriously amiss. Dr Stumpf has said in a public statement afterwards, 'We will get an end-user statement from China before the plant leaves South Africa.'

The background to the zirconium plant is interesting. Originally it had been part of a nuclear fuel production complex for the Cape Town nuclear power plant at Koeberg and cost $42 million to build. Since final qualification of the plant for nuclear-grade zirconium alloy cladding was achieved in 1988, it had produced 75,000 tubes for the Cape's reactors. The plant was shut down in 1993 after international sanctions against South Africa were lifted and cheaper tubes became available from France. The AEC has since stated that it had tried to convert the zirconium factory to non-nuclear use but failed because of 'the very specialized nature of the installation.'

According to a statement issued at the time by the South African Ministry of Foreign Affairs, 'there are three pieces of equipment in the zirconium plant which require official authorization under the Nuclear Suppliers' Group dual-use guidelines.' Stumpf described these as CNC machine tools used to make complex moulds. Washington's comments on the subject included a statement that, independent of a pledge provided by China to cease nuclear trade with Iran (in exchange for non-proliferation certification by the Americans), it was not impossible that Beijing could still go through with the export to Tehran. Questioned about the Iranian link, Stumpf said that the sale to China was limited only to equipment in the plant. 'China won't get any transfer of technology,' he added.

The Iranian connection with South Africa did not end there. Following the appearance of an article about the sale of the tube factory in *Pointer*, another Jane's publication, ('Is Iran in RSA–China Zirconium Deal?') South African Minister Abdul Minty wrote a letter of protest to Jane's Information Group in Britain. Dated 9 March 1998, it states: '...the article is filled with half truths and innuendo and the author's "investigation" uses as a basis another inaccurate report appearing in *NuclearFuel*' (published in Washington DC 12 January 1998). Minty also made the point that South Africa's relations with the United States in regard to nuclear matters were exemplary.

The thrust of the article is inaccurate, he goes on:

'It indicates incorrectly, that the whole contract was done under cover of darkness and even with the hope that the zirconium tube plant could leave (the country) without anyone knowing that South Africa had not complied with all the requirements of the Nuclear Suppliers Group (NSG).'

That is 'clearly not part of this government's policy, nor its style,' Minister Abdul Minty declared.

So what are the facts of this disturbing event that clearly attempted to elude government oversight?

- Details of the contract came to light after police, acting on a tip–off, raided Pelindaba because the Chinese group involved had originally entered South Africa on business visas. On prima facie evidence, they had no right to be in the country for any other purpose, never mind have access to and work in a nuclear-sensitive installation.
- As a result of that action, a journalist with the *Independent* newspaper group broke the story.
- The application to export the equipment on the Nuclear Suppliers' Group dual-use equipment list was made five days *after* the paper first reported the account of the planned sale to China. This was confirmed in a letter from Stumpf, to the editor of *NuclearFuel* dated 13 January 1998.
- According to a subsequent report in *NuclearFuel* (9 March); only after the story appeared in the press, was it disclosed that the Chinese had been working at Pelindaba. This, too, was in Dr Stumpf's letter.
- Following these developments, according to *NuclearFuel*, 'Western officials and experts raised concern that South Africa's export control regime was not functioning smoothly.'

*Chapter 14*

# Lessons Learned from the Nuclear Experience with Saddam Hussein

Much has been made by the inability of Coalition Forces to find weapons of mass destruction following Gulf War 2. That was markedly different from 'Operation Desert Storm' (Gulf War 1), when Allied Forces invaded Iraq the first time after which United Nations inspectors went on to uncover Saddam Hussein's nuclear weapons' programme. It was an enormous venture and at one stage employed something like 20,000 people. Massive chemical and biological weapons facilities were also eventually uncovered, though it took time because they were very cleverly concealed. All these WMD assets were destroyed by UNSCOM, the United Nations Special Commission and for those who still do not believe that the Iraqi dictator had been dabbling in such things, a simple Google search will reveal all.

After Iraq lost the First Gulf War and international weapons inspectors arrived under the auspices of UNSCOM, they uncovered what was termed at the time 'a remarkable clandestine nuclear materials production and weapons design of unexpected size and sophistication'[1]. The total value of the nuclear project alone was initially estimated at about $5 billion. Later considerations put it at double that. In his testimony before the United States Senate Foreign Relations Committee in October 1991, Dr David Kay – a weapons inspector – reckoned that there were about 7,000 scientists on the nuclear side alone, never mind all those still working on a multitude of chemical and biological programmes as well as missile delivery systems.

One of the most comprehensive reports on the way that the Iraqis managed to befuddle the West is contained in a report that Kay wrote for the Centre for Strategic and International Studies at Boston's Massachusetts Institute of Technology. Another was authored by Dr Khidir Hamza, the most senior Iraqi nuclear physicist to defect to the West and still more came from Dr Mahdi Obeidy, former head of Iraq's gas centrifuge programme. Both scientists detailed the extent of their (and others') work in a series of CIA debriefings which I was able to subsequently peruse. Dr Hamza now lives in the United States with his family, all of whom were successfully smuggled out of Iraq by the Americans.

Kay pointed out that in terms of Security Council Resolution 687, Iraq was required to give the United Nations precise and accurate details of the quantities and locations of all its nuclear, chemical, biological and ballistic missile stockpiles. These were to provide a touchstone for subsequent inspection activities and were to have led to the dismantling of Iraq's WMD. Dr Kay told me:[2]

'What really happened was that just about every detail that emanated from Baghdad thereafter was misleading … On the nuclear front, the scale of deception was even greater. Iraq's initial declaration on 19 April 1991, was that it had no proscribed nuclear materials. This was amended eight days later to acknowledge that it had only what was reported to the IAEA before the war, as well as a peaceful research project centred on the Al-Tuwaitha Nuclear Research Centre.'

Subsequent inspections found something altogether different. It soon became clear that Iraq had been involved in a massive nuclear weapons programme (certainly the largest in any Third World country) for some years. Kay writes:

'At the time of the invasion of Kuwait, (Iraq) had begun the start-up for industrial-scale enrichment using calutrons and had acquired the material, designs and much of the equipment for 20,000 modern centrifuges. Design, component testing and construction of manufacturing facilities for actual bomb production were well advanced.'

United Nations inspectors reckoned about then, that the electromagnetic isotope separation programme had put Iraq just eighteen to thirty months away from having enough material for between one and three atom bombs.

The UN Action Team uncovered a great deal of sophisticated European centrifuge technology. This seemed to indicate that there had been a leak of substantial – as yet, unspecified – proportions from the triple-nation (Germany, the Netherlands and Britain) Uranium Enrichment Company (URENCO). What soon became apparent was that there were detailed plans for building an 'implosion' nuclear device (which can use either HEU or plutonium). This type of weapon contains a mass of nuclear material – in this case, HEU – at its core. This was no easy task. Vienna's IAEA discovered early on that the Iraqis appeared just to be starting to comprehend the extremely complex principles linked to this kind of weapons' research.

Another IAEA inspector told this writer that Iraqi scientists were planning a device with a solid core of about forty pounds of weapons-grade uranium. It would have included a reflector of natural uranium metal and a tamper of hardened iron. An atom bomb of this type would weigh about a ton with an outer diameter of a little more than three feet, making it significantly smaller and lighter than the devices developed by Robert Oppenheimer and his Los Alamos club in the mid-forties, though the circumference would still have precluded it from being fitted to SCUD missiles.

The IAEA – and by inference, the major powers – were very much aware that when coalition forces launched Operation Desert Storm, Iraq had in stock a total of almost 60 pounds of enriched uranium, about half of it originally from Russia and enriched to about 80 per cent, and the rest that came from France that had been irradiated to 93 per cent. All had been subject to IAEA scrutinies which, according to Kay, had been deviously manipulated by Baghdad. The fact that Saddam was in possession of HEU did give him certain leverage, Kay conceded.

The Iraqis have since admitted to UN inspectors that after the IAEA made their routine inspection of this material in November 1990 – following the invasion of Kuwait (but before the Allies started their bombing campaigns) – they intended to divert all their HEU and further enrich a portion of it[3]. They were planning to convert it to metal 'buttons' for the final weaponization process, which should have taken place by April 1991. The intention was to present the world with a fait accompli; that Iraq had its bomb.

Israeli sources in Washington suggested that in order to do this, Saddam Hussein might have exercised one of two options:

- He could have test fired his bomb in the desert at a site to be built near the Saudi border. This would have demonstrated to the world that Iraq had a nuclear capability (and thus, possibly, bring about a stalemate in the Kuwaiti issue with his forces still ensconced at the head of the Gulf). As it was, he was pre-empted by the invasion.
- Alternatively, there is a school of thought that believed that he might have considered trying to get such a bomb to Israel, possibly by boat, for detonation in the Haifa harbour roadstead. This is a premise that was doing the rounds in Beirut and is thought to have originally been mooted by Iran's Pasdaran or Revolutionary Guards (My visit to Lebanon in August 1997).

Significantly, these people have maintained all along that it is not necessary to *physically* land a nuclear weapon on American soil in order to cause destruction. Such a device could be detonated while still onboard a ship in New York (or any other) harbour.

It is clear that the biggest shock of post-war IAEA inspections was the discovery that Iraq had a very substantial Electromagnetic Isotope Separation (EMIS) programme for the envisaged production of an A-bomb. It was vast. Numerous buildings had been constructed at Al-Tuwaitha, about twenty miles south of Baghdad. These housed the research and development phases of both the EMIS and gaseous diffusion enrichment programmes. The diffusion programme (which lasted from 1982 until mid-1987) occupied three large buildings. Interestingly, the EMIS project was located in other structures at Al-Tuwaitha which disconcerted a lot of the staff who were working there. They were only too aware of what had happened at Osiraq in June 1981, when the Israelis bombed that reactor. They knew too, that Israel had already complained about the huge conglomeration of buildings at the complex and when Saddam added still more buildings, it did little for morale.

For the while though, EMIS had a home. This process is such a large and energy-intensive technology that intelligence agencies have always assumed that with modern electronic and satellite-surveillance techniques, they would be able to detect such a development in its infancy. More significantly, neither Russia nor America believed that any nation would pursue 'obsolete' calutron technology in a bomb programme. It was outdated, Second World War stuff, the pundits argued. In any event, the US abandoned that route soon after Japan capitulated. Yet, the detail is all there, in print, among documentation that was declassified decades ago and has been available for public inspection by anybody who knows where to look.

Astonishment has always been expressed at the 'true breadth of Saddam's nuclear weapons enterprise', as well as the amount of manoeuvring – both adroit and malfeasant – that was needed to keep it hidden from prying eyes both on the ground and above it, says David Albright. He spent time with the IAEA Action Team in Iraq and takes a professional interest in all such developments, legal and illegal. As he said, these discoveries shook the international non-proliferation regime and the tremors persist. What was revealed were critical weaknesses in inspection routines, export controls as well as in intelligence gathering and the sharing of these assets. Albright reckons that the reality of those first disclosures – and the well-founded suspicion that more lay ahead – led to the initial assumption that Saddam was 'on the brink' of putting his own atomic weapon on the international table. While the Iraqi nuclear project involved tens of thousands of people, no one in the West was even vaguely aware until long afterwards of the numbers of Iraqi students that had been sent abroad to acquire the necessary expertise.

These youngsters – and some, not-so-young academics – were rarely sent to the same universities or countries, which made it difficult for any single authority to appreciate the breadth of technical skills being established by Baghdad. It also presented problems for the world community to be able to keep track of individual Iraqi scientists. The two exceptions, peculiarly, were France and Italy, who together hosted about 400 Iraqis; yet none were officially approached about the subjects or courses they were actually following. Dr Hamza states that nearly all the leaders who were to a play a prominent role in developing the bomb were drawn from those batches of trainees.

Dr Kay highlighted all this with a single disturbing observation. While in Iraq, he said, he dealt for months with a senior Iraqi scientist whose entire university training – from undergraduate level, all the way through to his doctorate – had been in the US. His first real job had been at a US nuclear power plant. Yet, he declared that all basic data on or pictures of this key individual could not be found. In retrospect, the issue has a something of Dr Strangelove resonance about it. It is interesting that the Iraqi experience has since led to a considerable tightening up of IAEA inspection procedures, which is essentially to prevent such things from happening again. Yet, if one were to observe from up close recent developments in Iran, history appears to be repeating itself[4].

There have been other anomalies. It is no longer a secret that prior to Operation Desert Storm, the Iraqis received generous amounts of tactical aid from what later became their chief antagonists, the Americans. During the Iran-Iraq War, while Washington was providing arms to Iran in the hope of getting their hostages in Lebanon freed, it was also rushing through classified satellite intelligence to Baghdad almost as soon as it came in. This gave Baghdad a very good idea of what the Americans were able to detect, and, by inference, they also knew how they could be fooled. With time, they would use this knowledge to good advantage[5].

Before that, Baghdad managed to gain acceptance by Vienna's IAEA by placing Abdul-Wahid Al-Saji – a mild-mannered Iraqi physicist – in a position to serve his country as a bona fide IAEA inspector. Gradually, the Iraqis came to understand the machinations of the agency. This knowledge ultimately proved useful to Baghdad's weapons programme in obtaining nuclear technology. According to Dr Hamza, the agency accepted Iraq's importation of HEU for its research reactor without ever evaluating the possibility that it might be diverted for military use. Most importantly, Iraqis were able to gain a complete understanding of IAEA inspection procedures and processes. Iraqi officials were also alerted to the success of satellite remote sensing in uncovering clandestine, and especially, underground activities. For this reason, Saddam built nothing underground.

Kay makes instructive comments about the way that the Iraqis demonstrated their ability to understand the limitations of U.S. technical collection systems and of how data gathered by such systems were interpreted by the experts:

'The catalogue of these techniques is long. It includes the erection of buildings within buildings (Tuwaitha); deliberately constructing buildings designed to the same plans and for the same purposes to look different (Ash Sharqat and Tarmiya); hiding power and water feeds to mislead as to facility use (Tarmiya); disguising operational state (Al Atheer); diminishing the value of a facility by apparent low security and lack of defences (Tarmiya); severely reducing off-site emissions (Tuwaitha and Tarmiya); moving critical pieces of equipment as well as dispersing and placing facilities underground.'

Hamza points out that even though Al-Tuwaitha had 100-ft high berms (which from the start should have attracted suspicion) a lot of effort went into carefully escorting IAEA inspectors each time they arrived to look around. Customarily they were shunted along pre-designated paths that exposed none of the buildings where secret research was being conducted. Also, some of the answers to possible questions would be endlessly rehearsed, sometimes for days beforehand.

It was only after Operation Desert Storm, when Vienna received aerial photos of the site that the IAEA learned about many structures they had never entered. In fact, this subterfuge was so effective; they did not even know they existed. And, when the bombings were done, the Pentagon had to concede that while Iraq had suffered through the most sophisticated aerial bombardment in history, the country emerged – in the words of former US Air Force Chief of Staff Merrill A. McPeak – with enough nascent nuclear capability to produce weapons early in the new millennium.

What became clear over time, is that Iraq tended to be devious throughout the IAEA inspection period. As one observer stated: 'The Iraqis lied fluently from day one.' He told this correspondent that among those who had originally worked with the U.N. in the region before they were ignominiously kicked out, it was common knowledge that the Iraqis had stalled, obfuscated, covered up or confused wherever and whomever they could. They did what they had to in order to hide the truth. It says a lot that the North Koreans have followed a similar path; Pyongyang continues to do so each time its demands are not met. For instance, he declared, one of the conclusions already reached in 1992[6], was that while the Iraqis claimed to have had little success with the centrifuge enrichment programme, a mismatch surfaced between the sophistication of the materials they admitted to having imported and those turned over to U.N. inspection. This gap raised real concerns that a hidden centrifuge facility still remained to be found. There are other examples.

It took the defection of Saddam's son-in-law, General Hussein Kamel, the former Iraqi head of the Ministry of Industry and Military Industrialization (MIMI), to expose the full extent of what Iraq had achieved since Operation Desert Storm. Once he was safely ensconced in Jordan, Iraq had no option but to hand over to the IAEA half a million pages of secreted documents (they had all been hidden in what became known as the 'Chicken Farm') as well as almost twenty tons of high-strength maraging steel and stocks of carbon fibre for more than a thousand gas centrifuges, all of which (and much more) Kamel had detailed in his debrief. Soon afterwards, General Kamel and family were lured back home by assurances from Saddam himself that all was forgiven. The same day he arrived in Baghdad, the son-in-law was murdered.

The Israeli Air Force bombing of the facilities at the Osiraq reactor (and subsequent developments) highlighted at a very early stage that Iraq was fostering an interest in nuclear weapons. Saddam Hussein had bought two nuclear reactors from France; a 40 megawatt thermal research reactor which was destroyed; a fuel manufacturing plant; and nuclear fuel-reprocessing facilities, all under cover of acquiring the expertise needed to eventually build and operate nuclear power plants and recycle nuclear fuel. What is amazing is that nobody in the West questioned the logic of these developments, coming, as they did, from oil-rich Iraq, with the second largest reserves in the world. Two decades later Iran is involved in exactly the same kind of duplicity, and one needs to ask why because Tehran has equally formidable resources. Indeed, Iran is the last nation on earth that needs to generate electricity by burning uranium. The very last!

The deals surrounding Osiraq were followed by a further purchase from Italy of a radiochemistry laboratory in 1978 which included three 'hot cells' used for the reprocessing of plutonium. Until destroyed in the Gulf War, they were operating at Al-Tuwaitha. Meanwhile, Baghdad had signed the Nuclear Nonproliferation Treaty. Dr Jafer dhia Jafar, leader of Iraq's nuclear-weapons effort (even though his curriculum vitae includes the notation that he was jailed for twenty months by Saddam for 'political crimes') claims that it was the Israeli bombing of Osiraq that had originally prompted his government to proceed with a secret enrichment programme. Educated at Manchester University as well as at Imperial College, London, he also spent four years working at CERN, the European accelerator centre in Switzerland.

Jafar reckons that the attack cost his country almost a billion dollars. Yet, he says, the world community did not punish Israel for what was clearly an act of war. This was one of the factors, he maintains, that caused his nation to resort to subterfuge. As he described it to United Nations inspectors, '[we] let Israel believe it destroyed our nuclear capacity. Accept the sympathy being offered for this aggression and then proceed in secret.'

Already, in 1982, the Iraqis had begun to explore electromagnetic isotope separation at Al-Tuwaitha which eventually became the principal focus of nuclear research in the country. Baghdad was said to be confident that its scientific establishment had the necessary skills and technology to master this extremely difficult process. They also reached out in other directions: gas centrifuge, gaseous diffusion, chemical enrichment and laser isotope separation. To begin with, time, money and effort went into gaseous diffusion. This route was abandoned when some of the technical problems proved insurmountable.

Also, Saddam's agents were having trouble getting their hands on essential equipment on the open market, much of which had been embargoed by the West. Looking at the lists, they appear, nonetheless, to have been remarkably successful. Starting in the late 1980s, Iraqi scientists began working on centrifuge enrichment as a possible alternative for a source of low enriched uranium (LEU) for EMIS. They had ultimately hoped to achieve a production output of about thirty-three pounds (seventeen kg) of 93 per cent weapons-grade uranium a year at each of the EMIS production units they intended to build. 'Originally, the gaseous diffusion elements would have provided low-enriched uranium as a feedstock for the EMIS plants, dramatically increasing HEU production,' Jafar explained during one of his interviews.

The Tarmiya complex on the Tigris River (built by a Yugoslavian firm, Federal Directorate of Supply and Procurement) and its 'twin' at Ash Sharqat (a few hundred miles to the north of Baghdad) were designated to support industrial-scale EMIS production. While there were numerous problems of a technical nature, both plants together, ultimately, might have produced between 100 and 220 pounds of weapons-grade HEU a year had they operated successfully, though clearly, this would have been pushing it. It would have given Iraq the capacity to build three or four A-Bombs a year.

A small plutonium separation programme was started in the mid-1970s. Following contact with SNIA-Techint of Italy, a facility was established in Baghdad for research on fuel processing under IAEA safeguards, the Italians being told that it was all intended for 'peaceful purposes', which begs another question; how gullible can a sophisticated nation like Italy get? This laboratory was eventually able to separate small quantities of plutonium, again, contrary to the NPT safeguards agreement.

Kay's observations about some of the deception techniques employed by Baghdad are interesting. Iraq, he maintains, was able to use the strong desire of Western providers of technology to make sales in order to effectively conceal the true purposes of its efforts. Thus, they were able to extract a considerable amount of proprietary information from these firms without compensation. He gives the classic example which lay at the heart of Iraq's efforts to obtain technology for the chemical enrichment (Chemex) of uranium.

At the time, there were two suppliers in the world of chemical enrichment technology; one was Japanese, the other French. In the mid-1980s Iraq initiated preliminary discussions with both and indicated a desire to acquire this capability. In the end, they concentrated on France. Iraq engaged the European company in lengthy negotiations which would soon take a familiar pattern. Each time Iraq would say that it needed 'only a little more data' to make a decision. The French would reveal more and the cycle would begin again later and this rigmarole went on for several years. Finally, after the suppliers had disclosed just about all the technology involved with the process, Baghdad announced that it was just too expensive and was abandoning all interest in pursuing it. Iraqi scientists were then able to begin the clandestine development of Chemex on their own.

David Albright stresses that in the evaluation of enrichment technologies, the Iraqis saw many advantages in EMIS technology, the first that this procedure involves large and static pieces of equipment[7]. Baghdad regarded this as preferable to gas centrifuge which required advanced engineering technology and was ill-suited to a developing country with a limited industrial base. For example, the rotors on gas centrifuges move at an astonishing speed and the slightest instability can cause bearings to fail and rotors to crash in an instant. It is worth mentioning that Pakistan battled with this technique for years and only lately succeeded in mastering it.

The advantages of following the antiquated EMIS route are important, especially since they might well apply to other developing countries intent on following this path. These include: EMIS is well-documented in the open literature; the basic scientific and technical problems associated with the operation of EMIS separators is relatively straightforward to master; the computational software and main equipment are often not on international export control lists, making procurement easy; the design and manufacture of the main equipment for prototypes can be accomplished indigenously; the feed material is relatively easy to produce and handle; final enrichment can be handled in two stages in machines that act independently of each other (one or more separator failures do not affect the operation of other separators) and a LEU feed can be used for a substantial increase in productivity.

Now, as recent disclosures have indicated, Iran appears to be heading the same way. Like Iraq, Tehran likes to keep its options open with regard to gas centrifuge technology, laser as well as chemical separation.

In Iraq, meanwhile, actual weaponization of the bomb was the responsibility of the scientists and technicians at Al Atheer, which the minister said when he opened the plant about 30 miles south of the capital, was to be 'like Los Alamos'. By the time that David Kay and his IAEA Action Team associates visited the site – which was bombed by the Allies during the war – the Iraqis had managed to acquire a variety of advanced equipment, much of it on Western export control (and thus embargoed) lists. Included were such items as high-speed streak cameras (from Hamamatsu Photonics of Japan) and maraging steel (which was found elsewhere in Iraq) from European suppliers.

Al Atheer was also involved in sophisticated work in metallurgy, chemistry and detonation engineering. Here, the Swiss company Asea Brown Boveri provided a state-of-the-art, cold isostatic press which could be used to shape explosive charges. More Swiss firms which supplied equipment to Iraq included

Acomel SA of Neuchatel (five high frequency inverters suitable for centrifuge cascades) and, among other shipments, 700 uranium hexafluoride-resistant bellows-valves from Balzer AG and VAT AG (together with the American company Nupro). There is no doubt that in pursuing his objective to acquire a bomb, Saddam relied heavily on foreign aid. The bulk of it, curiously, came from not from his old allies the Soviets and their cohorts, but from free Europe.

David Albright and Mark Hibbs stated in their reports that Iraq's 'Petrochemical Project Three' – the codename for the secret project (conducted under the auspices of MIMI) – received massive infusions of money and resources. Like America's redundant Manhattan project, Iraq sought a number of different technical avenues to the bomb[8].

The Iraqi leader sent out a minor army of agents to establish an elaborate procurement network which had operatives throughout the developed world. Even Africa was covered; South Africa (through Armscor) had great potential. By then the apartheid regime had supplied Iraq with the vaunted G-5 gun, a 155mm artillery piece which, until silenced, was used to good effect against Coalition Forces in Desert Storm. The entire issue was subject to the most stringent secrecy. There was not an Iraqi legation abroad that was not involved. Curiously, Jerry Bull, the Canadian maverick arms developer who was involved in Saddam's 'Super Gun' when he was assassinated in Belgium by the Israeli Mossad, also had a hand in developing the G-5. Ostensibly, everything that was acquired was intended for civil or peaceful use. Purchases were hidden behind such innocuous pursuits as dairy production, car and truck manufacture as well as oil refining. But it did not take the major powers long to click; Iraq was involved in something that was different, more disconcerting, and it was happening on a breath-taking scale and pace.

Many of the bulky calutron pole magnets used to enrich uranium were produced in Austria by a state-owned firm that shipped the finished products to Iraq – half by truck through Turkey and the rest through Hamburg. The Austrians never asked the purpose of this equipment. In turn, the Iraqis volunteered nothing. Much the same story applied to the high-quality copper that was used to wrap these magnets. It was produced in Finland to Iraqi specifications. Hundreds of tons of HMX high explosives – the 'big brother' of the better-known RDX (some of which would be used in the A-bomb programme) – was imported from Carlos Cardoen of Chile, already very well known to the old Pretoria regime. This man was eventually to build a plant in Iraq to manufacture cluster bombs. Cardoen was later investigated by the U.S. Justice Department.

Germany (both pre-and post-unification) featured prominently in almost every phase of what Iraq was doing nuclear-wise, so much so that it is impossible that Bonn could *not* have been aware of the extent of it. German companies included international conglomerates like Siemens AG (a workshop for what was termed 'tube processing'); H & H Metalform (flow-forming machines to make maraging steel rotor tubes for centrifuges); Neue Magdeburger Werkzeugmachinen GmbH (aluminium forgings and a CNC machine to machine casings); Rhein-Bayern Fahrzeugbau GmbH (240,000 magnetizable ferrite spacers for centrifuges); oxidation furnaces from Degussa AG and Leybold Heraeus (electron beam welder); centrifuge balancing machines from Reutlinger und Sohne KG; Arthur Pfeiffer Vakuum Tecknik GmbH (vacuum induction furnace) and a host of other companies and products. It is disturbing to some Western intelligence agencies that some of these companies now have Iranian interests.

H&H was contracted by Baghdad for centrifuge assistance and while doing so, served as a conduit for advanced technical know-how, material and equipment for the Iraqi nuclear effort. Much of the finance for the project was handled by the scandal-ridden Bank of Credit and Commerce International (BCCI) before it folded. Subsequently, the Atlanta-based branch of an Italian bank, Banco Nationale da Lavore (BNL) was placed under investigation in the US.

There were British companies involved too. These included Endshire Export Marketing which met an order for ring magnets which had to come from Inwako GmbH, a firm directed by the German arms dealer Simon Heiner. British Special Intelligence Service (MI6) was aware by now that the magnets were for an Iraqi nuclear weapons programme but it let the shipment proceed in order to try to establish what technical route the Iraqis were taking. London tends to work closely with Washington on such matters.

It transpired that the Technology Development Group, a company co-directed by an Iraqi intelligence agent, Safa Al-Haboudi, was an associate of some of the German firms involved in the transactions. Al-Haboudi eventually implicated Matrix Churchill; he was on that company's senior management. Matrix Churchill offered a lucrative, long-term contract for a tool shop (ostensibly for automobile parts manufacturing) to the Swiss metal-working combine Schmiedemeccanica SA. The records show that some of these exports never got through. Once the West had been alerted, they came down hard.

Swiss and German customs officials halted a shipment of special computer numerically-controlled (CNC) machines for making the endcaps and baffles of centrifuges. Earlier, Iraqi operators were caught trying to smuggle detonation capacitators from CSI Technologies of California. All would have been used in an Implosion-Type bomb. For all the help that Baghdad received from abroad, there were some serious technological gaps. Iraqi electronics expertise, for instance, did not warrant close scrutiny. It was discovered later that the Iraqis were having difficulty developing adequate capacitators and bridge wire detonators. Rolf Ekeus, the former head of UNSCOM, said that while Saddam's scientists had all the blueprints together with a considerable body of knowledge, they tended to lag in the engineering aspect. Also, Baghdad had been noticeably slowed by the inability to obtain several critical items required from overseas suppliers as soon as Western government controls began to stymie deliveries.

It is important to accept that Iraq is not alone in this sort of subterfuge. The newsletter *NuclearFuel* reported on 20 June 1994, that several shipments of preformed tubes for scoops in gas centrifuges from the German metalworking firm Team GmbH were shipped to Pakistan after being declared in customs documents as bodies for ball-point pens. There are other examples, many still under wraps.

Looking at the broader picture, it is clear that this embattled Arab nation was able to demonstrate an astonishing level of enterprise in getting as far as it did. It is important that this be noted since there are other nations that might wish to emulate Iraq. Basic items – factories, electrical supply, power equipment – were easy to buy. But, as Albright explained, 'the more specific the equipment Iraq sought, the more export controls began to bite. Crucial transfers of components were thus effectively blocked.'

Orders were subdivided into subcomponents which, on paper, looked innocuous. Or machines were bought to manufacture something back home. Middlemen and unethical companies in their hundreds were bribed to disguise final destinations or to falsify end-user's certificates in much the same way as South Africa (under UN sanctions) stocked its arsenal with embargoed items of choice.

German technicians were secretly hired to work on the Arab bomb project. Once the IAEA went to work and uncovered names, some of these people were charged with treason. Several were jailed. Among these individuals were Bruno Stemmler, Walter Busse and Karl-Heinz Schaab. It was Schaab who provided Saddam with classified centrifuge blueprints. The three men had worked on the centrifuge programme at MAN Technologie AG of Munich. Busse and Stemmler came to Iraq under the sponsorship of the German company H&H Metalform. Together they operated efficiently as a team and met many of Iraq's technical requirements. They also assisted in locating international suppliers. Some were companies with whom they had previously been associated. In the end, says Albright, their assistance greatly accelerated Iraq's gas centrifuge-design process. 'It sped the acquisition of necessary materials, know-how and equipment for manufacture.'

*Chapter 15*

# Is Tehran Building the Bomb?

*'Ever since the atom was split, governments have struggled to control a force with potential for good that can also wreak awful destruction. Some argue it is impossible to stop technologies that can keep the lights on from being used to make bombs. That is a sobering thought in a world ready to re-embrace relatively carbon-free nuclear power. But David Albright, a respected chronicler of undercover nuclear shenanigans, tells a more alarming story: just how little most governments have done to halt the bomb's spread.'*

*The review in the British weekly Economist of David Albright's Peddling Peril: How the Secret Nuclear Trade Arms America's Enemiest[1]*

In the past two decades, there are few countries that have raised as many issues related to weapons of mass destruction as Iran. Barely a week goes by without the major powers making pronouncements about Iran's nuclear aspirations. That the mullahs are determined to acquire nuclear parity is no longer a matter for discussion: they are almost there and the *New York Times*, *Le Monde*, Germany's *Frankfurter Allgemeine Zeitung*, the *Washington Post* and a host of British dailies are full of it.

With new revelations surfacing just about every week – including details about secret nuclear facilities, Iranian nuclear physicists defecting to the West, Moscow's role in building the Bushehr reactor and more war games and grandstanding in the Gulf Region than we have seen for years, issues have become problematic.

Iran's neighbours are aghast at some of these developments. They are also fearful, worried about Tehran's new-found militancy, especially since the theocracy remains a formidable advocate of the Shi'ite Islamic doctrine while all other countries in the region are preponderantly Sunni. There is also a real fear among some Middle East countries that the old-time Persia will, after Pakistan, become the second Moslem country to acquire the bomb and that they might be caught on the periphery of a nuclear firestorm. More worrying is the uncertainty about what the international community is likely to do should Iran detonate its first test Atom Bomb; on the face of it, absolutely nothing.

Following Pyongyang having detonated nuclear weapons in October 2006 – and again in May 2009 (there have been several nuclear tests so far, with more promised) – no effective action followed on the part of the major powers to attempt to curtail or possibly limit these developments. In fact, apart from usual low-key censures in the United Nations and other international bodies, nothing has really changed. That North Korea had become a member of the so-called 'Club of Nine' was a *fait accompli* and there is little anybody could or would do about it[2].

Tehran has obviously been a keen observer of these developments. Iran's mullahs argue that if an obscure and impoverished country like North Korea can get away with it, then so can they. Iran, they correctly point out, is not only oil-rich, almost beyond compare, but it also possesses the largest natural gas deposits in the world. Moreover, it straddles a strategic corner of the globe that is the source of more than half the carbon fuel oil needed by the West, if only to survive.

Nor are Washington, London, Paris and Berlin under any illusions that either Moscow or Beijing would actually censure Iran should it emerge with deployable nuclear devices within the near or medium-term future. The reasons are simple. Tehran supplies a fair proportion of China's oil, while the Russians are making good profits from building a succession of nuclear reactors for the maverick Islamic state. Nobody is likely to rock those boats in a hurry. Which begs the immediate question; how far advanced is Iran in acquiring nuclear weapons?

The reality is basically that nobody knows. Regular pronouncements are made by Tehran from time to time, often conflicting and contentious and invariably varying – depending on perspective – from anything between six months to three years or more. What has become apparent to several authorities including the Israelis is that Tehran is a lot closer to building the bomb than anybody is prepared to concede, backed in part by intelligence leaks that regularly feature in Western Media.

David Albright's Institute for Science and International Security is regarded by the majority of 'Iran Watchers' as closest to the mark[3]. Quoting an 18 February 2010 report issued by Vienna's International Atomic Energy Agency, Albright declared that Iran's gas centrifuge programme at its Natanz Fuel Enrichment Plant (FEP) could produce enough weapon-grade uranium for an atom bomb 'in six months or less'. He also provided details about the largely underground Fordow enrichment facility near the revered religious centre of Qom.

Lying under a mountain, it is a deeply buried centrifuge facility that the IAEA reported is at 'an advanced stage of construction' with 'centrifuge mounting pads, header and sub-header pipes, water piping, electrical cables and cabinets' put in place but not yet connected. In addition, Albright disclosed that 'passivation tanks, chemical traps, cold traps and cool boxes were also in place but had not been connected.' Inspectors noted that a utilities building 'containing electricity transformers and water chillers had also been erected.' Thus, declared Albright, the Fordow plant is suitable as a military facility in any Iranian effort to produce nuclear weapons. The bottom line here is that Fordow is large enough to produce enriched uranium for a nuclear weapons project and, of course, by now that facility is in full working order and pushing out in quantity whatever it was designed to produce. Concurrently, there had been significant work done on fuel fabrication lines at Isfahan, a city until recently better known for its quality Persian carpets than any kind of nuclear-related enterprise and by now that work is also complete.

While Vienna's IAEA reported no progress with Iran in addressing outstanding issues related to the possible 'military dimensions' of its nuclear programme in its disclosures, 'and continues to await Iran's reply to overtures for information about its alleged activities', successive reports note that information available to the IAEA is 'extensive and has been collected from a variety of sources over time.'

It also added – several times – that 'altogether, this [information] raises concerns about the possible existence in Iran of past or current undisclosed activities related to the development of a nuclear payload for a missile.'

Some of this information undoubtedly came from an Iranian nuclear scientist, Shahram Amiri who was persuaded to defect to the United States by the CIA. While nothing has been confirmed, it is known that Amiri worked at Malek Ashtar University in Tehran, reportedly located across the street from FEDAT, the name of the secret nuclear weapons research and development headquarters that operates under Iran's Ministry of Defence run by Mohsen Fakhrizadeh. On December 14, 2009, ISIS was able to release documents that reportedly showed the organizational structure of FEDAT as well as its exact location.

Additionally, Iran's then President Ahmadinejad unveiled what he termed a 'Third Generation' centrifuge on the country's National Nuclear Technology Day on 9 April 2010. While very little information was provided about this machine – its potential performance, the number of centrifuges produced, the quantity it eventually plans to install, or when Natanz or other enrichment facilities like the heavy water production plant at Arak would become part of the equation – the revelation did provide valuable insight to the Iranian nuclear programme.

A lot of controversy surrounds putative Iranian nuclear issues. After I published my book *Iran's Nuclear Option* in 1995, one of the first titles to appear on the subject[4], there were a number of 'specialists' who suggested that Tehran was doing nothing of the kind. It was all innocent research on the part of the Tehran Government, one expert suggested. Not long afterward I was personally attacked in print by Samuel 'Sandy' Berger, former United States National Security Advisor under President Bill Clinton from 1997 to 2001 for suggesting that Iran might be doing something illegal. The e-mail he sent declared there was no evidence that Iran was going nuclear, and that coming from somebody who has been at the heart of American intelligence for years. When I countered with the argument that he was possibly too busy to have noticed since he had since spent a good deal of his time stuffing classified material dealing with his own tenure of office down his underpants, the onslaught ceased.

What we do know is that America's Central Intelligence Agency has repeatedly told Congress that there is every indication that Iran is driven to build nuclear weapons and that it does so for a variety of reasons. One of these is to achieve dominance in the Islamic world. Another is to counter what Tehran likes to refer to as the 'Israeli nuclear juggernaut'.

On the face of it, Langley does not have a clear answer. What it told American lawmakers several times over the years was that if Tehran ever managed to acquire sufficient weapons-grade uranium or plutonium – possibly clandestinely, from contacts in the Former Soviet Union (FSU) – then, in all likelihood, it might be able to build the bomb within a time span of between three to five years. That has obviously not happened.

There are still more pointers that indicate that more might be taking place in Iran than most Western observers would like to believe.

Apart from its own efforts to enrich uranium, there have been numerous attempts by Iranian agents to buy highly enriched uranium (HEU) and plutonium on the East European black market that are both sourced and documented. Tehran has also been shopping for nuclear technical know-how. The West is also aware that the Iranians have recruited foreign specialists for its WMD research and development programmes, including South African scientists who were formerly involved in their own country's now-defunct missile programmes.

On the nuclear development side, research is taking place at various locations and in a country as big and, in places, as remote as Alaska, it is impossible to keep track of all developments. Some details are known and a variety of intelligence agencies are aware of dozens more locations where nuclear work might presently be taking place.

While not all the sites are directly related to weapons manufacture, some are. Israel recently highlighted Tehran's efforts at fragmenting its nuclear research and development efforts, mindful that on a previous occasion, Jerusalem launched pre-emptive raids against an adversary's nuclear assets.

Israeli warplanes, it will be recalled, destroyed Iraq's 40-MWth materials test reactor Tammuz-1 at Osiraq in June, 1981.

Consequently, Iran's nuclear assets are widespread. Some are to be found in the north of the country at Tabriz and Bonab (close to the Turkish border) as well as Chalus and Neka (both adjacent to the Caspian Sea). Also in that geographical sphere are Tehran (at Sharif University), Mo'allem Kalaych as well as at Karaj. Natanz, Arak and Fordow followed. In the central regions, there are nuclear assets at Esfahan, Saghand and Yazd. So too, at Tabas, to the east of Birjand, near the border with Afghanistan. In the south, there is the huge Bushehr facility at the coast. Still more is at Darkhovin to the east of Basra and close to the Kuwaiti and Iraqi frontiers and at Fasa, east of Bushehr.

What is enormously significant is that any of these developments took place at all. Shortly after the death of Iran's revolutionary leader, the Ayatollah Ruholla Khomeini, the country's leading mullahs – quoting excerpts from the Holy Quran – declared that harnessing nuclear energy, whether for civil or military purposes, was contrary to the precepts of Islam. That fundamental approach has since been reversed, even though the public line remains clear. 'Iran is not, nor will it ever be a nuclear power', its diplomats routinely proclaim.

In 1989, former premier Ali Akbar Rafsanjani (who was always vocal about wiping Israel off the map) observed, 'Iran simply cannot ignore the nuclear reality in the modern world.' Nor was the possibility of Iran exploring chemical and biological warfare discarded. At a speech to a group of military officers, he stated:

'Chemical and biological weapons are the poor man's atomic bombs. They can easily be produced. We should at least consider them for our defence ... Although the use of such weapons is inhuman, the [Iran/Iraq] war taught us that international laws are only scraps of paper.'

Since then, there has been much effort in trying to acquire foreign WMD expertise and technology in all three NBC disciplines: nuclear, biological and chemical. Pakistan, for instance, was asked for uranium gas centrifuge technology and agreed to train Iranian nuclear scientists at its Institute for Nuclear Science and Technology near Islamabad. Argentina too, had overtures from Teheran and until US pressure was brought to bear, responded favourably. So did Cuba. Concurrently, reactors were sought from China, Russia and India. Others contacted were Poland, Czechoslovakia and Italy. The results have been mixed since Washington was able to block only some of these efforts.

Meanwhile, Beijing entered the picture. US officials believe that China constructed a uranium hexafluoride ($UF_6$) plant under a secret nuclear cooperation agreement signed in 1991. This allows raw uranium dioxide concentrate to be transformed into 93 per cent pure weapons grade HEU using gas ultracentrifuges.

That was followed by a report in the American publication *Nuclear Fuel* that it had uncovered a joint US/German sting operation in which former Soviet nuclear warheads were offered to the Islamic Republic of Iran for $3m apiece[5]. All this came to light when a Hanover businessman – who suggested the deal to an Iranian procurement officer in 1993 – told German prosecutors everything he knew.

While specifics remain classified, what did emerge was that attempts to buy nuclear warheads – as well as a variety of other military items – appeared to fall within the jurisdiction of Iran's Defence Industries Organization (DIO) which – German Intelligence insists – is a clandestine nuclear and military procurement agency. The list was originally brought to the attention of Bonn's Ministry of Defence by an Iranian who had shown a German a letter of introduction from the Atomic Energy Organization of Iran (AEOI). The witness disclosed that terms of sale were discussed after the prospective Iranian buyer had cleared the matter with the Ministry of Defence in Tehran.

Not to be ignored either was the visit to South Africa shortly afterwards by Reza Amrollahi, then head of AEOI and deputy president for Iran's atomic affairs. Curiously, this event continues to elicit denials from both parties.

On the Pakistani front, there were several disclosures made about the help that Tehran received from the A.Q. Khan nuclear proliferation network. Khan actually boasted in a television interview that he and other senior Pakistani officials – who were eager to see Iran develop nuclear weapons – guided that country to a proven network of suppliers and for several years helped advance its covert efforts[6]. Khan told a television interviewer in Karachi that if Iran succeeded in 'acquiring nuclear technology, we will be a strong bloc in the region to counter international pressure. Iran's nuclear capability will neutralize Israel's power.' Although Khan previously claimed nationalist and religious justifications for helping to spread the kind of sensitive technology which made him a fortune, several experts said his statement – there were quite a few - were unusually direct claims of broad, official Pakistani support for an Iranian nuclear weapon. Much of the information emerged as a consequence of an historic association between A.Q. Khan and former British journalist Simon Henderson, a senior fellow at the Washington Institute for Near East Policy with whom the Pakistani scientist shared information. Quoting Khan's original summary of events relating to Iran, the deal was apparently worth US $10 billion to Pakistan.

The intelligence service's summary provided by Henderson disclosed that General Mirza Aslam Beg, a former army chief of staff who for a long time was arguably Pakistan's most influential figure, was 'in favour of very close cooperation [with Iran] in the nuclear field in lieu of financial assistance promised to him toward Pakistan's defence budget.' Khan's written statement to Henderson stated that after Shamkhani's arrival in Islamabad on a government plane, he told the chairman of Pakistan's Joint Chiefs of Staff committee that 'he had come ... to collect the promised nuclear bombs'. It should be recalled that A.Q. Khan always denied being involved with the *actual* production of nuclear weapons: his line throughout was that his sphere of influence lay in enriching uranium, though obviously, with illegal proliferation, certain parameters were likely to be overstepped.

What also emerged was a 2006 Associated Press article that reported Beg's recollection of a 1990 visit by an Iranian delegation: 'They asked, "Can we have a bomb?" My answer was: By all means you can have it, but you must make it yourself.' On Pakistani television thereafter, Beg declared that he had 'always' urged the transfer of nuclear arms to Iran. The former Pakistani official said, 'Shamkhani thought he had a deal when he came to Pakistan.' Various top officials, the former official suggested, were aware that Beg told the Iranians, 'You have the money, we have the technology. Beg saw this as a win-win . . . a way to take care of the Army's endless budget problems...'

Among all the obfuscation surrounding much of Iran's nuclear weapons issues, the West is aware that Tehran has been most active in trying to acquire weapons-useable nuclear materials, plutonium or HEU. It is not surprising therefore that there are reports of Iranian agents having been active in the independent states of the Former Soviet Union (FSU) trying to buy the stuff. One example will do:

In November 1994, the United States disclosed that it had completed an airlift of 600 kilograms (1,300 pounds) of weapons-grade uranium from Ust-Kamenogorsk in Kazakhstan to the United States. The shipment, packed in IAEA steel transport drums was flown to Dover Air Force base in Delaware and then moved by road to Oak Ridge, Tennessee. Ostensibly – after long and complicated negotiations – the material was handed over in exchange for US aid.

The uranium at the Ublinsky Metallurgical Plant had apparently been left behind in the confusion of the Soviet collapse, which was possibly not all that surprising since the plant was believed to have been specializing in low enriched uranium (LEU) and exotic metals. In any event, work on HEU in Kazakhstan (as elsewhere in the former Soviet Union) was supposed to be secret. What worried the Americans was that there had been reports that even before Washington came to know that there was HEU stored there, Iranian agents had visited the plant. This is not unusual, since Iran maintains the second largest embassy in Kazakhstan. Even the Russians conceded at the time that Tehran's intelligence infrastructure throughout the region was better than average, often using the talents of dissident Muslims and liberal dollar handouts to achieve objectives.

Throwing money about was a useful ploy in a society where some officials had not been paid for half a year. It is also instructive that the US initially asked the Kazakh Government to block any possible Iranian transactions from the Ublinsky facility. As subsequent events proved, there was clearly enough doubt in the minds of Washington's security chiefs that the authorities at Ulba were either unable or unwilling to resist Iranian offers to take appropriate action. Of real concern for quite a few years was that Ulba was only one of dozens such nuclear storage depots in former Iron Curtain states where security, until fairly recently, was tenuous.

Of more concern are recent reports out of the CIS that indicate that the Russian *mafiya* is active in this field. Operators linked to the Russian underworld are known to accept bids from all comers. Worse, there is little regard for long-term political or security implications. How else in a society where, by March 1994, the Russian Federal Counterintelligence service (now the FSB) reported that there had been 900 thefts from military and nuclear plants? There were also 700 items of secret technology stolen in the second half of 1993 alone, much of it insider activity.

The South African Iranian connection puts matters further into perspective, especially since Pretoria has vehemently denied that the events originally described in a report I wrote for Jane's *International Defence Review* in March 1998. Significantly, the key individual involved at the time – and the source of all this information – was Dr Waldo Stumpf, former CEO of the South African nuclear facility at Pelindaba, near Pretoria. After the report appeared, Stumpf vigorously denied that a meeting, or meetings, with the Iranians had ever taken place. I was accused of fabricating the episode; he called it 'fictionalizing the event, if it even took place at all'.

Then early 2009, for reasons best known to himself, Dr Stumpf recanted and admitted that he had met the Iranians after all. The story, as it emerged, is interesting. Quite by chance, in late May 1997, I asked for and was given an opportunity to meet Dr Stumpf. The six atom bombs that had been built in the 1970s and 1980s were history, but Stumpf, a quietly-spoken, round-faced scientist, had been around in the industry for many years and I requested help with a few questions about an article I was doing for Britain's Jane's Information Group. It was nuclear related, I explained, something about Iraq. From Johannesburg, I called Stumpf's office on the outskirts of Pretoria for an appointment.

I managed to get through to him immediately and though he was interested, he said it was difficult because of timing. He was leaving the next evening for Syria. 'But come along anyway and let's see what we can do.' The drive to Pelindaba should normally have taken an hour, but I got there in about forty five minutes. After stringent security checks at the gate, I was ushered into the office of the man who was the chief executive officer of NECSA, a position he held from 1990 to 2001. Because of constraints, I had expected the meeting with the man who has worked in the nuclear industry for three decades to last perhaps ten minutes. Instead, I departed Pelindaba after an hour.

It was an informative meeting. Stumpf, a Fellow of the South African Academy of Engineering, has an impressive academic record. He holds a Bachelor of Science degree in Engineering (Metallurgy) from the University of Pretoria and a PhD from Sheffield University, apart from a string of other qualifications, most of them linked to engineering. After completing his studies at Sheffield in 1968 on microstructural aspects of ferritic chromium steels during hot working, he regularly taught a postgraduate course on phase transformations in solids within the department. Professionally, his particular area of interest lies in the optimization of physical properties of metals and alloys through microstructural optimization by the design of heat treatment or hot working processes or by alloy design. Quite a mouthful!

Having finished our business, Dr Stumpf questioned me at length about my own activities abroad as a writer and correspondent: I had published more than a dozen books by then and he was familiar with my work. Had he not been, I probably would not have been allowed in the door; this was a busy man. He was also curious about my own forays into some of the Arab countries, especially since I had only recently returned from Damascus.

It was then that his mood turned conspiratorial. Almost offhand, he admitted that only recently, late May that year, he had played host to a group of Iranians at Pelindaba. Among them, he confided, was Iran's deputy minister of atomic affairs, Reza Amrollahi:

'I got a call from the President's office in Cape Town soon after getting in that morning – not from President Mandela himself, but one of his aides. I was told that a high level Iranian party, including Amrollahi – who I already knew from international meetings we had both attended – was on its way to Pretoria. There were no ifs or buts: they would be here by about noon.'

What was immediately troubling, Stumpf confided, was the haste in which the meeting had been arranged. Nothing was according to form. Had there been time, he would have liked to arrange for one of the international observers to be present, someone from the International Atomic Energy Agency. However, there was no time. In any event, the IAEA has a strictly monitoring role and the IAEA does not have personnel permanently stationed at Pelindaba.

By his own account, Dr Stumpf first reaction was to have somebody else in the office while these obviously sensitive discussions took place:

'These were clearly delicate matters: it wouldn't be in either my or Pelindaba's interest to meet alone with an Iranian deputy minister, especially someone involved with matters nuclear. So I called Pik Botha, until a short time before, my immediate superior. He had been South Africa's minister of Energy and Minerals Affairs until the post was taken over by Penuell Maduna. Fortunately, Pik was in Pretoria that day.'

As Stumpf explained, Pik Botha was one of the few white cabinet ministers that President Mandela had appointed to his new Coalition Government and Pelindaba had fallen within his bailiwick. 'I called and told him what was taking place and asked that he be present at the meeting. He would be with me within the hour, he replied.'

To Stumpf, the implications of the visit were obvious, which was why he was determined not to meet the Iranian alone:

'The encounter was formal but friendly. For a short while we talked about his visit to South Africa, what he had seen and what he still hoped to do. Then Minister Amrollahi handed me a file and, for a moment or two I just knew what was happening. It wasn't a big pile of papers, just a few details.'

The documents, he explained, contained a comprehensive list of items needed for the manufacture of an atom bomb. According to Dr Stumpf, there were some fairly advanced things requested by the Iranian party; blueprints, industrial, chemical and laboratory equipment and other essentials required for this kind of weapon production. 'Obviously we were stunned,' he recalled afterwards.

The two South Africans had to reject the request. Stumpf told Amrollahi that in accordance with the provisions of the Non-proliferation Treaty, there was no way that either he or members of his staff at Pelindaba could comply. He pointed out that not only had South Africa recently signed the NPT, but, as everybody present in the room was aware, the country had destroyed its entire nuclear weapons arsenal. Additionally, all documents relating to the manufacture of atom bombs had been shredded:

'Then I told him that since Iran was a NPT signatory, the nature of the visit was understandably compromising. We South Africans are being asked to break international law.'

Stumpf reminded his guest of what had happened not very long before in Iraq following 'Operation Desert Storm'. Once the names of some of the German scientists recruited by Saddam Hussein to work in Iraqi nuclear weapons programme had become known in the weapons strip-search by the IAEA Action Team and the UN Special Commission on Iraq (UNSCOM), warrants of arrest were issued. Two of those involved in the Iraqi effort were charged with treason. Last heard, one was still in jail, he added:

> 'So I made it quite clear that, with respect, it would simply not be possible for us to comply with his request. Besides, there were international safeguards in place at Pelindaba to prevent exactly that from happening.'

Aware that he might have exceeded his brief in telling me all this, Waldo Stumpf edged closer and insisted that everything was to remain off-the-record. For a month or two afterwards, it stayed that way. At the same time, I was deeply troubled by what I heard, specifically because of long-term international security implications. This was simply too potent a matter to let it rest.

Back in London shortly afterwards, I mentioned my meeting at the Pelindaba nuclear establishment to Clifford Beal, at that time the American-born editor of Jane's *International Defence Review*. Now it was my turn for confidences. I was worried by what I had been told, I told Beal. I suggested that if it were true that Iran was interested in building nuclear weapons, then the ramifications of such actions were incalculable. The lives of people could be at stake if this thing ever got to the fruition stage. Not only that, I declared, but the new South African government would be complicit in helping a maverick Islamic state develop something that could unalterably tip the balance of power in a region half the size of Europe. 'The world has a right to know,' I said, explaining in some detail the nature of my meeting with Stumpf.

On the last point, Clifford Beal's view was that I should follow the dictates of my conscience. He knew my style as well as the way I worked. By then I had been contributing to IDR – first in Geneva, and afterwards in Coulsdon, Surrey – for almost a quarter century. As for getting the story out, Beal was emphatic. 'It is hardly for me to tell you what to do, but let's face it, you do owe that much to the society in which you live.'

Having thought the matter through, the article was published shortly thereafter in the September 1997 issue of the magazine, which came out in late August. Days later, it was picked up by *The Times* under the headline: 'Iran Sought Pretoria Nuclear Deal'. In the interests of veracity and because I was aware that I had betrayed a trust, I went a step further after speaking to my editor. Just before IDR went to press, I contacted Phillip van Niekerk, an old friend from Sierra Leone's mercenary days – we had covered the activities of Executive Outcomes together. At that stage Phillip was editor of South Africa's most politically outspoken weekly, the *Mail & Guardian*, then still partly owned by Britain's *Guardian* newspaper. His job as editor gradually evolved into something of a personal crusade, a watchdog role in covering polemical government activities. I was in a quandary, I told him and I explained why. Up to that point my report was based solely on the basis of 'I said, he said'. I felt that I needed a bit of help to back up what had taken place, if only to assuage my own worries. Phillip van Niekerk agreed to look into the matter. If it shaped the way he thought it might, he would run the story a week after it appeared in the IDR, he told me.

In retrospect, I am pleased that he did. Van Niekerk immediately tasked Mungo Sogget, the *Mail & Guardian's* senior investigative journalist to look into what had happened. It was a good choice: there are those who refer to Sogget as 'the pit bull', though never to his face. When Pik Botha was asked by Sogget in a phone call to his home in Pretoria a day or two later whether Amrollahi's visit had in fact taken place – and whether Dr Stumpf had been presented with a nuclear 'shopping list' – Botha replied that he was not only aware of the event, 'I was there when it happened.'

Once the articles were out, the South African government reacted with uncharacteristic vigour. Within days, the matter was raised in Parliament in Cape Town and I was branded a liar. In answer to a Parliamentary Question, Stumpf declared that 'the entire story is fiction …Venter made it all up'. He made a statement saying that the only time he had ever met with any Iranian official was at a dinner in the presence of a large number of people. Stumpf also denied that Deputy Minister Reza Amrollahi had ever visited South Africa. Clearly, the man had been well primed.

Nor was Botha ever quite so forthcoming again. Shortly after returning to America, I related the whole sorry saga to another old friend, Dr Jonathan Tucker, then head of the Chemical and Biological Weapons Nonproliferation Programme at the Monterey Institute of International Affairs in California. I gave him Pik Botha's personal phone number. Only later did I hear that the South African minister slammed down the receiver as soon as Tucker raised the Iranian issue.

With that, Pretoria went into overdrive. The South African government issued a statement on 11 September that 'the country's Atomic Energy Corporation (AEC) had never been involved in any business transactions with Iran, nor were any being considered at present,' said Mineral and Energy Affairs Minister Penuell Maduna. 'Atomic Energy Commission CEO Dr. Waldo Stumpf never held a meeting with Iran's deputy minister of atomic affairs Reza Amrollahi, as claimed by local and foreign news media,' he declared in a written reply to National Party member Johan Marais.

Stumpf confirmed that the only meeting that he, or any other AEC official had ever had with any Iranian government official, took place in March 1995 in a public restaurant in Cape Town with Iranian petroleum minister Gholamreza Aghazadeh. Stumpf had been asked to attend the courtesy dinner by former Mineral and Energy Affairs Minister Pik Botha during Aghazadeh's visit to South Africa in connection with a possible oil storage deal at Saldanha Bay on the country's west coast. 'Botha did not attend the dinner, although other Iranian petroleum officials and South African officials were present,' Maduna said.

If all this were true, one must ask why Stumpf would chose to be evasive about such a sensitive issue, especially at a time when it must have become clear to several nations that Tehran was committed to covertly building an atom bomb of its own? His move was exacerbated by Botha – irrespective what he told Mungo Sogget – when the minister came out in strong support of his statement,

More pertinently, why did both men, respected professionals, chose to lie about something so vital? This was an issue that might ultimately result in the course of history being irrevocably changed in the most volatile region in the world. Clearly, both men know the answer to that one. So did several South African cabinet ministers who were involved. Reza Amrollahi had been in the country at the time and as we have seen, the meeting did take place. Both Botha and Stumpf were obviously put under severe pressure to recant, and, one must ask, for what reason? It is interesting that though this writer was vilified in Parliament, this matter – controversial as it is – was allowed to rest there.

It is also a fact that in an effort to get to the bottom of it and possibly claim defamation damages, Stumpf, highly regarded by his peers, had recourse to the country's courts where my claim could have been tested. Instead, he did nothing. Nor did the government, even though nuclear weapons issues in South Africa are still subject to restrictions, especially something as disputatious as supplying a foreign state with information related to WMD. One can only speculate whether the reticence of both men might have had something to do with their state pensions being withheld if they refused to cooperate. They are going to have to live with that reality.

Though Stumpf did eventually admit that the meeting with the Iranian minister Amrollahi did actually take place, he has never apologised for publicly calling me a liar.

## Chapter 16

# The Illegal Proliferation of Nuclear Materials Out of the Former Soviet Union

*Let me throw a hypothetical operation onto the table. The Islamic State has billions of dollars in the bank, so they call on their wilāyah in Pakistan to purchase a nuclear device through weapons dealers with links to corrupt officials in the region. The weapon is then transported overland until it makes it to Libya, where the mujahedeen move it south to Nigeria. Drug shipments from Columbia bound for Europe pass through West Africa, so moving other types of contraband from East to West is just as possible. The nuke and accompanying mujahedeen arrive on the shorelines of South America and are transported through the porous borders of Central America before arriving in Mexico and up to the border with the United States. From there it's just a quick hop through a smuggling tunnel and hey presto, they're mingling with another 12 million "illegal" aliens in America with a nuclear bomb in the trunk of their car.'*

John Cantlie, a British correspondent kidnapped by militants in Syria in November 2012 whose prognosis for a nuclear terror attack appeared in the May, 2015 edition of *Dabiq*, the Islamic State's English-language online magazine.

In a sobering assessment of radical Islamic aspirations to drop a nuclear bomb on the heads of a million Americans, David Albright and Sarah Burkhard succinctly spelled out this prospect in an article which appears on the website of Washington's Institute for Science and International Security. Titled 'Daesh Hype about Stealing Nuclear Weapons,' both writers go straight to the nub of the problem and in the process, they manage to encapsulate Islamic State sentiments by quoting Cantlie.

Though things have moved on a bit in embattled Iraq and Syria, both authorities maintain that with Daesh (Islamic State) entrenched in parts of the Middle East and their influence growing in North Africa and Pakistan, the risk of the terrorist group or one of its allies trying to acquire nuclear weapons is likely to increase. Or at least this is what they want the world to think since their publications imply these intentions, they aver, adding that Daesh's public claims of ways to accomplish that goal are unfounded and mainly seem intended to simply incite fear.

'[In Washington] we assess that the risk of Daesh acquiring nuclear weapons is low. However, that characterization needs to be carefully considered. The chance of [this terror group] acquiring a nuclear weapon – either through theft of a functioning nuclear weapon or of nuclear explosive material followed by the manufacturing of a crude nuclear explosive – is assessed as low, similar to the risk of a major nuclear reactor accident, such as the Chernobyl and Fukushima disasters,' said Albright and Burkhard.

However, they maintain, the outcome would be horrible and extraordinary efforts would be necessary to ensure that the risk becomes even lower. 'A nuclear explosive going off in a major city would have catastrophic consequences, probably far worse than those of Chernobyl or Fukishima,' is their take on such an eventuality. 'While the threat of Daesh stealing or otherwise acquiring a nuclear weapon needs to be taken seriously, Daesh writings on the subject should be discounted.'

The scenario as propounded by John Cantlie is indeed frightening but, they say, the prospect of it happening is highly unlikely, for many reasons:

'Stealing a nuclear weapon in Pakistan would be extraordinarily difficult. Moreover, if such a weapon were stolen in Pakistan, that theft would likely be detected; it would lead to a massive worldwide hunt for it and the perpetrators. Under these conditions, getting the weapon out of Pakistan and transporting it through Africa to the Americas, and finally into the United States, would be extraordinarily difficult. Detection and interdiction would almost certainly be assured before it reached its target in the United States.

'However, if the theft were not detected, would the authorities discover and seize the bomb in time? Likely, but that outcome is not as assured. Nuclear weapons can be notoriously difficult to detect during shipment if authorities are not on heightened alert. As a result, the priority remains ensuring that the theft of functioning nuclear weapons is practically impossible and that, in the chance that one is stolen, its theft is rapidly discovered and resources are quickly deployed to get it back before it is detonated. All the major nations of the world have agreed on those goals and are working to make sure they are achieved.

'In conclusion, the threat of Daesh seeking nuclear weapons must be taken seriously, and countries need to constantly improve their nuclear security over nuclear weapons and nuclear explosive materials, both against external and insider threats. Moreover, the threat of Daesh acquiring radiological materials that it could use as a terrorist weapon deserves special concern, scrutiny, and further remediation. However, the chance of Daesh stealing a nuclear weapon is currently very low.'

That said, there has been a good deal of clandestine movement of potential nuclear bomb-making components over past decades. London's *The Economist*, in a report headed 'A Weighty Matter' reported on 27 February 2010 that

'between 1992 and 2007 seventeen kg [almost forty pounds] of highly enriched uranium was seized from smugglers around the world, along with 400 grams of plutonium [about a pound]. In neither case is that enough for a proper atom bomb, but is still worrying…'

The magazine was drawing on a series of studies made by Dr Ian Hutcheon of the Lawrence Livermore National Laboratory in California. That followed his presentation of a paper in San Diego a short while before which dealt with analysing this captured material. His conclusions were disturbing and suggested that there is more of this sort of thing going than the international community might be aware of.

To understand why there are so many Third World countries currently engaged in illegal nuclear programmes, we need to understand how they have been able to acquire the kind of fissile materials that might be used in constructing a 'Dirty Bomb'.

Following the collapse of the old order in the Soviet Union, Washington expressed disappointment at the inability of Moscow to 'adequately safeguard its nuclear bomb-making materials'. America had poured millions of dollars into Russian nuclear complexes, but still, these facilities remained off limits. This effectively prevented anybody from being able to determine whether the money was being appropriately spent. In hindsight, looking at the broader canvas with regard to safeguarding (or trying to protect) Russian fissile material since the collapse of the Former Soviet, an awful lot of American money was wasted. Much was misappropriated, some of it ending up in Swiss bank accounts.

For all that, the United States Congress in 2009 authorized around $1.2 billion for American programmes that provide non-proliferation and threat reduction assistance to the former Soviet Union. And while such projects resulted in a considerable amount of fissile material being taken off the market and removed from vulnerable storage sites, and have made it far harder to obtain fissile material today than it was in 1990 or even 2000, it is only part of the story.

Earlier, the so-called Nuclear Material Production, Control and Accounting Program had provided more than $150m for about 100 projects. But what soon became apparent was that some of the money had not been used for the purposes for which it was intended. Rose Gottemoller, at that time head of the Department of Energy (DoE) Office of Non-proliferation, attributed some problems to the 'difficulty of opening doors to Russia's weapons-making facilities'. Because there was fissile material leaving Russia illegally, she declared, it was simply not possible to check how well Moscow's nuclear assets were being guarded, or in the case of some of the remoter dumps, being properly guarded at all. That comment was made as more instances of nuclear smuggling emerged, specifically of plutonium ($^{239}$Pu) and highly enriched uranium ($^{235}$U or, more commonly, HEU or highly enriched uranium) and the reality that the Russians were unable to account for these lapses.

There were many such cases in the past and more emerge with time. For instance, the interception of a cache of stolen uranium at Batumi, a few miles from the Georgian/Turkish border in the late 1990s prompted a strong reaction by Washington, with the State Department emphasizing that this was the second such incident within weeks. There have been many others since. According to an American intelligence source with whom the author made contact these – and many other such events – suggested a possible security breakdown either at a Former Soviet Union (FSU) nuclear fuel fabrication factory or an atomic energy plant, and that, despite the two superpowers having signed an agreement on cooperation in the monitoring and safeguarding of nuclear material.

These events were followed by a Tbilisi report that mentioned a quantity of uranium pellets found in the possession of Valiko Chkmivadze, a sixty-year-old Georgian with a history of illegally trading in fissile materials. He had previously been arrested by the Ankara authorities on suspicion of dealing in smuggled uranium but was never brought to trial. Worse, nobody was prepared to say why.

Turkish nationals (with their country bordering on several countries with dubious political agendas) seem to have taken the lead in smuggling prohibited material in recent years. There are known to be scores of attempts at trying to move such contraband to countries in the Near East using Turkey as a conduit. There are probably a lot more that we do not know about, because the felons would have got through undetected. In early 2000 for instance, a man was apprehended with a 'certificate for the purchase of uranium-235' together with a quantity of the radioactive metal in a 2kg lead container. Its origin was given as Moldova, while the illegal substance was recovered at Dounav Most, a village on the Bulgarian/Turkish border.

About the same time, roughly 6kg of 'non-active' solid uranium together with 8kg of 'active' plutonium from the 'secure' Upounda Metallurgy Plant in

Ust-Kamenogorsk, Kazakhstan, was taken from a man who had been arrested in Istanbul. It was established later that he was linked to a smuggling gang involving four Turks and three Kazakhis. A member of this group was a Kazakh army colonel which gives some indication of the measure of protection the gang was afforded.

That was followed by thirteen cylinders of uranium marked 'UPAT UKA3 M8' destined for Iran and seized at the Turkish town of Van. In a separate incident at Bursa, also in Turkey, 200 grams of enriched uranium from Azerbaijan was taken. Interestingly, also recovered were two shipments of about 2kg each of HEU out of Georgia. One lot was impounded in Switzerland, the other in Yalova, Turkey and both were destined for Libya. Those hauls were followed by 2kg of enriched $^{235}$U intercepted in Istanbul. Once it was established that it was intended for Iran, several Turkish nationals and suspect Iranian secret service agents were taken into custody.

Following these disclosures, a US State Department official told me in an unofficial briefing at Hanford, Washington while I was still living in America, that there were other nuclear-related issues that remained unresolved. For instance, United States non-proliferation and disarmament experts were having difficulty in trying to get the Russians to disclose specific details of their fissile material stocks. Again, these referred to both plutonium and HEU. The imbroglio, he stated, stemmed from the fact that US nuclear facilities, curiously, had the same problem with their accountability.

'Each time we ask them to give us an *exact* rundown, they countered by asking us whether we could do the same. Of course, we cannot, because this is an incredibly complex issue,' the specialist disclosed. Speaking on a condition of anonymity, he told me that the last time a survey of stocks of US plutonium was done, 'there was an uncertainty of about 2.8 metric tons (MT) of plutonium at American nuclear plants. In addition, losses to waste were put at about 3.4 MT.'

Part of the reason, he explained, was that while the plutonium manufacturing process is very well understood in general, there were some specifics about which the scientists were still a little uncertain. This was more marked in the early days. For instance, numerous computational irregularities at the beginning were really only resolved in the 1970s and might have included specifics as to how much plutonium a certain reactor might produce or how long it had been operational. 'One needs to keep in mind that apart from some pretty obvious uncertainties, a lot of this stuff is still classified. Restrictions apply as much to Russia as to America,' he stated, stressing that the so-called 'missing' plutonium at US nuclear establishments had not actually been stolen. Instead, there were several other factors involved. 'These range from trying to estimate the amount of plutonium still trapped in trans-uranic waste (TRU), to possibly something as mundane as inadequately kept books.' Since the first plutonium was produced in 1944, the industry had to gingerly 'feel its way' through a series of difficult phases that had never been dealt with before and establish its own parameters. Moscow has in the past been faced with exactly the same problems.

In order to comprehend how and why fissile or nuclear material goes missing in Russia, one needs to look carefully at how DoE stocks are stored and managed in America. Some striking differences emerge. For example, the US Department of Energy disclosed that before 1978, inventory differences were identified as 'Materials Unaccounted For' or MUF. At various times, MUF included the fractional amounts of nuclear materials lost in regular day-to-day operations. These were listed as normal operating losses. There were also accidental losses as well as materials possibly removed from a facility for quality control and safeguards analysis.

He made the point that since it was not prudent to discount the fact that a small inventory difference in US stocks might be due to theft, all losses were investigated, analysed and resolved to ascertain whether an actual theft or diversion had taken place. If necessary, he stated, an entire operation might be shut down until these differences were resolved. It was his view that matters for the Americans had improved markedly since the earlier period. It was worth noting, he added, that almost 70 per cent of inventory differences had occurred during a period when the learning curve was being established, largely through a complex process of trial and error.

In answer to a query, the DoE released details relating to American plutonium removals from the period 1944 to September 1994 (the period under review at the time). Of a total of 111.4 MT of plutonium produced or acquired in the half century (of which 85 per cent was weapons grade), only 12 MT was removed from the DoE/Department of Defence inventory. Of this, 3.4 MT was expended in wartime and nuclear tests; 2.8 MT was due to inventory differences; 3.4 MT was waste (normal operating losses); 1.2 MT was consumed by fission and transmutation while 0.4 MT was lost to decay and other removals. A total of 0.1 MT was transferred to US civilian industry for use in power reactors and 0.7 MT went to foreign countries, details of which remain secret.

Another source at the Hanford nuclear facility disclosed that the core of the problem with shortages lay with the production process. The system had always been fraught with uncertainties. For instance, nuclear physicists were aware from the start that plutonium was subject to a variety of natural losses. 'Some of it was trapped in process lines and waste streams (and it is still there) some tons of it,' he disclosed. There is even more in liquid waste dump grounds. About a half-a-ton of it had decayed.

Until fairly recently it was believed that radioactive waste products that had been left standing for many years (and sometimes for decades) might be close to criticality. Consequently, for a long time the authorities were simply unwilling to tamper with it. Some of this fissile material was certainly unstable, but at facilities like Hanford, Savannah River and Los Alamos, clean-up programmes resulted in much of it being stabilized and stored in preparation for the move to the Waste Isolation Pilot Plant at Carlsbad, New Mexico.

Thus, claimed the man from the State Department, exactly the same situation prevailed for Russian or FSU nuclear processing plants when faced with similar problems:

'The only difference between the two countries is that while it is all but impossible to get into Hanford or Colorado's Rocky Flats undetected – never mind try to take something out illegally – that has not always been the case in Russia since the collapse of the Soviet Union.

'Not only are the FSU installations badly guarded, but we have discovered that some of the sophisticated monitoring equipment supplied free by Washington was sometimes not put into service. Or it was declared unworkable, perhaps not properly understood, faulty or subjected to power cuts.'

In one or two instances, he confided, the equipment was never installed. More importantly, he said, 'Russian security personnel in the earlier, transitional period were often not paid for months at a stretch,' though he conceded that things had much improved since then. It was so bad, he suggested, that staff sometimes lacked the motivation to do a proper job, especially during the winter months when some were more interested in keeping themselves warm than watching dials. 'You can accept that it was probably a lot worse on an empty stomach.'

One result of Russian nuclear disparities was that such issues were somewhere near the top of most agendas each time there was a meeting between Russian and American heads of state. As one official at State phrased it, 'George W. Bush and Putin took on very much where Clinton and Yeltsin left off.' Early in 2000 for example, Reuters reported that a woman had been arrested in Vladivostok for trying to sell radioactive metal. Although she was employed at a base at Bolshoi Kamen (near the home of the Russian Pacific Fleet), the alloy was not from there, insisted Grigory Pavlenko a director of the Zvezda maintenance plant. What he did confirm, however, was that his company serviced nuclear submarines and much of the work was with nuclear fuels.

In a statement, the police in Vladivostok said that their investigation showed that the stolen HEU and other rare metals probably came from one of the many atomic plants in the region. Police and factory investigators subsequently carefully checked stocks but could find no missing atomic materials. The woman was arrested after she tried to sell a 4kg piece of the metal for $65,000. It had been kept in a local lock-up garage near her home and at the time of the arrest, had been wrapped in newspaper and was being carried about in a shopping bag. What astonished the investigators was that the radioactive substance exceeded safe radiation levels by more than 2,500 times, a Russian source disclosed[1].

In another incident almost immediately afterwards, Kyrgyz security service agents arrested an Uzbeki national trying to smuggle 8kg of plutonium aboard a flight to the United Arab Emirates. The man said that he had been offered $16,000 to smuggle the shipment out of the country. The plutonium – used in the detonation devices of nuclear bombs – had been carefully packed in a rubber container. Unconfirmed reports indicated that it was intended for Iran. As with the Vladivostok incident, *Itar-Tass* said afterwards that the origins of the radioactive metal could not be established.

Richard Meserve, former chairman of the US National Research Council (part of the US National Academy of Science) issued a statement not long afterwards. He declared that while joint efforts by Russia and America had strengthened security at many sites, 'we believe that terrorist groups or rogue nations have more opportunity to gain access to Russian plutonium and highly-enriched uranium than we had previously estimated'. A Moscow spokesman Yuri Bespalko immediately countered, maintaining that 'the safety and protection of Russian nuclear materials met and, in some ways, even exceeded international standards'.

Not long thereafter, the Norwegian nuclear watchdog organization Bellona reported that the Russian security police had arrested five people in St Petersburg for trying to sell a radioactive Californium-252 as well as about 20kg of mercury from the nuclear icebreaker base Atomflot, in Murmansk. Police made the interesting comment at the time that the radiation source 'could be used for the perfect murder'. Californium-252 is a strong emitter of neutron radiation and is used as a starter for nuclear reactors. It was customarily stored in quarter-ton containers onboard the *Imandra*, a Russian fleet supply ship. To transfer this radioactive material to an icebreaker, a bucket-sized container, carried by one man, was used.

Norway's Bellona has made the point many times over that there are certain aspects of the case that simply do not make sense. In recent years, it says, the DoE (through a project called Material Protection and Accountability) supplied both the *Imandra* and the Atomflot base with physical protection equipment. Also, radiation detectors had been installed at the entrance to the Atomflot base. Because the stolen material emitted radiation 350 times higher than background levels, it should have automatically triggered electronic alarms already in place (again, courtesy of the Americans). They conceded that the stuff might have been taken through a hole in the fence, or that the equipment wasn't working or possibly that the guards might, with some kind of financial incentive, have been encouraged to look the other way.

Interestingly, questions were also raised about the ease with which the Russian FSB security police made the St Petersburg arrests and whether the operation was not a set-up to convince Washington that they were doing a good job protecting Russian nuclear assets[2].

In a related comment, the US Department of Energy's Pacific Northwest National Laboratory (PNNL) in Washington State suggested during this writer's visit to the facility that what was often overlooked in trying to assess the Russian problem was 'weapons-radioactive materials that could be used in terrorist acts as pollutants rather than as fissionables.' Part of the reason why this issue was not being confronted, it was suggested, was that 'it would need to expand coverage to include literally everything radioactive...that would encompass radon waste-storage sites, medical waste and the rest...'

In the long term, stressed PNNL's Dr Michael Foley, radioactive contamination by hostile elements could become a serious security threat, a sentiment echoed by several other specialists dealing with these issues. Other incidents involving the illegal movement of radioactive materials or equipment include the following:

- A theft at the Kola nuclear power plant in 1999, when thieves removed two items that were part of the automatic radiation monitoring system at the facility's fourth reactor unit. For a full day, the plant lost control over radiation levels but managed to regain it[3]. The thieves were never identified and there were indications that the goods might have been targeted for outside or foreign interests.
- A month before that incident, a theft in the Kola plant's turbine machinery led to an automatic shutdown of its No.1 reactor unit. Kola Nuclear Power Plant at the time operated four VVVR-440 reactors commissioned between 1973 and 1984.
- A conscript onboard one of Russia's Northern Fleet's nuclear submarines at the Vidyaevo base pillaged more than twenty lengths of palladium-vanadium wire from the reactor room at about the same time. The significance here is that it could have been highly radioactive. The Murmansk newspaper *Polyarnaya Pravda* reported that the wire was used in communications systems of vital control devices on board nuclear submarines. When removed, they prevented the installation from being operated. The next day the sailor sold the wire to a Russian Navy petty officer for $45. It should be mentioned that Vidyaevo was the main base for Russian Akula class submarines, at that stage the most advanced attack-class submarines. In September 1998, another conscript shot eight of his colleagues and hijacked an Akula Class submarine at Skalisty on the Kola Peninsula. He was killed by Spetsnaz troops after a twenty-three-hour standoff.
- Six containers containing caesium-137 were stolen from a refinery in Volvograd in May 1998. Each of the 180 kg containers held a single capsule with about 1 cm³ caesium-137. If taken out of its container, the deadly capsule could radiate up to

400 roentgens/hr. Volvograd police spokesman Pyotr Lazarev disclosed that the caesium was used in electronic equipment that monitors chemical processes in the oil refinery and that the thieves would probably try to sell the isotopes abroad. He added that there was a certain demand on the black market for caesium, which could be used by terrorists in Radiological Dispersal Devices (RDDs or 'Dirty Bombs') and other terrorist acts. The Volvograd theft was the second that month: Two containers of caesium were also stolen from a cobalt smelter in the southern Siberian republic of Tuva but later recovered.

- The previous March, a number of radioactive pipes were stolen from the premises of the Chernobyl nuclear power plant. In a theft characterized by *Deutche Presse Agentur* as 'not the first of its kind', thieves removed irradiated pipes.
- Smugglers attempted to move a quantity of weapons-grade uranium that had been stolen in Novosibirsk in March 1997 into Kazakhstan, according to a local paper *Novoya Sibir*. A year later, the gang was smashed by a police follow-up team shortly before they were due to hand over the uranium pellets. Again, the origin of the fissile material was never identified. Questioned about the incident, Vladimir Orlov, Director of the Centre for Political Studies in Moscow, said that by then, more than twenty criminal cases had been launched in Russia and that all were related to the theft of radioactive materials. In a subsequent article in *Nuclear Control*, Bellona quotes Orlov as saying that 'the possibilities to smuggle nuclear materials for organised professionals remains quite high'.
- Also in 1997, a cache of almost 5kg of uranium was seized by police at the home of a man in the north Caucasus town of Ivanov. Police traced the HEU to the nuclear research centre at Sarov (formerly Arzamas-16) from where it had been stolen three years before. Meanwhile, the report said, it had been kept at the man's home in a metal cylinder inside a lead isolator[4].

Discussing conditions in present-day Russia, where security controls are far more stringent today compared to the earlier Perestroika or glasnost period, Kevin O'Neill, erstwhile deputy director of Washington's ISIS declared that 'Russia today cannot guarantee that nuclear explosive materials have not found their way to proliferating countries such as Iran or Iraq or to terrorists seeking nuclear weapons,' O'Neill's comment came during one of my early visits to Washington, though he did concede that much had improved in the new and revitalized Russia after President Putin took over. His comments are nonetheless instructive since much damage had already been done because of inadequate security controls. 'The lack of security and accounting of these materials has been one of the most troubling and immediate proliferation threats in the post-Cold War world,' he declared.

O'Neill said that the Russian economic free-fall that followed Gorbachev becoming president had had a dramatic impact on Moscow's ability to implement upgrades at its nuclear sites. For example, he said, 'US Department of Energy officials relate stories of MVD guards leaving their posts to look for food. Also, there were numerous cases of inadequate clothing and heating units for guards, coupled with unreliable communications, as well as cuts to electricity supplies at the various sites housing nuclear materials.' Meantime, there were several nations eager to take advantage of a situation that took time to correct, among them Iraq and Iran. In a last-ditch effort to help the Russians cope, the US provided emergency rations, portable generators, warm clothes and other items at sites participating in the upgrade programmes.

Elsewhere – around the northern ports of Murmansk and Archangel in the Kola Peninsula in the Russian Arctic, way north of Moscow, hundreds of redundant nuclear submarines were then being dismantled (as they still are today). To assist the Russians in their efforts to upgrade nuclear safety, the West pumped tens of millions of dollars into the region. But because this naval work was then – and still is – handled in what are termed 'closed cities', there was simply no way of telling whether the money was devoted to the purposes intended. The Kremlin assured the West that it was. Others have been more sceptical[5].

As O'Neill explained, the problem, essentially, was that by the time the Soviet Union collapsed in 1991, the former superpower had produced the world's largest stockpile of plutonium and highly enriched uranium. These materials come in many forms – in nuclear weapons and components, metal and oxide reactor fuel elements (including both fresh and spent fuels), bulk oxides for processing, metal 'buttons' as well as in a phenomenal amount of radioactive waste. Moreover, O'Neill elaborated, fissile materials were located in hundreds of buildings and in dozens of sites spread across the entire former Soviet Union, but principally in Russia. Most of it (and all the nuclear weapons) were under the control of either the Russian Ministry of Atomic Energy (Minatom) or the Ministry of Defence[6].

While nuclear weapons in the FSU were generally better accounted for and protected than non-military fissile materials, a number of Western authorities regarded some storage sites to be vulnerable. Transporting these nuclear assets also presented gaps which might have been exploited by those wishing to acquire fissile materials. Still worse, many of Russia's fissile material production facilities and other related locations lacked fundamental material protection, control and accountancy systems (MPC&A) which were essential to detect or prevent theft.

The chief of the Federal Security Service (FSB) in the Chelyabinsk region at the time told the Russian newspaper *Itar-Tass* that in December 2000, his agents had prevented the theft of 18kg of fissile material[7]. O'Neill maintained that while he hadn't seen the specifics, he was told on good authority during a visit to Moscow that the stuff was 'radioactive materials used for nuclear weapons production'. Another source mentioned weapons-grade uranium. According to a submission made to a Senate Select Committee on Intelligence in January 1998, 3kg of HEU was seized by the Russian police in St Petersburg.

Mayak, Russia's principal facility for processing nuclear materials for weapons (where over thirty tons of HEU is stored at any one time) was also in the news when an overhaul of security measures went into effect. Mayak also handles spent nuclear fuel as part of the Chelyabinsk-65 nuclear complex, one of Moscow's main weapons development facilities. According to Bill Gertz of the *Washington Times*, the CIA told a Senate Intelligence Committee that while nuclear warheads in Russia were relatively secure, 'declining morale and discipline in the military as well as economic conditions, raise our concerns about the potential for warhead theft'. The report added[8] that Russian nuclear weapons-useable fissile material – plutonium as well as HEU – 'are more vulnerable to theft than nuclear weapons or warheads'.

Significantly, the Mayak plant in the South Urals (and its associated residential community) has been listed under several different names over the years. It was originally Chelyabinsk-40, then Chelyabinsk-65, all with anonymous Chelyabinsk post office box numbers. Recently, the residential side (a closed Russian city) was allowed to rename itself Ozersk – City of the Lakes – because it nestles up against Lake Kyzyltash and has a beachfront park. The reactor/reprocessing/industrial complex is called the Mayak Production Association and is now distinguished apart from Ozersk.

In a presentation to the Defence and Security Committee of the North Atlantic Assembly in 1998, William Potter, a director of the Centre for Nonproliferation Studies, Monterey Institute, disclosed that at some Russian facilities, recently-installed security equipment was not being used because there was not enough money to maintain it. Similarly, at some installations entire security systems – alarms, surveillance cameras, portal monitors and more – had been shut down because electricity was cut off for non-payment of bills[9]. Thereafter, Barbara Slavin reported in *USA Today*[10] that at other facilities 'guards had intentionally turned off alarm systems or even cut their cables because they were annoyed by frequent false alarms'.

In several instances, in non-Russian republics, after being asked by plant officials to help measure the fissile stocks at their sites, Vienna's International Atomic Energy Agency found fissile stocks to be in excess of what was on record. In one area, dozens of kilos of fissile materials were discovered. Still more disconcerting, nobody was certain what the actual tally should have been. O'Neill also disclosed that American DoE officials and some Russian scientists were concerned that many of the facilities in the FSU lacked accurate records of their stocks[11].

V.N. Obarevich, Head of the Inspectorate for State Oversight of Nuclear Weapons Security, told the Russian *Duma* not long before President Putin came to power that at Russian nuclear warfare facilities, roughly 70 per cent of the technical security devices have become worn out and 20 per cent have been in operation for two or three service life periods[12]. 'Attempts [were] being made to repair them but this [was] no longer possible. Most control and check points do not have resources for detecting the unauthorized transport of nuclear materials, metal or explosives,' was the gist of a statement made to the Russian Parliament by Lev Ryabev, Deputy Russian Federation Ministry of Atomic Energy.

In 1998, a US team visiting the Kurchatov Institute in Moscow was shown a building containing roughly 100kg of HEU that was totally unguarded[13]. The Institute apparently could not afford the $200 a month salary for one guard, never mind the full quota for round-the-clock surveillance that would have been regarded as essential anywhere else. A report in *NuclearFuel*[14] stated that an almost 3kg cache of HEU found in a vehicle in Prague late in 1994 matched the specifics of similar material seized in Germany four months earlier. Following a tip-off, a number of people (including a Russian atomic scientist from the Nuclear Research Centre at Rez) were arrested. The report stated that the material found in containers identifying them as from the ex-Soviet Black Sea fleet had been stolen from a stockpile at Chelyabinsk 65. A correction later said that all of it had originally come from Mayak and was only part of what had been seized in Prague and Germany. A year later, 0.4gms of the same material was being offered as a sample for sale in Prague.

There are other serious issues in the Former Soviet Union that need attention, some of them urgently, because they are also nuclear linked. For instance, nuclear safety in the Russian Arctic, where redundant former USSR strategic missile submarines are being dismantled, is a cause for serious concern, in Western Europe especially. Conditions there are bad enough to have prompted Nikolay Yegorov, Russia's former deputy atomic energy minister to comment that with nothing being done, 'matters worsen every year … and could turn into a catastrophe worse than Chernobyl'.

Oslo's Bellona, with its own website, specifically targets work (or more appropriately, the lack of it) being done in several 'closed cities' in the remote Kola Peninsula. Some nuclear storage sites are only a twenty-minute drive from the Norwegian border. Bellona issued a report[15] that stated that more than 45,000 spent nuclear fuel elements were being stored in the region. Some of these assets were in temporary on-shore storage tanks. Others had been placed aboard a variety of service vessels, many of them in need of repair and badly run-down.

Under normal conditions, excess or spent nuclear fuel are transported by rail to the Mayak reprocessing plant in Siberia, but for some time these shipments became intermittent, though with American pressure and financial incentives, regularity has to some extent been re-established. In the past, issues were hampered by a lack of funds and specific orders from the Mayak county administration that declared that no more nuclear waste was welcome in this already-contaminated South-Ural region.

Other complications abound. Not only is space limited at Mayak (because for a while, storage facilities were filled to capacity) but the reprocessing plant was sometimes inoperative because of technical problems. Here, too, still more cash is needed for spares. In fact, the facility is so dated that an entirely new system needs to be installed but Moscow has consistently argued that it had not the cash to do that.

In some of the Arctic naval ports, reckons Bellona, many of the discarded reactors of 'Yankee' and 'Delta'-class dismantled submarines still harbour their nuclear fuel elements and a number were left unattended for years. These can sometimes be found lying where they were abandoned along the shore. More ominously, the report states, concrete tanks (in which spent nuclear fuel elements were being stored) were so dilapidated that the stability of their radioactive contents was threatened. The report explained that the distance between each element was only about an inch and that the concrete separating them, because of extreme temperatures, had developed cracks.

'There is consequently a substantial risk for criticality' (initiating a chain reaction such as occurred at Chernobyl). Because of the sheer volume of nuclear fuels stored there, a meltdown in the Russian Arctic would in all likelihood be on a much bigger scale than anything yet experienced this century. It could, conceivably, affect the entire Northern Hemisphere.'

Dr Michael Foley, a geologist specializing in nuclear-related issues at PNNL who was responsible for producing, in English, a Russian book on the subject, *Deep Injection Disposal of Liquid Radioactive Waste in Russia*[16], disputed this in an exchange of letters[17]. He maintained that:

'we have never taken the criticality threat very seriously. Perhaps we are being naïve, but that is one of the first and last things nuclear workers worry about and, let's face it, the Russians have had enough criticality accidents to be serious about preventative measures ... criticality developing from infrastructure degradation would start locally rather than involving the whole mass of a storage area. That would limit the consequences and allow remediation before things got too far out of hand.'

As Dr Foley explained, the submarine reactor accident at Chazhma Bay was an example of how things could go bad once a criticality gets going 'and it's interesting that we discovered that it was a fresh fuel accident and that the released radioactivity was less than 500 Curies after the first few weeks.'[18] He added that since the accident occurred in a reactor, the geometry of the event was designed to promote criticality. 'Accidental fuel proximity criticality would probably not be so efficient; however, this is a judgment-call area and we're still thinking about it.' Dr Don Bradley, a nuclear engineer and group leader at PNNL for decades, backed Dr Foley's comments. An acknowledged expert on the former Soviet Union's nuclear waste management programmes, he suggested that any meltdown of spent fuel cells could never be anything as bad as the Chernobyl disaster.

Fortunately, a good deal of all this is now history because, with US assistance, conditions in the FSU have markedly improved. At the same time, nobody would put good money on whether some shipments of fissile material had not been clandestinely filtered out of the country. On the face of it, he stated, 'there seems to have been thefts galore, but only those instances where the perpetrators have been apprehended, have become public knowledge. The bulk of it we'll never ever know about...'

There is very good reason for Moscow to put its house in order in this department and it is called Chechnya. For decades, the Russians faced a powerful Islamic-led insurgency in the enclave that claimed many thousands of lives. The situation there is more or less stable, though powerful security measures are in force. What is of concern to the West is that traditionally, Muslims from Chechnya have maintained strong links to Islamic dissidents and Jihadis elsewhere, including Osama bin Laden's al-Qaeda. It is also known that Chechnyan fighters have been involved in a dozen anti-Western/anti-American conflicts in recent years in places as far afield as Iraq (as snipers) Afghanistan (as combatants with the Taliban), the Philippines (as both training personnel and occasionally, as combatants), Indonesia and, more recently, Somalia.

Moscow is aware of all this. Russian Security Services maintain a specially-trained division that is responsible for nuclear security, well aware that 'Chetnik' dissidents have shown much interest in former Soviet nuclear installations and, the rumour mill has it, stolen nuclear warheads. Nor do the Russians need to be warned by Washington that if any of this material is acquired by Chechnyan separatists (or any other FSU rebels), it will almost certainly end up in some sort of device that may have Moscow's name written on the shell casing.

There are several international moves afoot to stop the trafficking of nuclear materials. One of these involves intrusive new advances in the United States that allows fibre-optic technology to be embedded in roads of several East European and East Asian nations. These are being laid specifically to detect smuggled nuclear weapons. A research project launched at PNNL has developed what the laboratory calls 'a one-of-a-kind scintillating optical fibre for sensing both neutrons and gamma rays'. Named PUMA – for Plutonium Measurement and

Analysis – the sensor is designed to be embedded in a variety of materials or literally, 'wrapped like fingers' around objects of different sizes for content analyses. It is adaptable to a wide range of applications including environmental restoration, cancer treatment and non-proliferation of weapons of mass destruction. Most importantly, it can be embedded into asphalt roads to detect the transportation of unauthorized or diverted nuclear weapons material. Alternatively, it can be wrapped around drums and other containers to inventory contents.

Head of research was Dr Mary Bliss. She advised that developments at the laboratory were quite revolutionary and that the sensors could be used for body-worn detectors for nuclear materials and airborne weapons detection. Portable monitors, she reckoned, were the single biggest commercial application. Unlike the gas tube, she explained, 'PNNL sensors are less sensitive to vibration, they are rugged and flexible and versatile in both length and numbers, ranging from about a quarter inch to two yards long. Also, they may consist of a single fibre or clusters of tens of thousands of fibres.' There was an important advantage. High-speed electronics could be utilized to give detectors 'an improved, dynamic range, which is simply not feasible with gas tubes'.

Though things have moved on since my 2008 visit to Department of Energy's Pacific Northwest National Laboratory, the PUMA concept remains based on the rationale that ionizing radiation interacts with the scintillating fibres and produces light. It works like this. Light is trapped within the fibre and goes to its end where conversion to an electrical signal takes place. This can be interpreted as either a neutron or a gamma-ray interaction, depending on size. A spokesperson for PNNL stated that teams of materials, nuclear, optical and electrical scientists began testing applications of fibre-optic radiation sensors at the lab almost decades ago and work has been going on ever since.

Until now, the single biggest problem facing the West has been detecting secret nuclear blasts. There is a global fear that more countries might follow India, Pakistan and North Korea in testing nuclear weapons. If we were to judge by the quantity of illegal fissile sporadically intercepted while headed for the Near East, so does Iran. Tehran's putative uranium enrichment programmes are a daily feature in American media, all of which tends to suggest that Tehran is eager to join the 'Nuclear Club'. The refusal of the US Senate to ratify the global (CTBT) test ban treaty complicates matters still further.

Several new nuclear monitoring developments have had an impact on the industry and a succession of revolutionary American monitoring procedures is likely, if not to permanently eliminate secret nuclear tests, then at least detect them. Systems developed involve technology many times more sensitive than those previously available for detecting atomic testing. Monitoring stations on every continent cover applicable seismic, hydro-acoustic, infrasound and radionuclide data.

Dissident Islamic groups like al-Qaeda and rogue nations like Syria and Myanmar (Burma) have been interested in acquiring nuclear capability for some years. Should they ever get to test the bomb, new scientific developments will immediately register the blast and identify the culprit. The same would happen were Russia to clandestinely start testing nuclear weapons again, or, for that matter, the United States. The system is all-enveloping.

With the CTBT stymied, advanced monitoring systems are now shown to be urgently needed to provide for what the pundits like to term 'total global verification'. What has emerged in recent years is a more intensive monitoring of nuclear testing and several new systems are being put in place. These include a network of hundreds of stations worldwide incorporating new instruments such as those developed by PNNL and operated for the DoE.

During treaty negotiations, the US Department of Defence was tasked to spearhead an international effort to develop a prototype international data centre (IDC) at the Centre for Monitoring Research in Arlington, Virginia. There are several reasons. The first of these is to support future test ban treaty negotiations and second, as we have seen, to check on illegal nuclear testing by rogue states or organizations. There is also a need to test new concepts necessary for effective global monitoring and yet another to establish an infrastructure for cooperative, international verification. Finally, the objective is to provide the foundation for an international data test ban centre, located in Vienna, Austria. Such a centre is envisaged to include a communications system, the prototype IDC as well as an international on-site inspection component to monitor compliance.

PNNL has produced two systems to monitor nuclear debris: A Radionuclide Aerosol Sampler/Analyzer (RASA) that measures radioactive debris from aboveground nuclear weapons testing (regardless of where or when the bombs were detonated) and ARSA, an Automated Radioxenon Sampler/Analyzer. This device fills the CTBT requirement for near-real-time, ultra-sensitive field measurement of short-lived noble gases. Like RASA, ARSA operates automatically. All are remotely programmable and both are funded by the DoE's Office of Nonproliferation and Security from Washington. Dr Harry Miley of PNNL was originally responsible for the development of RASA (in conjunction with researchers at DME Corporation, Orlando, Florida).

Again, things have moved on, by essentially, Dr Miley explained, the original system operated on the basis of the analyser passing air through a large area, low-pressure drop filter at a high rate of flow for selectable time periods. This action was intended to capture verifiable airborne trace particles on six strips of filter paper that are packaged in a single bundle to be analysed by a gamma-ray detector. 'In so doing,' he said, 'the system actually captures a part of the nuclear weapon: tiny, yes, but still a verifiable part.' He explained that the resultant spectra were then transmitted to central data locations thousands of miles away. It simultaneously achieved a very high sensitivity coupled with a low-power/small footprint. Since short-lived fission products have no natural background, weapon blasts, he said, could also be easily discriminated from reactor accidents. Thus, 'a simple one kiloton atmospheric blast will be detected by multiple isotopes at multiple stations'.

Another feature of this system was that special features incorporated within it, archived each sample. They then identified them with their own unique bar codes. Containing a 90 per cent relative-efficiency germanium detector, he reckoned that the new technology, which identified debris in an environment of ubiquitous radon background, was many times more sensitive than its nearest commercial rival.

Crucial to all these counter-proliferation procedures has been the establishment of a new European Union training centre to combat illicit trafficking of nuclear and radioactive materials. In the second decade of this century, the European Commission launched a new nuclear security training centre (EUSECTRA) in Karlsruhe. The training centre instructs front-line officers, trainers and experts on how to detect and respond to illicit trafficking of nuclear or other radioactive materials. Effectively, EUSECTRA offers hands-on training using a wide variety of radioactive and nuclear materials and a broad selection of equipment and measurement instruments.

Indoors, one of the training areas simulates airport conditions, equipped with a pedestrian portal monitor and an x-ray conveyor. Outdoors, training is provided on a variety of scenarios, providing four different types of radiation portal monitors. Overall, more than thirty measurement and detection tools are employed in training. The centre enhances the European Commission's Joint Research Centre's (JRC) training activities carried out in this field at the Karlsruhe and Ispra sites. Located at the JRC's Institute for Transuranium Elements (ITU) premises, the training centre was set up in the framework of the EU chemical, biological, radiological and nuclear (CBRN) action plan adopted by the European Council in 2009. The training programmes were developed in collaboration with the International Atomic Energy Agency (IAEA) and the US Department of Energy. Representatives from these organisations also took part in the inauguration.

Aside from the focus on trafficking of materials, EUSECTRA will enhance cross-border cooperation and experts' networking, and provide a centralised knowledge management tool. Advanced training in material detection and identification, management of radiological crime scenes and development of national response plans are also provided.

## Chapter 17

# Interdicting Nuclear Scams Out of the Former Soviet Union

*'Smuggling throughout the whole of Central and Eastern Europe has been on the upswing since the breakup of the Former Soviet Union. Economic conditions are prompting smugglers to transport items ranging from blue jeans to nuclear reactor components. Because border crossings lack funds, adequately trained personnel and technology, the smuggled goods have a better chance of making it through.'*

*Dr William Cliff, erstwhile programme manager for international border security in Pacific Northwest's National Security Division at Richland, Washington State.*[1]

Nuclear scams have been big business for a while now. Most transactions that involve radioactive materials have been between former FSU countries and three or four pariah states in the Middle East. American sources maintain that they are aware of several transactions where both Iranian and Iraqi agents have been hoodwinked and millions of dollars involved in some of the deals have gone sour. 'The trouble is,' warned a spokesman for America's Pacific Northwest National Laboratory (PNNL) at Richland – one of the Department of Energy's nine multi-programme national laboratories – 'what the seller or smuggler actually offloads may well be dangerously radioactive'. The authorities are aware that deaths have resulted from individuals unknowingly handling radioactive materials.

In the shadowy world of non-proliferation of weapons of mass destruction, say the Americans, times are bad. That is why there are groups of Russians, Slovenians, Georgians and Azerbaijanis as well as border enforcement personnel from a host of other Central and East European countries manning posts in the sand and sagebrush around the American government nuclear facility near the banks of the Columbia River at Richland, not far from the Hanford mostly decommissioned nuclear facility in Eastern Washington.

The first batch of twenty four Russians – many of them paramilitary customs officers and headed by a Major General – arrived at PNNL's Hazard training facility for a two-week course shortly before I got there early in the New Millennium. More kept coming over the years, some representing the 50,000 customs officers in the Russian Federation who complement more than 250,000 of that country's border guards. The Hazard programme was developed under the sponsorship of the Pentagon's counter-proliferation programme with technical direction by the US Customs Service.

The job is complex. PNNL specialists warned that with the global miniaturization of weapons of mass destruction, the most basic 'gun-type' atom bomb might have a diameter of only six inches (fifteen centimetres) and could weigh in at something like twenty kilograms. Similarly, a miniaturised thermonuclear device would not be very much bigger and weigh sixty or seventy kilos. Part of the course is devoted to demonstrating that chemical or biological weapons could arrive in any country on the globe in a variety of containers. These include grenades, mines, artillery shells, aerial bombs, spray canisters or storage tanks or, possibly, a missile warhead. PNNL science and engineering associate Ann Jarrell warned that a pathogen could be smuggled into a country in something as basic as powdered eggs.

Elaborate procedures on the best ways of preventing weapons smuggling are being held several times a year on a rotational basis at the $30 million facility. Training sessions when I was there were code-named Interdict/RADACAD (interdiction of materials associated with mass destruction weapons and RADACAD for Radiation Academy) and run for two weeks at a stretch. Courses are held with the full range of props that you are likely to find at any east or central European border post, harbour, railway station or airport. Inspections cover the full gambit and include cars, trucks, railway cars, passengers, freight, oil tankers and a lot else scrutinized for nuclear, chemical, biological and missile components and technology. The US Customs – in conjunction with the Departments of Defence, Energy and State – not only briefly lifted the veil on procedures that only a short time ago was secret, but, they stressed the American taxpayer is picking up the tab for all the cross-border instruction that takes in Eastern Washington State.

An unusual aspect of the course is the time spent on scams related to illicit nuclear trafficking, and as one authority suggested, they are extensive. Until recently, few outsiders were aware that a multi-million dollar industry involving some of the best swindlers in the game even existed. Many of those who are doing this kind of 'trading' are either Russian or Ukrainian, but increasingly there are other nationals from former Soviet Union states involved.

Also, the work can be dangerous. The number of people murdered because they were involved in 'red mercury' scams in South Africa and other parts of the world ran into double figures in spite of it being a barefaced scam. 'Red mercury' simply did not exist, but that did not prevent traffickers in Europe and the Middle East making a mint from selling purported supplies of the stuff. Two British writers, Peter Hounam and Steve McQuillan even wrote a book on this and related subjects titled *The Mini-Nuke Conspiracy* and 'red mercury' was very prominently featured. They even showed exploded drawings of 'red mercury' nuclear devices as published in an article by nuclear analyst Dr Frank Barnaby in Jane's *International Defence Review* in 1994.

Hounam and McQuillan claim that South African nuclear scientists had built 'hundreds' of atom bombs, which would have resulted in the apartheid regime having more atom bombs in their arsenal than either Britain or France. Of course it was all nonsense. Their reasons for going in hard on 'red mercury' was because it was an extremely sophisticated technological fraud that generated millions. Though purported to be a 'substitute radioactive component' in nuclear weapons development (and compared by some crafty operators to the heaviest hydrogen isotope, tritium), that was also fiction. Other nuclear scams involve Osmium-187, Philippine 'uranium', Southeast Asian 'uranium' as well as radiation gauges. The Americans state that osmium only recently emerged as a common nuclear trafficking scam in the FSU. PNNL officials told me that it has no known weapons application, nor is it radioactive. One of the tasks being taught by American specialists at the Richland facility is the ability of customs or border guards to recognize this danger and blow the whistle, 'not only for their own protection but for others as well,' an instructor explained. What is true is that there are a variety of osmium isotopes and they are found in abundance. Osmium-186, for example, while produced only in milligrams in the US (and in kilogram quantities in Russia) is a naturally occurring, radioactive alpha emitter. Non-nuclear uses include it as an alloy agent and, in the past, the production of phonographs and ballpoint pens. Also, PNNL scientists point out, there are no international laws against the sale or transfer of osmium and also that there is no need to separate the isotopes of osmium for commercial purposes.

Scam prices can be awesome. Candium (another fake Russian radioactive substance) would sometimes sell upwards of $50,000/kilo. One hustler tried to offload a kilo of Osmium-187 to an Iranian agent for $70 million. 'Obviously if there weren't takers, the market wouldn't exist,' the specialist declared. He added that there were 'a lot of basket cases out there and some of them have millions of dollars.'

Nuclear physicists at Richland stress that in the wrong hands, some radioactive materials or sources might be used for terror or extortion. The facility's six-inch thick, 600-page handbook – which is given to every student on arrival in his own language (including Cyrillic script for Russian speakers) – cites the case of a group of Chechen separatists who, in 1995, threatened to use radioactive dispersal devices in Russia. They even staged a media event to prove that they actually possessed a radioactive substance. Clearly, one of the scientists involved with training said, there are also a lot of legal radioactive isotopes around and that most serve good purpose. Technetium-99, for instance, is used for brain images, thyroid and lungs; Chromium-51 is involved in red blood cells tests; Cobalt-60 is used for external beam radiotherapy and Ytterbium-169 in spinal fluid studies. Likewise, Iridium-132 is used as an internal, radiotherapy source, and the two Xenon isotopes, Xenon-133 and Xenon-127 feature in lung ventilation function tests.

At the same time, there are numerous legal applications of radiation sources. These include examining welds in the steel industry, well logging, medical research, moisture sensing and others such as smoke detectors, airport runway lights, lighthouses in Russia, space programmes (for power on spacecraft) and the dismantlement of old reactors are other applications that might emit radiation.

Subjects handled at Interdict/RADACAD are diverse. They include arcane issues such as the threat assessment of WMD, nuclear concepts, advanced detection techniques, nuclear technology identification (both trigger list and dual-use list) as well as missile technology, which includes on-site examination of the innards of a Scud missile and its components which I was able to photograph.

Russia's Scud missile – and updated versions that flowed from the original design – get a lot of attention at the site. Many countries that have the missile, including several Islamic states, have been developing WMD of their own, like Iraq, Iran, Syria, North Korea and others. Indeed, Syria tipped hundreds of its Scud-2s with sarin as well as other nerve gases and deployed them along the border with its arch-enemy Israel. The smuggling of Scud components, consequently, has been a problem for years. This was underscored by the UN Special Commission (on Iraq) investigating that country's illegal acquisition of dozens of rocket gyros. Originally retrieved from redundant Russian nuclear submarine ICBM missiles, many were smuggled to Baghdad when Saddam Hussein was still around. One of the conclusions subsequently reached was that it would have been impossible to remove such sophisticated devices from the original missiles without the authorities being aware of it. More to the point, it would have been equally difficult to take them out of the country had there not been some sort of collusion from 'on high'. Moscow has never adequately explained how large numbers of such sensitive devices were clandestinely shipped to the Middle East.

While some of the gyros did reach Baghdad (and were later dumped into the Euphrates after UNSCOM got wind of them) more were seized at Amman Airport when American agents, acting in concert with the Jordanians, acted on a tip-off. And though some of those involved were arrested, the big fish linked to the transfer were never identified. Because the outdated Russian missiles are notoriously inaccurate, the gyros were apparently to have replaced those of an earlier generation in Iraqi Scuds. Specialists accept that late generation ICBM gyros would have markedly increased their reliability. There are still about two dozen more gyros sent to Iraq which the UN never recovered. Prior to the withdrawal of UN inspection teams, a number of Iraqi Scuds were modified for long-distance flight.

Among Scud components which participants are instructed to look for are several instrument section components (range accelerometers, horizon gyros, vertical gyros/lateral accelerometers, flight computers and gyro mounting boards). Engine components include regulator and stabilizer valves (including balance diaphragms), turbo pumps (both turbine wheels and inducer impellers) fuel and oxidizer injectors as well as thrust vector control sets and jet vanes. The latter are made of high-grade steels to counter excessive temperatures generated by rocket engines. Other WMD component parts listed as having been smuggled abroad include chemical weapon spray parts (actuators, swaybraces, dissemination nozzles, outlet cutters and a lot else besides). Similarly, instructors accentuate the illegal transportation of the 152mm chemical tube artillery shell of which the students are given a cutaway diagram. They are also provided with nuclear weapons schematics and a cutaway of a chemical or biological cluster bomb.

Subjects for study are diverse and include radiation protection as well as the elements of biological warfare. Time is also spent viewing the operations and use of sensitive equipment at a fully functional international border crossing, in this case at Blaine, on Washington State's Canadian border. In typical American fashion, the training sessions cover an inordinate lot of ground. Usually numbering a couple of dozen participants from two *compatible* East European countries (representatives of Chechnya and Russia, for instance, on the same course, might lead to problems), classes are conducted in English with simultaneous translation into home tongues.

The first morning's sessions deal with weapons of mass destruction, followed by a WMD-threat assessment. There are many breaks for practical demonstrations by experts. Then follows targeting and selectivity as well as risk assessment.

Radiation in all its facets is covered in depth. Lectures include practical demonstrations with items such as gamma spectrometers and pagers. Altogether, many different types of cutting-edge, portable technology are provided for detection and identification of suspect materials and components and students return to their home bases with all this paraphernalia in hand, hopefully to instruct their colleagues.

The esoterics of export/import documentation and a string of conspiracies related thereto also get prominence. Also targeted is what is termed 'the New International Criminal.' Even behind the old Iron Curtain, said one authority (who goes there often), 'crime associated with the illegal movement of WMD has achieved an incredible level of sophistication'. Taken together, the Richland courses are the most comprehensive anti-proliferation sessions held anywhere in the world.

The PNNL laboratory – with a staff of 3,500 and – when I visited the place – an annual budget of $500 million, is one of nine national multi-programme laboratories in the US. It was created in 1965 when the government's research laboratory at the Department of Energy's site at Hanford along the upper Columbia River was separated from Hanford's mostly nuclear operations. The Hanford Project, also known in its time as Hanford Works, Hanford Engineer Works and Hanford Nuclear Reservation, was established in 1943 as part of the Manhattan Project in south-central Washington State. The site was home to the B Reactor, the first full-scale plutonium production reactor in the world. Plutonium manufactured at the site was used in the first nuclear bomb tested at the Trinity site and immediately thereafter in Fat Man.

As a result of 'Project Amber' (a classroom programme initiated in 1994) the Interdict/RADACAD programme has resulted in many hundreds of foreign officers from scores of countries having been trained in a variety of anti-WMD detection disciplines on US soil over the years. Many more were put through their paces in similar disciplines on site in Poland, Estonia, and Uzbekistan and a number of other Central and East European states. Extensions of 'Project Amber' have included Cyprus and Malta, and other far-flung outposts, underscoring their strategic potential in the Mediterranean and elsewhere.

There have been some notable interdictions over the years, some of them involving past students:

- Twenty-two tons of radioactive contaminated concentrate detained near Krasnoyarsk. The stuff appears to have been sent to Russia to be dumped.
- An American company in 1996 shipped seventy-eight tons of radioactive scrap steel from Houston to China.
- Radioactive sources sent scrap metal from the Czech Republic to Italy. Many people near the path of the train were given medical exams.
- Contaminated scrap copper from Poland got turned back at the German border. It eventually found its way to Slovakia where it was processed and went out as product
- Two tons of radioactive tungsten was found entering Lithuania from Belarus. The driver transporting the load was seriously radiated.

- Mexican kitchen tables contaminated with radioactive metal sent to the United States
- A large consignment of Uranium 235 was interdicted in Bulgaria, apparently en route to the Middle East.

Among items offered to participants are a couple of state-of-the-art portable detection devices; a Material Identification System (MIS) and an Ultrasonic Pulse Echo (ultrasound) instrument. An unspecified number of these instruments were sent to other Central and East European as well as FSU governments. The first device discriminates between a variety of strategic metals; some of them used in WMD; composed of a laptop computer with a plug-in instrument card, it operates with a hand-held probe.

The problem countered here is that most metals – including those used for strategic purposes – are very similar in appearance. It is difficult, if not impossible, for a border inspector to *visually* determine whether a particular metal is what it is said on its accompanying documents to be. And since advanced weapons programmes require advanced types of steel, MIS – based on non-contact electrical conductivity – can tell whether a batch of metals in a cargo is pressure vessel steel or cold rolled. Similarly, with graphite (which might be used for nuclear reactor development). Participants are warned to regard any batches of sharp-edged carbon with great suspicion; its only potential use is nuclear-related.

The ultrasonic pulse echo, in contrast, is based on advanced ultrasound technology and was developed to inspect chemical weapons stockpiles and discarded munitions by UN officials after the Gulf Wars. It can also determine – virtually in real time – hidden packages or cavities in a container that might hold drugs or other prohibited material. US Government agencies have ordered many sets over the years for use at East European border crossings.

Other advanced equipment used in the training include:

- a gamma and neutron spectrometer to identify radioactive isotopes such as nuclear weapons material ($^{239}$Pu, $^{235}$U and $^{233}$U) as well as commercial and medical isotopes
- a radiation pager which alerts border guards that there might be a radioactive substance present
- a gamma densitometer which is used to locate items hidden behind walls and in tyres or other cavities in shipping containers or liquid tanks
- a fibre-optic scope for viewing inside dashboards, fuel tanks etc., and
- an electronic measuring tape for exposing hidden compartments and false walls

It is interesting that the US Government is also providing almost every Central and East European customs service with numbers of X-ray detection vehicles. Costing about $300,000 each, these have also gone to Russia with more to follow.

For their size, the vehicles are well equipped. While 10,000 ordinary packages might be scanned without prompting a reaction, anything radioactive triggers an alarm. For this purpose, each vehicle is fitted with a forward scanner and backscatter X-ray, together with a variety of other systems able to detect the full spectrum of nuclear-related materials. These include plutonium, uranium, carbons, lithium, beryllium and zirconium, all substances covered by the Nuclear Suppliers' Group.

At the core of it, the thrust of Interdict/RADACAD training at Richland's Hammer facility centres on the material components and commodities associated with the development, deployment and delivery of weapons of mass destruction. Consequently, there is emphasis on the full nuclear fuel cycle – from yellowcake – to weapons-grade highly enriched uranium, plutonium as well as substances which might already have been weaponised.

A feature of some of the classes involves trying to track actual smuggling patterns. Other sessions concentrate on the routes that operators are likely to use, if only because, once acquired, the stuff still needs to cross frontiers. One instructor explained that, once a border crossing or an airport is regarded as 'unsafe' by those involved in this sort of business, they will seek a border exit with less stringent controls. 'You need to pre-empt such developments. If you don't, you could be wasting your time. It all takes time and effort coupled with a good bit of imagination,' he added.

In one important aspect of training, participants are shown procedures that need to be followed in primary and secondary searches. For this purpose, courses have involved some of the best inspectors and agents active in US Customs. There are also specifics about the need to follow through on cross-border arrests in order to ensure that suspects as well as contraband do not disappear into what one official described 'the usual Eastern European bureaucratic labyrinth'.

While Washington has been low-key on the nature and the extent of help being extended, several authorities fear that this rigmarole might possibly be 'too little and too late', though personally speaking, I was enormously impressed because there is nothing like what is going on in Richland anywhere else in the world.

One specialist who asked not to be named, said that considering the huge distances (across seven time zones in Russia) and the manifest interest of so many rogue states in acquiring nuclear, biological and chemically-related materials, it was almost impossible to keep track of everything that is going on. 'In the past, following the break-up of the Soviet Union, the fact that they were able to produce large sums of cash didn't make it any easier when people who had not been paid in months were involved,' he added. This was specially marked since the Russian *Mafiya* had become involved in some scams and transactions, he reckoned.

That trend goes on.

## Chapter 18

# Egypt, Saudi Arabia and Algeria

In Egypt, a country in international focus almost since the end of the Second
World War, one of the discussion points that has been doing the rounds in
the Middle East runs along the lines that if Egypt wished to do so, it could
probably go nuclear. I did a report along those lines for one of the publications
in the stable of Britain's Jane's Information Group. Despite the subject matter,
it was fairly well received and there were no protests out of Cairo[1]. Indeed,
questioned on the issue in recent years, several Egyptian nuclear scientists
contended that their country had both the expertise and the raw materials
to enrich uranium or produce plutonium. A glance at the country's 'Nuclear
Map', prepared by California's Monterey Institute of International Studies a
few years ago explains why Egypt might have good reason to desire some kind
of nuclear parity.

For decades Cairo has maintained a delicate (and objective) balance of
championing nuclear prowess in the Middle East, essentially to address its
economic and industrial needs, while at the same time seeking a guarantee
of security against the Israeli nuclear threat. There were attempts in earlier
years to develop something resembling a nuclear device but time and money,
or lack of funds, played negative roles. Nor did successive wars with Israel
help in fostering this ambition. For a while, political and security issues were
compounded by a rigid approach by some senior Egyptian military officers,
government officials and scholars who sought to develop what the Cairo
newspaper *Al Ahram* routinely referred to as 'The Arab Deterrent'. They
pointed to Israel consistently refusing to ratify the NPT. Also in contention was
the perceived double standards regarding the development of nuclear weapons
by the Jewish State in one of the most volatile regions on the globe. The finger
pointed – and continues to point – directly at Washington.

Notable, there is no shortage of raw material. There is a solid depth of
uranium resources throughout the country, coupled to an industrial base that
is not dissimilar to that of Pakistan and in this respect Egypt might have been
regarded by some as a couple of generations ahead of North Korea. Or, were
Cairo to do it illegally, there are a host of out-of-work nuclear physicists in
countries such as Russia, Iraq, Brazil and South Africa where such matters have
been either placed on the back burner or abandoned altogether.

At the same time, Egypt has not been altogether inactive. According to evidence uncovered early in 2004 by US and British inspectors attached to the International Atomic Energy Agency, Libya and Egypt engaged in some kind of nuclear technical co-operation until late 2003. That matter was further compounded when the French newspaper *Liberation* made certain claims late 2004; it declared that before Libya abandoned all its work on nuclear-related matters, it had actually been working 'secretly for the Egyptians'. As we saw in Chapter Eight, Libya's uranium-enrichment programme on the outskirts of Tripoli was a lot more advanced than was at first conceded.

There are also IAEA reports that Egypt might itself have made some illegal nuclear material. Quoting diplomats at the UN atomic watchdog agency, George Jahn of the Associated Press said the agency had found evidence of secret nuclear experiments in Egypt that could be used in a weapons system. The material was taken to Europe for analysis and evaluation. While most of this work was carried out in the 1970s and 1980s, an IAEA source has since said that the agency was looking at some of it possibly having been performed more recently. This revelation came months after the IAEA discovered plutonium particles in an area adjacent to an Egyptian nuclear facility.

Israel has views of its own. According to a report in *Jane's Intelligence Review*, Major-General Aharon Zeevi, former head of Israeli Military Intelligence (AMAN), gave the Knesset Defence and Foreign Affairs Committee a similar judgment in October 2004. He noted that he and other Israeli officials have talked of seeing 'worrying signs' of nuclear ambitions in Algeria and Egypt, although they noted that the evidence was circumstantial and any programmes based on uranium enrichment would be in their infancy. The consensus was that Cairo was likely motivated by early steps being taken to hedge against the possibility that Iran would develop nuclear weaponry[2]. Interestingly, the Pakistani nuclear smuggler A.Q. Khan had by now arrived on the scene.

It went on to say that 'Khan had ties to Egypt through nuclear-related conferences he hosted (including the International Symposium on Advanced Materials in 2003) and parts of the Egyptian government outside of the Atomic Energy Commission published a number of scientific papers which suggested that they might have been thinking about hedging bets in the event that it could decide to commence a nuclear weapons project in the future.'

Joseph Bermudez revealed in the 4 February 2010 edition of *Jane's Intelligence Review* that satellite imagery taken over suspect Egyptian sites revealed significant and continuing WMD infrastructure expansion at the country's Jabal Hamzah facility, though with a new government in place under General Sisi and strong ties having developed between Egypt and the United States, that programme has been put on the back burner.

As he explained, the missile facility was located in the governorate of Al Jizah (Giza) where, in the late 1960s it was designated by the CIA as the Jabal Hamzi Surface-to-Surface Missile Complex because it is on the road from Cairo to Alexandria just a few miles south-southwest of the abandoned Jabal Hamzi Airfield.

> 'The original installation…consisted of a small cluster of facilities built on the edge of a low sandstone escarpment. Between 1967 and 2000 the original installation had only minor infrastructure development. However, since 2000, not only has there been significant expansion there but a major related construction project at a site approximately [two miles] to the south was started. The two sites, which are here referred to as the north and south sites, are connected by an asphalt road that was paved between 2008 and 2009.'

For all this, Washington's Nuclear Threat Initiative gave Cairo a clean bill of health[3]. One of its reports stated:

> 'While suspected of harbouring nuclear weapons ambitions at various points in history (and especially under President Gamal Abdel Nasser in the 1960s), the Egypt of [today] is a member in good standing of the Treaty on the Non-Proliferation of Nuclear Weapons (NPT) and the leading proponent of establishing a weapon-of-mass-destruction-free zone in the Middle East.
>
> 'Many scholars and practitioners worry that Iran's nuclear activities could provoke an Egyptian policy reversal, but currently Egypt seems to perceive developing nuclear weapons as counter to its national interests.'

For its part, Israel is not so sure. Jerusalem has a particular interest in the prospect that Egypt might be developing a clandestine nuclear capability. Efraim, while still chief of the Mossad, was of the opinion that it was not only Egypt that was linked to reports of illegal nuclear activity, but also Syria and Saudi Arabia. In respect of the former he was proved right while the jury is still out on the Saudis, but, as we have seen above, there have been disturbing developments there.

Referring to what he called a 'nuclear leap', Halevy revealed that A.Q. Khan – who we know visited Cairo during this critical period. – had visited Egypt but whose purposes have never been made clear. Neither Cairo nor Islamabad have been willing to explain.

Reacting to what was construed in Cairo as a challenge, Ahmad Ali Abu el-Ghait, the then Egyptian Minister of Foreign Affairs, denied that Cairo was involved in running secret nuclear experiments. He stressed that its nuclear

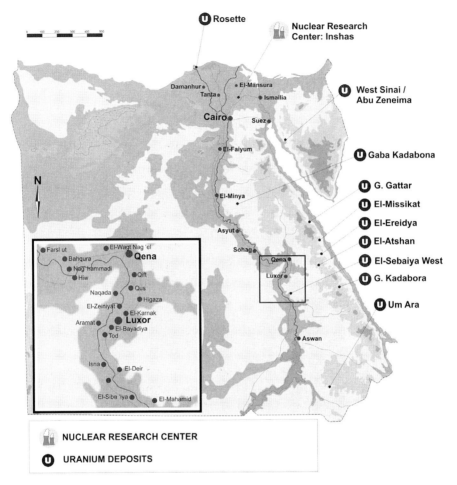

## EGYPT'S NUCLEAR CAPABILITIES

programme was strictly for peaceful purposes, but then as we have seen, so do they all. However, he could not refute news leaked by an IAEA source that 'some pounds' of uranium metal had been found during an inspection. Also recovered was an undisclosed amount of uranium tetrafluoride, a precursor to uranium hexafluoride gas, customarily enriched into weapons-grade uranium.

These developments seem to have taken place even though Egypt signed the Nuclear Non-Proliferation Treaty in July 1968, as well as an active safeguard agreement with Vienna. But as one European critic observed: 'Iraq[4], Iran and Syria also signed that accord, and look where all that led...'

As Nuclear Threat Initiative says, there are some analysts who have characterized Egypt's nuclear fuel cycle as being one of a 'dual-use' nature. For instance, in 1996, the authors of the *Risk Report* claimed, 'Argentina is building a nuclear reactor in Egypt that will give Cairo its first access to bomb quantities of fissile material, with possibly enough plutonium to make one nuclear weapon per year.' Argentina's 22MW pool type light water reactor does burn enriched uranium and produce plutonium[5]. However, in 1997, when the Argentinean ETTR-2 reactor was built and began operating, it went under full scope IAEA safeguards, making diversion of its spent fuel improbable. This does not preclude possible irradiation of uranium targets which may go undetected. Egypt also has a hot cell laboratory which may be used to reprocess irradiated targets or fuel on a laboratory scale and might also have other facilities that would help it to develop nuclear weapons.

Obviously, in the ongoing uncertain political climate of the Near East, there is a very real possibility that Cairo might once again be seeking new technologies from either Russia or China, or possibly both. Recently, reports surfaced of the willingness of both countries to sell Egypt a nuclear power reactor.

It is necessary to look back over past decades in order to assess the extent of Egypt's earlier forays into nuclear technology and to clearly understand the potential for Cairo possibly entering this endeavour again. As Nuclear Threat Initiative tells us on its website, Gamal Abdul Nasser, who became Egypt's first president in 1954, also presided over his country's earliest notable forays into nuclear technology.

Nasser founded the Egyptian Atomic Energy Commission (AEC) in 1955, after which the AEC was transformed into the Atomic Energy Establishment (AEE) in 1956 – an organization now known as the Atomic Energy Authority (AEA).

'Until the 1967 Six Day War, the AEE made impressive progress in developing an Egyptian nuclear infrastructure – whether Nasser intended this infrastructure to serve military or exclusively peaceful purposes remains a matter of debate among scholars. Under Nasser, Egypt also pursued a ballistic missile set-up, which might have yielded a nuclear weapons delivery system had the country decided to pursue that route.

'A United Nations Conference on Peaceful Uses of Atomic Energy, held in Geneva in 1955, afforded representatives from Egypt and numerous other countries invaluable insights into beginning their own nuclear initiatives, while a 2008 report by the London-based International Institute for Strategic Studies (IISS) asserted: 'The conference not only provided the basic structure for the AEE's programmes, but was also the foundation for a series of negotiated bilateral cooperative agreements with foreign countries. Arguably, it was this willingness on the part of foreign countries to assist that allowed Egypt's programme to develop in the first place[6].'

According to Washington's Nuclear Threat Initiative: 'Ibrahim Hilmy Abdel Rahman, the first Secretary General of the AEE, presided over nuclear developments in Egypt until 1958.' During Rahman's tenure, Egypt pursued a number of nuclear cooperation agreements, most significantly concluding one with the USSR in 1956. This was followed by a 1958 bilateral reactor deal through which the USSR supplied Egypt with a 2MWt light water research reactor (the ETRR-1, which went online in July 1961) and associated fresh and spent fuel services. Sources mentioning the deal are quick to point out that the reactor – built at Inshas and not placed under the non-proliferation inspection 'safeguards' system of the IAEA until the 1980s – produced only insignificant quantities of plutonium, a material potentially useable for nuclear weapons. 'Nonetheless, Egypt's decades of experience operating a research reactor provided it with extensive dual-use experience and the opportunity to train generations of scientists and nuclear engineers.'

A subsequent chain of Egyptian statements and incidents – sometimes well documented, and in other cases alleged – are the basis for many scholars' conclusions that from 1960 to 1967 Nasser's government was pursuing nuclear weapons[7]. James Walsh, who wrote one of the most comprehensive studies of Egypt's nuclear programme concluded: '... it is fair to say that Egypt's most intensive efforts to acquire nuclear weapons (or the capability to produce them) occurred during this phase – that is, just after the disclosure of the Dimona reactor, but before the 1967 Arab-Israeli war[8]'.

It is indisputable that Egypt stepped up its rhetoric on the issue of nuclear weapons following the Israeli announcement. For example, in 1961 Nasser warned that if Israel acquired such weapons, 'we will secure atomic weapons at any costs[9]'. It has not happened yet, nor – with the new-found friendship between President Trump and Egypt's sometimes erratic President Abdel Fattah Saeed Hussein Khalil el-*Sisi* – is anything like it to take place in the foreseeable future.

Unless, of course, Tehran detonates its first nuclear test device.

## Saudi Arabia

Things are very different with regard to Saudi Arabia's nuclear ambitions and proliferation risks in late 2017. In a report issued by Washington's Institute for Science and International Security (ISIS) titled 'Saudi Arabia's Nuclear Ambitions and Proliferation Risks' by Sarah Burkhard, Erica Wenig, David Albright, and Andrea Stricker, published on 30 March 2017, the situation was fluid. I quote lengthy extracts from their findings, an encapsulated version of their Executive Summary and Recommendations – a full pdf version is available on their website:

'The Kingdom of Saudi Arabia has an uneasy relationship with Iran. The Iran nuclear deal, or Joint Comprehensive Plan of Action (JCPOA), which went into effect in January 2016, has limited Iran's sensitive nuclear programme and subjected it to greater international monitoring. Many hoped that the JCPOA would also ease regional security tensions between Saudi Arabia and Iran, yet they have actually increased despite the deal. The JCPOA has also not eliminated the Kingdom's desire for nuclear weapons capabilities and even nuclear weapons, but rather reduced the pressure on Saudi Arabia to match Iran's nuclear weapons capabilities in the short term. In that sense, the deal has delayed concerns about nuclear proliferation in Saudi Arabia.

'However, there is little reason to doubt that Saudi Arabia will more actively seek nuclear weapons capabilities, motivated by its concerns about the ending of the JCPOA's major nuclear limitations starting after Year 10 of the deal or sooner if the deal fails. If Iran expands its enrichment capabilities, as it states it will do, Tehran will reduce nuclear breakout times, or the time needed to produce enough weapon-grade uranium for a nuclear weapon, to weeks and then days. With these concerns, the Kingdom is likely to seek nuclear weapons capabilities as a hedge. A priority of the administration of Donald J. Trump is to prevent Saudi Arabia from developing such capabilities, in particular acquiring reprocessing and uranium enrichment facilities. The administration's stated commitment to better enforce and strengthen the JCPOA provides a sounder foundation to achieve that goal.

'Saudi Arabia has little nuclear infrastructure today, and acquiring nuclear weapons is a difficult process for any country. At this point in time and at its current pace of nuclear development, Saudi Arabia would require years to create the nuclear infrastructure needed to launch a nuclear weapons effort. Our open source research, which includes translations from Arabic of official Saudi statements, nuclear infrastructure plans, and domestic research, shows that Saudi Arabia is not likely to have launched any domestic covert nuclear programmes to create the wherewithal to build nuclear weapons. Instead, like other cases of proliferant states and territories, such as South Africa, Iran, and Taiwan, it appears that Saudi Arabia is concentrating on building up its civilian nuclear infrastructure. It is acquiring nuclear or nuclear-related facilities and committing to placing them under international inspections according to international norms. Saudi Arabia has thus far embarked on a path to seek civil nuclear assistance from several nations, including Russia, South Korea, and China. It is also researching civil nuclear applications and developing a robust nuclear engineering and scientific workforce.

'Any research on the weaponization of nuclear material would of course be cause for international alarm, as it was in the case of Iran and its secret programme to develop a nuclear weapon. However, preventing proliferation in Saudi Arabia should focus first on preventing enrichment and reprocessing capabilities, even in the absence of work on a nuclear weapon. Nuclear suppliers should reach consensus on not exacerbating security concerns in the Middle East by agreeing not to sell Saudi Arabia sensitive fuel cycle capabilities. Moreover, Western governments should enhance their efforts to monitor, detect, and prevent the illicit spread of enrichment and reprocessing capabilities to Saudi Arabia.

'A major uncertainty in this analysis is the nuclear relationship between Pakistan and Saudi Arabia. Although reports that Pakistan has promised Saudi Arabia nuclear weapons appear inaccurate, some level of agreement relating to nuclear cooperation appears likely.

'Based on other proliferation cases, unresolved, chronic security concerns can foster nuclear weapons development. For many cases, only the resolution of such concerns led to the avoidance of nuclear weapons. Thus, in the long term, diplomatic and other initiatives should be aimed at regional threat reduction efforts to prevent Saudi Arabia and other Middle Eastern nations from seeking nuclear weapons. Perhaps more important, remedying the relatively short-term nature of the Iran deal's nuclear constraints is critical in preventing Saudi Arabia from building a nuclear weapons capability over the next five to 15 years.'

## ISIS Key Findings:

- Saudi Arabia is in the early stages of nuclear development. Saudi Arabia does not possess much nuclear material. It has a Comprehensive Safeguards Agreement (CSA) with the International Atomic Energy Agency (IAEA) which entered into force in 2009. That CSA has an old model Small Quantities Protocol (SQP), which holds certain reporting responsibilities in abeyance until nuclear material inventory exceeds one effective kilogram or the Saudis have a nuclear facility such as a reactor. At that time, Saudi Arabia will need to negotiate subsidiary arrangements, including facility attachments, which will specify in more detail the reporting requirements and inspection arrangements. As of early 2017, Saudi Arabia has neither power nor research reactors, nor are any under construction. The general belief in the non–proliferation community is that Saudi Arabia is a nuclear 'newcomer.'
- It is unclear at this point whether Saudi Arabia will sign and ratify the Additional Protocol to its CSA.
- As of 2016, there is no evidence of technical research or development of the production of fissile material, namely highly enriched uranium or

separated plutonium. However, a European government official confirmed to our Institute in 2014 that the pursuit of scientific and engineering expertise necessary to take command of all aspects of the nuclear fuel cycle is ongoing in Saudi Arabia.

- Saudi Arabia appears genuinely committed to importing many nuclear reactors and has pursued numerous cooperation agreements with other countries. The country's declared nuclear focus is on peaceful applications of nuclear energy, affordable power plants, desalination reactors, and environmental protection. According to recent plans, it intends to install over 16 nuclear reactors during the next few decades. This nuclear development programme is expected to remain strictly civilian in nature, focused mainly on deploying nuclear power reactors for generating electricity and desalinating sea water. However, it appears on a trajectory to create domestic appendages that could provide a nuclear weapons capability, even if for some time these capabilities would likely be under international safeguards. The conditions necessary for Saudi Arabia to operate unsafeguarded nuclear facilities or leave the Nuclear Non-Proliferation Treaty (NPT) to build nuclear weapons appear onerous today. The disincentives far outweigh the incentives for such a path. However, this could change depending on the fate of Iran's nuclear programme.

- As Saudi Arabia moves towards the operation of nuclear reactors, it will have to revise its safeguards agreements and replace the SQP with a CSA. It is unclear at this point whether Saudi Arabia will also ratify the Additional Protocol.

- Saudi Arabia has conducted at least one feasibility study on its 'involvement in all stages of the nuclear power generation cycle.' According to this study's results, using Saudi Arabia's natural uranium deposits to enrich uranium is among the feasible options.

- Although there is no evidence that Saudi Arabia is currently seeking to acquire or build uranium enrichment or reprocessing plants, this could change as its nuclear infrastructure develops and regional tensions fester. Once it establishes its knowledge and industrial base over the next five to 10 years, however, Saudi Arabia will be in a more favourable position to decide on building fuel cycle capabilities, albeit under safeguards. A former IAEA inspector interviewed for this paper judged that Saudi Arabia may seek such technologies in as soon as five years.

- Saudi Arabia's interpretation of the NPT appears to include a view of what some have called a 'right to enrich.' The country has not taken advantage of nuclear energy assistance from the United States, possibly because U.S. reactor purchases would need a signed memorandum of understanding (MoU) stating that Saudi Arabia would 'not pursue sensitive nuclear technologies,' which include enrichment and reprocessing.

- Saudi Arabia has expressed interest in developing an indigenous capability to manufacture nuclear reactors. KA.CARE, the national agency at the forefront of Saudi Arabia's nuclear agenda, has identified several steps within the nuclear fuel cycle as having high potential for local manufacturing, including fuel fabrication, processing, and enrichment. Going beyond the import of technologies, Saudi Arabia appears to have intentions to acquire intellectual property rights and become an exporter of small modular reactors (SMRs).

- Saudi Arabia appears to have a domestic supply of uranium sufficient for a small-scale, clandestine nuclear weapons programme. However, Saudi Arabia has not yet mined or processed any uranium from its domestic sources.
- Overlooked by many experts evaluating Saudi Arabia's nuclear future is the fact that the country's nuclear workforce is increasing at a rapid pace in both quality and quantity. The academic nuclear engineering sector is growing substantially, constantly launching new graduate programmes and expanding Saudi Arabia's five nuclear research centres. Already in 2014 Saudi Arabia considered it had a "high" comparative advantage in "operations and maintenance" of nuclear reactors and a "medium" advantage in other relevant steps.
- The bulk of its published nuclear research is of a theoretical, rather than experimental nature, and it does not involve significant quantities of uranium or other nuclear material. Nevertheless, Saudi Arabia is pursuing front-end nuclear fuel cycle research, such as studies on the extraction of uranium from ore.
- The growth of its academic nuclear energy sector in past years emphasizes the Saudi ambition to modernize and equip the future generation with technical nuclear capabilities.
- Saudi Arabia is highly invested in medical applications of nuclear science, such as gaining hands-on experience with nuclear reactions and housing at least five hot cells of unknown size. Hot cells over a certain size are of concern because they could be used in small-scale plutonium separation or irradiated fuel reprocessing experiments. In the case of Iran, hot cells exceeding six cubic meters are banned unless expressly allowed by the executive body of the JCPOA, and allowed ones are subject to IAEA monitoring. Regardless of the size of the Kingdom's hot cells, Saudi Arabia does not currently have any irradiated fuel (or targets) it could use in such experiments. Nonetheless, learning more about these hot cells and limiting the size of any future ones makes sense. In addition, the IAEA should report to member states on its knowledge of these hot cells.
- Official statements by Saudi Arabian officials suggest a commitment to acquire nuclear weapons, or at least advanced nuclear fuel cycle capabilities, in the event that Iran's nuclear programme is not adequately constrained by the nuclear deal. Recent statements indicate that officials are for now content with the temporary restrictions on Iran's nuclear capabilities brought by the JCPOA. The opinions of society and prominent Saudi analysts are mixed.
- Under the JCPOA, restrictions on Iran's enrichment programme start to conclude from year 10 to 15 of the deal's implementation (or in the period 2026-2031), and Saudi Arabia may again come to fear a renewed Iranian nuclear threat. This threat could be viewed as greater than prior to the agreement due to the international legitimization of Iran's nuclear weapons capabilities under the JCPOA, in particular. If the JCPOA ends prematurely, Iran's actions and those of the United States and UN Security Council to constrain Iran will likely dictate whether the nuclear programme is seen as a threat that Saudi Arabia must match.
- It is likely that Saudi Arabia did not pursue nuclear weapons capabilities following the IAEA's discovery of Iran's covert nuclear programmes in 2003. The exact reasons why are uncertain, but part of the rationale appears to be that the

international community refused to legitimize Iran's enrichment programme and instead enacted United Nations Security Council and other unilateral and regional sanctions against Iran. Those actions may have discouraged Saudi Arabia from seeking uranium enrichment technologies out of concern of being stigmatized and possibly subjected to international pressure and sanctions. However, Saudi Arabia's concerns over the Iranian programme likely contributed to its decision to pursue nuclear energy projects on a large scale as part of a hedging strategy.

- Unfortunately, the ability of the international community to detect potentially small-scale proliferation-relevant research and development by any nation is questionable, including today in Saudi Arabia. As Saudi Arabia has no major nuclear facilities, the IAEA's familiarity with its research and procurement efforts is limited.

- An on-going concern is that Saudi Arabia may plan to receive nuclear assistance from Pakistan. The Institute uncovered evidence that the assistance would not involve Pakistan supplying Saudi Arabia with a full nuclear weapon or weapons; however, Pakistan may assist in other important ways, such as supplying sensitive equipment, materials, and know-how used in enrichment or reprocessing. An unanswered question is whether Pakistan and Saudi Arabia may be cooperating on sensitive nuclear technologies in Pakistan. In an extreme case, Saudi Arabia may be financing, or will finance, an unsafeguarded uranium enrichment facility in Pakistan for later use, either in a civil or military programme.

- Saudi Arabia secretly purchased a controversial set of ballistic missiles from China in the 1980s, the DF-3 missiles, which can carry nuclear weapons. The United States detected the purchase after the fact. They appear to remain operational.

## Algeria

Until fairly recently, the United States was concerned about what was happening along the south-western shores of the Mediterranean. Although this is going back some time, David Albright did express disquiet at the fact that Algeria might, at least for a while, have had the capacity to produce nuclear weapons-useable plutonium. Though Moscow was not a direct participant, it certainly knew that 'backward' Algeria had shown interest in getting its own atomic bomb. Until February 1992, Algeria was secretly building a Chinese-supplied reactor at Ain Oussera, a remote site in the Atlas Mountains south of Algiers.

Albright told me that recent disclosures indicated that China had been the principal supplier of nuclear technology to Algiers since the two countries had signed a secret accord in 1983[10]. This involved the construction of the nuclear complex near Birine. It also included the Es Salam reactor, a hot cell laboratory and another for the production of radio-isotopes. For a country as impecunious and as historically troubled as Algeria, these were significant developments.

Of note was the fact that Es Salam was a heavy water reactor with 15 MW capability. Such a plant, said Albright, was capable of producing military grade plutonium that might be used in the construction of a nuclear bomb. The facility was opened in 1993 and, an American intelligence source told him, the Algerian atomic programme, as a consequence, exceeded its civil need. It was significant too, that they did receive some Argentinean technical assistance.

A Spanish intelligence report subsequently disclosed that Algeria had also concluded the second phase; the construction of the hot cell laboratory where it would be able to dismantle nuclear fuel produced from the reactor, one step prior to obtaining plutonium. The third and final phase would consist of the construction of a radio-isotope production laboratory with the capability to extract plutonium from the nuclear fuel first irradiated in the reactor and then dismantled in the hot cells.

Argentina's role was that in 1989 it sold Algeria the Nur research reactor. Though irrelevant from a military point of view, the step did commit Buenos Aires to a level of cooperation with the Arab state in nuclear matters. There was also a direct link to developments at Es Salam and the IAEA found this disquieting.

What worried the Americans (and the Spanish, in particular) was that while Algeria officially renounced nuclear weapons and signed the Nonproliferation Treaty (NPT) that has been circulated among the major powers and submitted voluntarily to International Atomic Energy Agency (IAEA) controls, this embattled government continued with its nuclear programme.

ISIS maintains that this information was the basis of a report recently produced by the Spanish secret service, Cesid and presented to the Madrid government. Cesid, said Albright, was unequivocal about the development. It described the clandestine work as a danger and warned of the implications of tolerating an Algerian deception regarding military objectives. Meanwhile, in a confidential Washington DC intelligence briefing a short while later, U.S. officials warned that the Algerian armed forces were in possession of a variety of delivery vehicles including bombers, missile launchers and Soviet-made rockets, all of which were quite capable of carrying nuclear weapons. Algeria, it disclosed, also had access to underground sites where, before independence, France carried out its own tests with nuclear weapons. More seriously, there are several other Islamic states interested in what is happening in Algiers. The Sahara desert sites, it is argued by pundits, might be ideal for testing an Iranian-built atom bomb. The fact that Algeria maintains strong ties with Tehran has not been lost on Western observers.

One of the reasons why concern was again raised about Algeria's nuclear aspirations was the alarms triggered by nuclear tests conducted by India and Pakistan. American satellites had originally discovered the construction of the nuclear reactor at Es Salam south of Algiers. That led to this North African government – already enmeshed in a particularly brutal civil war – acceding to the NPT. However, tensions did arise when, as a consequence of Vienna's International Atomic Energy Agency (IAEA) inspections, it was discovered that five pounds of enriched uranium, 'some litres' of heavy water and various pieces of natural uranium supplied by China had not been declared.

The Es Salam reactor had the theoretical capacity to produce up to five pounds of plutonium annually and it would not be difficult for small quantities to be diverted for military purposes. Furthermore, Algeria depended on outside suppliers of nuclear fuel. The IAEA has also confirmed the purchase of 150 tons of uranium concentrate from Nigeria in 1984. Its main limitation now, the Spanish document stated, was Algeria's inability to undertake a military nuclear programme on its own. However, the discovery of uranium in the southern Hoggar Mountains puts Algeria in a special category within the Third World context.

It is interesting that all documentation related to the project has been classified as secret by the Algerian authorities, which, says the Spanish report 'is surprising due to the supposed peaceful use to which Algeria's nuclear programme was to have been put.' On the other hand, there is not a country involved in nuclear research, at whatever level, that does not restrict information. Secondly, with Algeria's abundant energy resources, especially natural gas, it is the view of the Spanish intelligence agency that Algeria has no need to choose the nuclear route for power production. The only conclusion that Cesid could reach – and which was contained in its confidential report – was that the development of Es Salam was with strictly military objectives.

It is significant that at the time, Washington concurred.

*Chapter 19*

# A Nuclear Weapons Programme in Burma?

*'There remain sound reasons to suspect that the military regime in Burma might be pursuing a long-term strategy to make nuclear weapons…'*

*Washington's Institute for Science and International Security, January 28, 2010*[1]

Within the international community there can be few countries that are as poor, as politically isolated or as oppressed as Myanmar, formerly Burma. The country was ruled by a military dictatorship that had a history of either killing or jailing its political opponents, like Aung San Suu Kyi who, over decades, gained the same international measure of status as Nelson Mandela. Thankfully, those days are hopefully over and the nuclear issue has receded; but that it could have happened is what worries cognoscenti who deal with such matters.

Great secrecy surrounded the day-to-day machinations of the country's former leaders and in this respect Myanmar would appear to have shared some of the nuclear aspirations of its closest ally, Kim Jong-il's North Korea. The country's junta was even paranoiac enough to have moved its capital city from graceful old Rangoon (Yangon today), which had captured both the imagination and the minds of travellers and writers for centuries. Yangon, it seems, simply was not safe enough. The generals' new home was to be known as the Abode of Kings; more commonly as Naypyidaw.

There were other developments, including a series of persistent reports – the majority little more than rumours – of the possible development of a nuclear alliance between Myanmar and North Korea. There was little substantive, but the flow of information – conflicting and sometimes contradictory – was disturbing enough to have resulted in various groups trying to establish veracity. David Albright's ISIS was among the first to publish a report. While he and his co-authors remained cautious, they published a report that underscored not only close links with Pyongyang but also the possibility that both countries might have pooled efforts in possible nuclear procurement. The warning that ISIS proffers was clear:

'North Korea's past proliferation activities and the failure to promptly detect the Syrian reactor cannot but lead to more scrutiny over whether North Korea might sell Burma a reactor or other nuclear industrial equipment and facilities, or the means and guidance to manufacture things related to this industry.

'When one adds Burma's own efforts to acquire abroad sophisticated dual-use goods that can be used for nuclear purposes, it becomes essential to determine and constrain as necessary the military junta's nuclear intentions. Another dimension was whether Burma was helping North Korea obtain items for its illicit activities.'

ISIS went on to declare that Burma could act as a cooperative transhipment partner for goods ultimately destined for North Korea's gas centrifuge uranium enrichment programme. At the same time, this Washington think-tank came up with a report titled 'Exploring Claims about Secret Nuclear Sites in Myanmar' and while numerous satellite photos were shown, nothing conclusively nuclear emerged. In fact, the authors reached a contrary conclusion.

There were a few smoking guns to ponder. David Albright's team revealed that the Naypyidaw Government asked the International Atomic Energy Agency for assistance in acquiring a research reactor. 'The IAEA said that it would help with such an endeavour once Burma had achieved a set of milestones that included bringing its reactor safety and regulatory infrastructure up to a minimally acceptable standard.' Meanwhile, without telling the nuclear monitoring body, Burma started negotiations with Russia over the supply of a ten megawatt thermal research reactor. A draft cooperation agreement was approved by Moscow in May 2002 for the construction of a nuclear research centre that would include the reactor, two laboratories (believed to include hot cells for radio-isotope production) as well as facilities for the disposal of nuclear waste.

The draft agreement did not represent an approved sale, maintains ISIS:

'The two countries finally signed a nuclear cooperation agreement in 2007 for the sale of the reactor complex, but no construction of the research centre had started. In addition, neither side publicly announced the planned location of this reactor project. Under the terms of its cooperation, Russia reportedly conducted training of Burmese in fields related to the building and operation of research reactors'.

With that much established, more recent disclosures showed evidence of Burmese cooperation with North Korean trading entities that include the presence in Burma of officials from Namchongang Trading (NCG), which was sanctioned by the United Nations Security Council after it was proved that Syria's illegal reactor project depended on assistance from NCG.

Then Japanese newspapers reported the arrest of three men who had attempted to illegally export a magnetometer to Burma through a Malaysian intermediary. That effort took place under the direction of a company associated with illicit procurement for North Korean military programmes and successfully delivered other nuclear dual-use equipment to Burma.

ISIS at the time was clear about these developments:

'Burma is seeking abroad a large quantity of top-notch, highly sophisticated goods with potential missile and nuclear uses. Yet, no pattern emerged in these procurements that lead to a specific missile or nuclear end use. Nonetheless, the procurements are often suspicious or highly enigmatic, according to one senior European intelligence official.

'The consensus was that the repressive military regime might use North Korean trading entities to acquire overseas sensitive nuclear and nuclear dual use goods. Moreover, its military cooperation with North Korea had increased exponentially, fuelling concerns about nuclear cooperation. North Korea could also supplement Burma's own foreign procurement networks, and it could sell nuclear goods made in North Korea.

'For its part, North Korea would find such an arrangement lucrative, and it could use Burma as a willing transhipment point, or "turntable" for illicit sales for itself or others. Another, albeit less likely, possibility was that North Korea could build sensitive facilities in Burma for its own use.

'There were also lingering questions about two Pakistani nuclear scientists who reportedly went to Burma in late 2001, during a time of intense interest over any help these same Pakistani nuclear scientists could have provided al-Qaeda in Afghanistan before the fall of the Taliban.'

ISIS tells us that Suleiman Asad and Muhammed Ali Mukhtar, reportedly left Pakistan with the agreement of the Pakistani government to elude questioning by the United States. Burmese officials subsequently denied giving sanctuary to any Pakistani nuclear scientists and their whereabouts or activities remained unknown.

According to the Federation of American Scientists, Burma's purported nuclear ambitions originally surfaced in an unlikely source. Details initially surfaced on 1 August 2009 in the *Sydney Morning Herald* in an article titled 'Revealed: Burma's nuclear bombshell' written by Hamish McDonald, the newspaper's Asia-Pacific editor[3]. McDonald explained that there were two Burmese defectors involved. Both were extensively and separately interviewed over a period of two years by Desmond Ball, an Australian National University strategic expert and Phil Thornton, a Thai-based Irish–Australian journalist who has followed Burma for years.

Ball and Thornton said that what had emerged from these interviews was that the secret nuclear complex was centred largely in caves that had been tunnelled into a mountain at Naung Laing in northern Burma. 'It runs parallel to a civilian reactor being built at another site by Russia that both the Russians and Burmese say will be put under international safeguards', wrote McDonald.

For the purpose of anonymity and the sake of the safety of their respective families, source names have been changed. One of the principle informants is listed as Moe Joe, who revealed that the regime had sent him to Moscow in 2003 to study engineering. He was in a second batch of trainees to be sent to Russia as part of an effort to eventually train a thousand personnel to run Burma's nuclear programme. Before leaving, he was told he would be assigned to a special nuclear battalion.

'You don't need 1,000 people in the fuel cycle or to run a nuclear reactor,' said Moe Joe. It is obvious that there is much more going on. Moe Joe alleged a second, secret reactor of about the same size as the Russian plant had been built at a complex called Naung Laing. He said that the army planned a plutonium reprocessing system there and that Russian experts were on site to show how it was done. Part of the Burmese army's nuclear battalion was stationed in a local village to work on a weapon.

An operations area was buried in the nearby Setkhaya Mountains, a set-up including engineers, artillery and communications to act as a command and control centre for the nuclear weapons programme, he disclosed. 'In the event that the testimonies of the defectors are proved, the alleged 'secret' reactor could be capable of being operational and producing a bomb a year, every year, after 2014,' say Ball and Thornton. For all the hype, this has never happened.

The second defector was given the nom de plume of Tin Min. He claimed to have worked as a bookkeeper for a tycoon closely linked to the Burmese military regime and whose company had supposedly organised nuclear contracts with Russia and North Korea. He believed that the deal with North Korea on nuclear co-operation dated back nine years, covering construction and maintenance of nuclear facilities. 'Tin Min spoke excellent English and presented his reports to us with a touch of self-importance,' wrote Ball and Thornton, adding that he had good reason to know what it was like to feel important; 'before defecting he had scaled the heights of his country's high society and had reaped the benefits of that position.'

Tin Min dismissed the regime's rationale for requiring nuclear technology. 'They say it's to produce medical isotopes for health purposes in hospitals. How many hospitals in Burma have nuclear science? Burma can barely get electricity up and running. It's all nonsense.' He also claimed that his boss once told him of the regime's nuclear dreams. 'They're aware they cannot compete with Thailand with conventional weapons.'

Shortly after the story was released the *Kang Nam I*, a North Korean freighter, headed towards Burma carrying undisclosed cargo. A South Korean intelligence expert claimed satellite imagery showed that the ship was part of clandestine nuclear transfer and also carried long-range missiles. Shadowed by the United States Navy, the vessel eventually turned around and returned home.

Not everybody accepts these disclosures at face value. For one, the ISIS report written by Robert Kelley, Andrea Scheel Stricker and Paul Brannan demonstrates that while little is certain, there is almost nothing to show in a series of satellite photographs that Burma has a nuclear programme up and running.

Mark Fitzpatrick, a senior fellow at the International Institute for Strategic Studies and a Burma watcher who is to publish a book on South East Asian nuclear plans concurs. He is certain the Russian reactor has not been built already. He sees 'nothing alarming' in the prospective Russian deal – Russia is a signatory to the NPT which governs the export of civilian nuclear technology – and he doubts whether Moscow would attempt to secretly supply a reactor to a pariah state. Nor has the IAEA raised questions about Burma's nuclear ambitions.

But Fitzpatrick is sceptical about the stated reasons offered by Burma's rulers to explain their interest in nuclear technology, whether for research or power generation. Of the defectors' claims, Fitzpatrick says that he had heard the reports and paid attention to them and they shouldn't be dismissed out of hand. 'North Korea is willing to sell anything to anyone', he says, and points to evidence that Pyongyang secretly sold a nuclear reactor to Syria.

## Chapter 20

# Biological Weapons: A Real and Agonising Threat has Come Back to Haunt Us

*'It is an agonizing way to die. First there is fever and dreadful aching pains. Then come pus-filled boils which appear all over the body and scabs develop. Slowly, inexorably, the immune system surrenders...'*

*'Smallpox: The New Bioweapon' The Times, London, 8 January 2001*

It is a reality of the age we live in that new (and quite a few old) weapons of war have returned to modern society and might present some serious problems for all generations in the near future. There have been any number of films and TV programmes made over decades where disease and germs – biological warfare, in modern parlance – has been a consistent theme. These days we take it all for granted: the denouement invariably ends well and everybody (or almost everybody) emerges alive and well. However, with smallpox, the reality of this horrendous threat is terrifying because the disease remains a threat. A slew of international agreements has been signed by just about every country on earth that biological warfare is illegal, but its presence lingers.

Using this example, we have smallpox, eradicated worldwide almost two generations ago. Yet it remains a real and identifiable threat, so much so that United States Special Forces were inoculated against the disease prior to going into Iraq in 2003. The late Dr Jonathan Tucker, an international and much respected authority on biological warfare and a very good friend with whom I shared many notes, highlighted an accident in 1978, a year after smallpox was supposed to have been eradicated worldwide. A smallpox virus escaped from a research laboratory at the University of Birmingham Medical School in Britain. A medical photographer who was working on the floor above the laboratory became infected (through air vents, it was thought at the time) and she later died. The disease also spread to her mother, who survived. It was only luck that a major smallpox outbreak did not result.

More to the point, could terrorist groups use smallpox as a weapon? Since the virus no longer exists in nature, the only way dissidents could acquire seed cultures would be on the international black market. For this reason, smallpox would be an unlikely weapon for 'ordinary' terrorist groups, which would not exclude either Islamic State or al-Qaeda. There is certainly a possibility that state-sponsored terrorists linked to rogue states like North Korea and possibly Iran could be used.

What is of concern is that should a group intent on causing injury or disease on a continent-wide basis manage to acquire and produce the virus in liquid form, it would be a relatively easy matter to disseminate it. A compact aerosol device in an enclosed space – such as the London Underground or the New York City subway would be an ideal terror scenario.

The pattern of infection is chilling. Within two weeks the first victims would come down with fever, aches and other non-specific symptoms before developing smallpox's distinctive pustular rash. By the time the first patients were diagnosed, they would have infected the next wave of cases. So it would go on.

It is notable that the reality of the smallpox threat was made clear much more recently by Bill Gates, the Microsoft Founder, when he addressed the Royal United Services Institute in London (RUSI) on 19 April 2017. He could not have been more explicit when he warned that an outbreak of a lethal respiratory virus like smallpox would be more dangerous than even a nuclear attack: it could kill 30 million people were it to get a hold. Gates declared that it was more important than ever to help foreign countries monitor diseases to prevent a global tragedy. 'Bioterrorism is a much larger risk than a pandemic,' were his words, adding that:

'All these advances in biology have made it far easier for a terrorist to recreate smallpox, which is a highly fatal pathogen, where there is essentially no immunity remaining at this point.

'When you are thinking about things that could cause in excess of 10 million deaths, even something tragic like a nuclear weapons incident wouldn't get to that level. So the greatest risk is from a natural epidemic or an intentionally caused infection bioterrorism event.

Yet, smallpox does get into the news from time to time, including a report that somebody had contracted the disease in India about a decade ago. Yet the Indian sub-continent is supposed to be clear of this dreadful disease. According to Dr. Richard Spertzel, in a submission before the House Armed Services Committee[1], the Middle East remains the locus. Others named by him before Congress as possibly having access to the deadly *Variola major* (smallpox) virus for military use are Iran, North Korea and of course, the Russians.

Almost as if preordained, Dr Jonathan Tucker published his book on smallpox almost exactly a year before. Some of his observations are compelling[2]. Dr Tucker quotes a Defence Intelligence Agency (DIA) report from May 1994 stating that virologists from one of the Soviet Ministry of Defence's military microbiology institutes transferred smallpox virus cultures to Iraq in the late 1980s or early 1990s. There was also (unsubstantiated) evidence he stated, that the Russians 'assisted the Iraqis with their biological warfare programme'.

Significantly, Dr Kathleen Vogel, a scientist at Cornell University who toured biological warfare facilities in the former Soviet Union, told a meeting of the American Association for the Advancement for Science not long before that, that she suspected secret stocks of smallpox virus were still being held at Russian military microbiology facilities. These were outside the WHO-approved repository in Novosibirsk, she warned, reporting at the time that scientists formerly employed by the Soviet biological warfare programme had been offered lucrative jobs in countries categorized by the US State Department as 'supporting international terrorism'.

She expressed concern that samples of smallpox virus might have been sold to some of these rogue states which might include Iran, Syria, Libya and others. Gadaffi's revolutionary North African state had since agreed to end all its chemical and biological warfare programmes, as well as its much-publicized efforts at achieving nuclear parity.

Then we had news after the Iran-Iraq War (1980 to 1988) that out-of-work Russian scientists had been recruited by Iran to work on its biological warfare programme. In a publication titled *Iran: Arms and Weapons of Mass Destruction Suppliers*, Kenneth Katzman, a Washington-based specialist in Middle Eastern affairs disclosed that Iran had also sought chemical weapons technology and chemical precursors from Russia as well as China. He made the point that official American statements on efforts to dissuade Russian WMD-related technology sales tended to omit discussion of chembio technology. Outside assistance to Iran's chemical and biological programme, says Katzman, 'is difficult to prevent, given the dual-use nature of the materials, the equipment being sought and the many legitimate end-users'. In one sense, he intimated, it was almost like UNSCOM's Iraqi WMD debate of the mid-1990s.

Katzman is much more effusive about China's role. Since the early 1990s, he says, US officials identified firms on the Chinese Mainland as suppliers of Iran's chemical weapons programmes, though some US officials attributed the assistance to Iran to a lack of export controls by the Chinese government. With these facts in mind, the spectre of scientists closely linked to the Tehran regime dabbling in things like smallpox, becomes very real.

Suddenly, after decades of smallpox being a non-issue, Western intelligence services are again focusing on its use as a weapon of mass destruction (WMD).

The US government is taking the threat seriously enough to prepare the nation for a possible germ attack in which smallpox might be involved. As Jonathan Tucker pointed out, 'while the disease itself may have been eradicated, laboratory stocks of the virus continue to exist and may have fallen into the hands of pariah countries'.

There are several reasons why international terrorists might be tempted to use smallpox as a weapon sometime in the future and why Western nations are quickly pushing through with as many immunizations among health workers as possible; as quickly as is feasible, all health workers in Britain will their shots and, as in the US, it will be available to others who want it. The first reason for this uncharacteristic haste is that the United States stopped vaccinating its civilian population against the disease in 1972. All other nations had taken the same approach by the early 1980s.

Given this vulnerability, Atlanta's Centres for Disease Control (CDC) has since warned that even 'a limited terrorist release' of the smallpox virus would constitute a major emergency. In the absence of sufficient stocks of the vaccine worldwide, smallpox could potentially result in the return of a global health threat, the Atlanta spokesperson declared.

Smallpox apart, there are several diseases brought onto European and American soil by the flood of illegals who have been entering Western countries illegally over the course of the past decade. Bubonic Plague is only one of them and another is the biological agent botulinum toxin, which is made from spore-forming bacteria found all over the world in the soil. According to Allied intelligence reports during the Second World War, the highly toxic nature of this substance was recognized by the Nazi regime and it was feared that the Germans might develop a mechanism which could unleash botulinum on the forces landing on the beaches at D-Day.

Several other diseases recently reported by Atlanta's Centres for Disease Control to be near eradication are making a comeback in the United States. A Health.com report disclosed that a 16-year-old girl from Oregon was sickened and hospitalized with plague after apparently being bitten by a flea on a hunting trip. This would not be of too much concern, except that the disease actually persists in parts of Africa, Asia, and South America and there have been sixteen reported cases of plague, with four deaths, in the United States in recent years. Symptoms of bubonic plague include fever, chills, headache, and swollen lymph glands.

Other 'comeback' diseases that have recently entered our system, some of which are prevalent among foreign born residents of the US and foreign visitors, also need to be countered. These include zika, flesh eating parasites – coetaneous leishmaniasis – ebola, leprosy, intestinal parasites, HIV, scabies, and diphtheria. In the USA, there have been two serious outbreaks of mass illness as a result of infected dairy produce: in 1985, 170,000 people were infected by the contamination of pasteurized milk by the virus *S. typhimurium*; while in 1994, contaminated liquid ice cream transported as a pre-mix in tanker trucks affected a quarter million people in forty one states. In the same vein, Shanghai's enthusiasm for the consumption of clams unintentionally led to the spread of hepatitis A in 1991, with nearly 300,000 people affected. Even recent *E-coli* scandals pale beside the food poisoning tragedy in Spain in 1981, when 800 people died and 20,000 became ill – many of them permanently – from a chemical agent that had been added to cooking oil.

Political dissidents have also a hand in spreading disease and the idea of making large numbers of innocent people sick by contaminating water has long been a fantasy of terror groups, from the radical Weathermen in 1960s America to the Red Army Faction in 1970s Germany, where thirteen members of the extremist outfit were reported to have received instruction in how to poison urban water supplies in at least twenty European cities. The obvious danger from this source was also highlighted in the US with several unintentional incidents of mass water poisoning, as in Milwaukee in 1993, in which the spread of the pathogen cryptosporidium led to the deaths of 111 people and illness for another 400,000.

Events of recent times have underscored the risks we face in our increasingly sophisticated, complex and over-crowded world. As the former Iranian leader Akbar Hashemi Rasfanjani once said of the threat to the West, 'It is not necessary to develop nuclear weapons when much cheaper and more portable chemical or biological agents can kill the enemy in their thousands.'

According to some experts, it is not a matter of *if*, but rather of *when* we witness a major biological terror attack. We saw something of this potential in the quiet American town of Dalles, which nestles along the Columbia River in Oregon. It was as if a terrible Biblical plague had been visited on the community. In September 1984, hundreds of residents were suddenly struck down by violent sickness, made all the more terrifying because of the speed at which it raced through the area. First the victims felt nausea and stomach cramps. Soon afterwards they were gripped by dizziness and disorientation. Then followed fever, chills, extreme vomiting and diarrhoea, which forced many of them to be hospitalized. No age group was safe, with the afflicted ranging from infants to the elderly. As the casualties mounted, a mood of bewilderment and panic resulted.

At first investigators concluded that the apparent mass poisoning was the result of poor personal hygiene by food handlers working in local restaurants and bars. But most believed this to be an inadequate explanation: it could not account for either the virulence or the scale. They were right to be suspicious. On further investigation – by then, Federal law enforcement agencies and CDC had been brought in – it emerged that there were far more sinister origins. The reality was that the town had been subjected to North America's first bio-terrorist attack. The residents had been deliberately poisoned with a salmonella virus by power-crazed members of an extreme religious cult.

In a bizarre political plot that would have been laughable had it not been so harmful, the fanatics – all followers of the Asian mystic the Bhagwan Shree Rajneesh – wanted to incapacitate the local electorate so that they could seize control of the Dalles municipal council and promote the expansion of the commune they had set up nearby. It was the cult's chosen method of attack. In a series of experiments to test the effectiveness of their pathogens, they first put salmonella in the drinking glasses of two municipal officers, one of whom became seriously ill.

Then they stepped up their operations, contaminating ten salad bars in local restaurants with salmonella. They did this either by smearing the virus directly onto the produce, or by placing it in the salad dressing. Eventually 751 people were infected, with 45 of them hospitalized. The truth about the conspiracy came out partly because of splits in the cult, some of whose members gave evidence to the police.

It is a sign of how much more innocent the world used to be about terrorism that the conspirators, led by a zealot called Sheela Silverman, only received light sentences and were out of prison in four years. At the time, there was no such crime as bioterrorism with which they could be charged, so they had to be convicted on far lesser offences.

Much more serious is the role played by nations that oppose us, North Korea and the former Soviet Union in particular. Both countries can be implicated in apparently trying to acquire stockpiles of the most terrible infection of them all, the notorious Ebola haemorrhagic virus. The victims of this brutal disease die a horrible death. There is evidence that the Russians conducted experiments using Ebola virus; indeed, one Soviet scientist is reported to have been observed in a Moscow laboratory with appalling symptoms of blood emitting from his body, even from the pores in his fingers.

In the Soviet era, Moscow's agents are said to have acquired their samples of Ebola by visiting plague-infected areas of the remote parts of the Congo in Africa. This was a practice that the late Dr Margaret Isaacson – a family friend – told me was also followed by the North Koreans. As an advisor to the World Health Organization and based in Johannesburg, Dr Isaacson was often first on the scene during outbreaks of the haemorrhagic virus such as Ebola. She could sometimes be spotted in the background in CNN news clips taken during the course of visiting such catastrophes.

She recalled one event that particularly disturbed her. On a visit to an extremely remote part of the Congo that had been afflicted – she needed to charter a small plane to get there – she came across groups of North Koreans, posing as tourists, but they were almost too interested in the infected corpses. Another source indicated that they had surreptitiously taken blood samples. She approached the group leader and he responded aggressively: 'we are tourists ... why do you want to know', he asked.

The disturbing aspect of Ebola is that, just like smallpox, it can be transported and ultimately spread around in a container no bigger than a jam jar. As Dr Isaacson suggested, should a group like al-Qaeda, ISIS, or the North Koreans – who might be intent on causing injury or disease on a continent-wide basis – manage to acquire and produce the virus in liquid form, it would be a relatively easy matter to disseminate it. Again, spreading it about in the London Underground or the New York City subway in aerosols might come into play. And though the 'disseminator' would also die in spreading the disease, that fate would be of little concern to fanatic jihadis who, as recent events in the Middle East and elsewhere have shown, welcome death in the glorious service of their Prophet.

One needs to understand how these diseases actually work when disseminated and prior to entering the human body. Professor Vincent Fiscetti, head of the Department of Bacterial Pathogenesis and Immunology at The Rockefeller University observed that in a mass transport environment there are people from all over the world travelling together. 'It takes several days for the symptoms to show, by which time they will have carried it back to their own countries.'

An interesting aside here, is that exactly this pattern of infection (out of Hong Kong) was instrumental in transmitting China's much less potent SARS virus early in 2003: It did not take long to spread the virus to many countries, though comparisons end there. Smallpox deaths, among those who have *not* been vaccinated, could, by comparison, be measured in terms of hundreds of millions.

Professor Fiscetti is of the view that an even more effective delivery method might be to use a low-flying aircraft to disperse an aerosol of the virus over an international event like the Olympics or a World Cup football game or, unthinkably, those making the *Haj* (pilgrimage) to the Saudi Moslem holy cities of Mecca and Medina. Geographically small countries such as Sri Lanka, Israel, Singapore and Jordan would be especially vulnerable. Because of fears that smallpox could be used as a terrorist weapon Washington announced not long ago that it was pouring money into developing new drug treatments for the virus.

The most feared of all infectious diseases, smallpox was first identified in ancient Egypt and gradually spread throughout the world. Over the centuries it caused untold numbers of deaths; it killed rich and poor, royalty and commoners. Repeatedly the disease changed the course of history. Highly contagious, the smallpox virus spreads through the air and it takes only a few particles to infect. The more potent form of the disease, *Variola major*, kills about 30 per cent of its victims. Survivors in the past were almost always disfigured with ugly scars.

Almost forty years ago a worldwide vaccination campaign organized by the World Health Organization (WHO) successfully eradicated the disease. The last natural outbreak occurred in Somalia in 1977. Three years later, the WHO declared the disease extinct and urged all member-countries to halt routine vaccination because it entailed a significant risk of complications. Even after smallpox was eliminated from nature, some countries retained laboratory stocks of the virus for research purposes. Although Soviet leaders had been the driving force behind the WHO smallpox eradication campaign, they cynically exploited the world's new vulnerability to the disease by turning it into a strategic weapon.

It is no longer a secret that during the 1980s, the Soviet army mass-produced the smallpox virus as a biological weapon. We now know from several scientists who defected to the West that tons of the virus in liquid suspension were stored in refrigerated tanks. In wartime, they reckoned, the agent would have been loaded into aerial bombs and ICBM warheads and dropped onto residents of US and Chinese cities.

Dr Ken Alibek, who served as First Deputy Director of Biopreparat, a major component of the Soviet biological weapons programme, provided Western intelligence agencies with all the details after his defection to the United States in 1992. He also claimed that stocks of smallpox virus were distributed 'to places in Russia beyond the known laboratories – possibly where there was less effective security controls'. Alibek added that while smallpox was an effective weapon, Soviet scientists had attempted to make it even more deadly by adding foreign genes from other viruses such as Ebola, although this work was apparently halted after the breakup of the Soviet Union.

Specialists at a Johns Hopkins University conference on bioterrorism at the turn of the Millennium said that much of Dr Alibek's information had been confirmed by other sources. At the same time, there are chemical weapons specialists who remain sceptical of the genetically engineered 'double kill' concept (reinforcing the acknowledged lethality of one virus by adding another).

There are two basic types of biological weapons, those that are contagious and those that are not. Anthrax, for instance, is not contagious: people do not spread it among themselves. Also, you cannot catch anthrax from someone who is dying of it. Smallpox and Ebola in contrast, are virulently contagious; both spread rapidly, the virus magnifying itself, causing mortality and chaos on a massive scale.

One source described the most powerful bioweapons as dry powders formed of tiny particles, anthrax especially; 'bio-dusts', in fact, that are almost designed to lodge in the human lung:

'The particles are amber or pink. They have a strong tendency to fly apart from one another, so that if you throw them in the air they disperse, invisible to the human eye, normally within seconds after the release.

'You cannot see a biological weapon, you cannot smell it and you cannot taste it. You don't know it was there until days later, as with anthrax – when you start to cough and bleed – it ends up spreading the spores around once more. Moreover, the particles of a bioweapon are exceedingly small, about one to five microns in diameter. You could imagine the size this way: around 50 to 100 particles lined up in a row would span the thickness of a human hair.

'The tiny size of a weaponized bio-particle allows it to be sucked into the deepest recesses of the lung, where it sticks to the membrane, and enters the bloodstream. Then it begins to replicate. A bioweapon can kill you with just one particle in the lung. If the weapon is contagious in human-to-human transmission, you will kill a lot of other people too.

'Given the right weather conditions, a bioweapon will drift in the air for up to a hundred miles. A couple of hundred pounds of anthrax spores in optimal atmospheric conditions would kill up to three million people in any of the densely populated metropolitan areas of the United States.'

What we do know is that like smallpox, anthrax is an insidious disease that has long been associated with human history.

The fifth and sixth plagues described in *Exodus* may have been anthrax in domestic animals followed by cutaneous anthrax in people – the same form of the disease that appeared to have affected most of those involved in the sporadic attacks in America in 2001/2002. The disease that Virgil described in his *Georgics* is clearly anthrax among animals. We also know that anthrax was intimately associated with the origins of microbiology and immunology; a disease for which the French scientist Louis Pasteur developed a live bacterial vaccine in 1881. For centuries, anthrax in humans was associated with exposure to infected or contaminated animal products.

In 1958 it was estimated that, worldwide, between 20,000 and about 100,000 humans were infected by the disease. In recent years, anthrax in animals was reported from more than 80 countries, the largest epidemic in modern times occurring in Zimbabwe from 1978 through 1980 with an estimated 10,000 cases. It was about then that I landed at a small airstrip near Fort Victoria on the way back from a diving trip in Northern Mozambique: there were animal carcasses strewn everywhere along the length of the runway. More lay where they had fallen in the adjacent bush.

Military interest in anthrax in the West in the past half-century or so – such as research being conducted today at the US Army USAMRIID germ warfare facility at Fort Detrick, Maryland – has been linked strictly to defend *against* its use as a biological weapon. That is not the case in some other countries. By the start of Gulf War 1 in the early 1990s, Iraq had weaponized tons of it and American intelligence sources maintain that scientific groups appointed by Vladimir Putin are still dabbling in both weapons of mass destruction at a variety of secret locations, very much as it was during the communist period. Saddam Hussein's intent while still in power in Iraq (recently confirmed by declassified CIA and DIA reports) was to spray it over allied forces moving up from the south. He had even modified several MiG-21 aircraft, complete with special tanks adapted for the purpose, though all were destroyed in the first day's air strikes of Operation Desert Storm. Were his scientists able to master the intricacies needed to fit Scud missiles with warheads containing anthrax and botulinum toxin, these would almost certainly have been showered over Israeli cities. The panic that resulted from the few Scuds that did land in Israel shortly afterwards underscores the level of fear that would almost certainly result from such an attack.

The process of using anthrax as a weapon involves an extremely complex system of disseminating huge volumes of spores that have been 'weaponized', in itself a sophisticated process necessitating government involvement rather than private individuals or terror groups. Again, as with smallpox, quantities of the pathogen might be sprayed over a specific area by an aircraft. Or it might possibly be delivered in the warhead of a missile, very much as the Soviets planned to do in their darkest days. What is important is that in order to become contaminated with the disease (which, untreated, is fatal about 80 per cent of the time) each subject needs to inhale between 8,000 and 50,000 anthrax spores[3]. According to Eric Croddy who has detailed his findings in one of the best books on the genre titled *Chemical and Biological Warfare: A Comprehensive Survey for the Concerned Citizen*, these numbers probably need to be revised: a range of 4,000 to 8,000 is more likely, and is also conservative. In fact, he feels, it may take considerably less[4]. While such an attack might result in terrible loss of life, that will only occur if a variety of other factors such as spore size, wind, temperature and climate are ideal, the conclusion here is that anthrax is an inordinately difficult medium to deploy as a weapon.

In the incidents involving sections of the postal system in Florida, New Jersey and New York being contaminated with anthrax after the World Trade Centre attack, the consensus of most authorities was that the perpetrators, while deadly in their intent, were amateurs. The subsequent attack on Congress, however, placed them in a different league.

Let us look then at the implications of a full-scale anthrax attack. The potential threat from aerosol clouds is evident from a WHO estimate that about 80 pounds of dry anthrax used against a city would kill as many as 36,000 people and possibly incapacitate another 50,000 or so. Other estimates are higher still. But why go aloft when a simple subterranean option would provide the terrorist with a much better prospect?

Dr Seth Carus, former Visiting Fellow at the National Defence University's Centre for Counterproliferation Research in Washington DC, told me that in order to disperse anthrax in a New York subway or through the London Underground, you would need to produce a dried, milled, powdered agent. Also, size is critical; the spores need to be from 1-10 microns in diameter. 'Anything smaller and they don't deposit in the lungs. Bigger and the body starts its natural filtering process,' he declared.

Also, the *bacilli* would tend to settle more quickly instead of remaining suspended in the atmosphere. Carus stressed that it is extremely dangerous to handle agents of this kind: Those involved need to have an extraordinarily efficient containment programme. 'If you don't, you could end up killing everybody involved.' As he points out, producing a dry agent is a much more difficult task than actually growing the organism. In theory, a schoolboy with the right paraphernalia might be able to do that. However, he would first need to find a source of anthrax seed stock. 'But once you get to a more advanced level, it becomes relatively easy in military terms to disseminate the agent and infect a large number of people.'

What is clear is that with *Bacillus anthracis* spore in powder form, the perpetrator will encounter none of the problems usually found with a liquid agent where nozzles and pressure have to be just right. However, the slurry has to be just the absolute correct  consistency or wrong-sized particles might result, he pointed out.

Preparing anthrax as a large-scale biological weapon requires a good level of technological skill. The essentials include industrial centrifuges, repeated washings and intensive drying of the spores, all of which take place inside a specially built sealed environment. That is hardly the stuff of some primitive lab in a cave in Afghanistan. Even the Russians had difficulty with some of the more arcane aspects of these disciplines. In one instance in 1979, as a result of an accident at a biological weapons factory in the industrial city of Sverdlovsk (now Yekaterinburg) east of the Urals, some of their own people died when the disease was unintentionally released into the atmosphere and disseminated by wind. The figure officially quoted was almost seventy dead, though sceptics of this unsolicited Russian candour tend to put the fatality figure much higher, if only because only civilian deaths were tallied in an accident that took place in a military establishment.

Anthrax remains potent for a very long time, largely because it is a remarkably hardy pathogen. This was illustrated by the British, who used Gruinard Island off the coast of Scotland as a bombing site for the testing of dropping anthrax during the Second World War. Decades later the area was still contaminated and the place stayed off-limits. Only in recent years has the island been declared clear of anthrax.

An interesting hypothesis regarding the use of anthrax as a biological weapon was submitted as a paper in the *Journal of Emerging Infectious Diseases* in July/August 1990. It dealt with an aerial anthrax attack on an outdoor stadium where a football game was being played before tens of thousands of spectators. This is *extremely* noteworthy because it fairly accurately tracks what could still happen in actuality if terrorists were able to dispense anthrax at a large gathering. The scenario envisaged was a truck passing along an elevated highway at a stadium. For thirty seconds it released an invisible, odourless anthrax cloud about a third of a mile long into the atmosphere. About 16,000 fans – or about a fifth of those present – were infected and so were another 4,000-plus people living in adjoining areas. Two days after the game, hundreds of people become ill with fever, coughing fits and, in some cases, shortness of breath and chest pain. Some of the sick self-administered. Others went to their doctors. Because it was that time of the year, influenza was commonplace, nobody made too much of the outbreak to begin with. A day later however, a large number of serious upper respiratory illnesses were reported. By nightfall some victims were dead.

Though the study was fictitious, it does make the point that when anthrax is properly disseminated among the unsuspecting and left untreated, the disease becomes a potent killer.

*Chapter 21*

# Chemical Weapons – A Scourge That Threatens Our Future

*'President Bashar al-Assad continues to retain hundreds of tonnes of his country's chemical stockpile after deceiving United Nations inspectors sent in to dismantle it,' said Syria's former chemical weapons research chief and other experts. Brigadier-General Zaher al-Sakat – who served as head of chemical warfare in the powerful 5<sup>th</sup> Division of the Syrian military until he defected to the West in 2013 … Assad's regime failed to declare large amounts of sarin precursor chemicals and other toxic materials…*

*Daily Telegraph London 14 April 2017*

That all emerged earlier in the month after an intensified aerial attack by Syrian and Russian aircraft on a small town that lies on the main road that connects the city of Homs with Turkey left 86 people dead, many of them children. A short while before that, residents of the besieged Iraqi city of Aleppo have been struck down by mysterious chemical gasses sprayed on residents by air force helicopters.

In response to the revelations made public by General Sakat, President Assad stressed that Syria was not in possession of any chemical weapons, despite sarin nerve gas bombardments against rebel elements active in the country having become a regular feature of the war. In a declaration made to the United Nations, President Assad declared that his country had handed over all the chemical weapons it possessed. He is lying, said General Sakat, and explained that he and others were well aware of the fact that while the Syrian regime had admitted to only 1,300 tons of nerve gas held in several military arsenals, 'we were aware that Assad had almost double that…'

In truth, the use of chemical weapons in the modern period is nothing new and it would be unwise to ignore the reality that chemical weapons might be used in some future conflict. The Egyptian Army used nerve gases against rebel fighters in the Yemen Republic in the 1960's. Also, chemical agents were deployed on a massive scale by both sides in the almost decade-long Iran/Iraq war of the 1980s.

Then, in March 1988, Saddam Hussein went on to murder 5,000 of his own people by using chemical weapons against the civilian residents of the northern Kurdish town of Halabja. According to reports that emerged after Gulf War One, the Iraqis repeatedly bombed the town with a variety of nerve gases that included sarin, soban, VX, tabun as well as the blood agent hydrogen cyanide. Human Rights Watch subsequently reported that survivors recalled that the gas smelt of 'sweet apples'. They said people died in a number of ways, which suggested a combination of toxic chemicals. Some of the victims 'just dropped dead' while others 'died laughing'. Still more took a few minutes to die, first 'burning and blistering' or coughing up green vomit. It was not a pretty picture.

In all, it was estimated that another 12,000 people were injured, almost all civilians while thousands more have subsequently succumbed to complications that include related diseases and birth defects. Now a handful of others – almost exclusively Russian - have entered the scientific lexicon and among them is novichok.

This is a new class of extremely potent binary nerve agents that make civilians thousands of miles from any war front as vulnerable as people in the Middle East. It also gives chemical weapon an altogether different dimension, one about which most chemical warfare specialists until recently were only able to speculate because there was so little known about it. Eric Croddy, author of *Chemical and Biological Warfare: An Annotated Bibliography*[1], told me that 'for a while I thought that novichok might never have existed, but then I learned the truth'. What he discovered was that the Soviets had created a unique, toxic compound that was seven or ten times more potent as other CW agents such as VX, sarin and soman. He admits to having been awed by novichok's remarkable potency.

Early reports spoke of novichok – a revolutionary nerve gas that dates from the soviet era (in Russian, the name means 'newcomer') – as being able to defy medical treatment, that it could filter through all known Western gas masks and that CW field detectors were not able to spot it. Strategically, said one of those who had worked with it, novichok has another advantage; it can be used in ultra-cold temperatures and will not freeze on the battlefield like most other chemical warfare agents.

Worse, says Croddy, for a long time attached to the Centre for Nonproliferation Studies at the Monterey Institute of International Studies and more recently to the Pentagon's Pacific Command or PACOM in Hawaii, 'novichok binary components were specifically designed to be indistinguishable from civilian pesticide manufacture. It can, or so it is claimed, be made in any fertilizer factory'.

Though a violation of the Chemical Weapons Convention (CWC), novichok until recently, was not listed among the controlled scheduling of chemicals.

Significantly, a binary weapon is made of two ingredients that become lethal only after they are combined – usually a short while before detonation – which makes them easily and safely transportable. In contrast, with unitary chemical weapons – such as VX and sarin (which Syria, Iraq, Iran and some other Middle States have acquired) – the ingredients are already combined in the manufacturing process. Unitary weapons, consequently, are lethal from the start.

When first disclosures that Moscow had been working on a succession of top-secret binary weapons programmes became public, the news could not have come at a worse time for the Russians. It followed the signing of a bilateral agreement between the US and the USSR in 1990 for both countries to reduce their respective CW stockpiles. The end of the Cold War was in sight. In any event, the 1972 tripartite convention between the US, Britain, and Russia precluded such activity. The revelations were a public relations disaster.

Thus, in 2002, the intelligence community was rocked when they read a report titled 'A Poisoned Police' in the weekly *Moscow News*. Written by a Russian scientist Dr Vil S. Mirzayanov, he disclosed that Russia, all along, had been clandestinely building a new class of secret, highly effective binary weapons. This programme was so successful, he declared, that those involved were actually honoured with the Lenin Prize at a Kremlin function.

Dr Mirzayanov, a twenty-six-year veteran of the Soviet CW programme and his associate Lev Fedorov[2] went public about novichok in what he termed were 'the interests of humanity.' For his efforts Mirzayanov was arrested and jailed for revealing state secrets. Also associated with the exposure was Valdimir Uglev, another Soviet scientist. He said in an interview that he had helped invent the agent. Though he was locked out of his laboratories by the authorities, Uglev warned that unless charges against Mirzayanov and others were dropped, he would disclose publicly the chemical formula of the controversial binary agent.

The ploy worked, even though it had been a bluff. After Yuri Baturin, security advisor to the Russian parliament convinced him to keep the details secret, Uglev admitted that he really did not have the information. Mirzayanov, meanwhile, once he had been released from prison, immigrated to the US where there were Americans who badly wanted to talk to him. For his part, Fedorov has since written two historical accounts of the Soviet Union's development of chemical weapons.[3]

Another scandal followed not long afterwards. Russian Lieutenant General Anatoly Kuntsevich – a graduate of the (Soviet) Military Academy of Chemical Defence in 1958, and himself an author of over 200 works – was dismissed from his position as head of Centre of Ecotoximetry at the Academy of Sciences Institute of Chemical Physics. In a furious exchange with his fellow generals, he was charged with helping smuggle a quantity of CW nerve agent precursors to Syria. Unlike most of his colleagues who often made no secret of the fact that they despised Arabs, this dissident officer had apparently always maintained close ties with the Syrian President's advisors.

Kuntsevich's political sentiments can perhaps be gauged from the fact that while all this was unravelling, he tried to win a parliamentary seat in the Duma with Zhirinovsky's reactionary party which has been tainted by numerous anti-Semitic utterances. It is of note that Kuntsevich (who shared the Lenin Prize for his work in binary chemical weapons with A. Gayev, A. Kiseltsov and V. Petrunin) never denied his actions[4]. He justified his contacts with Syria on the basis that it was all part of a deal that had been authorized under a 'long-standing contract obligation' with the Assad regime.

Novichok was in the news again shortly afterwards. Following a visit to several Former Soviet Union (FSU) states, Judith Miller of *The New York Times* visited the so-called Chemical Research Institute in Nukus, Uzbekistan shortly after the collapse of the Soviet Union, where Soviet defectors and American officials say was the site of major research and testing site for novichok[5]. At that stage, the US and Uzbekistan had quietly negotiated a bilateral agreement to provide $6 million in American aid in decontaminating and dismantling one of the FSU's largest chemical weapons facilities. In an interview in Tashkent with Isan M. Mustafoev, the Uzbeki deputy foreign minister, the comment to Miller was that 'we were shocked when we first learnt the real picture.'

The Soviet Union was crumbling in 1992 when more than 300 scientists at the plant packed up everything at the plant and headed home. Following a refusal by the Russians to disclose what went on there, Ms Miller was able to visit the Chemical Research Institute, a closed military complex in Nukus in the semi-autonomous republic of Karakalpakstan:

'…in one room stood a large test chamber into which smaller animals were placed for testing…another room contained treadmills for dogs and dozens of testing harnesses, to cram dogs' muzzles into gas masks, leaving their bodies exposed.'

The device enabled scientists to expose either the dogs' skin or lungs to lethal chemical agents, Uzbeki and American experts told her. Ms Miller expressed the view that information is slowly emerging about hundreds of open-air chemical tests at the Nukus plant and on the neighbouring Ustyurt Plateau in the Turgey steppe. This she describes as an equally inhospitable desert several hundred miles west of the Aral Sea which Uzbekistan and Kazakhstan share.

The question most often asked by Western Defence and intelligence analysts is what exactly is novichok? Croddy has consistently maintained that 'the answers are hidden in classified reports somewhere'. He explained what it is not:

- It does not owe its toxicity to being an acetylcholinesterase (AChE) inhibitor, at least according to Vil Mirzayanov; it might inhibit AChE, but that may be only a minor or secondary affect
- If it is not covered by the technical parameters of the substance and precursor lists of the CWC, it does not have a direct P-C bond (if it contains phosphorous at all)

Croddy goes on:

'If the reports that we already have are to be interpreted literally, and novichok can be produced (at least one of the binary components, anyway) at a fertilizer plant, then we need to think very carefully about what is produced at a real fertilizer plant. The chemical kind of fertilizer that I buy at my local store is your basic ammonia, potash and phosphate.

'Now potassium is a dead end, at least for our purposes of finding a compound that might be used as a weapon. Nitrogen and phosphorus are, of course, readily found in all kinds of chemical weapons, serving different purposes and depending on how they are attached to other organic and inorganic structures.

'There are some organophosphoric compounds called "caged" which are reasonably toxic, but the analogs that I am aware of are nowhere near as toxic as soman or VX.

'Truth is, the general-purpose criterion of the CWC notwithstanding, such compounds are technically not listed under CWC control lists. But again, it should be stressed that any nation that has signed on to the treaty, cannot (and should not) make chemical weapons regardless of whether or not they are explicitly listed in the schedules.'

Inconclusive disclosures in a Decision Brief by the Centre for Security Policy[6] claimed that:

'...soldiers can mix the innocuous starting materials [of novichok] to create the lethal product in the field: one by means of a simple addition of alcohol [presumably ethanol] and another by mixing it with acetonitrile'.

Novichok's pedigree goes back a long time. Lev Fedorov writes[7] that the USSR Council of Ministers in 1973 initiated a 'Flora' programme in order to develop herbicides to be used in war. As he explains, various programmes fed off a bureaucratic windfall to fund both chemical as well as biological weapons projects entitled 'Flute', 'Fouette', 'Fagot', 'Flask', 'Ferment' and 'Factor'. That was followed ten years later with a special decree tasking the 'Foliant' programme to work on a new and very advanced generation of binary weapons. According to Fedorov, five 'promising' nerve agent prototypes were later developed. Novichok-5 included A-232 and its 'ethyl analogue' A-234.

The late Dr Jonathan Tucker, the director of the Centre for Nonproliferation Studies at the Monterey Institute for International Studies (and Croddy's boss) provided this writer with a footnote. Quoting an interview in the Russian publication *Novoye Vrema*[8] Mirzayanov claimed that under the 'Foliant' programme, the Former Soviet Union secretly developed and tested three new unitary CW agents. The first was Substance 33, a compound similar to the persistent nerve gas VX, of which 15,000 tons were produced in the early 1980s (in a full-scale production facility near the city of Novochebokarsk in the upper Volta Region). Mirzayanov claimed that while the West was under the impression that the Novochebokarsk facility was involved in VX production, it was actually Substance 33.

Of interest here is that more than one authority has since asked whether it was not Substance 33 that was used by Iraq during the Gulf War, including Howard T. Uhal, formerly of Clemson University, South Carolina[9]. Two other unitary agent substances were also developed: A-230, which was officially approved by the Soviet Army in 1988 and A-232 (an agent similar to A-230) that was never formally approved. These three unitary agents became the basis for later research into the development of the novichok series of binary weapons started at the State Union Scientific Research Institute of Organic Chemistry and Technology (GosNIIOKht) in Moscow and its affiliate in Volsk-17 (near Shikhany).

The first Soviet binary agent, novichok-5 was derived from the unitary nerve agent A-232. A test batch of five to 10 metric tons of it was produced at a pilot-scale plant in Volvograd and field-tested at the CW testing ground at Nukus, the same one that Judith Miller visited. GosNIIOKhT also developed a binary form of Substance 33 that has no established name, but which Mirzayanov calls novichok-#. It too was tested at Nukus and adopted as a CW in 1990. Mirzayanov stated that the organization developed a third binary agent called novichok-7 which has a similar volatility to soman but is about ten times as effective. It was produced in experimental quantities (tens of tons) in Shikhany, as well as Volvograd. Two other binary nerve agents, novichok-8 and novichok-9, were under development but never produced.

Dr Mirzayanov goes on:

'Although the chemical structures of the novel CW agents are unknown, they are reportedly organophosphate compounds derived from accessible raw materials.' He quotes Valdimir Uglev, the inventor of A-232 in saying that 'the weapon's originality lies in the simplicity of its components, which are used in civilian industry and which cannot, therefore, be regulated by international experts.'

Moreover, he stated[10], 'since binary components are much less toxic than unitary nerve agents, the novichok series might well be produced at commercial chemical plants that manufacture fertilizers and pesticides.' In its final form, he warned, it is deadly. 'Even accidental exposure to it is invariably fatal,' he said. Those who came into contact with it remained disabled for the rest of their lives. Also, its effects are incurable[11]. Croddy says that the disabling effects of novichok as described by Russian scientists remind him of tri-ortho cresol phosphate poisoning which has a low anti-ache activity but permanent neuropathy can follow.

Questioned by Uhal as to whether Russia sent any CW to any Middle East countries, Dr Mirzayanov was certain that they had not. But, he added, Baghdad might have received Substance 33, an analog of VX gas. All Soviet/Russian CW agents have their own 'substance' code numbers: sarin, for instance is referred to in the Soviet lingo as Substance 35; as soman is Substance 55. Substance 33, the Russian expatriate said, was also known as Soviet V-gas and was produced in the USSR instead of VX gas.

When discussing agents with Americans, the Russians always referred to their V-gas as VX-gas which was incorrect since V-gas has its own unique structure and properties. Mirzayanov felt that this subtle but vital piece of Soviet deception might, ultimately, have had some very tragic consequences, especially with regard to Allied forces in Iraq, though that never happened.

For while US troops in the Gulf were prepared for the full range of known CW agents (including mustard), they could not have known about Substance 33 and certainly, they might not have been able to recognize it if it had been deployed, accidentally or otherwise, Mirzayanov told Uhal. He qualified that statement with another, saying that he was not sure whether Iraq actually used the Russian V-gas.

Conversely there is evidence that Washington wasn't quite as unprepared as Dr Mirzayanov suggests. A recently declassified Defence intelligence assessment titled 'Subject: Defence Intelligence Assessment – Iraqi Military Developments' – stated already in 1989 that 'Iraq was expected to begin producing the persistent nerve agent VX or an analog of VX within a few years'[12].

Thankfully, that will never happen.

# Epilogue

With so many disturbing factors having emerged from these chapters to consider, we are clearly living in an unsettled world. Yet, it is a kind of cyclical condition and some of us have visited it before.

I was in New York for the first time in 1960 and images of children being instructed on how to survive a nuclear strike remain vividly etched in my mind. On black and white television programmes, the American people were shown how to seek shelter under their school desks, or if they were at home when disaster struck, under their beds. All these images were stark and realistic and I reckon that if our American friends were asked to do the same today, they would probably think you were joking.

Yet in Seoul, within heavy artillery range of the North Korean border, there are emergency kits for use in the event of a nuclear attack in many public places including the country's subways: millions of them.

I recall too, the Soviet leader Nikita Khrushchev coming to New York while I was in the city and addressing the United Nations in September 1960. At one stage, in trying to make a point that he believed demanded attention, he removed one of his shoes and banged it on the desk before him; those were 'Crisis Years' as the period was dubbed by the media. A particularly nasty piece of work, Khrushchev was not all bluster and hot air. In striking down multitudes of his adversaries over many years in his bid to reach the top of the Supreme Soviet pole, this podgy, balding quasi-dictator seemed to have acquired a broader vision of his world. That was one of the reasons why he had enough common sense to back down when John F. Kennedy called his bluff.

The American president clearly indicated that he was prepared to take the world to war if the Soviet Union did not halt the delivery of nuclear warheads and missiles to Castro. That was the Cuban Crisis, the last time that the world was taken to the brink and, as history tells us, Moscow acquiesced.

More than half a century later, we have somebody else calling the shots in the Kremlin and there is one stark difference between then and now. Khrushchev and his cronies – and the Soviet leaders who came afterwards – never ever threatened to 'reduce the United States to a pile of radioactive dust' as one of Putin's senior functionaries threatened not very long ago. In the 'old days', it was accepted that a nuclear war between the great powers was, very appropriately, a MAD option, as in 'mutually assured destruction'. These days the possibility of somebody hurling nukes about hardly rates consideration.

Take another example, the new Royal Navy aircraft carrier HMS *Queen Elizabeth*. That fine ship was still on its sea trials in 2017 when a news report out of Communist China said something about the carrier being an 'easy target'. So it might well be, as are all the other aircraft carriers in Western navies, including a dozen in Washington's.

What nobody in the West has said anything about – though it is obviously on the cards – is Beijing's extreme vulnerability in any potential exchange of nuclear missiles. A single low-kiloton nuclear bomb dropped on or near the giant wall of China's Three Gorges Dam – the largest man-made stretch of fresh water on the planet – and about a third of that country's industries and probably half its residents would be unceremoniously dumped into the China Sea. The length of the reservoir behind the great wall runs to close on 600 kilometres and there is enough force of water there if unleashed – the dam having displaced about a million and a half people and flooded 13 cities, 140 towns and 1,350 villages – to just about do the trick. Granted, this is an extreme example and we all rather blindingly trust, it will never happen, unless of course somebody does something stupid.

Which brings us to South Africa, only the tenth country in the world to have actually built the bomb and more pertinently, the only country to have voluntarily dismantled its nuclear weapons programme. My old friend David Albright, head of Washington's Institute for Science and International Security makes a closing point in his book *Revisiting South Africa's Nuclear Weapons Program: Its History, Dismantlement, and Lessons for Today* that there was a lot to learn from a relatively modest effort that eventually turned out six atom bombs. I quote him directly:

'Deception was critical to South Africa's nuclear weapons program. It was fundamental in keeping its adversaries and allies guessing about its nuclear efforts and intentions. Its nuclear strategy depended on the ability to maintain a highly sophisticated concealment effort. Moreover, illicit procurement required a great deal of deception about the end-use of the goods Armscor and the nuclear establishment bought overseas.

'Failures to hide the program, such as unfortunate statements by uninformed or misguided South African government officials, were denied officially; however they were also used to create uncertainty about the existence of South Africa's nuclear weapons as part of Phase One of its nuclear strategy.

'Frank Pabian has pointed out that despite the 'shining success story' of South Africa's nuclear disarmament, there 'are the concealment efforts that continued despite outward signs of cooperation and transparency.'[1]

'These continued until March 1993. Even after, there were further efforts to hide parts of the nuclear weapons programme and downplay certain aspects, such as the delivery systems of the nuclear weapons, the full nuclear strategy, the sophistication of the nuclear weapons, and foreign procurements. Likewise distortions were readily disseminated in expert and governmental communities.[2]

'Both Iran and North Korea also use deception as a tactic. Despite the overwhelming evidence, including IAEA judgements, Iran still denies it ever had a nuclear weapons program. It is also still hiding parts of nuclear efforts of which the IAEA had evidence. North Korea both hides activities, such as it did for years with the centrifuge program, and exaggerates its accomplishments. For example, North Korea recently claimed that it could strike the United States with a nuclear-tipped ballistic missile.

'One obvious implication of the South African case is to treat official Iranian and North Korean statements with a high degree of scepticism, along with the echoes of their supporters. The simple act is that Iran and North Korea, like South Africa and others, lied about nuclear weapons. They did so out of a recognition that their success depended on maintaining secrecy and out of knowing that lying can minimize the international consequences of the truth.'[3]

Albright concludes by declaring that countering the nuclear deceptions of countries such as Iran and North Korea requires robust international inspections and intelligence operations:

'It also requires an independent non-governmental community willing to uncover and challenge their deceptions. North Korea's exaggerations need to be guarded against lest they increase instability and overreactions among the United States and its allies.'

One of the world's foremost authorities in nuclear proliferation is Dr Siegfried S. Hecker, a senior fellow and affiliated faculty member at Stanford University's Centre for International Security and Cooperation and the Freeman Spogli Institute for International Studies. He is a research professor in the Department of Management Science and Engineering at Stanford and director emeritus of the Los Alamos National Laboratory where he served as director from 1986 to 1997 and as senior fellow until July 2005. In the website 38 Degrees North, which provides 'informed analysis of events in and around North Korea', a project of the US-Korea Institute – under the auspices of the Johns Hopkins School of Advanced International Studies – this eminent physicist attempted to master two related issues in answer to a question raised after the September 2016 detonation of another nuclear device by the Pyongyang regime.

The first was what to make of North Korea's latest nuclear test? Also at issue was how many nuclear warheads can the Democratic People's Republic of Korea produce? And finally, can North Korea produce lighter, smaller warheads (as claimed by the DPRK Nuclear Weapons Institute), that have been 'standardised to be able to be mounted on its ballistic missiles', of which there have been many test firings in the past year.

The article which followed, dated 12 September 2016, is both balanced and prescient, as is all of this eminent scientist's work. He also provides us with an insight to a rather arcane environment on the far side of the world to which he obviously has had access and his revelations are fascinating. I quote several extracts:

'On September 9, 2016, seismic stations around the world picked up the unmistakable signals of another North Korean underground nuclear test in the vicinity of Punggye-ri. The technical details about the test will be sorted out over the next few weeks, but the political message is already loud and clear: North Korea will continue to expand its dangerous nuclear arsenal so long as Washington stays on its current path.

'Preliminary indications are that the test registered at 5.2 to 5.3 on the Richter scale, which translates to an explosion yield of approximately 15 to 20 kilotons, possibly twice the magnitude of the largest previous test. It appears to have been conducted in the same network of tunnels as the last three tests, just buried deeper into the mountain. This was the fifth known North Korean nuclear explosion; the second this year, and the third since Kim Jong-un took over the country's leadership in December 2011.

'Unlike previous announcements, such as the claim of having detonated a hydrogen bomb in January 2016, the current statement can no longer be dismissed. This time, KCNA reported North Korea's Nuclear Weapons Institute claiming:

'The standardization of the nuclear warhead will enable the DPRK. to produce at will and as many as it wants a variety of smaller, lighter and diversified nuclear warheads of higher strike power with a firm hold on the technology for producing and using various fissile materials. This has definitely put on a higher level the DPRK.'s technology of mounting nuclear warheads on ballistic rockets.[4]

'This statement brings up some fundamental questions, including the seminal issue of how many nuclear warheads the DPRK is able to produce.

'North Korea's capacity to produce plutonium remains limited to six kilograms, or approximately one bomb's worth, per year. We estimate that it may have a stockpile of thirty-two to fifty-four kilograms (roughly six to eight bombs' worth) of plutonium now. Whereas plutonium production can be estimated reasonably accurately because of telltale signals resulting from reactor operation, production of highly enriched uranium (HEU) remains highly uncertain.

'However, based on what I saw at the Yongbyon centrifuge facility during my last visit in November 2010, the expanded footprint of the facility since, and our probabilistic estimates of how much it could make in covert facilities,[5] it is possible that the DPRK could add 150 kg of HEU (roughly six bombs' worth) to a current stockpile of perhaps 300 to 400 kg.[6] In other words, a stockpile of sufficient fissile material for approximately 20 bombs by the end of this year and a capacity of adding approximately 7 per year makes the DPRK claim sound plausible.'

Which brings us to the second issue: Can North Korea produce lighter, smaller warheads and as claimed by the DPRK Nuclear Weapons Institute, ones that have been 'standardized to be able to be mounted on its ballistic missiles?'

As Dr Hecker declares, with several successful nuclear tests in recent years, the international community must assume that the DPRK has designed and demonstrated nuclear warheads that can be mounted on some of its short-range and perhaps medium-range missiles. He goes on:

'Its ability to field an ICBM fitted with a nuclear warhead capable of reaching the United States is still a long way off—perhaps five to ten years, but likely doable if the program is unconstrained.

'As much as a doomsday nuclear shot at the United States worries Americans, it is not what I consider to be the primary threat from Pyongyang's unrelenting drive to more bombs and better bombs. At a minimum, the current state of the North's nuclear arsenal is an effective deterrent to potential hostile external intervention. It has reinforced Kim Jong-un's legitimacy as leader of what the North considers a beleaguered nation.

'The current situation is very different from what my Stanford colleagues and I encountered during our November 2006 visit a few weeks after the North's first nuclear test. At each of our stops—the Ministry of Foreign Affairs, the Department of Atomic Energy, and the military—we found their pronouncements of having achieved a deterrent against the United States to ring hollow.

'Nevertheless, Kim Jong Il [North Korea's previous leader and father of the present one] appeared sufficiently confident of the state's security that he accepted the Bush administration's change of heart and new willingness to find a diplomatic solution.

'The years 2007 and 2008 marked significant diplomatic progress, which resulted in a rollback of operations at the Yongbyon nuclear complex, the return of international inspectors, and the presence of an American technical team. However, in the summer of 2008, the Bush administration pulled back followed by a similar response by the North in August.

'By the time our Stanford team visited Pyongyang in February 2009, we were told that times had changed—the North was going to launch a long-range rocket and that matters would get much worse. And, so they did. The launch was followed by UN condemnation and Pyongyang's expulsion of the international inspectors and American team. Then in May, the North conducted its second nuclear test, which, unlike the first, appeared successful. Seoul and Washington apparently rebuffed Pyongyang's overtures in the summer of 2009 to get back on a diplomatic track and the DPRK was off and running on a determined path for more and better bombs, combined with greatly increasing its missile threat.

'The death of diplomacy, namely the Obama administration's retreat to 'strategic patience' and the demise of the Six Party Talks, opened the door to an unrelenting expansion of the North's nuclear weapons program, as best as one can tell, unconstrained by international opprobrium and escalating sanctions.'

Dr Hecker concludes with the question: 'So what to do?' As he declares, the latest nuclear (and missile) tests demonstrate conclusively that attempting to sanction the DPRK into submission and waiting for China to exert leverage over Pyongyang's nuclear program simply do not work, to which he adds

'Increasing sanctions and adding missile defences in South Korea to that mix will also not suffice and make China even less likely to cooperate.

What's missing is diplomacy as much as Washington may find it repugnant to deal with the Kim regime.'

# Notes

## Chapter 1

1. Christopher Andrew: *The Defence of the Realm – The Authorized History of MI5*, Allen Lane, London, 2009 pp 819/821
2. Al J. Venter: *Allah's Bomb: The Islamic Quest for Nuclear Weapons*, Chapter 5, The Lyons Press, Guilford, Conn. 2007. See also *Iran's Nuclear Option,* Casemate Publishers, Philadelphia, USA 2006, by the same author.
3. Nicholas Paul Badenhorst and Pierre Lowe Victor: *Those Who Had the Power - South Africa: An Unofficial Nuclear Weapons History*, privately published, Pretoria, 2006.
4. Al J. Venter: *War Dog: Fighting Other Peoples Wars*: Casemate Publishers, Philadelphia, 2006.
5. The author was a regular contributor to *Jane's Islamic Affairs Analyst* and *Jane's Security and Terrorism Monitor* while Stephen Ulph was editor of these, and other publications.
6. Bill Gertz, *The Washington Times, 2* May 2007.
7. *Allah's Bomb*: (Ibid)
8. Dr Nic von Wielligh and Linda von Wielligh-Steyn: *The Bomb: South Africa's Nuclear Program;* Litera Publikasies Pretoria, 2015
9. George Tenet - former Director of Intelligence: *At the Centre of the Storm: My Years at the CIA* by, HarperCollins, New York, 2007
10. Con Coughlin and James Kirkup 'Britain's Al-Qaeda Hub is the Biggest in West': *The Daily Telegraph*, London, 16 January 2010.

## Chapter 2

1. Cynthia C. Kelly: *Manhattan Project: The Birth of the Atomic Bomb in the Words of Its Creators, Eyewitnesses and Historians*, Black Dog & Leventhal, 2011
2. Richard Rhodes: Dark Sun – *The Making of the Hydrogen Bomb*, Simon and Schuster, 1996
3. David Fisher: *History of the International Atomic Energy Agency - The First Forty Years*, IAEA Publications, 1997

## Chapter 3

1. *Time*, 16 December 1960
2. *Bulletin of the Atomic Scientists*, September/October 2002 pp73/75
3. Federation of American Scientists: 'Nuclear Weapons': http://www.fas.org/nuke/guide/israel/nuke/
4. Nicholas Valry: 'Israel's Silent Gamble with the Bomb'; *New Scientist*, 12 December 1974,
5. 'Israel Begins test of Nuclear Missile Submarines' Irish Times, 2 July 1998
6. Seymour, Hersh M., *The Samson Option: Israel's Nuclear Arsenal and American Foreign Policy,* Random House, New York, 1991
7. Nashif, Taysir: *Nuclear Weapons in the Middle East: Dimensions and Responsibilities;* Princeton, New Jersey, Kingston Press, 1984.
8. Robert S. Norris and Hans M. Kristensen 'Indian Nuclear Forces, 2008' Bulletin of the Atomic Scientists, November/December 2008 doi:10.2968/055006016
9. Ibid

10. Institute for Science and International Security, Washington DC: http://www.isis-online.org. Federation of American Scientists, Washington DC :'Nuclear Weapons': http://www.fas.org and navigate to the entries dealing with nuclear weapons

11. David Albright and Susan Basu: 'India's Gas Centrifuge Enrichment Program: Growing Capacity for Military Purposes': Institute for Science and International Security (ISIS), 18 January 2007

12. Ibid

13. Hassan Abbas, 'Pakistan's Drift into Extremism. Allah, the Army and America's War on Terror' Pentagon Press, 2005, p142

14. R. Jeffrey Smith and Toby Warrick, 'A Nuclear Power's Act of Proliferation', *The Washington Post:* 13 November 2009 and Simon Henderson, *Sunday Times*, London September 20, 2009.

15. Al J. Venter, *Allah's Bomb: The Islamic Quest for Nuclear Weapons*, Lyons Press, New Haven, 2007

16. Pakistan announced that it tested five nuclear devices on May 28 and one on May 30. But seismic records do not discriminate the May 28 tests, and it is possible that only one device was detonated that day. See Robert S. Norris and William M. Arkin, 'Known Nuclear Tests Worldwide,' *Bulletin of the Atomic Scientists*, November/December 1998, p. 65.

17. 'Pakistan Nuclear Forces, 2007': Prepared by the Natural Resources Defence Council, *Bulletin of the Atomic Scientists*, May/June 2007 pp71.74

18. Ibid

19. David Albright and Paul Brannan 'Pakistan Expanding Plutonium Separation Facility near Rawalpindi', Institute for Science and International Security, Washington DC: 19 May 2009

20. Seymour Hersh 'Defending the Arsenal – In an Unstable Pakistan, Can Nuclear Warheads be Kept Safe?': *The New Yorker*, November 16, 2009 pp 28–35

21. 'A Primer on the Future Threat' (Secret), in Defence Intelligence Agency, The Decades Ahead: 1999–2020, July 1999, p. 38. Reprinted in Rowan Scarborough, *Rumsfeld's War: The Untold Story of America's Anti-Terrorist Commander* (Regnery, Washington DC, 2004), pp194–223.

22. Ibid: *Bulletin of the American Scientists*

23. More specific details can be found in Chapter 9 of Al Venter's *Iran's Nuclear Option* published by Casemate in the United States in 2005.

## Chapter 4

1. George Tenet: *At The Centre of the Storm: My Years at the CIA*: Harper Collins, New York, 2007

2. 'Mohamed ElBaradei Warns of New Nuclear Age': Julian Borger, Diplomatic Editor, *Guardian*, 14 May 2009

3. Abdul Hameed Bakier 'Leader of Yemen's Mujahedeen Claims al-Qaeda has a Nuclear Weapon': *Terrorism Focus Volume*: Issue # 6: 4 February 2009

## Chapter 5

1. 'Investigators Suspect Nuclear Smuggling Network is Still Active', Andrew Koch, *Jane's Intelligence Review*, London, 1 July 2006

2. Al J. Venter, *The Iraqi War Debrief*

3. 'Nuclear Saudi Arabia Risks Inflaming Middle East Tensions', Christina Maza, *Newsweek*, 30 October, 2017

4. A. Q. Khan Nuclear Chronology, by Michael Laufer, Proliferation Brief, Volume 8, Number 8, Carnegie Endowment for International Peace, Washington DC

5. The World in Which We Live: Elizabeth Dougherty, *The Atlantic*, November 2005

## Chapter 6

1. Christopher Andrew: *Defence of the Realm: The Authorized History of MI5*, Allen Lane, London, 2009

2. 'British Terrorist Dhiren Barot's Research on Radiological Weapons', by Robert Wesley, *Terrorism Focus* Volume 3, Issue 44 (14 November 2006): Jamestown Foundation, Washington DC.

3. CRS Report for the United States Congress Radiological Dispersal Devices: *Select Issues in Consequence Management* by Dana A. Shea Analyst in Science and Technology Policy Resources, Science, and Industry Division.

4. BBC news report by Frank Gardiner, Chicago, 2 August 2007. See BBC link: http://news.bbc.co.uk/go/pr/fr/-/2/hi/technology/6925584.stm.

5. Federation of American Scientists website: www.fas.org.

6. CRS Report for the United States Congress: *Terrorist 'Dirty Bombs': A Brief Primer* by Jonathan Medalia, Specialist in National Defence Foreign Affairs, Defence, and Trade Division, updated 1 April 2004. See also Don Olenburg: 'How Bad Would a Dirty Blast Be? Here's What the Experts Say'- *The Washington Post*, 13 June 2002, p. C1.

## Chapter 7

1. *Erich Follath and Holger Stark: 'The Story of "Operation Orchard"*: How Israel Destroyed Syria's Al Kibar Nuclear Reactor'; *Der Spiegel*, 2 November 2009

2. Noah Klieger: 'A Strike in the Desert'; Y-Net News.com, Israel, 2 November, 2009

3. David Albright and Paul Brannan: Suspect Reactor Construction Site in Eastern Syria: The Site of the September 6 Israeli Raid? Published by Washington Institute for Science and International Security (ISIS) October 24, 2007

4. Duncan Gardham: *'Mossad carries out daring London raid on Syrian official'; The Daily Telegraph*, London 15 May 2011.

## Chapter 8

1. Paul Kerr: 'IAEA: Questions Remain About Libya' - *Arms Control Today (published by Arms Control Association:* Vol. 34, No. 6 (July/August 2004), p. 28

2. Judith Miller; 'How Gadaffi Lost his Groove', *New York Times*, 16 May 2006

3. G.R. Heald; 'South Africa's voluntary relinquishment of its nuclear arsenal and accession to the treaty on the non-proliferation of nuclear weapons in terms of international law': Master's dissertation, University of the Witwatersrand, Johannesburg, 2010.

4. William Langerwieche: 'The Wrath of Khan': How A.Q. Khan Made Pakistan a Nuclear Power': *The Atlantic Monthly*, November 2005.

5. Bruno Tertrais, Senior Research Fellow, *Fondation pour la Recherche Strategique*: 'Pakistan's Nuclear Exports: Was There a State Strategy?' Final Draft, 12 August 2006, Paper prepared for the Non-proliferation Education Centre; *fn* 43 pages 6/7

6. Nigeria has also recently emerged in the sites of al-Qaeda. A document issued by the movement in 2005 stresses the vulnerability of this West African country and the economic harm that might result should it be destabilized and its huge oil industry disrupted. One report mentions a jump of $100 per barrel in the oil price should that be allowed to happen.

7. Full details are to be found in the author's book *'War Dog: Fighting Other People's Wars'*

## Chapter 9

1. Graham Allison: 'Nuclear Disorder: Surveying Atomic Threats', Foreign Affairs, pp74-85, January/February 2010.

2. Dan Yurman's Blog: Idaho Samizdat - http://djysrv.blogspot.com: Personal communication 6/10 February, 2010.

3. Andrew Koch: 'Investigators Suspect Nuclear Smuggling Network is Still Active' *Jane's Intelligence Review*, July 1, 2006.

4. Kongdan Oh and Ralph C. Hassig: *North Korea: Through the Looking Glass* Brookings Institution Press, Washington: 2000.

5. 'DPRK Succeeds in Nuclear Warhead Explosion Test,' KCNA, 9 September 2016.

6. John Bistline, et al. 'A Bayesian Model to Assess the Size of North Korea's Uranium Enrichment Program,' *Science and Global Security* 23 (2015): 71-100.
7. Chaim Braun, Siegfried Hecker, Chris Lawrence, and Panos Papadiamantis, 'North Korean Nuclear Facilities After the Agreed Framework,' Centre for International Security and Cooperation, Stanford University, 27 May 2016, http://fsi.stanford.edu/publication/north-korean-nuclear-facilities-after-agreed-framework.

## Chapter 10

1. Helen E. Purkitt: 'The Politics of Denuclearization: The case of South Africa.' Paper presented at the Defence Nuclear Agency's Fourth Annual International Conference on Controlling Arms, Philadelphia, 21 June 1995. (Earlier draft presented at the Institute for National Studies [INSS], U.S. Air Force Academy, Colorado, 9 November 1994), p7. For more in-depth discussion of this period of South African covert nuclear weapons programmes, Helen Purkitt and Stephen Burgess, *South Africa's Weapons of Mass Destruction*, Bloomington: Indiana University Press, 2005. Also, A.R. Newby-Fraser, *Chain Reaction*. Published by the Atomic Energy Board, Pretoria, 1979, pp 20-21, p 42.
2. Peter Hounam and Steve McQuillan, *The Mini-Nuke Conspiracy Mandela's Nuclear Nightmare*. Faber and Faber Ltd., London, 1995, p137.
3. Helen Purkitt, 'The politics of Denuclearization: The case of South Africa.' *op. cit.*, pp5-6.: See also 'A Problem Centred Approach for Understanding Foreign Policy: US Foreign Policy towards Southern Africa', in S. Nagel (ed.) *Global International Policy Among and Within Nations*: Marcel-Dekker, 2000.
4. Al J. Venter: *Coloured: A Profile of Two Million South Africans*: Human & Rousseau, Cape Town, 1974.
5. See Al J. Venter, *Iran's Nuclear Option:* Casemate Publishers, Philadelphia and London, 2005
6. A.R. Newby-Fraser: *Chain Reaction*, Published by the Atomic Energy Board, Pretoria, 1979
7. Megawatt Thermal
8. Hannes Steyn, Richardt van der Walt and Jan van Loggerenberg: *Armament and Disarmament: South Africa's Nuclear Experience*, Network Publishers, Pretoria, 2003

## Chapter 11

1. Al J. Venter, in association with Nicholas Paul Badenhorst and Pierre Lowe Victor's illustrations: *How South Africa Built Six Atom Bombs*; Ashanti Publishing, South Africa, 2008
2. Access Institute for Science and International Security at http://www.isis-online.gov
3. Tyler Drumheller and Elaine Monaghan: *On The Brink*; Carroll & Graf, New York, 2006
4. While South Africa's population in the 1980s was more than thirty million, it was politically structured along racial lines, thus the concept of racial separation or apartheid. Only white South Africans were allowed to work on the nuclear weapons programme and they were drawn solely from this community which then numbered roughly five million
5. Stephen Laufer and Arthur Gavshon: 'The Real Reason for South Africa's Nukes', *Weekly Mail*: 26 March 1993, p3
6. *The Message*, 'The Jewish Broederbond Syndicate', Chapter Two, Arms Industry.

## Chapter 12

1. Al J. Venter, *Allah's Bomb: The Islamic Quest for Nuclear Weapons*, Lyons Press, New Haven, Conn. 2007
2. Seymour Hersh: *The Sampson Option: Israel's Nuclear Option and American Foreign Policy*, Random House, New York, 1991
3. Purkitt, Helen E., 'The politics of Denuclearization: The Case of South Africa.' Paper presented at the Defence Nuclear Agency's Fourth Annual International Conference on

Controlling Arms, Philadelphia, Penn. 21 June 1995. (Earlier draft presented at Institute for National Studies [INSS], US Air Force Academy, Colorado, 9 November, 1994), p10.

4. Peter Liberman, 'The Rise and Fall of the South African Bomb'; *International Security*, Volume 26, # 2 (Fall 2001) as well as 'Israel and the South African Bomb': *The Nonproliferation Review*, Centre for Nonproliferation Studies, Monterey, California, Summer 2004, Volume 11, Number 2

5. See Carey Sublette's *Nuclear Weapons Frequently Asked Questions*: http://nuclearweaponarchive.org/Nfaq0.html .

6. A.R. Newby-Fraser: *Chain Reaction*, Published by the Atomic Energy Board, Pretoria, 1979

7. Former US President Jimmy Carter: *Palestine: Peace Not Apartheid:* Simon & Schuster, New York 2006.

8. For the purposes of this book, the author identifies the following as WMD: nuclear fission, enhanced radiation, and thermonuclear fusion explosive devices; weapons or delivery vehicles capable of being armed with any of the aforementioned; suitable platforms able to carry, launch, or fire such weapons or delivery vehicles - such as aircraft, submarines, and artillery; and lastly, elements of command, control, communications, computers, intelligence, surveillance, and reconnaissance (C4ISR) which, in concert, facilitate executive decision-making to this end.

## Chapter 13

1. Blog: Idaho Samizdat - http://djysrv.blogspot.com

2. Michael Wines: 'Break-In at Nuclear Site Baffles South Africa' *New York Times*: 15 November 2007

3. Al J Venter: *Iran's Nuclear Option*, Casemate Publishing, Philadelphia 2005 pp156-162 and by the same author, *Allah's Bomb: The Islamic Quest for Nuclear Weapons*, Lyons Press, New Haven, 2007 pp181-185

## Chapter 14

1. Jay C. Davis and David A. Kay: 'Iraq's Secret Nuclear Weapons Program'; *Physics Today*, July 1992.

2. Personal communications with Dr Kay by phone.

3. David Albright and Robert Kelley, 'Has Iraq Come Clean at Last?' *The Bulletin of the Atomic Scientists*, November/December 1995

4. Until Iranian opposition groups pinpointed several nuclear sensitive sites, among them the one at Natanz, the Iranians prevented IAEA staff from setting up environmental monitoring units in some areas where the Atomic Energy Organization of Iran was active, particularly at some newly-established uranium processing plants. See also 'Inspectors in Iran Examine Machines to Enrich Uranium' *New York Times*, 23 February 2003.

5. William Burrows and Robert Windrem: *Critical Mass*: Simon & Schuster, New York, 1994

6. *Pointer*, supplement to *Jane's Intelligence Review*, London, March 1988

7. David Albright, Frans Berkhout and William Walker: *Plutonium and Highly Enriched Uranium 1996:* Oxford University Press 1997.

8. David Albright and Mark Hibbs: 'Iraq's Shop-Till-You-Drop Nuclear Program' *Bulletin of the Atomic Scientists*; April 1992

## Chapter 15

1. David Albright: *Peddling Peril: How the Secret Nuclear Trade Arms America's Enemies. Free Press, New York, 2010*

2. It was dubbed 'Club of Nine' after it became known that South Africa had built atom bombs. With the help of the US, Britain and the IAEA, Pretoria dismantled that programme prior to the ANC taking power in the early 1990s. With North Korea having detonated nuclear

devices, it has nine members again. Soon, some pundits maintain - with Iran about to enter the ranks – it will be the 'Club of Ten'. After that, who knows?

3. IAEA Report on Iran: Enrichment at Natanz improving; entire LEU tank moved to PFEP; no progress on weaponization, 18 February 2010

4. Al J. Venter: *Iran's Nuclear Option: Tehran's Quest for the Atom Bomb*, Casemate, Philadelphia, 2005. See also his book *Allah's Bomb: The Islamic Quest for Nuclear Weapons*, Lyons Press, New Haven, 2007

5. *Nuclear Fuel:* 27 August 1997

6. Pakistani Scientist Khan Describes Iranian Efforts to Buy Nuclear Bombs: R. Jeffrey Smith and Joby Warrick, *Washington Post*, 14 March 2010.

## Chapter 16

1. Internal State Department memo; 6 Sept 1999

2. Igor Kudrik: 'Nuclear Icebreakers Base Robbed', Bellona, Norway: 14 July 1999: See website http:// bellona@bellona.no

3. *Polyarnaya Pravda*, a Murmansk daily, 28 May 1999

4. Interfax, Moscow

5. Bellona: 'Five Subcritical Nuclear Tests': Oslo, Norway, 29 December 1998

6. David Albright and Kevin O'Neill (Editors); *The Challenges of Fissile Material Control:* The Institute for Science and International Security, Washington DC, 1999.

7. Jump-Start: Retaking the Initiative to Reduce Post-Cold War Nuclear Dangers: *Arms Control Today*, Washington DC, Jan/Feb 1999

8. *Washington Times:* 21 October 1998

9. Todd E Perry *Preventing the Proliferation of Russian Nuclear Materials: Limit to the Current Approach:* paper prepared for the Annual meetings of the International Security Studies Section (ISSS), International Studies Association, Monterey, California, November 8, 1998

10. 24 November 1998

11. Albright and O'Neill: Ibid

12. *Yaderny Kontrol Digest #5:* Stenographic Record of the Parliamentary Hearings on Issues Concerning the Security of Hazardous Nuclear Facilities, October 1997

13. Elisabeth Rindskopf: 'Where Nuclear Peril Lies Waiting', *The Chicago Tribune*, 12 October 1998

14. Mark Hibbs: 'Smuggled HEU Seized in Germany, Prague Came from Mayak Stockpile, Police Say', *Nuclear Fuel;* 21 September 1998

15. *Naval Nuclear Waste Management in Northwest Russia*: Bellona, Norway: Edited by Michael J Foley and Lisa MG Ballou: Battelle Press, Columbus: Richland, WA 1998

16. A series of personal communications with me.

17. The modern unit of radioactivity (the number of radioactive disintegrations per second) is the Becquerel, symbol Bq. In the past it was measured in curies. A curie is approximately the number of disintegrations per second in 1 gram of radium. 1 Curie = $3.7 \times 10^{10}$ Bq. Because the Bq is such a small unit, in practice one usually finds that the activities of materials are expressed in G(giga)Bq and T(tera)Bq. One kg of natural uranium has an activity of about $25 \times 10^6$ Bq and 1 kg of radium an activity of $37 \times 10^{12}$ Bq, i.e. more than a million times that of uranium.

18. Don Bradley: *Behind the Nuclear Curtain: Radioactive Waste Management in the Former Soviet Union*: Edited by David R Payson: Battelle Press, 1997

## Chapter 17

1. Personal observations made and briefings I attended during a visit to these facilities in Eastern Washington State. At the time his British passport sufficed for clearance to a highly restricted security series of facilities. That all changed after 9/11.

## Chapter 18

1. Al J Venter: 'Is Egypt Going Nuclear?': *Jane's Islamic Affairs Analyst*, London: 1 February 2005
2. 'Investigators Suspect Nuclear Smuggling Network is Still Active' Andrew Koch: *Jane's Intelligence Review*, 1 July 2006
3. 'Egypt Nuclear Overview,', *Nuclear Threats Initiative (NTI)*: Access at http://www.nti. org/e_research/e1_egypt_nuclear.html
4. Prior to Gulf War One, Saddam was involved in a major nuclear weapons that employed upwards of 20,000 people. All these facilities were subsequently destroyed by UNSCOM, the United Nations Special Commission (on Iraq). A complete rundown on the Iraqi nuclear programme can be found under the heading 'How Saddam Hussein Almost Built His Bomb' in my book *Iran's Nuclear Option*: Casemate Publishers, Philadelphia, 2005; Appendix D; pp 341/357
5. *Risk Report* Volume 2, Number 5: September – October 1996 (http://www.wisconsinproject. org/countries/egypt/nuke.html )
6. *Nuclear Programmes in the Middle East: In the shadow of Iran*, ed. Mark Fitzpatrick, The International Institute for Strategic Studies, London, 2008, p. 18.
7. Maria Rost Rublee, 'Egypt's Nuclear Weapons Program: Lessons Learned,' *Nonproliferation Review* (November 2006), p. 556. Robert J. Einhorn, 'Egypt: Frustrated but Still on a Non-Nuclear Course,' in *The Nuclear Tipping Point*, ed. Kurt M. Campbell, Robert J. Einhorn, and Mitchell B. Reiss (Washington, DC: Brookings Institution Press, 2004), p. 45.
8. James Walsh, *Bombs Unbuilt: Power, Ideas, and Institutions in International Politics*: PhD dissertation, Massachusetts Institute of Technology, 2001.
9. Etel Solingen, *Nuclear Logics: Contrasting Paths in East Asia & the Middle East*: Princeton, NJ: Princeton University Press, 2007, p. 239.
10. Personal communications.

## Chapter 19

1. David Albright, Paul Brannan, Robert Kelley and Andrea Scheel Stricker, 'Burma: A Nuclear Wannabe; Suspicious Links to North Korea; High-Tech Procurements and Enigmatic Facilities': Institute for Science and International Security, Washington DC, 28 January 2010.
2. Robert Kelley, Andrea Scheel Stricker, and Paul Brannan
3. Burma's Nuclear Secrets: Federation of American Scientists, Washington. Maintained by Stephen Aftergood and Hans M. Kristensen: See http://www.smh.com.au/world/burmax2019s-nuclear-secrets-20090731-e4fv.html

## Chapter 20

1. House Armed Services Committee, Congress, Washington DC, 10 September 2002
2. Jonathan Tucker 'Scourge: The Once and Future Threat of Smallpox': *Atlantic Monthly Press*, New York 2001
3. There is a significant difference of opinion within the scientific community on actual quantities needed for an infection to take place: some authorities opt for the higher figure, others for much less.
4. Eric Croddy, with Clarisa Perez-Armendariz and John Hart: *Chemical and Biological Warfare: A Comprehensive Survey for the Concerned Citizen*; Copernicus Books: New York, 2002

## Chapter 21

1. Eric Croddy: *Chemical and Biological Warfare: An Annotated Bibliography* (Scarecrow Press, London & Lanham Maryland), 1997
2. Lev Fedorov: 'We Were Preparing for an All-Out Chemical War,' *Obsgchaya Gazeta*, in Russian #4: 26 January *Ibid*

3. Lev Aleksandrovich Fedorov has followed up on his *Chemical Weapons in Russia: History, Ecology, Politics (Khimicheskoye Oruzhiye V Rossii: Istoriya, Ekologiya, Politika*, 1994, pp 1-95, (translated in FBIS) with another monograph not yet available in English.
4. J. Michael Waller, 'The Chemical Weapons, *The Wall Street Journal*, 13 February 1997 p18
5. Judith Miller, *New York Times* 25 May 1999 p3
6. Decision Brief, The Centre for Security Policy, No 97-D-19, 4 February 1997 using a *Washington Times* report as a source
7. Fedorov: *Ibid*
8. With Lev Fedorov: No 44 (October 1992) pp 4-9 in JPRS-TAC-92-033 (14 November, 1992)
9. Howard T. Uhal; The UKOPRP: 'Soviet Chemical Warfare Agents Novichok and Substance 33
10. Mirzayanov: *Ibid*
11. Uhal: *Ibid*
12. Department of Defence GulfLINK file 02200639.89

## Epilogue

1. Frank V. Pabian, 'The South African Denuclearization Exemplar,' *Nonproliferation Review, 2015*, Vol. 22, No. 1, pp. 27-52. http://dx.doi.org/10.108 0/10736700.2015.1071969
2. See for example, Waldo Stumpf, 'South Africa's Nuclear Weapons Program: From Deterrence to Dismantlement,' *Arms Control Today*, December 1995/ January 1996. Here, he downplays the sophistication and deliverability of the weapons and the nuclear strategy. That he likely knew differently is confirmed by a statement of Nic von Wielligh in his book *The Bomb* [Nic von Wielligh and Lydia von Wielligh-Steyn, *The Bomb:* p. 513.] The authors write that von Wielligh had obtained the set of official documents, which discuss missile delivery of nuclear devices, the more detailed nuclear strategy, and plans to expand the arsenal, from the AEC and Armscor 'at the time of the IAEA's investigation of South Africa's nuclear weapons programme.' Given that von Wielligh reported directly to Stumpf and both interacted heavily with Armscor and the IAEA, these omissions in such journals as *Arms Control Today* must have been deliberate.
3. For more reading on preventing illicit nuclear procurement, see David Albright, Houston Wood, and Andrea Stricker, *Future World of Illicit Nuclear Trade: Mitigating the Threat* (Washington, D.C.: Institute for Science and International Security, July 29, 2013). http://isis-online. org/uploads/isis-reports/ documents/Full_Report_DTRA-PASCC_29July2013-FINAL.pdf
4. 'DPRK Succeeds in Nuclear Warhead Explosion Test,' KCNA, September 9, 2016.
5. John Bistline, et al. 'A Bayesian Model to Assess the Size of North Korea's Uranium Enrichment Program,' *Science and Global Security* 23 (2015): 71-100.
6. Chaim Braun, Siegfried Hecker, Chris Lawrence, and Panos Papadiamantis, 'North Korean Nuclear Facilities After the Agreed Framework,' Centre for International Security and Cooperation, Stanford University, 27 May 2016, http://fsi.stanford.edu/publication/north-korean-nuclear-facilities-after-agreed-framework.

# Bibliography

**ALBRIGHT, David**: *Peddling Peril: How the Secret Nuclear Trade Arms America's Enemies*, Free Press, 2010

**ALBRIGHT, David and STRICKER, Andrea**: *Revisiting South Africa's Nuclear Weapons Program: Its History, Dismantlement, and Lessons for Today*, CreateSpace Independent Publishing Platform, 2016

**ALVARES, L.W**: Adventures of a Physicist, Basic Books, 1987

**BADENHORST, Nicholas Paul and VICTOR, Pierre Lowe**: *Those Who Had The Power South Africa: An Unofficial Nuclear Weapons History*, 2006

**BIRD, Kai and SHERWIN, Martin**: *American Prometheus: The Triumph and Tragedy of J. Robert Oppenheimer*, Vintage Books, 2006

**BLIX, Hans**: *Disarming Iraq – The Search for Weapons of Mass Destruction, Bloomsbury*, 2004

**BRACKEN, Paul**: *The Second Nuclear Age: Strategy, Danger and the New Power Politics*, St Martin's Griffin, 2013

**COLEMAN, David G. and SIRACUSA, Joseph M.**: *Real-World Nuclear Deterrence: The Making of International Strategy*, Praeger, 2006

**CROCKER, Chester**: *High Noon in Southern Africa – Making Peace in a Rough Neighbourhood*, Norton, 1993

**DEGROOT, Gerald**: *The Bomb - a Life*, Jonathan Cape, 2004,

**DELPECH, T**: *Nuclear Deterrence in the 21$^{st}$ Century – Lessons from the Cold War for a New Era of Strategic Piracy*, Rand Corporation, 2012

**FISHER, David**: *History of the International Atomic Energy Agency - The First Forty Years*, IAEA Publications, 1997

**FRANTZ, David and COLLINS, Catherine**: *The Nuclear Jihadist – The True Story of the Man Who Sold the World's Most Dangerous Secrets*, Twelve, 2007

**GALE, Robert Peter**: *Radiation: What it is, What You Need to Know*, Vintage, 2013

**GROVES, Leslie**: *Now It Can Be Told: The Story of The Manhattan Project*, Da Capo Press, Reprint 1983.

**HERZOG, Rudolf** : *Short History of Nuclear Folly: Mad Scientists, Dithering Nazis, Lost Nukes and Catastrophic Cover-Ups*, Melville House Publishing, 2014

**HOUNAM, Peter and MCQUILLAN, Steve**: *The Mini-Nuke Conspiracy: How Nelson Mandela Inherited a Nuclear Nightmare*, Faber and Faber, 1995

**JUNGK, Robert**: *Brighter than a Thousand Suns: A Personal History of the Atomic Scientists*, Harvest Books, 1970.

**KELLY, Cynthia C.**: *Manhattan Project: The Birth of the Atomic Bomb in the Words of Its Creators, Eyewitnesses and Historians*, Black Dog & Leventhal, 2011

**LEATHERBARROW, Andrew**: Chernobyl 01:23:40: The Incredible True Story of the World's Worst Nuclear Disaster, Andrew Leatherbarrow publ.

**LEVY, A and SCOTT-CLARK, C**: *Deception: Pakistan, the United States and the Secret Trading in Nuclear Weapons*, Walker Publishing, 2007

**MAHAFFEY, James**: *Atomic Accidents: A History of Nuclear Meltdowns and Disasters: from the Ozark Mountains to Fukushima*; Pegasus, 2015

**MALLEY, Marjorie C.**: *Radioactivity: A History of a Mysterious Science*, Oxford University Press, USA, 2011

**NARANG, Vipin**: *Nuclear Strategy in the Modern Era: Regional Powers and International Conflict*, Princeton University Press, 2014

**NEWBY-FRASER, A.R.**: *Chain Reaction; Twenty Years of Nuclear Research and Development*, Atomic Energy Board, 1979

**PAGE, Christine Wing B. and SIMPSON, Fiona**: *Detect, Dismantle, and Disarm - IAEA Verification, 1992-2005*, United States Institute of Peace, 2013

**PANT, Harsh V.**: *The Handbook of Nuclear Proliferation, Routledge, 2015*

**PELLA, Peter**: *The Midlife Crisis of the Nuclear Nonproliferation Treaty*, Morgan & Claypool Publishers, 2016

**POLAKOW-SURANSKY, S.**: *The Unholy Alliance – Israel's Secret Relationship with Apartheid South Africa, Pantheon, 2010*

**PURKITT, Helen E. and BURGESS, Stephen F.**: *South Africa's Weapons of Mass Destruction, Indiana University Press, 2005*

**REED, Bruce Cameron**: *The Physics of the Manhattan Project*, Springer, 2014

**REISS, Mitchell**: *Bridled Ambition – Why Countries Constrain their Nuclear Capabilities*, Woodrow Wilson Press Centre with Johns Hopkins University Press, 1995

**RHODES, Richard**: Dark Sun – The Making of the Hydrogen Bomb, Simon and Schuster, 1996

**RHODES, Richard** : *The Making of The Atomic Bomb*, Simon and Schuster, new edition, 2012

**RHODES, Richard** : *Twilight of the Bombs: Recent Challenges, New Dangers, and the Prospects for a World Without Nuclear Weapon*, Vintage Books, 2011

**RHODES, Richard** : *Arsenals of Folly: The Making of the Nuclear Arms Race,* Vintage Books, 2008

**ROSE, Gideon and TEPPERMAN, Jonathan** (Ed); *Iran and the Bomb: Solving the Persian Puzzle*, Council on Foreign Relations, 2012

**SCHLOSSER, Eric**: *Command and Control: Nuclear Weapons, the Damascus Accident and the Illusion of Safety*; Penguin, 2014

**SERBER, Robert**: *The Los Alamos Primer: The First Lectures on How to Build an Atomic BOMB*, University of California Press, 1992

**SIRACUSA Joseph M**: *Nuclear Weapons: A Very Short Introduction*, Oxford University Press, 2015

**SOLINGEN, Etel**: *Sanctions, Statecraft, and Nuclear Proliferation*, Cambridge University Press 2012

**SOLINGEN, Etel** : *Nuclear Logics: Contrasting Paths in East Asia and the Middle East*, Princeton University Press, 2007

**STEYN, H., VAN DER WALT, R. and VAN LOGGERENBERG, J.**: *Armament and Disarmament: South Africa's Nuclear Experience*, iUniverse, 2003

**VENTER, Al J.**: *Iran's Nuclear Option: Tehran's Quest for the Atom Bomb,* Casemate, 2005

**VENTER, Al J** : *Allah's Bomb – The Islamic Quest for Nuclear Weapons*, Lyons Press, 2007

**VENTER, Al J** : *How South Africa Built Six Atom Bombs – And then Abandoned its Nuclear Weapons Program*, Ashanti, 2008

**VENTER, Al J** : *The Iraqi War Debrief – Why Saddam Hussein Was Toppled*, Earthbound Publications, 2004

**VON WIELLIGH, Nic and VON WIELLIGH-STEYN, Lydia**: *The Bomb – South Africa's Nuclear Weapons Programme*, Litera, 2015

# Index